The Re-Enchantment of Everyday Life

The
Re-Enchantment
of
Everyday Life

Thomas Moore

HarperPerennial
A Division of HarperCollins*Publishers*

Grateful acknowledgment is made for permission to reprint excerpts from the following material: "If they want me to be a mystic" from *Keeper of Sheep* by Fernando Pessoa. Copyright © 1986 by The Sheep Meadow Press, Riverdale-on-Hudson, New York. Reprinted by permission. • From "The Jesus Papers," *The Book of Folly*. Copyright © 1972 by Anne Sexton. Reprinted by permission of Houghton Mifflin Company. All rights reserved. • From "Peter Quince at the Clavier," "Asides on the Oboe," "Anything is Beautiful if you say it is," and "Notes Toward a Supreme Fiction." *Collected Poems by Wallace Stevens*. Copyright © 1954 by Wallace Stevens. Reprinted by permission of Alfred A. Knopf, Inc. • From "Ship of Death" (page 965) by D. H. Lawrence and "The New Word" (page 513) by D. H. Lawrence, from *The Complete Poems of D. H. Lawrence* by D. H. Lawrence, edited by V. de Sola Pinto & F. W. Roberts. Copyright © 1964, 1971 by Angelo Ravagli. Used by permission of Viking Penguin, a division of Penguin Books USA Inc. • From "Suzanne" written by Leonard Cohen. Copyright © 1967, 1995 by Bad Monk Publishing. Used by Permission. All rights reserved. • From *Blue Moon Soup Spoon* by Mimi Otey. Copyright © 1993 by Mimi Otey. Reprinted by permission of Farrar, Straus & Giroux, Inc.

HarperCollins books may be purchased for educational, business, or sales promotional use. For information please write: Special Markets Department, Harper-Collins Publishers, Inc., 10 East 53rd Street, New York, NY 10022.

FIRST INTERNATIONAL EDITION

Text design and production by David Bullen

ISBN 0-06-092769-0

96 97 98 99 00 ❖/RRD 10 9 8 7 6 5 4 3 2 1

For a free listing of all books, audio tapes, and video tapes by Thomas Moore, send a self-addressed envelope to:
Green Table Productions
145 Grove Street
Peterborough, NH 03458

Contents

Acknowledgments

Ye elves of hills, brooks, standing lakes and groves,
... and you whose pastime
Is to make midnight mushrooms ... by whose aid,
Weak masters though ye be, I have bedimmed
The noontide sun ...

SHAKESPEARE, *The Tempest*

Even Prospero, the great magician, required the help of friendly spirits to work his magic. There are those invisible spirits that have helped put these words together, but I would like to acknowledge, too, friends and coworkers whose crafts are present here:

As usual, Michael Katz performed his splendid magic, from the beginning to the end of the project, and beyond.

Hugh Van Dusen offered enthusiastic support exactly when it was needed and, as always, fathered the book into life with great heart and charm.

I've developed a deep appreciation of the magic of publishing and publicity, and I'm pleased to acknowledge the skills of Rose Carrano, Anita Halton, George Kushner, and Steven Sorrentino.

Paul DuBois Jacobs expanded the limits of my understanding of enchantment through his research excursions into the land of faerie.

Carol Williams deftly soaked the raw text alchemically to remove the dross, and Cynthia Merman offered skepticism and sympathetic reverie as she weeded my words.

My friend Bill Burford acted as consultant on certain themes that required a poet's spell.

David Bullen's legerdemain makes all this into a book.

And Joan Hanley is the *soror mystica*, the soul of the work, present on every page, between the lines, in the margins, and in the gossamer lace of irony and implication that wraps my words and thoughts—the love element in the text.

Thanks to all, and now, as Prospero says, "I'll drown my book."

Introduction

Magic and Enchantment

*E*NCHANTMENT IS a spell that comes over us, an aura of fantasy and emotion that can settle on the heart and either disturb it or send it into rapture and reverie. One day you fall in love, and a person who yesterday was like anyone else has suddenly become translucent with grace and infused with otherworldly value. You stumble across a roaring, resplendent waterfall, as I once did, in the middle of a quiet forest, and you become profoundly entranced. The stunning vision fixes itself in memory, and you wish you could have other moments of similar transporting charm.

An enchanted life has many moments when the heart is overwhelmed by beauty and the imagination is electrified by some haunting quality in the world or by a spirit or voice speaking from deep within a thing, a place, or a person. Enchantment may be a state of rapture and ecstasy in which the soul comes to the foreground, and the literal concerns of survival and daily preoccupation at least momentarily fade into the background.

The soul has an absolute, unforgiving need for regular excursions into enchantment. It requires them like the body needs food and the mind needs thought. Yet our culture often takes pride in disproving and exploding the sources of enchantment, explaining away one mystery after another and overturning precious shrines, dissolving the family farm that has housed spirits of civility for eons, or desecrating for material profit a mountain or stream sacred to native residents. We have yet to learn that we can't survive without enchantment and that the loss of it is killing us.

A culture dedicated to enchantment recognizes our need to live in a world of both facts and holy imagination. It doesn't explain everything away in materialistic terms but understands that wisdom and deep intelligence require an honest appreciation of mystery. It seeks out experiences that quiet our mental ambitions and open a pathway toward some kind of transcendent vision, experiences that swell the heart and stretch the limits of belief and understanding. Enchantment is both a dulling of the mind and a sharpening of perception.

Enchantment is not always positive; we can be seized by fear, paranoia, jealousy, envy, depression, rage, and disillusionment. Sometimes intense, difficult emotions take hold of us in a "seizure," to use an old word, a spell that falls over us like a bubble, clouds our understanding, and seems to impede our freedom. In our disenchantment, we often seek psychological explanations and chemical tonics for these troubling emotions and states, and yet even disturbing spells and episodes have their necessity.

I began my book *Care of the Soul* saying that all our problems are due to a loss of soul, and here I want to extend that idea, suggesting that one important aspect of the loss of soul is disenchantment. An enchanted world is one that speaks to the soul, to the mysterious depths of the heart and imagination where we find value, love, and union with the world around us. As mystics of many religions have taught, that sense of rapturous union can give a sensation of fulfillment that makes life purposeful and vibrant.

In an enchanted life, we're not always in a state of rapture, of course, but we do have frequent, even daily opportunities to enter a different level of experience that has more charm than practicality. In many societies, regular festivals offer enchantment to the community, and houses may be designed, painted, and decorated in ways that appeal strongly to the imagination and offer comfort and attachment. Tradition may be strong, and people may find many occasions for festival and celebration—all aimed at bringing rich fantasy into daily communal life.

It isn't easy to discuss enchantment in a disenchanted society, one that suffers the lack of a deep, solid, communal fantasy life, because enchantment stands our usual values on their head. What is central in the hardcore, hardware, hardworking world of the disenchanted has little or no place in a soft life of enchantment, and what is important to the charm of daily life may appear as a distraction to those who are dedicated to the kind of seriousness that excludes enchantment. Yet there is no essential conflict between enchanted living and practical, productive activity; they can serve each other: one delighting the spirit of ambition, the other comforting the heart.

Enchantment is an ascendancy of the soul, a condition that allows us to connect, for the most part lovingly and intimately, with the world we inhabit and the people who make up our families and communities. Without enchantment we try rationally to forge those intimacies and make those connections, but our efforts are futile. Just consider the common complaints voiced against modern culture: the modern family is falling apart, marriages can't hold, neighborhoods are disappearing, and nature is being ravaged. We're not holding together, and that is a problem of eros—love and attachment. But if we were to live in an enchanted world, we'd be motivated toward intimacy and closeness.

On almost every page of this book I feel as though I have to defend the absurdity of what I'm writing, because the particulars of enchantment are simple in comparison to the complexities of modern life, and because the principles of enchantment are so directly opposed to those of modernism. Enchantment is tinged with play and eros, for example, elements that are suspect in a culture of extreme ambition, and it always implies an escape from logic, one of the prized tools in a society bent on understanding. Still, I keep in mind the enigmatic and yet oddly noble words of the early Christian theologian Tertullian: "I believe because it is absurd." Enchantment is often colored by at least soft hues of absurdity, which is only a sign of its saving distance from excessive rationality.

Magic

I base a large part of this work on the writings of serious Western philosophical magicians whose interesting work has been excluded from our history books, or has been rarefied into such abstraction that the flesh and blood of magic is nowhere to be found. I find in their literature and rich illustrations that the magus of the past was a devout, intelligent, well-read, thoughtful, and compassionate individual, sincere in his or her quest to explore all the powers of nature, especially those capacities hidden by our focus on reason and purely mechanical means of control.

I'm not interested in reviving old magical practices that contain naive understandings of the physical world that we have surpassed with our science, but I think we can gain immeasurably from reconsidering the worldview of magic treatises and even apply many of the principles of magic in simple ways in our own daily lives. I'm drawn to magic primarily as a way of recovering enchantment, and I'm convinced that by approaching these forgotten ideas intelligently and carefully we can restore soul to everyday life.

We might rediscover some of the magical terms that now lie hidden in our everyday speech. "Grammar," for instance, is a fairly rigid subject full of rules and traditions, and yet the word metamorphosed at some point in history into "glamour," the original meaning of which was enchantment or spell. The *Oxford English Dictionary* indicates that in 1721, Allen Ramsay wrote: "When devils, wizards or jugglers deceive the sight they are said to cast glamour over the eyes of the spectator."

"Spell" is another fascinating word linking language with enchantment. You spell a word, and you cast a spell on someone. In Hobbes's *Leviathan,* enchantment is defined as the working of strange effects by spells and words. In *Kabbalah* and in other magical systems, the spelling of a word and the arrangement and count of its letters are all part of its magic.

"Charm" is a form of *carmen,* a song, adding the idea of voice and music, the "chant" in enchantment. Deep in enchantment is the experience of being lured into reverie, dreamland, by the musical charms of the enchanter. The world is a lullaby, giving us a lull in our daily activity so that the soul can come out and find its refreshment. It must be sheer coincidence that one of the early medieval magicians was named Ramon Lull, and that his approach, based on letters of the alphabet, is known as Lullism—another instance of grammar acting as glamour.

In considering magic seriously, we may have to stretch the borders of our scientific assumptions and insist that the moon is not dust and rocks, the human body is not a machine or a gene factory, and the earth is neither inert nor without a personality. We may have to push the limits of psychology and insist that human beings are not aggregates of social influences or brain-driven packets of emotion that can be tweaked by chemicals into well-functioning social machines. Anyway, I'd rather be a dysfunctional soul than a well-adjusted robot.

The approach of magic is different from the way we're used to dealing with the world. For us, understanding something about the world leads first to *application;* we translate science into technology. Then we often become involved in *exploitation,* overusing the materials of the world for our own narcissistic purposes. Finally, all of this leads to the *abuse* of nature and persons, as we use both for the compulsive advancement of a disenchanted culture.

An alternative is to translate science into wonder, philosophy, story, and intimacy with nature. In place of the excesses of exploitation, we could appreciate simplicity in life, reserve in our use of things and people, and respect for the limitations nature asks of us. Instead of being obsessive about spreading modern culture around the globe and into the future, we could realize that other cultures have much to teach us and that the Third World is in many areas more advanced and sophisticated than we are. We could have the modesty to question our own "advances" and the humility to learn from others. Magic offers an unusual but deep-seated rationale for an ecological posture in daily living.

If these suggestions seem naive or unworkable in a culture neurotically driven in its own productivity and self-advancement, one reason is that we don't think we have control over the engine of our own hyperactivity. For instance, we have made a god of evolution, taking it not merely as a scientific rule but as a necessity that can't be stopped, hindered, or modified. We give up our responsibility toward humanizing culture by appealing to the inexorability of evolution. It's no wonder that some religious people see our theory of evolution as a threat to their religious convictions: for us, evolution is not just a theory but a demanding imperative that we never question. We seem to be victims of evolutionary processes instead of makers and artists of our own culture and individual lives.

Science and technology have their underlying mythology, rituals, and eschatology—an interpretation of the future and a sense of goal. Our disenchanted society is not without its beliefs, but they are unspoken or presented as discoveries, inventions, hypotheses, and theories. Many of our scientists, politicians, and businesspeople are ardently at work building the cathedrals of their own religion of secularism, and in response, religion in its desperation is falling apart or becoming defensive and reactionary.

Yet for all the problems that science and technology present to a world in need of soul, they are not the cause of our disenchantment. They are both full of magic, and I'm certain that magicians of the past would have readily appropriated many of the methods and discoveries of science along with the accompanying technologies. The tendency of reason and science to take up too much room in modern life is just another symptom of disenchantment. The root problem is not science. It is religion.

Religion and Enchantment

"Religion" means many things to different people. When I say that religion is the main issue in enchantment, I'm thinking not of eighteenth-century Deism and the reasonable religion of the American founders, but of an appreciation of the sacred and the holy in every aspect of life: nature, work, home, business, and public affairs. I call this "natural religion," taking the wording from many authors of the past—Marsilio Ficino in the fifteenth century said that religion is as natural to a human being as barking is to a dog—because I want to distinguish it from religion as an intellectual commitment buttressed by strong emotion and sheltered in an institution like a church or tradition.

Many people define their religion as a belief, and they pin their hopes and understanding on a provisional understanding of life. But there isn't much room for faith in a religion that is reduced to belief, and there isn't any place for an open-minded appreciation for the world's sacredness. In a disenchanted world, for all its concern for morals and social action, religion separates itself from everyday life and becomes obsessed with its own brand of belief and moral purity. In this kind of setting, the people who pollute our rivers and

oceans and exploit workers and families may go to church and profess strong moral values, and yet they don't have any conscience
about the water, the earth, or the human community.

There is something dreadfully wrong with this kind of religion,
which creates a kind of psychotic dissociation. A person feels morally pure because he is blissfully adhering to ideas of morality that
have little to do with the world in which he lives, and at the same
time he is committing heinous sins that are not cataloged in his disenchanted morality. The source of our modern discontent is the
loss of natural religion, a base for any other kind of religious sensibility.

If we define magic without its usual connotations of duplicity or
self-aggrandizement, and if we define religion in basic terms, prior
to traditions, institutions, and beliefs, then at this level magic and
religion are barely distinguishable, and one serves the other. The re-
enchantment of our everyday lives then becomes a matter of seriously shifting our priorities, developing a sense of the sacredness in
the particulars of ordinary life, and making them part of our personal lives more by imagination than by brute force.

Re-Enchantment

Why *re*-enchantment?

When I was a child in school, I would sit at my desk half listening to the teacher telling us how many square miles made up the
state of Michigan and how to do compound interest. My mind was
occupied with more serious issues: Do dragons exist? Was there
ever a Flood? Were Adam and Eve real?

It took many years of education, a Ph.D. in religion, and then
more years of independent reading and writing before I felt I had
answers to my pressing questions. I passed through a period when I
was convinced through elaborate theories of metaphor and psychological projection that fairies and dragons were symbols and metaphors, or were real in fantasy only. For a long time, I believed in
Jung's unconscious and considered it a good explanation for such
things. But now, finally, I've come to realize that dragons are real,
fairies do indeed dance, and the Flood of the Bible is more real than
flooding on the evening news. Our reduction of figures of imagina-

tion to psychological categories steals the magic away from a poten-
tially rich poetic participation in life.

As we "grow up," we get sophisticated out of enchantment and
become too smart about the things that cause children to wonder.
We try seriously and heavy-handedly to find a world that is different, more conscious, more theoretically elegant than the charming
one we knew as children. This is one reason for naming this book
the *re*-enchantment of everyday life. We may have to return to
childhood and recover its truths, its vision, its logic, its sense of time
and space, its extraordinary cosmology, and its creative physics if we
want a way out of the black-and-white world of disenchantment.
The authority for many passages in this book is the wisdom I have
gained from my children, who are experts in enchantment and
would probably wonder why this book has to be written.

Re-enchantment also asks us to search for the lost childhood of
the human race and discover, in a larger social sense, what we have
forgotten. Judeo-Christian religion teaches that human life began
in a garden, Eden, where there were no worries or work, a place of
pure play. Religion also teaches that ultimately we will return to
paradise, again a garden and a place of happiness. These two images
give good reason for spending some time in our gardens, perhaps to
find a piece of lost enchantment among the flowers, plants, and
humus just outside our homes.

But at the same time, while in the garden we might keep in mind
these and other great stories of gardens, so the dialogue between
lived life and imagination will be constant and the two dimensions
indistinguishable. This is one of the secrets of enchantment: Never
leave the yin and yang of poetry and life, and never abandon the
steady rhythm of experience and imagination.

The beautiful Gnostic story "The Hymn of the Pearl" tells how
we all once lived in a far-off place with our true parents and then
were exiled into this cool, remote realm called human life with the
charge to recover the pearl of the soul. I, for one, am visited once in
a great while by what feels like a memory of events and persons that
could have no historical reality for me, but the mystery of their visitation makes me feel that life was indeed once paradisical.

Here is another way we can find enchantment *again*, in a mythic
way and not as historical memory. The idea of lost paradise, a one-

time Golden Age, a long-past era of wholeness and perfection, is to be found in the lore of most people and also appears in the fantasies of persons who imagine a golden time in the recent past—the era of their grandparents, or the forties, fifties, or sixties, depending on their age.

We remember in a Platonic sense, a mythic memory, an imagined period when things were in harmony, and we can re-enchant our lives in this way as well, knowing in our sophistication that life has never been perfect and yet feeling that somehow, heading toward enchantment is at the same time a return. We may have only passing sensations of enchantment, lasting minutes or seconds, and yet these brief epiphanies are sufficient, and they may bring with them a sense of deep memory.

Restoring Paradise

The idea of enchantment lends itself to sentimentality, and I have noticed a countereffort to make enchantment appear difficult, highly abstract, and convoluted. In some cases, writers on enchantment disalign themselves from magic, charm, and childhood, apparently in an attempt to be serious about a topic whose seriousness appears to be always slipping off the edge.

Some psychological theories equate childhood with paradise and conclude that to live as mature adults we should separate heroically from childhood and enter this vale of tears called maturity. They're afraid that if we don't overcome childhood, we'll become stuck in infantile illusions. Some experts believe that life is fundamentally disenchanted and that those who think otherwise are naive or psychotic.

During my years of practice as a psychotherapist, I felt that people bringing me their stories of a foundering career, a failing marriage, a tenacious depression, or an overpowering addiction were suffering from a deeper malaise. They had fallen out of love with life itself, which, in their adult years, had become an absorbing collection of problems. Psychology sometimes gives the impression that life is a problem, and it is always difficult to love a problem.

On the other hand, as I travel for lectures and readings, I encounter many people who are able to avoid falling into easy modern despair, who love their lives and themselves, who have endured all kinds of suffering, from divorce to cancer, and yet express and cultivate their love of life in gardening, painting, travel, music, and community service.

Another secret for re-enchanting everyday life is to refuse to leave Eden, to be in the garden for life. If we imagine paradise deeply enough, we won't be literally childish or naive, but we can live with a positive love of life amid many kinds of torment. As the philosopher Epicurus taught, no matter how much suffering afflicts us, we can always find a modicum of pleasure, and that is sufficient.

Another relatively easy way to restore paradise is to let children be children. When I was young, my parents let me be a child and didn't wound the innocence that was so precious and delicate in me. They created a world for me that was safe, nonviolent, and caring. Yet even with this generous upbringing, I myself don't find it easy to let myself be a child or let children be themselves. I can feel the stern voice in me that demands order and control, and, of course, I see it in the world around me as parents yell at their children and shake them into obedience. It seems we're afraid of paradise, anxious, perhaps, that the orderly world we know will fall apart if the angel guarding Eden's gates lowers his sword for a second of rest.

The re-enchantment of our personal lives may very well feel like going back to Eden: taking a job that delights our heart, being in or out of a marriage according to our heart's deep desire, living where the spirit of the place soothes our tired body and emotions, following through on our eccentric interests and mad inclinations. Many times I've seen people suffer the most tormenting agonies, only because they won't allow themselves to enter the garden they can see at a distance but for some undefinable reason is closed to them. In some cases, there comes a day when the obstacles don't seem so remarkable, and calmly and easily they stroll through its entrance.

Naturally, I don't mean to suggest that life can be utterly carefree; that would be taking paradise too literally. But it is a theme that can be lived amid all the other dimensions of an engaged human life. You may have to take suffering close to heart as the price of admission to paradise, and you may have to decide to live as wholeheartedly as possible in order to enjoy just a taste of Eden. But that taste makes all of life enchanted and seasons even our suffering with its pleasure.

Writing About Enchantment

This book is a logical third volume in a series on soul. *Care of the Soul* portioned out the realm of soul among the concerns of everyday living. *Soul Mates* moved into a discussion of intimacy and community, natural haunts of soul. Now I turn to the soul in nature and culture, and from that aspect soul appears as an enchanting voice, as the things of nature and culture speak and sing their magical, haunting whispers and alluring siren songs.

In these pages I try to restore legitimacy to certain practices, such as astrology and divination, which are considerably misunderstood and denigrated by a culture that has lost its taste for enchantment. I realize that I risk being misread, as I try to find a middle path between the psychological reduction of enchantment to projection or metaphor and a literal, too simple belief in a spirit world. As I write, I'm always searching for an alternative to belief and explanation, for a midrealm where imagination is taken seriously, though not literally.

I take magic seriously, as a source of effectiveness in a world that is more mysterious than our scientific achievements imply. A word, a gesture, or an image may be more powerful than a reasoned argument, a ritual or a ceremony more beneficial for human community than any machine or technical development. Becoming a person of deeply grounded and rich imagination may be more desirable than being healthy, politically savvy, or well informed.

I also write out of passion, anger, and longing, as one who has spent years listening to the tragedies of families and the despair of individuals, as a parent who can hardly tolerate hearing of the suffering of children, and as a world citizen frustrated at our failure to end bloodshed at home and in foreign wars. I'm convinced that none of these problems can be solved directly, but they can be countered positively by turning our backs to the disenchanted values that dominate modern life.

The answers to our problems surround us in the many voices of enchanted nature and in the haunting words and images of our artists and religious visionaries. All the insight we need could be found in a library, in the great literature of the arts, humanities, and religions, or in meditation on a single flower in a tiny garden outside the most ordinary house, because nature, as the medieval monks taught, is a book too, teaching those who are willing to be its pupils.

The world is shouting at us, offering us guidance, but when we're too busy making up our own inadequate answers, we can't hear its voice. We have to become as children, as Jesus taught without any sentimentality when he said, "Whoever among you becomes as a child shall know the Kingdom," or as Zen master Shunryu Suzuki advised when he wrote: "How important it is to resume our boundless original mind. Then we are always true to ourselves, in sympathy with all beings."

There is a sophistication prior to adult learning and modern development of culture, an appreciation for the interiority of nature and the hidden power of persons and places. It's a sophistication that can be lost behind the illusion that our own developed intentions, observations, and values are supreme. The first step in enchantment, then, is to recover a beginner's mind and a child's wonder, to forget some of the things we have learned and to which we are attached. As we empty ourselves of disenchanted values, a fresh, paradisical spirit may pour in, and then we may discover the nature of the soul and the pleasure of being a participant, and not a master, in the extravagance of life.

Nature

I think is was from the animals
that St. Francis learned
it is possible to cast yourself
on the earth's good mercy and live.

JANE HIRSHFIELD

Nature Spirits

IT'S EARLY SUMMER, and the sunflowers are about seven feet high in the garden off the kitchen. I'm reminded that in the fifteenth century, Marsilio Ficino recommended that everyone turn toward the mystery of his own nature the way a sunflower turns toward the sun. In all things, even in the most recondite mysteries of the soul, nature is the first and finest of teachers.

All lessons in enchantment begin with nature: with animals that exhibit "pure soul," as Robert Sardello once remarked; with day and night, season and tide—natural rhythms; with our own instincts and sensations, our own nature, part of and reflective of the natural world around us. It's easy to speak philosophically and abstractly about being part of nature, but the important thing is to live that realization, to make local nature a concrete element in daily life. This is a necessary initial step in the re-enchantment of our individual lives, although it will take a while for society as a whole to discover that it can't survive humanely without surrendering some authority and initiative to nature.

Enchantment is to a large extent founded in the spirituality inherent in earthly nature. Religious and spiritual writers often symbolize their goal with images of light and sky that draw us upward and away from the particulars of life on earth. Our task in re-enchantment is to expand our very idea of spirituality to include the lowliest of things and the most particular and familiar haunts of nature. Without romanticizing nature, we could turn to it as the major source of our spirituality—a difficult task for most of us who have been brought up on moral and theological abstractions.

Although nature is usually thought of as the quintessential example of the material world, paradoxically nature gives us the most fundamental opening to spirit. Mountains, rivers, and deserts, enjoying a lifetime far exceeding our own, give us a taste of eternity, and an ancient forest or gorge reminds us that our own lives are brief in comparison. In nature, we become sensitive to our mortality and to the immensity of the life that is our matrix, and both of these sensations, mortality and immensity, offer the foundation for a spiritual life.

For all our well-equipped investigations and classifications, nature remains full of mystery: The farther the physicist explores the subatomic world, the more mysterious nature appears; and the more pictures we receive from beyond our solar system, the more it inspires awe and wonder. By confronting us with irreducible mysteries that stretch our daily vision to include infinity, nature opens an inviting and guiding path toward a spiritual life.

As we approach nature as fact finders, analysts, and classifiers, we tend to lose sight of the story we are living, the myth that gives shape to our very investigations. Are we like Prometheus, hoping to steal what we can for humanity from the mysteries of life? In our voracious pursuit of information, are we like the man in the fairy tale who gobbled up his world from a pointless, ravenous hunger? Or are we St. Francis, loving nature as the immediate presence of divinity? Or the Buddha, finding in the simple presentations of nature images of the mystery that is human life?

In religious practices around the world, we find spirituality and nature going hand in hand—among the Irish monks who built their stone monasteries on windy, raw islands and steep promontories inhabited mainly by goats, among the Tibetans who developed a highly sophisticated approach to the spirit in the thin air of their mountaintop monasteries, in the tropical rain forests where nature is revered in exotic ceremony and icon, or on the American plains where earth and sky are honored as divine sources of life.

Many of us who limit spirituality to a book or a church long for something more. Traditional peoples know that nature feeds the spiritual life as nothing else can. What is required is simple proximity, contemplation, ritual, and a spirit of piety. If we can allow ourselves to be stunned by nature's beauty, complexity, simplicity, devastating power, vast dimensions, and unexpected quirkiness, then lessons in spirituality will pour into us without effort on our part. But it isn't easy to be so naive and open in an age of scientific sophistication. We want to harness nature and not be directed by it, study it and not learn from it, get it under firm control and not let it have influence over us.

Nature is not only a source of spirit; it also has soul. Spiritually, nature directs our attention toward eternity, but at the same time it contains us and creates an intimacy with our own personal lives that nurtures the soul. The individuality of a tree or rock or pool of water is another sign of nature's soul. These intriguing natural beings not only point outward toward infinity; more intimately, they also befriend us. It's easy to love groves of trees or mountain ridges, to feel related to them as though by blood, and to be secure in their familial protection.

One of the great challenges we face as we develop technology and expand scientific knowledge is to preserve nature as a source of spirituality. Recent history has proven how easy it is to lose an appreciation for the sanctity of nature and to get so caught up in the material dimensions of our science that we fall deeper into materialism and lose touch with spiritual values. Then we not only destroy nature out of the shallowness of our appreciation but also lose nature's gift of spiritual sensitivity.

Too Busy for Nature

When I fly around the country, I usually leave from Bradley Field in Hartford, Connecticut. One day, as the shuttle bus approached the airport, the driver pointed to a grassy patch between the highway and the terminal, where a groundhog had made a home, and as we drove by we saw him sitting in the middle of the field, sunning himself. Behind him were the massive engines of the airliners and the typical busyness of the airport, and the odd combination appeared to me as a visual oxymoron, a woodchuck and an airliner sharing the same world.

In many ways, modern life shields us from the infusion of spirituality nature has to offer. In our busyness, a neurotic development of modern life, we believe we don't have time for nature. We put off looking at it until our senses have become weak with age, and we offer countless reasons for remaining focused on whatever is in front of us rather than on the mysteries of nature hiding in our peripheral vision.

In letters and essays written by previous generations, I'm struck by the absence of the common modern complaint "I didn't write because I'm too busy." People who had no computers or heating or running water wrote thousands of pages of letters, essays, novels, and treatises. World trade carried on at a good pace; people traveled widely by train, boat, and horse.

One could conclude that busyness is a fantasy, a story we live and talk about. When we say we're busy, we're really saying that we're caught in an emotional complex where our will is trapped and we're not free to do things we might wish for ourselves. One effect of this complex is to keep us divorced from nature, which asks for contemplation and other unproductive activities, or should I say "passivities."

In general, it's difficult to imagine being busy and enchanted at the same time. Enchantment invites us to pause and be arrested by whatever is before us; instead of our doing something, something is done to us. This is the way of the soul, which is primarily the receptive power in us; by letting ourselves be slowed down and affected by nature, we are fashioned into persons of substance, even if at a more active, conscious level we are forcefully engaged in becoming something else.

If busyness is an emotional complex, then it's likely that when we are busiest, we are doing least. We can be extremely active without being busy, and busy without accomplishing anything. We may be feverishly engaged in some task and yet not truly focused on the matter at hand. The job may be merely a means to accomplish some other goal: to make money, to impress, or to prove oneself to another. Our busyness may be a way to avoid difficult emotions and thoughts, or we may simply believe that it's important never to waste time.

One simple way, then, to re-enchant our lives is to divest ourselves somehow of this "busy" complex. We might do work that we love, give up the futile task of proving ourselves to anyone, keep money within perspective, and do whatever is necessary to enable us to walk away from our work and activities if our soul requires it.

Obliterating Nature

Recently two businesses started up in my town. One is a large, sprawling store that sells books and videotapes. It seems to be an efficient store, convenient for people who want to look for various kinds of entertainment in one place. It has a few comfortable reading chairs, though they're placed rather severely at the ends of aisles. Yet the store, for all its convenience, seems completely cut off from nature. All the materials are arranged in logical order, and the aisles are labeled alphabetically, creating a well-functioning utilitarian space, but I feel the absence of interior walls or pockets of interest, a nook or a cranny. There is nothing organic in the layout, and the light shines brilliantly, evenly, and relentlessly on every square inch. There are no shadows, no variation in the color or intensity of the light, no place for escaping into darkness or even a soft shade. When I venture into the place to look for an obscure recording of music, I'm reminded of the proverbial bare light under which criminals confess to their crimes, and I hurry off as soon as I find what I want.

The use of light to obliterate nature must be a trend. Just down the road, a new gas station manifests the latest in efficient design: a perfect rectangle of pumps where you can use a credit card so that there is no interpersonal exchange, not even with the clerk who sits in a box in the center of this perfectly geometric arrangement like a character in a Samuel Beckett play. At night the entire eerie project stands out against the darkness, with what must be superhalogen lightbulbs evenly distributing colorless, unblinking light. Nothing in this business has any relationship to nature in general, and certainly not to the natural woods and meadows that surround it. It must have been designed by someone who has spent years in a windowless workplace of right angles and plain walls and lives in "cyberspace," a nowhere area that enjoys no experience of locality. This gas station could be transplanted without adjustment anywhere on the globe and rest like a purely artificial "white hole" in the midst of natural shadows and hues.

We have been ingenious in this century finding ways to hide from nature, and in the process we have let enchantment recede piece by piece. Then we wonder why we now have a religious and

spiritual crisis. We blame each other for not having the moral forti-
tude to maintain traditional values and sustain church commitments, but we don't complain about the commercial obliteration of
nature by the great screen of advertising that lines every American
town and city road, or by the ever-present noise and light of an
insensitive culture that keeps nature's presence blissfully blocked
out.

The only explanation for our acceptance of these commercial
insensitivities is that we have forgotten that nature is the prime
source of the spiritual life. Block it out, and we obliterate the source
of the spirit that our souls thrive on. Erect another billboard, another neon sign, another rack of halogen lights, and we push spirituality farther into repression.

On the other hand, build a real market, invite the neighboring
farmers into the city, keep animals nearby and cared for, let the
songs of birds and insects penetrate the sounds of machinery, let the
darkness descend at night to gently envelop every business and
every home, and you will see the spiritual life begin to rise and glow,
and you might hear the voices of those spirits, nymphs, little people, and ghosts that were heard generations ago, that fed the quotidian imagination and excited a spirituality not yet divorced from
good creation.

Nature's Template

Our businesses don't have to all become "fern bars" and hang plants
to evoke the spirits of nature, although plants are generous spirit
providers. A business could itself be natural and organic rather than
artificial and mechanical in its organization and presentation. It
could balance abstraction and quantification with personality, individuality, and hints of raw nature.

Give me an old garage any day, owned and operated by generations of mechanics or by a new daring lover of cars, complete with
disorganized and greasy manuals, boxes of parts, and work bays.
Point me to a bookstore where the owners, managers, and salespeople know and love books, though they don't know exactly where
everything is by chart or abstract arrangement; a store that has private places to take a book for a few minutes of examination, where

the bright light won't expose me completely and where I can be deliriously and surreptitiously lost in contemplation.

When you walk into a natural forest, you can't go first to a card catalog or find the trees and plants arranged alphabetically or have enough light to see everything with the same degree of detail. Our homes and businesses could show more the influence of nature and not strike such a sharp dividing line between nature and culture.

I would expect most people who have dogs and cats in their homes or places of work to give testimony to the spirituality the animals bring to their places and the soul that settles into a room that is home to an animal. Spiritual awareness begins when we get a glimpse of life going on in ways that transcend or are at least different from human ways, and in the habits of animals we see nature revealing itself intimately.

Just as nature usually invites us into contemplation, wonder, and reverie, we might bring nature into our busyness by incorporating those same values. In business we have efficiency experts, but where are the inefficiency experts? We need them as well, because a workplace that is devoted only to productivity may suffer serious loss of enchantment. It's important to be heroic, ambitious, productive, efficient, creative, and progressive, but these qualities don't necessarily nurture the soul. The soul has different concerns, of equal value: downtime for reflection, conversation, and reverie; beauty that is captivating and pleasuring; relatedness to the environs and to people; and an animal's rhythm of rest and activity.

The beauty of nature's spirituality lies in its complete resolution of the problem of mind and body, spirit and matter. Give nature a place, and you introduce egoless and unambitious spirituality, a spirituality that serves well as the starting point and base for other forms. There need not be any conflict between this natural spirituality and more evolved forms of theology and church, and if there appears to be such a conflict, it may be a sign that the spirit has lofted too high above the earth, has forgotten the goodness of creation, and is serving human ambition more than the community of beings that inhabit the cosmos.

In a series of extraordinarily delicate paintings, Lucas Cranach, the sixteenth-century painter, depicted the "Nymph of the Spring," an image of Venus as abundant nature. In a corner of these paintings is a script that reads: "Do not disturb the sleep of the nymph of the spring." Scholars say that the motif in these paintings probably comes from the mysterious Renaissance book of magical images *Hypnerotomachia Poliphili* (The Dream Love-Battle of Poliphilo). As I "read" these paintings, the nymph is dreaming nature onward not only as literal life but also as the source of spirituality and imagination. We are warned not to disturb this dream, and I take Cranach's words seriously: As long as we do not disturb the subtle, nymph-like presence of nature, we will find our own lives enchanted and infinitely enriched.

Nature and the Workplace

While slight attention to the soul can go a long way, it isn't enough to maintain the active life and give the soul mere morsels. We could incorporate nature into our work and home life. A business could bring nature into the workplace. The placing and architecture of a building might reflect an awareness of the role of nature in work. Some businesses locate in areas of unusual natural beauty, like an architectural company near my home that took time to select an extraordinary piece of property, with no ostentation whatsoever, and then developed it with great care for its delicate contours, wetlands, and rock formations. The president of this company knows the geology of his place and its history, and one senses in his presence an unusually fertile mixture of business and nature.

Most businesses need to be in cities, of course, and yet they could also give special attention to nature, if only in providing their employees with natural light and fresh air. Plants and even paintings and sculptures of nature; interior gardens, atria, fountains, wind chimes, windows on nature; time for walks, access to parks—all of these can effectively bridge the gulf between nature and work. Today businesses will go to considerable expense to provide employees with exercise and fitness areas and equipment, but what about fitness of soul? The cost is usually minimal; it asks only for our sensitivity and awareness.

I am not proposing a Luddite, antitechnological world in which nature is romanticized and inefficiency glorified. As I write these days, I sit in a simple room that has a wood floor and a colorful rug.

The walls are a deep rust color, and some plain, natural-wood bookcases line part of the walls. I write at a computer. Next to me is an array of electronic musical instruments—synthesizers, tape recorders, a mixer, amplifier, speakers, and so on. I can write music simply by turning my chair in the direction of all these electronics that are hooked up to the computer on which I write books.

At the same time, I look directly out a large window at tall evergreens, a contemplative rock garden, and a grape arbor made of posts that still retain their bark. This important window allows me to keep track of the movement of the sun in the shadows and pieces of sky that peek through the trees. I work at home, so that the children can have easy access to me and I can take the dog out when she barks for a walk.

I don't present this arrangement as a model, and it is by no means exceptional, but for me it provides a fascinating and pleasing high-tech approach to work as well as a way to be attuned to nature and family. This is my workplace, thoughtfully arranged and persistently cultivated for efficient tools and instruments, and allowing for "intrusions" of family and the occasional need to stop and watch the life outside my window.

In a culture that has generally lost sight of the soul and has given most of its attention to the heroic and the ambitious, these values of the soul may appear more detrimental than advantageous. Yet it's clear that even in business, when soul appears in the form of emotional distress, symptomatic behavior, or failure in morale, work suffers and the economics of the business declines. An enchanted life is good for business, even though it requires a considerable turnabout in values and vision. As far as I know, no one has yet made a correlation between the decline of soul values and the lowering of productivity and morale in the workplace.

Business has an intimate relationship to nature, since usually it uses nature in some way—for materials, real estate, waterways, even air. It may seem obvious, in the industrial age, that the relationship is one of exploitation, but there are other possibilities. In an enchanted world, nature sets limits on what we can do commercially, and in that way it helps keep our work and productivity humane, at human scale. Incorporating nature into our vision gives work and business a context that has naturally spiritual values, so that nature can affect the character of a business or a home and the people who work and live there.

Perhaps the most difficult challenge to business in moving into an enchanted world is to be less pragmatic and coldhearted. Business often seems to be anxious about giving an inch to tenderness, to anything other than hard-nosed attention to financial success. But nature promotes a different kind of sensibility, one that I think would not threaten the financial goals of a business. On the contrary, deeper humanity would certainly help morale and character, two soul qualities that have much to do with the success of any business enterprise.

What if the businesspeople in a city bordering a river learned the history of that river, and songs and stories expressing its character, and what if they shed their modernism enough to engage in some rituals honoring that river—I suspect those businesses would be profoundly enriched in their personnel, their presence in the community, their image in the world, and the quality of their product. What if we all shed our modernism, so full of narcissistic pride in our own accomplishments and vision, and learned from *feng shui* experts how to place buildings and design rooms, from artists how to animate the workplace with color and image, from psychologists of depth how to shape time and space in the workplace for the souls of the workers, from traditional societies how to bless and honor our tools, and from spiritual leaders how to develop an adequate vision of the context of our work?

Manufacturers could learn that in an enchanted world, good function is only one of many qualities a product must have. Once, every tool from a simple drill brace to a manual typewriter had animation in its design. As a child, I was rocked in a chair that had swans' heads for armrests and some sort of animal feet on its base. These animal images transform an object from pure function to fantasy.

One day I hope to see little feet on my computer. Think of automobiles you have loved, and consider whether they had any fins or grilles that were not needed for function but encouraged a relationship of love and attachment. When you're in a room decorated with wallpaper designed by William Morris, founder in the last century of the English arts and crafts movement, you find yourself in a rich natural setting evoked by the art of someone who was intimate with the spirit of nature.

In our families and in our corporations, we might be better off putting effort into bringing enchanted objects into our lives rather than things that make life convenient. I once approached my wife with the idea of purchasing yet another machine to help make my work more efficient. I would have had to use family funds, and so I sought her opinion. "Yes," she said, "it makes a lot of sense to be able to work a little faster, but for the same amount of money you could buy a beautiful rug for your studio." I bought the rug.

If we put more money or thought into enchanted things than into technology, we might find our daily life and work profoundly enriched, for technology often promises enchantment but rarely delivers it. When I find myself considering increased efficiency in my work, on deeper reflection I realize that what I'm looking for is more satisfaction, more pleasure, and even more play in the serious work of writing books. I have plenty of machinery around me; what I really need is a more enchanting world in which to live and work.

Nature plays a central role in this enchantment of modern life, for its potential for charm and mystery seems infinite, and yet it is close and accessible. All that is required is to take it into consideration as we organize our daily lives. Its resources of enchantment and spirituality could give us the power and support we need to live a full life and to find deep satisfactions in work and business.

The Waters of Life

ACCORDING TO the Greek philosopher Thales, everything is water, and water is the basic element in all life. With our modern ears, we may hear that statement as a scientific fact, but over the centuries many philosophers have understood that water is not just H2O but also an element of the soul—fluid, deep, changing, tidal, cleansing, amniotic, nurturing, and threatening. To know water intimately is to know something about ourselves and to appreciate its presence as a means for increasing the life of the soul.

The enchantment water provides does not arise directly from its symbolism. Anyone who lives, or has lived, near water has that water in his or her soul by a process of evaporation and condensation that has nothing to do with science. I could write an autobiography based on water, and yet I've never lived on an ocean. The many waters I've known as part of my own personal world—rivers, streams, and lakes—have taught me, shaped me, and given me a sense of values. They have extended the process of transformation that began the day I was baptized, when a trickle of water flowed over the crown of my head and down its side, initiating me out of sheer physical existence into a life of alchemical, elemental, and religious change. Religion knows something of the mystery by which we become more human through our acquaintance with water.

My father was a water professional all his life, a teacher of plumbing who was fascinated by all aspects of water, especially its role in the life of a city, but he also perceived its enchantment. Once, as he was passing a store window on a small street in Syracuse, New York, he saw a faucet apparently standing in midair, with water pouring out of it into a sink. The effect was intended to be magical, but the apparatus was imperfectly done—thin wires holding up the faucet were visible to the casual eye. So my father went home and perfected the magic by bracing the faucet with a thin glass tube that was invisible in the flowing water, and he charmed everyone who beheld the miracle of water gushing from nowhere.

With a father devoted to water, quite naturally I've been drawn to the element's poetics. A literary image of water that has long appealed to me and that I frequently write about is Tristan adrift at sea in his small boat, playing his harp. When I first read Joseph Campbell's treatment of this scene, I was spellbound, because I saw my own life mirrored in that mythological moment:

> Tristan, resting trustfully on the bosom of those cosmic powers by which the movements of the heavens and all things on earth are controlled, has been carried on the concord of his Orphic-Irish harp, resounding to the music of the sea and spheres, to that very Dublin Bay where Joyce's hero Dedalus was to go walking centuries later, questioning his heart as to whether he would ever have the courage to entrust himself to life.

Like Tristan, I have taken the rudderless route in life, drifting from one barely familiar piece of land to the next, trusting fate, bringing my sources of stability with me—my music, my books, my small rituals. Like Tristan, I sailed to Ireland as a young man, although my boat was larger—the *Queen Mary*. Like him, I've been more interested in style than substance, in beauty more than fact, and I am easily distracted into new fateful adventures, just as he was carried off to sea as he was absorbed in a game of chess.

Tristan is a variety of the puer figure discussed by C. G. Jung and James Hillman, a figure often pictured in the air or on mountain peaks and sometimes recognized in dreams of flying. But there is also a puer of the waters, a boy afloat. I don't think his mindless drifting is the best way to live, and I certainly don't believe it's a path everyone should take. But for some of us, Tristan's is a watery fate that was set long before we were born, and we have no choice but to make music from its quick rhythms and frequent turns, and to accept the special melancholy—Tristan's name means "sadness"—that comes with this meandering style of life.

People have often come to me in therapy wanting a stronger grip on their rudder and demanding a map showing future turns in their life. They came to the wrong person, because my sensibilities are with Tristan, who trusts in the changing winds and sings in tune with the music of the spheres. Although I haven't been in many boats in my life, and I've never sailed, I think we all have to be sailors of a sort, because the soul is a universe of its own, with its own waters and its own rules of navigation.

I've never felt comfortable with the word "path" as a description of a way of life. It's a land word, dry and earthy, whereas the only way I make any movement in my life is by allowing myself to drift, to sail, unknowing, with a spirit of adventure, ready to adapt to the culture at hand, so absorbed in the play of the moment that I don't realize when the rope on the skiff has slipped loose.

Some would no doubt find a life modeled on the sailor Tristan as an irresponsible one, and I'm sure that's a reasonable judgment. But there is no doubt that it is an eminently responsive life, and in most things I prefer responsiveness over responsibility. Tristan drank a potion and immediately became enchanted with Isolde, and then was true to that enchantment for the rest of his life. I find a deep moral sensitivity in being loyal to one's deepest enchantment. It's a way of love rather than principle, and it's fluid rather than firm. We might deepen our sense of morality by thinking of it in elemental and humoral terms (according to individual humors or temperaments), recognizing that we are all led in our own way toward our fate and destiny.

Lake

Like Tristan, I have an intimate and mixed emotional relationship with water. When I was four years old, I went fishing one Sunday with my grandfather on a large Michigan lake. For some reason, with no explanation he suddenly stood up in the boat and stepped toward me. Immediately I began to feel cold water rising up over my ankles. Then I was in the lake, and at eye level I saw cans and cushions afloat around me and breathed in the pungent odor of outboard engine fuel. I clung to the bottom of the capsized wooden boat, feeling my grandfather's strong hands under my shoulders from the back, holding me above the water. I saw my uncle dive fully dressed into the lake from the shore, and then everything was blank and still. I awoke in a strange room in a large unfamiliar bed, sheets wrapped tightly across my chest, and I heard someone say "undertaker." I assumed I had died, but it was my grandfather who had passed away, giving me my life in the last moments of his.

Early in life I became intimately acquainted with the power of water and its fellowship with death. Campbell talks about the "music of the land below waves," and I think I've heard that music. For many years, I couldn't bring myself to put my face under water, and even now friends tell me I swim as though I'm going to panic at any moment. With profound envy I watch them move gracefully and effortlessly through beautiful, enticing, monstrous water, and I know that my memory is more than recall. It's my myth. There is some secret of my very existence linked to the deep and terrible music of water.

Tristan has unimaginable faith as he spends days and nights in his little boat, drifting to a love that would prove irrepressibly sweet and infinitely challenging. I have long felt that the capsized boat I clung to with my grandfather's help saved me for something, stripped me to my essential Tristan fate, to be forever without clear direction or firm control.

It is said that baptism is a ritual of death and rebirth. I learned early in my life that the sacraments are available not only in churches but also outdoors among the elements. I was baptized in the church, but then I was baptized again in the lake, and this later baptism had as much effect as the first. For all my deep appreciation for religions around the world, my Catholicism is set deep in my marrow, and for all my optimism about life in general, I know, from my initiation in the waters of the lake, that life is a body of water, beautiful and inviting, but always ready to swallow me up.

River

Away from the lake, in the city and down the street from where I grew up, flowed the powerful and beautiful Detroit River. As a child I played on Belle Isle, a lovely park island in the middle of the river. In wintertime, my friends and I played ice hockey on parts of the river protected from the winds, where the ice was deeply frozen and smooth enough for a puck and sticks. On summer evenings my father would drive us down to the river's edge so we could sit and watch the water and wonder about Canada on the opposite shore. Later, when I was a summer instructor at the University of Windsor, I would spend some of my free time on that other shore, watching the mail boat leave port several times in an hour to rendezvous with a passing freighter, and observing the natural life of a big river.

A river can give a city its very soul, and yet I know from traveling the country and visiting many cities built on rivers that we have largely forgotten that they are sources of spirituality. We think of them pragmatically, as conduits of commerce, which is certainly one of their major gifts to us, but generally we overlook the spiritual benefits they bestow on the community living on their banks. People who live in cities blessed with this kind of water need access to the river, to draw its nurturing spirit into their hearts, and yet in most places it's difficult to find the smallest piece of riverfront that is not privately owned or developed for business.

During those summers of teaching in Windsor, I would sit on the bank of the Detroit River and notice the tall silos of the Medusa cement factory on the other shore. I was teaching Greek mythology, and so I would reflect on the image of that frightful gorgon, a mistress of the underworld, whose chief weapon was a stare that could turn a person into stone, or possibly cement.

I had introduced my class to Freud's little essay on Medusa, where he interprets the many snakes that make up the gorgon's hair as an image of castration. Their large number is a sign of absence, and their power to petrify an image of castration. From the riverbank I could see many places of business lined up along the shore, blocking all views of the health-giving water to the citizens, and I realized that Freud was right: the more we multiply our heroic, egotistic activities, the more we castrate ourselves, turn ourselves to stone, a strong contrast to the moving waters that offer a city its very life.

A people attuned to enchantment, aware of the absolute necessity of soul to the sane and sanitary flow of life in their city, would make the protection of their river a high priority. They would realize that the water flowing powerfully and beautifully through the city is not just a physical element but an aesthetic and spiritual presence. In a real sense, the river is sacred and, more than that, is a primary source of the city's sacredness. Lose that sacredness, and civil chaos is bound to ensue.

We are accustomed to thinking of spirituality falling down from the sky without any work on our part, and yet religions teach that spirituality flows from nature and that it takes our constant care to protect natural sources of spirit and to discover the rituals, structures, and festivals—liturgies—that invite that spirit to bless the community with its gifts.

The Greek philosopher Heraclitus, in a famous statement, said: *"Panta rhei"*—Everything flows. He also said: "You can never step twice into the same river." Heraclitus was talking not only about actual rivers but also about the flow of life and the passing of time. Spending time by a river teaches us many things, one of them the flow of life, its constant movement, and it's clear that an enchanted life demands an appreciation of this flow. As soon as we try to stop it, problems arise, and the psyche of a person or a community begins immediately to show signs of its rigidity and dryness.

James Joyce's *Finnegans Wake*, an extraordinary modern example of metamorphosis literature, begins with the image of the river: "riverrun, past Eve and Adam's, from swerve of shore to bend of bay." Mythology tells of rivers so deep that they play a role in the fate of the dead and mark the barriers of the very memory of our lives, and the rivers of paradise pass through the land of Adam and Eve. The Greeks told entrancing stories of Proteus, the river who could change into a thousand shapes. These and many other stories instruct us in the enchantment of water and give good reason to protect rivers and contemplate their flowing life and celebrate the sounds of their experience. A river sings a holy song conveying the mysterious truth that we are a river, and if we are ignorant of this natural law, we are lost.

Ocean

Other kinds of water also feed the soul with knowledge, fantasy, and emotion. To the Greeks, Ocean was the son of Ouranos the

Sky and Gaia the Earth. With his bride-sister, Tethys, he spawned
the rivers of the world, including the terrible underworld river Styx,
and the three thousand Oceanids. Oceanids are nymphs of the
ocean, spirits that hover near the great water. James Hillman has
described nature nymphs as nature reflecting itself and inciting the
imagination in humans. They are a spiritual emanation of natural
places, felt in the atmosphere and mood that surround a particular
locale, and sometimes in the sounds and colors of a body of water or
a marsh or a moor.

When you walk along the Atlantic Ocean, feeling the wind and
noticing the unique vegetation of the shore, and start wondering
about yourself and your own life, and then notice the cultural life,
the houses and shops that have developed as an outgrowth of the
water, you may begin to sense the presence of oceanids. Go to the
Pacific Ocean, or to foreign shores on the same or other oceans, and
you will understand why mythology teaches that there are so many
oceanids, so many different kinds of spirit spawned by the presence
of the water. You may also come to understand the importance of
oceanids to your life and the life of your people, their role in the
enchantment of ordinary life and your corresponding charge to
protect them at all costs, for they are bearers of soul.

If with an ecological sensibility we protect the oceanids, care of
oceans will follow. We couldn't maltreat an ocean unless we had
begun to think of it as a mere body of water and not as a spiritual
entity. The Greeks and others who imagined the ocean as divine
were not beneath us in sophistication, but ahead of us. If anything,
we have lost the one thing that would sustain our intimacy with
nature—a religious sensitivity to the sacredness of all forms in
nature. The oceans are not only a bountiful source of fish, transportation, and recreation; they are also one of the supreme sources
on the planet for contemplation and other aspects of the spiritual
life, but we could know this only if we were deeply schooled in the
necessary virtue of reverence.

An imaginative psychology can also show how deeply the waters
of nature affect us. Freud's colleague Sandor Ferenczi, a man of
astounding powers of imagination, wrote a book on what he calls
"the thalassal regressive trend," a desire deep in the heart to return
to the "aquatic mode of life" experienced in the mother's womb, but

earlier, too, in our origins in the sea. He says he is describing not a literal world but a psychoanalytical one, a world of deep fantasy. He notes that the rhythmic rocking in the womb has been compared to the surging of the sea and that this comparison is more than a figure of speech. He points to the "fishy odor" many ascribe to the genital areas in mammals and humans, and he alludes to the twenty-eight-day female cycle and its relation to the moon, which controls the tides. His conclusion is that the erotic life, the very base of our desires, lies in a longing to return to this sea of imagination.

Psychoanalytic descriptions like this are difficult to appreciate unless we give up all literalism and realize how profoundly nature plays a role in the imagination. Ferenczi had an extraordinary intuition in his book on the sea and the psyche, full of echoes from ancient mythology and lore, which was nothing less than a glimpse of the soul's ocean, different from and at the same time inseparable from physical water. Desire and longing, he says, have their source in the ocean of our hearts.

Whenever I stand at the edge of the ocean, on the beach that separates a world of water from the earth where my life takes place, I am drawn into deep feelings and thoughts about my past and future, and I feel certain melancholic desires and longings to know the ocean better, to have a home at its edge, to travel to the other shores, to swim in it. But my thoughts always run farther and deeper, so that I never know just what it is I'm longing for as I listen to the waves and taste the brine in the air.

A great ocean creates a great soul in a people, and the diminishment of the ocean diminishes the people. Water ecology will find its necessary dimensions only when it has rediscovered a truth known by most cultures that preceded us: the ocean is a great spiritual entity that gives more to our souls than to our bodies. If we return to this understanding, we may discover a major source for the care of our souls, and we may find the motivation, which has been so elusive, for protecting the oceans with our very lives.

Trees That Talk

"OUT OF THE ground the Lord God made all sorts of trees grow that were pleasant to the sight and good for food, as well as the tree of life in the middle of the garden, and the tree of the knowledge of good and evil." These lines from Genesis follow immediately after the story of the creation of the first human being, and so they place human life and trees in the closest proximity, an intimacy that I feel, having been born in Michigan, a land typified by its tall firs and pines.

Every patch of ground that has a tree growing in it echoes Eden and is a reminder of our origins in an enchanted garden. Once we stop taking trees literally, we begin to see how they frame the world we look at every minute of our outdoor life, how they set a limit to the upward reach of the land, and how, tall and branching, they stand like nature's doubles of ourselves. If we stop to think about trees in our life, we begin to understand how fully capable they are of relatedness, intimacy, and meaning. Eden is always with us, unless and until we narrow our vision, forgetting myth and disregarding aesthetic perception, and the trees of Eden are also always with us, full of mystery and implication.

The "cosmic tree" appears in religions, mythologies, paintings, and dreams around the world, and is so central and richly elaborated in art and story that one is tempted to think that the tree, and not the chimp or the dog, is humankind's closest companion in nature. The vast, creative inner truth of the tree extends itself outward into paintings, decorations, sculptures, poems, and songs, with such extravagant fertility that the care of trees must at the same time be care of the human imagination. The tree teaches us so vividly to see eternity in our immediate environment that it is impossible to imagine art and religion without it.

At the same time, nothing is more ordinary than a tree, and I doubt that we can find enchantment merely in the symbol. We need real trees in our world, a wide variety of trees, individual trees, trees close to home and at work, trees in the city and trees in the countryside. We don't have to study the symbolism of trees to be affected by them emotionally and intellectually, but we may have to be aware of them and give them daily honest regard.

Individual trees can seize the imagination and win your heart, like a large, rounded maple in our town that hides in the background among all the other trees throughout the year but then, for a week in the fall, turns brilliant red and radiates like the sun. People driving by have to stop to gaze at it, paint it, and take a photograph of it. It won't suffer them to pass it unheeded.

Trees provide a rudimentary lesson in enchantment: We need not cling anxiously to our own subjectivity, will, and desire; instead we can place trust in the beings around us who demonstrate many alternative ways to be a contributing, outstanding individual. A tree tells us what gives it pleasure, and it is so good at offering us benefits beyond measure that we have no reason not to surrender ourselves to it. We can sit on a tree's limb, rest against its trunk, enjoy its fruits and nuts, sit under its shade, and watch it dance in the wind. The lessons we can learn from a tree are infinite, and its pleasures indescribable. There are moments in anyone's life when to be like a tree—tall, straight, fertile, rooted, branching, expressive, and solid—would be the most effective therapy.

The Community of Trees

During the years I lived in Texas, I learned to appreciate Tex-Mex food, "down home" ways of talking, and cowboy boots and western shirts, but I missed the tall trees of the Northeast. The ubiquitous dark, scraggly southwestern mesquite didn't do. I would drive out to east Texas sometimes in search of trees, but those I found were submerged in swampy waters, beautiful and haunting but not what I was craving. I would drive farther, to Oklahoma, where I found more familiar forests and streams, and to New Mexico, where the aspens were magical, and yet I still felt the need for trees. Painfully I discovered how much a tree is part of its place, and that my longing for certain trees was a kind of homesickness.

Now that I live once again in the Northeast, and I'm surrounded by hemlock, pine, beech, and birch, my longing has subsided, and I don't go driving all over the countryside looking for the proper trees; they're right outside my door. I can see them as I write, and they give me comfort in the sure knowledge that I'm home where I belong. But now and then I'd like a glimpse of a mesquite, and I still like to put mesquite chips in the fire when I cook or when I sit in front of a fragrant hearth.

Trees also create a special spirit in community with one another, whether in large gatherings in the forests or lined up along a road or path, creating an inviting archway of welcome. Orchards, too, have a spirit of their own, evoked by human art but at the same time as a "community" of trees. Many forests have cathedral trees—tall, Gothic congregations of trees that unmistakably evoke a spiritual atmosphere. People want to meet, have picnics, and get married under certain trees, and have their pictures taken with them. All of these are indications that trees are not mere material objects but have a body, soul, and spirit.

The landscape architect Dan Kiley said he felt that trees and green spaces were so rare in American cities that he had to go to Europe to find a place to sit down. With trees, he says, you can have quiet places, places of mystery and repose, in the middle of the city, and he made it his life's work to bring trees to cities, where, echoing the Genesis pairing of people and trees, they humanize civic spaces. This observation is plain and obvious, and yet in new housing developments everywhere the builders have uprooted the trees and leveled the land, "plaining" the earth just as we have mentally "explained" all of life. "We can plant new trees," they'll tell you in defense, as though you could kill off the children in a family and grow new ones.

Emily Dickinson wrote about trees many times, not surprisingly, since she spent most of her life next to a garden of trees that kept her company. Her poem about the resurrection of trees has a reference that demonstrates her role as a "poet of enchantment":

Nature—sometimes sears a Sapling—
Sometimes—scalps a Tree—
Her Green People recollect it
When they do not die—

Enchantment requires that we find some way to acknowledge the "Green People" who keep nature healthy more effectively than fertilizers and power saws. W. B. Yeats tells a story of a woman from faerie who was so close to human life that you couldn't tell immediately where she was from, until one day, as she was helping the family, she mysteriously disappeared.

Day after day, one summer, my wife lugged her watercolors to Emily Dickinson's garden and painted a single oddly bent tree, and now that we have those watercolors in our house, I can see the green people more easily in the paintings than in the actual garden. Painters sometimes capture more than they are aware of, especially in a landscape or still life, where the spirits remain hidden until the scene has been contemplated long enough.

Sometimes trees find their society with other trees, sometimes in intimacy with other forms of nature. The hawthorn tree guarding the holy wells of Ireland provides a canopy for the spring and creates a community of tree, water, and earth. The architect Christopher Alexander says that trees can be planted as an umbrella, a pair, a grove, a square, or an avenue, each formation suggesting a different kind of community. He also points out that trees may have a relationship with buildings and can invite human action or interaction—trees have the significant power to form and sustain communities.

I once had a memorable conversation with a friend in a village outside Brussels. We sat at the edge of a lake in the quiet of the evening, watching boats on the water, with a small fountain spraying in the distance, houses cozily crowding the water's banks, and the remarkable Belgian trees everywhere. I remember the soft meeting not only for the words exchanged and the pleasure of the company but also because of the enchanting nature of the place. My memories of Brussels focus, too, on the park of tall trees in the middle of the city, where I got lost and had to ask passing horse riders for directions, and on the Ardennes forest, where the timeless green beauty of the trees serves as a strong tonic for the crowded streets of the city. Trees are silent members of a community and attentive but mute partners in many kinds of intimacy.

But trees can also have disturbing connotations. The Ardennes was also the site of savage battles in World War II. In my book on the Marquis de Sade I recount a dream I once heard from a man in therapy who was having an affair. He dreamed that he and the woman were picking excrement off the branches of a tree, an odd but telling "fruit" of their passion. The dream echoes the story of Adam and Eve, suggesting not a moralistic condemnation of their action but a recalling of the fallen human condition, the idea that transgression and betrayal are an inevitable part of imperfect human life.

Genesis implies that the human condition owes its essential imperfection to a tree, suggesting, beyond all the moralism that has been attached to the story, that we have to be careful with trees. Their bounty is endless, but if we don't treat them with care, the consequences can be severe.

Trees of Myth

Currently the use of trees for wilderness and for building is the subject of angry debate, but often one has the sense that both sides advocate a disenchanted world. As long as the debate takes place in this context, there can be no solution, because without a sensitivity to the soul of trees, neither our protection nor our exploitation will benefit from the wisdom of the tree itself. Our arguments will all be human ones, when the issue is fundamentally a matter of theology: our use of the earth's materials has to be done in a sacred manner, or we will have no deep guidance in knowing how to build and how to preserve. The very last line of Black Elk's memoirs reads: "There is no center any longer, and the sacred tree is dead."

The North American Seneca people tell a story about a tree that at the beginning of time stood in the center of their village and bore lovely white blossoms, until one day, all the blossoms fell to the ground. A woman in the community dreamed three times that the tree should be uprooted, and she convinced the people to dig it up. The chief was angry and ordered that the woman be placed in the hole made by the uprooted tree, and from that hole the woman discovered this world in which we live.

We all have to find a world in which we can really live. Native Americans tell many stories of the ascent or descent out of a misty place of origins into actual life—a process that engages each of us as we find a way, through our ideas, influences, hopes, fears, memories, and especially our wishes for perfection to enter wholeheartedly into actual life. We are all like the woman in the hole made from the uprooting of the blossoming tree: we may have to give up our innocent thoughts of perfection to find the entry into life.

Much of my early life felt like a preamble, or like the Tibetan *bardo,* a getting ready to live, but then one day I noticed that my hopes and ideals were turning yellow, and I found life sprouting around me, crowding out my thoughts. I had to cut down the tree of my youthful innocence and make some space for actual life. It wasn't easy to make the change, and I resisted and fought against the necessity until I knew I had no choice but to stop preparing and start living.

Trees in the forest and the trees of myth have much to teach us. The Greeks believed that Zeus spoke to them as or through an oak tree. We could learn to see Zeus in the oak tree in our own neighborhood and listen to its oracle, or consult it in times of confusion. Conversing with a tree, we are not talking to ourselves or "projecting" in a psychological sense; nature can receive our thoughts and feelings, and often we may find some solution, or at least a fresh way of seeing matters, after consulting a tree. We have no need to explain how this dialogue takes place but only to find our way back into an enchanted world where nature becomes part of the community and is no longer mute.

The Greeks told stories also of the great ship *Argo,* which was made of special pine that could speak and give directions to its crew—another extraordinary image of enchantment. The *Argo* is the great "Ship of Life," parallel to D. H. Lawrence's "Ship of Death," the vehicle of our days and adventures. This ship, the thing itself and not the persons on it, speaks to us, says the story. Earth is our *Argo,* as is our culture, our family, our own personal fate, the world around us. They all speak to us, even as they ferry us through life, but to hear them we have to have ears of enchantment.

Many other sacred stories tell of the importance of trees to the religious vision. Gautama Siddhartha sat beneath the bodhi tree, determined to remain at its base until he was enlightened. There he became the Buddha. According to some traditions, Jesus was crucified on wood from the tree of paradise, and that wood has been venerated over the centuries. In the ancient stories of the Sumerian Dumuzi and Inanna, Dumuzi is described as the palm tree opening into fruit. The mysterious tales of Daphne, turned into a tree in her flight from Apollo, offer deep insight into the conflicts between pristine nature and ambitious culture.

One of the Arezzo frescoes of Piero della Francesca paints the scene of the Queen of Sheba venerating the holy wood of the cross. According to a long tradition, Seth, one of the sons of Adam and Eve, planted this tree. One day King Solomon saw it and wanted it for his home, but the builders couldn't find a way to fit it into the structure, so they made a bridge of it. As the Queen of Sheba was about to cross the bridge, she realized through spiritual intuition that this wood would one day be the cross on which the King of the Jews would be crucified, and so she refused to tread on it and instead bent over in worship.

Trees are the teachers, revealers, containers, companions, and protectors of the sacred, and our relationship to them, whether we meet them gently in a forest or, muscled and equipped, cut them down for the price of lumber, touches on our deepest values, emotions, and sense of meaning. Divinity resides somehow in the marrow of a tree and in the sanctuary made of the overarching branches of an avenue or the columns of a grove or the mere umbrella of a tree's foliage. "Cleave a piece of wood," says Jesus in the Gospel of Thomas, "I am there."

Trees and Human Creativity

We find nature in the world when we rediscover that our own natures are "nature" in the naturalist's sense. The soul of the tree overlaps with my own soul, so that we are more than siblings, indeed saplings, as we share the same air and space. Mysteriously, a tree, all trees, are implicated in the profound psychology and theology of our most intimate lives. This doesn't mean we can't use trees for furniture—because that use, too, is part of the mystery—but it does mean that the secularization of the tree is a threat to all human life, for secularization means a loss of soul through the diminution of enchantment.

The novelist John Fowles wrote a book on the role of trees in his life and work. "Again and again in recent years I have told visiting literary academics," he writes, "that the key to my fiction, for what it is worth, lies in my relationship with nature—I might almost have said, for reasons I will explain, in trees." Fowles writes about his father's trees, trees on his own land, and many other trees, and sees in them the poetic mysteries of his life and work. Intriguingly, he also places his relationship to nature somewhere between the green wild of the woods and the dry sophistication of learning.

We may not find our nature just by running into the woods or by spending our days in the company of books—which, after all, are trees shredded, soaked, and dried out. We may have to find a way to live in both moist nature and dry culture, forgetful of neither but deeply enough attached to both so that mutual engagement is possible.

Fowles concludes that we have to find nature for ourselves and not vicariously in the words and works of others, whether scientists or artists. "As long as nature is seen as in some way outside us, frontiered and foreign, *separate*, it is lost both to us and in us." A remarkable thought: Nature can become lost in us through an excessive interiorization of experience. But we can lose ourselves, too, in a mental rarefying of life. Conversely we can find ourselves by rediscovering the sibling relationship we have with trees.

The search for fructifying and animating nature requires of us a mental backflip, a profound reorientation of vision and imagination in which our interests shift, from a reduction of nature to our abstractions, interpretations, theories, and applications, to a restoration of enchantment, in which we know nature in a felt relationship that has all the overtones of a natural religion.

Standing tall with branches outstretched, trees can look very much like human beings. A Native American story tells how the first couple were trees, until a snake came and ate their roots so they could walk. Science informs us that we're close to the apes in the family of nature, but sacred story identifies us with trees. If we could recover the enchanting intuition that we are not simply related to trees in the natural chain of being but we *are* trees, then we might know how to be with the saplings and giants of the forest, and we might also know why in fairy tales the answer to the riddle of life is often found in the forest, the place where trees congregate and cast their spell.

Blood from Stones

ALL MY LIFE I have walked the sandy shores of Lake Huron and gathered stones from the water's edge. Three of them sit on the windowsill in front of me as I write day after day, feeding my memories of an adolescence on the Great Lakes and adding an element of beauty to my surroundings with their shapes, colors, markings, and even with the shadows they cast as the low sun streams through the windows. In their stillness and unchangeability they are comforting, the work of nature's art, giving me lessons in how to write, make things, and live my life.

The house in which I now live has a special beauty that comes mainly from its assortment of woods—cherry floors, maple cabinets and trim, mahogany shelves, even some cherry and pine furniture I have made. It was the wood that first drew me to this house, and the way it was joined and finished. Soon after moving here we learned that there can be too much wood in a home. The dominance of the wood gave our daily environment the feeling of being too soft and bucolic. We knew early on that we needed a different material in order to live in this building, and so, when it became possible, we looked for a stonemason to build a large fireplace.

He found stone in a nearby quarry, gray stone that had sparkle in it, and he and his sons and grandsons made us a hearth. They chipped away at small, bread-loaf pieces of schist and gave our home the stone it craved. We feel better now, having accomplished in our home what Marsilio Ficino described as "tempering" your world, tuning it to a number of different pitches the way a musician might tune a guitar, giving it the range and variety of materials it needs.

Stone, maybe more than any other material, has been known forever to be magical, to have powers to heal, guide, house divinity, and mark places of burial. Altars are usually of stone, as are temples, oratories, and sometimes houses. Rock gardens invite meditation, and stone walls, a common sight in New England, do more than mark boundaries; they evoke memories of the people who once lived on this land of ours and give rise to speculation about early visitors from Europe and ritual megaliths and dolmens.

The Greeks knew that stones contribute much to an enchanted life, and so they spread oil over them to honor the spirits, and decked them with flowers. They piled stones into herms, which later became the incarnation of the god Hermes, guide of roadways and souls. In many places in the world, people have looked at a pile of stones and have seen a phallus, which they've honored as a life-giving spirit. We might be scandalized by a public phallus, but in an enchanted world, erotic images are not reduced to human sexuality but, especially when carved in stone, are seen as totems of animation and vitality.

In burial monuments, stone evokes eternity, while the stone in bank buildings gives the impression of solidity and security. Scientists tell us that stone is always moving and changing, but to human eyes nothing is as fixed and stable as stone. It's really not so puzzling that alchemists, who sought up and down for sure and precise images of the soul, prized stone as the very heart of the work of making soul and as an image for the rock-hard, unchanging core of the human heart. *Lapis philosophorum*, they called it, the philosophers' stone.

In a letter to an English schoolteacher who reported a dream of stone, Jung mentions an "old tradition" according to which Adam was created as a stone statue, and then Jung blends alchemy with the New Testament, saying: "Transform yourselves into living stones." Elsewhere in his alchemical studies, Jung describes blood pouring from stone: when we have soul, we are made of stone; we have eternity, stability, toughness, and immutability in our very makeup, even though we are still blood and flesh and live brief lives and change from one day to the next.

Clearly, this is not the stone of the scientist, and yet the *lapis* has some relationship to the stones that I pick up every year on the sandy shores of Lake Huron. The stone figures on Easter Island and the huge circle of stones at Stonehenge teach us that stone is in the service not only of literal life but of religion and mystery as well.

I remember well the first time I saw Stonehenge. I expected it to be a disappointment, because travelers had told me it had been commercialized, fenced, regulated, and posted to the point where its magic had been diminished. Not so for me. As I rode with friends through the open English countryside and caught my first glimpse of the stone formation, I felt immediately that I was crossing the threshold of a genuine temenos, a true sanctuary. The fences didn't interfere with my immediate fascination, and I didn't have to spend a long time studying the circle and the placement of the dolmen. In fact, I didn't think much at all, but simply felt the impact of the magic of the place and its eternity and knew in my heart that these stones were among the precious living beings of this world.

If stones speak and bleed, then the wondrous stones of Stonehenge and the Irish beehive oratories and the building blocks of cathedrals and castles are indeed alive in their own way. In a letter to Maud Oakes, who studied Native American culture and had written Jung some of her ideas about the stone he carved at his retreat in Bollingen, Jung expressed this rule of enchantment: "When I hewed that stone I did not think, however. I just brought into shape what I saw on its face." In doing our part to make an enchanted world, we don't have to think ahead and know what we're doing. We can respond to something as dumb as stone, knowing that stones speak in their own way and teach us what we have to do. Jung listened to the stone and learned from it where and what to carve. We could make our entire culture in this way, and then we would live in a world with personality and voice, and our lives would not be divided from the nature that is our substance and our guide.

The Stone Heart

When my family traveled to Ireland, we visited several oratories made of stone, some of them in the shape of beehives. Following the narrow road that snakes along the ocean, we drove out onto the far edges of the Dingle Peninsula and came to a farm where the beehives stand, preserved for twelve hundred years or more. We paid a few coins to a young man of the family there—a mythic act in itself—and then walked among the sheep that kept guard at the oratories. I was aware that our young children, examining the stones in their hands, might be the first humans in many hundreds of years to dismantle these sacred oratories.

It was an extraordinary experience to stand there close to the cliff that rises over the ocean, feel the strong, cool winds from the sea, sense the nudges of pasturing sheep, crawl into the small earthen rooms within the unmortared rocks, and then imagine holy monks of our own era praying and living in community, their spirituality fed every moment by the proximity of nature and their very establishment, made entirely of stone. Mysteriously, it was all appropriate, a wonder of spiritual technology, like a vineyard or an orchard set in just the right soil, climate, and elevation.

We were surprised on our return home to New England to discover what looks exactly like a beehive oratory just a few miles down the road from us, big enough to hold about three people, facing east, lying cozily under three tall trees. Local historians told us they suspected Irish or other Celtic monks had made our local beehive, but it isn't certain, because some scholars are skeptical about the age and function of New England stonework. At around the same time, we found, even closer to home, on our very hill, stone hearths believed to have been set up by pre-European natives. They are perfectly preserved, suggesting, as stone often does, that the passage of time can sometimes be entirely irrelevant.

We need stones around us to echo the substance of our own lives—hard, solid, heavy, timeless, and subtly hued. People go to therapists to find answers to their problems and strategies for working out difficulties, but their real work might be to discover the heavy, solid nature that lies like stone in the very deepest pit of their heart, and the knowledge that is carved into that stone self at the quick of their being. Lives of the twentieth century sometimes seem to be too soft, impermanent, light, and unrelated to the earth. For all these symptoms, stone is an obvious tonic, so that I would advise anyone motivated to engage in therapy to seek out with the alchemists the stone that has blood, the heart stone or the stone heart, which will give you a feeling of your own substance.

Don't turn this stone into a symbol, but if you have trouble finding it in yourself, look first to the stones of nature. See if your environment has enough stone in it. Become the magus of your own life, and make an amulet if you must out of material that speaks to you clearly. Wear a stone around your neck, visit Stonehenge or make the trek to Easter Island, build stone into your house. You can't find the philosophers' stone in your head. You may have to realize that the earth is your teacher and gives you the wisdom you need to make your life magical and effective.

We use the earth and its materials to create a life full of materialistic wonders, but we have lost an appreciation for the earth as a source of our spiritual development and the life of our soul. Oddly, if we want an intensification of spirituality, it might be better to become more intimate with the things of the earth than to build a self in the sky.

Precious Stones

All stone is precious, but certain stones we value more than others, for their brilliance, hardness, and color. Ficino believed that some stone sparkles because it has material of the stars in it, so when we see a stone at the water's edge twinkling in the sunlight, we may be looking into the sky. Although obviously this is not a scientific fantasy about stone, it is a useful fiction for connecting earth and heaven, and it helps us perform one of the most important of all soul tasks—reconciling spirit and body—while at the same time it ritualizes the magical formula of the *Emerald Tablet:* "As above, so below."

Precious, sparkling stones also evoke the theme of the *scintilla,* the spark of vitality that resides in material, natural and artificial. This sparkle is a sign of the soul in matter, and, reflecting the brilliance of the stars, it's an indication that the material world always contains something of the eternal. Perhaps this is one reason for giving a precious stone as a token of engagement and marriage. In "On the Nature of the Psyche," Jung treats shine and sparkle as indicators of the very depth of the soul. Quoting several alchemists, he describes the soul of the world, *anima mundi,* as scintillae or sparks identical with the spirit of God. What is often lost in discussions of alchemy is the simple idea that today we can bring tokens of that divine spark into our everyday lives through the ordinary use of precious and sparkling stones.

When twenty years ago I wrote my first book, *The Planets Within,* about Ficino's astrological magic, I didn't mention enchantment, but now I see that his work is exactly that: a manual for the enchantment of everyday experience. My book was a commentary on the third volume of his *Book of Life,* entitled *How to Design Your Life in Accord with the Sky,* a manual of natural magic that became extremely popular in the decades after Ficino's death, in 1499.

In this book, Ficino often discusses stones, and nowhere more appropriate to our theme than in his description of the model of the cosmos he says we should each have in our homes. Chapter 19 of his book, captioned "How to Make a Model of the Universe," gives instructions on how to make such a thing and enchant our lives.

He says the model should be made of bronze on silver and begun at the exact minute the sun goes into the sign of Aries, the birthday of the world. Always the astrologer, Ficino recommends that we take careful notice of the timing of our actions and our work. We shouldn't work on it on Saturday—Saturn's day—the Sabbath, on which God rested. God, he says, finished the world on Venus's day, Friday, inviting beauty into his work, and we can do the same.

The primary colors of the world are green, gold, and sapphire blue. This blue, the color of Jupiter's stone, lapis lazuli, plays an important role in evoking solar spirit, and so has the power to cure the baneful effects of Saturn—depression, melancholy, and heaviness. Ficino was familiar with many traditions that relate precious stones to spiritual mysteries, like the mystical vision of the prophet Ezechial, in the Old Testament, who saw the upper part of the universe made of sapphire, and like Gregory the Great's description of Christ as a sapphire crystal.

Just as traditional teachings about colors, stones, timing, and choice of materials guided Ficino in the development of his magic, those same traditions could show us how to go about re-enchanting our world. We could choose sapphire, the stone or just the color, when we felt a need for the spirit of Jupiter, his joviality, conviviality, and creativity, and especially his strong but benevolent authority. We could wear a sapphire ring or amulet for the same purpose, or write the sapphire into our poetry for its magic, or place its color in the workplace we are designing or furnishing. We could bring the same spirit of enchantment to all colors and textures.

The Ficinian way of going about our daily business lies somewhere between an aesthetic approach and a purely practical one. His "natural magic" is not as esoteric as it may first appear, but simply offers a way to use natural materials for a spiritual purpose. In this regard, precious stones play a significant role because, without any self-consciousness or explanation, they give daily life sensations of extraordinary value, otherworldly brilliance, eternal hardness, and deep beauty in form and color.

All kinds of stones, of course, are available for our daily magic. Ficino was especially taken with solar stones, since he considered solar spirit the most important spirit for the cultivation of human life. He recommended serious use of gold, chrysolite, carbuncle, amber, and certain stones that are magnetic—drawing metals to them as the sun heliotropically draws flowers to itself—or stones that sparkle at night. His book provides long lists of such stones and other materials, divided according to planetary or, we might say, archetypal qualities.

Jewelry can be used as magic as well as for ornament. Like all fashion, it may appear to be a luxury, and a purely spiritual philosophy may judge it as superficial, but in the Ficinian philosophy of natural magic, jewelry may be of extraordinary value to the soul.

Polishing and arranging colorful stones, setting them in brooches and rings, imitating them in stained glass, and keeping them on our persons and in our homes, all have enchantment value. We don't need to mystify stones, making them too spiritual and exotic, for the soul disappears when we become too abstract, symbolic, and intellectual about such things. There may be more enchantment in luxury than in mysticism.

Enchantment doesn't require large sums of money, but it does require some degree of luxury. Over the centuries, luxury has been condemned, moralized about, and cautioned against, but in Ficino we find a fascinating, deep-seated, occasionally repudiated Epicureanism, an understanding that pleasure is not in itself an obstacle to the spiritual life. In the eighteenth century the philosopher Jeremy Bentham could say, "Necessaries come always before luxuries," but from a less spiritually pure position, we could re-examine his principle and see that the soul requires luxuries. The poet William Burford writes that "luxury helps us forget necessity, even the ultimate necessity, death," and he describes the precious jewels used in Egyptian tombs and medieval cathedrals as means of banishing death. While the saints' bones remind us of our mortality, cathedral windows with their rubies "are erected in praise of God."

All of us in our own ways can find luxury in our lives, and what may be luxury for one may be necessity for another. Certainly luxury can get out of hand and represent a division of society into the haves and have-nots, but luxury can be a virtue when it is part of a life-affirming, soul-centered way of life.

The sparkle of a precious stone can go a long way in teaching us the spiritual potentiality of material things. Writing about the scintilla or spark, Jung says that deep forms in life have a "certain effulgence," "a numinosity that entails luminosity." In the present context, I would reverse that statement and apply it to precious stones: They have a luminosity that evokes the numinous, the presence of the divine or a spiritual dimension. For all their luxury, precious stones do indeed mysteriously represent divinity as a spark within material life, and to children and adults alike they have real magic, offering a simple way to heal the breach between heaven above and earth below.

Home

I don't know what Nature is: I sing it.
I live on a hilltop
In a solitary whitewashed cabin.
And that's my definition.

FERNANDO PESSOA

Ecology's Home

"*E*COLOGY" IS A relatively new word. Coined by the naturalist Ernst Haeckel in 1869, it referred until recently to the study of inter-relationships among plants, animals, and the environment. Now it has become a word full of emotion, indicating the impact of human culture on the natural world, and it is often used morally, implying that an ecologist is someone who has an ethical concern for all living creatures and for the earth as a living system.

The idea that the earth is an organism is not new—two thousand years ago, philosophers spoke of a "world soul," and Marsilio Ficino referred to the cosmos as an animal, a being that lives and breathes and even has an expressive face. But the development of a materialistic culture has led to an image of the earth as inert, as a hoard of inanimate materials at our complete disposal, and so it sounds new, almost radical, to say that the earth is an organic being.

"Eco-logy"

"Ecology" is made up of two important Greek words, each of them a gateway to mysteries that lie at the very base of human life. Its etymology shifts attention away from science and focuses on emotion and mystery, religion and the heart. If we could think of ecology as a development of the internal as well as the external life, we might deepen and humanize our relationship with nature.

"Eco," an abbreviated form of the Greek *oikos*, means home, either a human home, a temple, or the home of the gods, and even the astrological "house" or domicile of a planet. A sacred word covering several profound areas of life, *oikos* embraces our emotional search for a home, the building and caretaking of churches and temples, and the astrological quest for the most fruitful arrangements of time and place. At the deepest level, ecology involves the spiritual practice of making a human home and, more mysteriously, finding a home for the soul.

Logos, the other part of "ecology," is another mystery word. Although it is commonly explained as "the study of," as in psychology and geology, the word is full of sacred implications. In the Gospel of John, Jesus is named *Logos:* "In the beginning was the *Logos,* and the Logos was with God, and the Logos was God." In the ancient Wisdom of Solomon it is written that the "all powerful Logos leaped from heaven, from the royal throne" (18:15). At the beginning of the *Corpus Hermeticum,* we find: "The lightgiving Logos who comes from mind is the son of god" (1:6). These important texts show that *logos* is so full of mystery that it is used to denote divinity itself.

Connect this vast notion of *logos* with the mysterious word *oikos,* and you get "ecology," an infinitely deep and mysterious notion of home. Thinking of ecology in this way, we move beyond the literalism and materialism of our usual image of nature and approach one of the great mysteries that motivates every day of our lives: we are always making a home for the heart and always looking for the house of divinity.

The Experience of "Home"

The need for home lies deep in the human heart: when our homeland is threatened we go into action to defend it, and when our family house is violated we are profoundly offended. We spend our lives trying to "make a home"—building, buying, renting, borrowing houses, staying in the old family homestead or moving from house to house according to the winds of fate. Few things are more important than finding a home and working at it constantly to make it resonate with deep memories and fulfill deep longings.

The experience of home is so deep-seated that when we find it in our own houses or in the homes of others, we may feel enchantment thick in the air, and when we lack it in our daily experience, we may be haunted by its elusiveness. One of the sharpest emotional pains I've ever experienced came to me when I left home at an early age to enter a Catholic seminary. I spent many sleepless nights with an ache in my heart, tormented by thoughts of the comforting family I had left behind. I had left home voluntarily, inspired by powerful idealistic longings, but the burning desire one day to be a priest won out over my homesickness only by a slim margin.

Sometimes even now I wish I had stayed at home, giving my soul the comforts and pleasures of a familiar family and place, but something else in me was caught by the spirit of adventure. For many years I lived, as perhaps we all do, suspended between the heart's longing for a stable past and the spirit's wish for an exciting future, and even in my current life I have to work out the practical details of staying home while responding to the call of a greater world.

It is a mistake to see a conflict between home and adventure, because obviously we can have both. We leave the home of our parents, some of us happy to do so, others reluctant, and then eventually make our own homes. But as time goes on, we may find, as the call to community and career grows stronger, that our idea of "home" becomes complicated.

Modern life favors work, social engagement, travel, and the development of a career over the needs of home. We're expected to overrule the complaints of the soul for stability and security, so that we can move without hindrance into an exciting and fulfilling future. We see homesickness of all kinds as a childish malady, inappropriate in the mature adult, who needs to keep home in perspective and become increasingly independent.

But the soul always complains when it has been slighted, and the emotional sicknesses associated with modern life show that the spirit of home has been violated. Aimlessness, boredom, and irresponsibility are common problems, and they may be traced back to a loss of home. All signs indicate that our society is suffering from profound homesickness.

The soul's need for home has to do not only with shelter and a house, but with more subtle forms, like the feeling that one is living in the right place, being around people who offer a sense of belonging, doing work that is truly appropriate, feeling maternally protected and enlivened by the natural world, and belonging to a nation and a world community. These larger sources of home ask for our attention and commitment, but they also have gifts for the heart, and each one of them can contribute to the enchantment of everyday existence.

"Ecology," then, is the "mystery of home." It's not a program of action as much as a sensibility, a set of feelings focused on the desire for and the experience of being in the right town or area, being connected with the place in which we live, and being enchanted by the sensation of home the place provides. As we grow older and expand our idea of what makes a home, many places in the world may become part of our personal ecology, and we may begin to realize that the entire planet is in a real sense our home. We may then feel in our hearts the need to take care of the planet precisely because it is our home, and our activism and sense of responsibility flow from our emotional attachment.

A Soft Approach to Ecology

Enchanted ecology is the work of religion more than science, love more than understanding, and ritual more than heroic action. It is rooted in both a love for home and a willingness to let the place where we live set limits on our lives, define our personalities, and shape our values. This kind of ecology is concerned not simply with the natural world but with our place in the human environment as well, and it has as much to do with meaning and emotion as with the protection of literal nature.

Enchantment can provide a solid basis for an ethical response to the world we live in; for morality doesn't come out of nowhere. It has to have a foundation. Sometimes we act morally from a sense of obligation, fear, custom, family values, religious instruction, or the desire to be a good citizen and good person. Enchantment is another strong motive, because when we are charmed by a person or place, we will feel a strong connection, and from that intimacy we may want to be protective or responsible. Furthermore, motives of love lie deeper than those of obligation and are less anxious than those of narcissism—the need to be right and even righteous.

If we felt at home on this earth and loved our home, we would do everything possible to keep it vibrant and healthy, and we would have a basis for human community. Any conversation about community that excludes the natural world is incomplete and headed toward failure, just as any talk about ecology is inadequate if it doesn't include all relations, from nature to persons. As mystics have taught for centuries, we realize who we are only in community with our fellow human beings and in the closest intimacy with the world of nonhuman beings, a spirit Henry Thoreau captures in his memoirs of Walden Pond: "A lake . . . is earth's eye; looking into which the beholder measures the depth of his own nature. The fluviatile trees next the shore are the slender eyelashes which fringe it, and the wooded hills and cliffs around are its overhanging brows."

Ecology: A Sacred Science

Enchantment arises on the threshold between human activity and nature's presence. It is always a liminal phenomenon, a momentary relationship, made of the right arrangement of stars and planets and elaborated with art by human consciousness. Enchantment is nature's song heard by a sensitive human ear, and it is the crafted work of human hands reflecting their admiration of nature's geometries.

Science and technology are sometimes at odds with enchantment, not because of the work they do and the cultural advances they bring, but rather because of the relationship to the world they fashion when they are carried out without sacred imagination. To the extent that they reduce understanding to materialistic dimensions, they create a secularistic worldview that infiltrates every aspect of daily life. An enchanted science and an enchanted technology would not drive a wedge between science and religion, or even between secularity and religion.

Enchanted science would not be devoted exclusively to facts, but it would be able to reflect back on its own mythic nature and its own fantasies and fictions. It would acknowledge that the very notion of facts is part of a mythological worldview. Taking itself literally and denying its place in the realm of imagination, science

often closes the doors on enchantment, keeps them shut aggressively and defensively, thinking that fact-free imagination would be
a contamination of its purity.

Enchanted science would not divide the poetry of nature, as
reflected for instance in mythology, lore, and legend, from physical
laws and characteristics, nor would it separate us in time so haugh-
tily from our ancestors. Knowing the geology of a region has not
inhibited us from overdeveloping and destroying places of natural
holiness, nor has awareness of the sociology of a neighborhood pre-
vented us from building unsightly overpasses, expressways, and
other enterprises that wound or destroy communities. A technology sensitive to enchantment would serve the soul as well as fulfill
our spirited ambitions, and therefore it would create and sustain a
humane environment.

Modern devotion to science convinces us that we should understand and classify all of nature, that we should explore every place,
and that we should manufacture everything that is inventable. The
owner of a manufacturing plant once told me that he was obsessed
with machinery and the assembly line and that every idea that came
to him demanded to be put into production. He felt choked by the
busyness such a productive life required of him, and it appeared to
me that his torment was a reflection of our society's obsession with
the invention and fabrication of things. We mark our progress as a
civilization by what we see as advances in hardware, and that crite-
rion, assumed so readily by the population at large, blinds us to
other possible values such as community, reverence, wisdom, the
care and education of children, and the condition of the natural
world. I would wish to be a member of a community that judged
itself on the happiness of its children rather than on the unhindered
flow of its mechanical inventions.

I remember reading as a child magazine articles that illustrated
what the future would be like—the 1990s, for instance. These articles always focused on technological advances: Everyone would
have a personal helicopter, and the air would be filled with individuals soaring off to work or play. Houses would be completely auto-
mated, and each home would be cleaned by a resident robot. I
remember many circles, lines, and squares in the geometry of the
imagined civic and commercial buildings—no images, no strong

presence of nature, no imaginative elaboration in the architecture. It was a cold, secularistic, unnatural future we imagined in those days.

What if we pictured our blissful possibilities in more human terms? I see hospitals built and run more on the model of home than of body repair, and schools where children were fed excellent food and learned how to be persons in community rather than skilled units stuffed with information, and cities where our long history was visible in architecture and monument and where nature was invited in and befriended. Rather than bringing robots into our homes, I see us hosting people of all races, genders, sexual preferences, and states of body and mind. By keeping "home" in our definition of ecology, we can imagine a more humane world and give heart to our very idea of environment.

Enchantment arises whenever we move so deeply into anything we're doing that its interiority stirs the heart and the imagination. An enchanted ecology comes into being when our concern for the environment goes beyond materialistic elements in nature and culture: to children rather than machines, trees rather than excessive paper products, and home rather than shelter. There need not be a conflict between technology and enchantment—driving a combine in a great field of wheat under a blazing sun can make for difficult but enchanting work, and standing at an office copying machine can quicken the soul, provided the context of the work is in accord with nature and the heart needs of the culture.

Debates about the environment develop out of emotional commitments to one side or other of a divisive view of life, where nature competes with culture and home with wilderness. One alternative to such divisiveness is to find intermediaries between these apparent polarities and thus diminish the gap between them.

Art, for instance, can present nature to us for our contemplation, so that we get to know it more deeply and intimately. My gardener friends are always telling me about the value of establishing a link, in the form of low bushes or tall grasses around the home, between the civility of the house and the wildness of the woods. Maybe there's a metaphor in that artistic suggestion: we may need a means of connection, a Hermes of the garden, between our feelings about culture and nature, about development and the conservation of land.

Nature has many gifts to offer, including beauty, a place of retreat, raw materials and space for development, purification of air and water, a habitat for creatures of all kinds, a place for play. "Green" awareness focuses on all but the development resources, while "steel-gray" consciousness gives its attention to the concrete inherent in gravel, the studs hiding in raw timber, and the girders lying in wait underground. It might help us to appreciate all these gifts of nature and to establish a buffer zone, as in a garden in the woods, so that we're not always on the embattled border between nature and civilization.

Both sides of the ecological argument are in battle gear, because nature itself has become a psychological "complex." In any matter, if voices are harsh and tempers hot, some powerful and unknown concern has got hold of us and we have lost our capacity for imagination in that area. We may need to explore more profoundly our needs for nature and home, and hope that a more vivid imagination might take us more sensitively and more effectively into their fulfillment and enjoyment.

When we become obsessed with anything, from sex to chocolate, we may be deluded into thinking that large quantities of it makes up for quality. Unhindered use of raw materials, with no limiting conscience or other feelings of inhibition, may not give us the home or business that we are searching for. Knowing what is enough is an element in all forms of creativity, but boundless exploitation is a sign of neurosis and ultimately offers little substantive reward.

Maybe we don't need as much space in our homes and workplaces as we think we do, so much paper for our business, or so much "nature" for our recreation. In all these instances, an ecological reflection on the way we live and work might note where our obsessions lie, in either the steel-gray or the green areas. We all need nature, we all need development, we all need home, and so we all have to look closely and honestly for signs of our own individual and collective neuroses, for it is in our obsessions and delusions that both nature and humanity are threatened.

I equate neurosis with disenchantment, for when we lose our religious sensibility and the captivating powers of imagination—the sources of enchantment—we are left with a soulless life and a flat, pragmatic, and literalized culture. Our problem then is not the lack of appreciation for human creativity and development or for the environment; our problem is the loss of enchantment, a much deeper problem, which has more to do with the very meaning of our lives.

Establishing a home or business is always an act of natural religion, and if we don't bring appropriate sensitivity to the mystery, depth, and sacredness inherent in that activity, then we increase our disenchantment. If our corresponding sense of community with our fellow humans, fellow animals, and fellow plants isn't deeply rooted, then disenchantment increases again, along with our voraciousness for both nature and development.

The disenchanted environmentalist and the disenchanted developer walk the same road, on opposite sides. Both suspect that there is enchantment in their own occupations, but neither knows the security and satisfaction that an enchanted world would give them. An enchanted building can be nature's partner and can add enormously to the soul of a place, but forty enchanted buildings on a plot of land can destroy nature's presence.

I always feel a pleasant shock when I visit a culture where commercialization is not a dominant factor, where there are no billboards and garish signs interfering with my view of nature and where stores and businesses appear to find their place in a landscape of homes and nature. I see no sign of the people's obsession with buying and selling, and yet I come across a colorful market where the sense of community and the quality of food and other goods are remarkable.

The way to an ecological way of life is to treat our houses as homes, our communities as homes, and nature as home. It is the intimacy in each relationship that serves the welfare of the other; at root, ecology is an erotic attitude of closeness, relatedness, and care. We have made it into a rational/activist project and lost sight of its heart. When eros and logos are lived deeply enough, they are so close to each other as to be barely distinguishable. Knowing fosters love, and love inspires the desire to know. A good scientist, who is not entirely captivated by modernist philosophies, knows the love of nature that arises from close study, and a good environmentalist knows the desire to learn that appears as a blossoming and sophistication of his or her innate attachment to nature. There is no room in this tight interrelationship for exploitation and uncaring analysis, and there lies deep in this fundamental intimacy the recognition that ultimately there is nothing in creation that is not a piece of the home that satisfies the soul and allows the security that is the *sine qua non* of all creative activity.

The Enchanted Child

I REMEMBER VIVIDLY the soft light of dawn and the gentle quiet that settled on the birthing room moments after my daughter was born. This was certainly one of the stillest and most treasured moments in my life. Her mother and I had just spent a night together that was extraordinary, as my daughter was hesitant to enter the world, just as now she's reluctant to leave childhood. It was the night of Thanksgiving, and the hospital staff was sparse, and, of course, many babies decided this would be a good time to make their entrance into the world.

We were alone all the night long, as her mother was in hours of fruitless labor until the doctor arrived. I stood with one arm behind my wife's shoulders and the other rubbing against his. "Cut there," he said, handing me a scissors and pointing to a place on the umbilical cord. The baby didn't cry, and as soon as her mouth and eyes were clear, the doctor and nurse shut off the bright lamps and left us for an hour in the gentle natural light and the merciful quiet. In the unfamiliar calm, we whispered, as a light rain drummed on the windowpanes, and got to know each other. Only at the end of the hour did the baby cry, letting us know she had a voice and a spirit.

Nothing is more magical than the birth of a child, except perhaps watching that infant grow into a person as the soul emerges gradually and shows itself in the individuality of a new being. I don't think for a moment that a child is a *tabula rasa,* an empty page that life experiences and culture make into a person. Clearly, a child is fully present in that moment of birth, and what happens later is simply an unfolding and unwrapping of a complicated and rich destiny and potentiality. James Hillman says a child is an acorn and that you can see the seeds of its life early on: "You have an acorn in you, you are a certain person, and that person begins to appear early in your life, but it's there all the way through your life."

A child lives in an enchanted world that is always alive and in dialogue. I will be writing in my studio and hear my daughter in the next room talking and singing to her large rabbit doll as she wraps a diaper around his soft velvet thighs. To her, the entire past is "yesterday." "Yesterday I went to New York and stayed at a hotel," she will say, referring to a trip the family took months ago.

Is this simply a cute childhood animism and a failure to know how time works, how to read a calendar or a clock? Or could it be a valid way of being in the world, the way of enchantment? Could we enter into relationship with the so-called inanimate world, and could we explore alternatives to a world governed by the clock and calendar?

Why not imagine the child's world as perfectly valid and complete: not something we grow out of or develop from, but one that we fall out of and forget. Could it be that in becoming adults we are educated away from the soul that is so vividly present in childhood? In some societies, adults don't seem to be nearly so different from children, or to have forgotten the values of childhood. They may paint their faces the way children do and ritualize all of life in dance, song, story, and many forms of play.

Keeping the Child in Childhood

Imagine a form of education that does not try to change the child or transform it into an adult, but rather provides a place where the child can flourish as a child, where "education" means "leading out" the child, not the adult trapped in the body of the child. Such an education would ask the adults to be full of faith and trust that the child would discover the world and learn its nature and ways over time. Maybe not every child would learn how to read at the same "stage of development," or to count or tell time. Would it be so unfortunate for a child to spend the early years without ever knowing the purpose of the clock on the classroom wall?

I have had more education in my life than is seemly or appropriate, and yet in all those years I never learned how to build, fix, or maintain a house; how to take care of the business of life—banks, taxes, economics, insurance; how to grow food and cook it; how to get along in nature. I was a born musician, and yet I was in my tenth year of school before someone introduced me to the study of music. Fortunately, in my childhood my father encouraged me to play a piano whenever we happened to be in a house that had one, and then later he bought a fifty-dollar piano and placed it cozily in the basement, which became my studio and a rehearsal hall where he played violin to my halting piano accompaniment. Although I was never given piano lessons as a child, I was enchanted by the instrument from the very first time I saw one, and a keyboard still casts a spell on me today.

The idea is often sentimentalized, yet I do think that artists maintain a connection to childhood through their work, as does anyone who can't distinguish work from play. Being an audience to art and sport is another way to keep the child active in the community of the soul. Parties, carnivals, celebrations, and even holy rituals speak to the child and help keep the connection to childhood vibrant.

A radio interviewer once confessed to me on the air that when he was a child attending services in his Jewish tradition, the stories, dress, music, and food were much more important to him than the teachings and moral admonitions he was subjected to. I thought it was interesting that he associated the soul elements in religion with childhood and the more spiritual dimensions with adulthood. The soul is indeed close to the things of the child, and the fact that we tend to judge those very elements as inferior hints at our more general disparagement of both childhood and the soul.

I was never athletically "inclined." Not good at baseball, I was always chosen last when teams were being formed and was usually assigned to right field, with the hope that I wouldn't get much business out there. I tried out for the grade school basketball team once, but no one had ever taught me how to play, and I was in the first batch of boys to be quickly cut from among the hopefuls. I was good at ice hockey, but it was never given a formal place in school.

And so I spent my education years without sports, not because I didn't appreciate their enchantment but because I couldn't play competitively.

I have long known that I have a piece of depression in me, though I'm not by nature a depressed person. I think it is the child in me who is depressed, the one who was born with his moon in Capricorn and then was taken from the warm embrace of home to be educated in a school that had no joy and where pleasure was equated with sin, and who finally left home for good to chase after a dream. Maybe for many of us depression, which we usually understand as a general emotional affliction, stems from harsh treatment and neglect of the soul's eternal childhood.

The secret of making a soulful adult may not be to bring up a child correctly; it may be to allow the child its own nature, its pleasures and interpretations. If we were to redesign child care and education on the model of the child, both might become enchanted. The child has no trouble seeing magic where adults find only mechanics and practicality. It makes sense that to restore enchantment to our lives, we could do no better than to reassess our attitudes toward our own childhood, childhood in general, and the children in our world.

A Child's Way of Knowing

A child looks at the world with eyes not yet trained to see literally and according to the laws of physics; children are not naturally Newtonian. I have a very strange memory of once riding in a car down Jefferson Avenue in Detroit. I must have been very young. An adult in the car pointed to the far side of the street—I can still see the scene vividly in my memory—and said, "There goes a drunk man." I looked over, and all I could see out of the ordinary was an inflated orange rubber raft—Jefferson Avenue runs along the river. I simply concluded that when you drink too much, you turn into a rubber raft, and I promised myself that it would be far better to swear off drink than ever to find myself in that condition.

The spirit in us that wants to teach a child out of such absurd perceptions is a spirit that doesn't appreciate enchantment. We assume it's natural to take a child from ignorance to learning, and these days we become active in the process as early as we can. A child's weekly schedule of lessons and "experiences" can sometimes compete with that of the CEO of a large company. This kind of education appears to arise out of anxiety, the fear that the child may become an adult and not be able to get along or "compete."

To avoid working against the magic of childhood in the name of learning, we may first have to confront our own bias against the enchanted life, our pragmatism, literalism, and exaggerated seriousness. The soul is essentially epicurean: its primary objective is pleasure. We might ask a child coming home from school not "What did you learn today?" but "Did you have fun in school today?"—an epicurean question that speaks for enchantment.

Another way to investigate our adult bias might be to look closely at the serious attitude we bring to education and consider its roots. When I was a child in a Catholic school taught almost entirely by nuns, it was common to observe a teacher slapping a child on the face until his skin turned red or taking a child into the hall with a long wooden ruler. Today we have laws that protect children from such torture, but we still sometimes imagine education with the seriousness of the sadist rather than with the playfulness of the epicurean.

We have little or no trust that a child's knowledge is real knowledge, that their play is important work, or that the animated world they inhabit is as true as the Newtonian world we prefer. We believe firmly that we have to teach them and that we have nothing to learn from them. In an enchanted world, it would make sense to let children do some of the teaching and to give lessons in what they know best—play, animism, and charm, the very things our culture lacks.

When a Child Is Present

When as adults we come up against the world of the child, often we find an emotional fence that keeps us out. We may, as the Jungian analyst Patricia Berry has pointed out, encounter a deep and disturbing feeling of inferiority. The child represents the experience of not being able to do many things, not being well-read, not understanding what is going on, and not being able to give full attention. As adults, we encounter qualities that make us feel inferior, and we react by wanting desperately and obsessively to correct them. Yet to gain the enchantment that children enjoy, we will have to live with feelings of inferiority, feelings that are occasioned by the sophistication of adult life.

Simply allowing the child into our lives represents a beginning in the process of re-enchanting life through the child. Internalizing childhood values is one way, but including actual children in day-to-day living is another effective means of gaining enchantment.

Once, when my daughter was an infant, my wife and I attended a lecture on Renaissance art at the Gardner Museum in Boston. We sat at the very rear of the auditorium, far from the last row of seats, and began to enjoy a lecture on themes of importance to both of us. My wife nursed the baby, who didn't cry or make any other noise. After a while, a woman in the audience came up to us and asked us to leave.

"But the baby's not making any sound," I said.

"Yes, but she's interfering with our concentration anyway."

I knew what she was saying: the mere presence of a child in adult company is a threat to the world created by and for adults.

A recent newspaper article told of wedding invitations asking that children stay home. Adults don't want children running all over the dance floor, it said. Once, our elementary school, widely known in the area as a progressive institution, sponsored a dance in the school gym. My wife and I attended, learning first how to do swing dances, and then enjoying an evening of old music and familiar dances. Our son and daughter were there too, and they also enjoyed themselves, while we took care to make sure they didn't get in anyone's way. Within a few days we received a note from the school, saying that the dance was a great success but many people had complained about the presence of children.

A society with soul appreciates the beauty and tolerates the interference of children, knowing that something essential disappears from life when children are excluded. Of course, it's necessary to have events for adults exclusively, and parents certainly need relief from the constant demands of their children, but we could be aware of those circumstances in which the exclusion of children adds to the soullessness of life.

Just by genuinely taking children into consideration, we have an opportunity to rediscover the enchanted life—not the orderly, functional, smooth-running life, but a life of magic. If we could imagine the conflict between adult order versus child chaos not as a matter of good and bad, or right and wrong, but rather as two different ways of life, then we might be able to find ways to include children in almost all of life, without sacrificing adult pleasures. With a child stationed in every corner of life, we don't have to theorize about enchantment but have only to watch it pour in.

The Interiority of Food

A FEW YEARS AGO my wife and I made our first trip to Italy and were charmed by almost everything we saw: extraordinary art, exquisite Renaissance architecture, mysterious Roman ruins, and the uniquely comforting hills of Tuscany. But now, when we talk about that trip, our stories focus on food: the unending lunch in Florence, the small *ristorante* in Rome with the bottomless tank of wine, the homemade multicourse dinner with friends, dining at sunset on a rooftop, a midnight repast in the Piazza Navona by the Bernini fountains, a night roaming through dark hills in search of a hilltop café, ubiquitous coffee bars, and fresh food at expressway stops. Food is a major source of enchantment.

In recent times we seem to have lost some of the enchantment of the kitchen, either by slipping unconsciously into thoughtless eating in fast-food restaurants or by focusing more on health than on taste. Food has become a problem, a threat to our hearts especially. At a certain level I appreciate being able to read the ingredients of the packaged food I eat, but at another level I wonder what impact those messages have on eating. If I place a skull and crossbones on an apple before I eat it, my experience of the apple will be seriously affected, because food is an experience of the imagination as well as the stomach.

Labeling food with its chemical components turns eating into an abstract, mental activity, weakening its sensuality. Chemists give us one view of the interiority of food—its chemical components— but there is another kind of interiority, the soul of food, which can be found in its traditional preparation, in its associations in history and the family, and simply in taste, color, smell, and texture.

Food is not an amalgam of chemicals designed to keep the organism alive. If that were true, we could eat tasteless wafers having the exact balance of fats, fibers, starches, and carbohydrates that our bodies require—"soylent green." Food is not just for the body; it also feeds the soul. Why else go to Italian, Indian, Thai, Chinese, Ethiopian, or French restaurants, unless the soul craves the culture that is provided by the food and all its accoutrements? One of the most important gifts of food is to convey a cultural imagination, giving us a "taste" of life. We eat certain foods, and our imagination gains weight.

I have yet to see a study of the health effects of spices, and yet spice is essential to food. Spice is to food as color is to a painting or instrumentation to music. Ginger, cinnamon, allspice, rosemary— they are all traditional remedies for both body and soul. As every good cook knows, a recipe and a menu are among the most imaginative and creative things in life, a form of literature that has direct and immediate appeal. Food requires a taste imagination, just as music requires an imagination of sounds and sculpture demands an imagination of materials and forms. Tasting is a form of knowing, a school for the senses, and is central in food's ability to enchant.

The preparation of food also serves the soul in a number of ways. In a general sense, it gives us a valuable, ordinary opportunity to meditate quietly, as we peel and cut vegetables, stir pots, measure out proportions, and watch for boiling and roasting. We can become absorbed in the sensual contemplation of colors, textures, and tastes as, alchemists of the kitchen, we mix and stir just the right proportions. The colors and the smells can take us out of "real" time, which can be so deadening, and lift us into another time and space altogether, the time of myth created by cooking. The kitchen is one of the most soulful rooms in a house, often the center of family life.

Kitchen utensils are part of the enchantment. One tool has been in the family for generations, another was received as a wedding gift; a favorite utensil might work particularly well or be oddly shaped and perform an unusual task. I have spent years in quest of the ultimate peeler, one that doesn't jam, break, or dull easily. To me, a good pan is worth a shelf of library books and gives an inordinate degree of charm to an afternoon in the kitchen.

Setting a table asks soul to be present as we transform eating into dining. Plates and cups and silverware may be objects of family memory or simply beautiful tools of the table. A tablecloth, cloth napkins, candles, and even a trivet can change an ordinary meal into an experience that magically holds the family together, invites needed conversation, stokes friendship, and swells the soul with the ordinary pleasures it craves.

These homespun ways of eliciting the soul of food have far more importance than we might imagine. A cousin of mine, who was always kind and attentive to me, developed cancer one year and had to spend Thanksgiving Day in a hospital room shortly before he died. I visited him there, and when I was leaving he said to me, with tears in his eyes, that he would give anything in the world if he could just have one last Thanksgiving dinner with the family. I've never forgotten the depth of feeling expressed in that simple wish.

The food and table I'm describing here can take countless forms, from family to family, from culture to culture, from time to time. They may be simple or ornate—a lunch in a park on an ordinary workday, an old table set with bent and stained knives and forks, a cup of tea in the afternoon, a hot dog at a ballpark, a festive dinner at a swank restaurant, a holiday meal with family and friends, a dinner alone for someone whose partner has gone on or whose family has grown. Every repast can have soul and can be enchanting; it asks only for a small degree of mindfulness and a habit of doing things with care and imagination.

As a therapist, I've worked with people who feel their lives are meaningless, aimless, and generally depressed. In a number of instances, after discussions of family and tradition, these people have brought soul into their lives simply by phoning a mother, father, or grandparent and asking for some old family recipes. The familiar but forgotten smells and tastes restore (the meaning of the word "restaurant") a long-dormant element in the soul—a comforted childhood, a feeling of belonging, the support of religious and cultural traditions, and family stories and personalities.

Over the years, when I've lectured on food, cynical listeners have complained that I'm reducing psychology to the themes of modern living and gourmet magazines. When I first heard such objections I felt defensive and concerned. Was I not being clear about the depth of these issues? Then I realized that magazines about food and home may be more important, even if they are intellectually light, than thick tomes of research and philosophy. Now I don't mind being associated with books of recipes and advice about furnishings and entertainment. Of course, they can be superficial and middle-class, but their simplicity is not a sign of their insignificance.

The Poetics of Food

The soul is not a mechanical problem that needs to be solved; it's a living being that has to be fed. I believe that if this simple, ancient idea were taken to heart, we would move close to the solution to many of our problems, but in this day of mechanistic thinking and problem solving, it isn't easy to appreciate such a simple notion. For some reason, we prefer to think of ourselves as a complicated apparatus in need of analysis more than a living being in need of good food.

The idea of feeding the soul is an old one, which can be found in mystical literature from around the world. Jesus said with utter simplicity: "I am the bread of life" [John 6:35]. Ancient notions of soul food are summarized in the words of the modern poet Anne Sexton, in "The Jesus Papers":

> Mary, your great
> white apples make me glad.
> . . . .
> I close my eyes and suck you in like a fire.
> I grow. I grow. I'm fattening out.

The soul needs to be fattened, not explained, and certain things are nutritious, while others are without taste or benefit. Good food for the soul includes especially anything that promotes intimacy: a hike in nature, a late-night conversation with a friend, a family dinner, a job that satisfies deeply, a visit to a cemetery. Beauty, solitude, and deep pleasure also keep the soul well fed.

Religion teaches that sometimes spiritual food for the soul is closely connected to the body's food. The story in Genesis about Adam and Eve eating forbidden fruit is worth years of meditation. Somehow, eating the wrong thing brings a curse on life. The story has far-reaching and sublime theological implications, but it may also speak to the simple truth that we can be nourished or poisoned with whatever we take into ourselves—the books we read, the people we associate with, the religion we follow, or the food we eat.

Jesus begins his public life with his first miracle, transforming water into wine at a wedding, and then later he presents himself, his body and blood, as bread and wine. In one of his great miracles, he feeds five thousand people with five loaves of bread and two fish. In Greek religion the infant Dionysus was cut up, boiled, and eaten by the Titans, and in Judaism the Israelites were fed in the desert with miraculous manna. The ancient story of Gilgamesh tells of the hero's quest for the plant of immortality, and in Chinese Taoism we find a peach of immortality growing in a garden full of rare flowers and colorful birds.

In fasting and in feasting, in proscriptions and blessings, religions around the world stress the importance of food for the soul, not just for the body. When I was a child, we ate fish on Friday and fasted for hours before communion and gave up certain foods in Lent, and these simple food practices helped link religion with daily life in a simple but effective form of enchantment. When practices like these disappear, the fantasy associated with food, and therefore its soul and charm, diminishes. These days even religion seems to have forgotten the importance of lacing food with sacred imagination, and so we are left with food as a mere means of sustenance and health. We are getting fat in body, but not in soul. We are eating apples from the corner stand, but not Mary's apples.

Shunryu Suzuki Roshi ends his excellent little book of spiritual guidance, *Zen Mind, Beginner's Mind,* with the sentence: "In Japan in the spring we eat cucumbers." Food is so ordinary that we overlook it as we make grand quests for spiritual understanding and enlightenment. Yet the religions of the world have understood its profound significance, its luscious imagery, and its weight in meaning. "Give us this day our daily bread"—is there a simpler yet more profound prayer in all of religious literature?

Many poets have recognized the secret of food's significance to the heart, and so we can turn to the poets to learn how to eat enchantingly. The American poet from Hartford, Wallace Stevens, tells us straight out: "The only emperor is the emperor of ice cream." In another poem he writes: "Meyer is a bum. What is it we share? Red cherry pie."

The fact that Meyer is a bum echoes the basic teaching of Shunryu Suzuki—"beginner's mind." To appreciate the importance of food, we may have to divest ourselves of our knowledge of chemicals and calories and, like a bum of the kitchen, discover food as if for the first time. We don't have to be self-conscious about our eating, yet we could give every kind of dining plenty of time and imagination. It's no accident that in our disenchanted times we have found hundreds of ways to short-circuit the production, preparation, and eating of food, and so it makes sense that to re-enchant our ordinary lives we could approach the supermarket, the kitchen, and the dining room differently, realizing that the extra time real food demands of us is not wasted but serves the soul.

Emily Dickinson, who once told her colleague Thomas Wentworth Higginson, "People must have puddings," makes a similar point about food's plainness and adds the rule of magic: the smallest ingredient is the most powerful, the slightest act the most potent.

> God gave a Loaf to every Bird—
> But just a Crumb—to Me—
>
> . . . .
> I wonder how the Rich—may feel—
> An Indiaman—an Earl—
> I deem that I—with but a Crumb—
> Am Sovereign of them all—

Give us this day our daily crumb, our ice cream cone, our cherry pie. The slightest things—a walk, a word, a breeze, a passing view—please the soul immeasurably, and feed it. A dinner with a hint of imagination and effort, a tree bearing fruit outside the kitchen, a favorite market, an old recipe, can all feed the soul even as they nourish the body.

The health fantasy of food is not enough. That has its importance, of course, but if it is allowed to dominate, especially as we at present imagine it—a medical, scientific, chemical-genetic reduction of the human person to a materialistic object—the soul in food will vanish, and we will have lost one more important source of soul and enchantment in everyday experience.

Food Rituals

Religion and poetry teach us how to recapture the soul in food, but we don't have to "baptize" food by surrounding it with pomp and circumstance or elaborate symbolism. We could maintain food's simplicity while at the same time safeguarding all the fantasy, memory, and emotion that are associated with or contained in it. Such ordinary activities as shopping, canning, boxing, making a pantry, and filling a shelf are rites of food that give as much to the soul as they do to the body.

Shopping can be one of the most rewarding soul activities in daily life, but it can also be done obsessively or mindlessly. Good shopping makes a soulful life. But good shopping means taking time and care, knowing well the varieties of food and their seasons, and buying whenever possible from people who have some imagination about food. Consumerism could be defined as disenchanted shopping, while in soulful shopping we are profoundly aware of the wealth of culture that surrounds food—its seasons, national varieties, natural characteristics, and recipes.

A good food market that has excellent produce, in great variety, presented with imagination, and filled with sights and smells and gustatory possibilities can be one of the most enchanting places on earth. But not all food stores are real markets. A soul-inspiring market can make you passionate about buying and preparing food. "Market" is a "mercury" word, like "merchandise" and "commerce." "Store" also has a rich background, since it has the same root as "restaurant"—a place where we can be restored. If there is mercury in a market, and if it promises real restoration, then it is a treasure.

Even the disposal of food has soul in it. Garbage, compost, and trash, the underworld of food, is obviously full of fantasy. In every bucket of garbage we see the alchemical law of all life—the decomposing, the smells and sights of corruption, and, in our gardens, the great fertility in refuse. Every day we come in contact with garbage and "putrefaction," a process that has parallels in our personal and social lives, as when a marriage goes sour or a job becomes rotten.

Garbage is the shadow side of food, perhaps, but it is nevertheless enchanting in its own way. Any effort to avoid garbage by living in a sanitized environment contributes to our disenchantment. One of my household chores is to take the garbage to the recycling center in our town. Every time I pour food scraps into the great stinking bin that stands in the very middle of the melee, I think of Dante's inferno and Hieronymus Bosch's vivid portrayals of hell—a real benefit of my visit to the "dump."

Food can bring rich cultures from all over the world to our own table. It's exciting to come across an excellent spice for Indian food or a great salsa from the American Southwest. It's worth traveling great distances not only to see unusual sights but to eat local food. These notions are obvious to anyone even slightly sensitive to the richness of experience food offers, and yet in our modern world we are losing this source of enchantment too. Great colorful, soul-drenching markets all over the world are gradually being replaced by cool, packaged, controlled supermarkets. At home, the American diet is filled with bland, overly processed, culture-poor, tasteless food that not only is inimical to our physical health but, worse, starves the soul of the enchantment calories it requires.

It wouldn't take much to change this unfortunate situation, and indeed there are signs here and there of movement back to soul food. In some cities, farmers come into town regularly to offer their fresh produce as well as their stories and advice. Some new supermarkets stock organic, locally grown food and positively refuse the overly processed food that bears the mark of the stainless-steel machine rather than the weathered hand. Some restaurants offer true seasonal menus and are always experimenting with ways to enrich the experience of food and dining.

Shops, restaurants, and our own dining room or kitchen tables can come to life quite easily with food that is ethnically evocative, individual, fresh, at least in part local, imaginatively prepared and presented, enjoyed, and lovingly disposed of. Food is an implement of magic, and only the most coldhearted rationalist could squeeze the juices of life out of it and make it bland. In a true sense, a cookbook is the best source of psychological advice and the kitchen the first choice of room for a therapy of the world.

The Presence of the Hand

ONE WAY TO appreciate the enchantment in a place or thing is to sense the presence of an invisible personality, either a ghost from the past or a current resident spirit. Once, when walking through Emily Dickinson's house, I felt distracted by the tour guide's informative but nevertheless intrusive running commentary. I wanted to sit and take in the ghosts of the place and somehow be receptive to the memories stored in the rooms and in the original furnishings. But the guide was intent on educating me rather than allowing me to be visited by the spirits that obviously lived in the closets and hallways, or to imagine myself sitting at the window with the poet by my side. There is a close tie between enchantment and haunting, and to have an enchanted world we have to do everything possible to preserve spirits of the past, to make and keep things rich in personality, and then to surrender ourselves to their presence.

Some sign that a human hand was involved in the making of a thing can often give it a degree of enchantment. In our house we have a small jelly cabinet that I crafted out of a few scraps of pine. I made it in strict Shaker style, and it's an extremely simple piece. Over the few years of its life, its door has sagged, the panels have shifted to reveal unpainted areas, and cracks and knots have darkened. I took trouble to find some authentic powdered milk-paint for it, but when I applied the paint, apparently I didn't mix it well enough, and now the white of the milk shines through the brilliant blue of the pigment. People mistake it for an antique. I didn't intend to make it look old, but it's easy to confuse the simplicity of old and sometimes outmoded techniques with the simplicity of an amateur carpenter.

In 1605, Francis Bacon noted that the Bible says God *made* the world. He did not bring the world into being by decree; he manufactured it, says Bacon, made it "by hand." We, too, are making a world, but now manufacture has come to mean making by some means other than the hand, and it could be said that the loss of enchantment coincides with the disappearance of the hand in crafting the things we use every day. The presence of the hand gives a thing at least the rudiments of personality, but a machine has to be quite extraordinary to animate the object it fashions.

You don't have to be an expert to sense the presence of the human hand in fabricated things, because the hand leaves marks that are different from those of machines. I have a mahogany bench in my house that still shows the hot, rapid, spinning teeth of the carpenter's circular saw, and those marks do not add beauty to the piece the way a hand scraper or a handheld plane might. On the other hand, when my children brush their teeth or wash their hands, they stand on a small stool I made with my hands, and every time it wobbles under their naked toes, we are all reminded of my loving but amateur woodworking fingers.

A few years ago I began to read magazines on woodworking with a passion that shocked me. I had never done any serious woodworking, and I knew I didn't have much natural talent. What was unusual about this new obsession was that it didn't require that I actually work with wood. I have a few objects around the house that I've made, but these are all out of proportion to the amount of reading I've done and the number of magazines I keep on my shelves. I've long thought of writing a piece for one of these magazines, confessing that I seem to get more from reading them and studying the pictures than from doing the work, but I assume no one would want to hear such a thing, especially not the no-nonsense craftspeople who constitute the readership.

I read woodworking magazines because I'm drawn to the culture surrounding handcraft: the questions amateur and professional craftspeople ask and answer for each other; the discussion of methods, materials, shortcuts, and traditions; the pictures of step-by-step construction. I'm often disappointed by the designs in the projects I see, but I can find beautiful design elsewhere. I'm captivated by the pictures of the partial bodies of the craftspeople, their hands on their work, their individualized workshops and homemade jigs. All this handwork seems to be an attempt to return to a kind of enchanted making that we have lost to the impersonality of the machine.

Nostalgia

Some would say that my interest in handcrafting is nostalgic. I don't give much attention to woodworkers who use power tools for every step of the work. I recall fondly receiving lessons in the use of old hand planes one summer afternoon at a Shaker farm near where I used to live in eastern New York State. I love the simple, elegant materials and designs of Shaker furniture, and I've found that by making furniture from hand-jointed wood, it isn't necessary to fake the aging process. The presence of the hand evokes the spirit one is looking for.

Anyway, I don't know what is wrong with nostalgia. The word sounds like a disease, and, in fact, it is by definition a kind of malady. *Nostos* means return home, and *algia* is pain. *Nostos* can be found frequently in the Homeric epics describing the journey home of Odysseus and the other heroes of the Trojan War. Nostalgia has to do with home and ecology, and could be understood as an emotion appropriate to enchantment as a calling home, a bittersweet feeling of longing for a life once enjoyed but now lost.

Once in a while I find myself overwhelmed with feelings of nostalgia, which seem to be a mixture of sweetness, longing, melancholy, and a touch of bitterness. When I watch movies filmed in the English or Irish countryside, I have the intense feeling that I'm looking at my home, and I want to go back, even though I know it is not my home in any literal sense. When these emotions pour over me, I feel enchanted, stung by an irrational longing that I can't explain, but the strength of the emotion makes me think that nostalgia has a role to play in re-enchanting our lives. Perhaps we can refrain, at least, from dismissing it as sentimentality, or maybe we could even follow up on those emotional fantasies and find ways to bring the object of our nostalgia more intimately and concretely into our lives.

In general, I think we suffer the loss of soul when we fail to heed strong emotions and irrational longings. They are strong voices, and it would be odd if they didn't have something important to reveal or to teach about living a soulful life. Following through on nostalgia could lead us into folly, but not following through could lead to a worse place—a disenchanted life.

Nostalgia is not idealizing the past as a way of defending against the demands of the present. Often in politics we hear expressions of an imagined "golden age" of the forties or fifties, and we sense an anxious avoidance of present life. Nostalgia is different. It's not an anxiety of the ego but an acidic action on the soul, in which one is called back to recover the past, particularly an experience of "home." The theme of nostalgia is home, not a generic past.

Sometimes I feel that I've never gotten over the homesickness that crept into the marrow of my bones when I left home at a young age to study for the priesthood. I often recall days at my grandmother's home in Detroit, a simple house across the street from where I grew up, a place that was always full of people and spirit. It wasn't a wealthy home by any means, and in fact I remember one day when the adults were sobbing because one of the children had lost a ten-dollar bill. But it was a real home, a place where I felt secure—more than secure; I felt surrounded by personality and vitality. In my memories I see old cars and clothes and a style of life that has now slipped away, and I feel a slight ache of longing.

Nostalgia is a haunting call asking us to return to the past and not to get completely caught up in the lure of the future. There is a spirit in us that wants to make progress and move quickly toward new worlds, but there is another part of the soul that offers a counterforce, an attachment to the past and a longing to return. Our society is goaded by "futurists," who frequently charm us with images of a carefree time to come, but we also need nostalgists to keep us mindful of the past—not its problems, but its values and beauty.

Familiar Hands at Work

And so I admit that my love of handcrafted objects is a part of my nostalgic soul. I don't want to leave behind anything that has contributed significantly to my feeling of being home, for "home" is such a fragile thing. The whole of modern life asks us to be independent, strike out on our own, become mobile and travel lightly, and be free to leave home when opportunity knocks. It's no wonder that our society struggles so with homelessness, that neighborhoods are falling apart, and that families can't seem to hold together well. We approve of independent wandering, but we consider morbid any dependency or attachment to our past, and we speak of nostalgia as if it were neurosis.

The presence of a hand in the manufactured world around us can be a tonic for the sensation of being homeless and rootless. If we live in a world made entirely by machines, with signs of their iron teeth and well-oiled shafts embedded in the things we use in everyday life, then we will be family to a machine rather than to humans. Maybe it would be foolish to try to re-create a world of the past when the work of the hand was ubiquitous, but the sentiment is never far from my awareness. It wouldn't take much for me to swear off airplanes and to sell my car in return for a horse and buggy. I don't want to be an anachronistic fool or to stand against modern technology—that kind of avoidance doesn't make any sense—and yet if that's what it takes to recover the sensation of home my soul clearly yearns for, then maybe it would be worth doing.

One motive for my nostalgia is the intimacy that has been lost as we have turned so many family-owned shops into chain stores owned by a distant corporation and run by executives who never once visit; or have made routine the building of houses from Sheetrock and factory-assembled doorjambs and windows. If you want to make a house by hand today, you have to be literally a millionaire or a clever expert craftsperson. To live in an intimate world is to feel at home, to have a soul in a world that is ensouled, and to have deep longings and cravings for home and comfort satisfied.

We tend to think that our problems of loneliness and emptiness are personal and interpersonal, but the intimacy the soul craves can be satisfied by the things around us as well as by the people in our lives. The warmth of the hand in things gives something to the heart and helps chase away the chill that so much of modern life instills with its machinelike efficiency, sharp corners, and smooth surfaces.

I look at a piece of wood that has been molded by a powerful and noisy router, and I admire the sharp edge and straight line, but I'd rather see a wavy line and a softer edge that exuded the spirit of a human hand. Machines increase production, shorten the time of manufacturing, and make work easier and more convenient, but these are not virtues of the soul. Anything of the soul requires time—and therefore a lowering of productivity—and effort. The sweaty hand working a piece of wood, cleaning a hazy window-pane, or hoeing a patch of garden leaves pieces of skin and flesh of smaller than microscopic dimensions on the work, humanizing and ensouling it.

Productivity has become, in the modern world, not a value but an obsession. We think it is better to make more copies of things than to make things beautiful, individual, and with personality and presence. In my home I have a room full of books, and I love books and know they can be beautiful, but not one of those books has the vibrant presence of a single page from the simple medieval hand-illuminated manuscript that hangs on the wall in that room.

Of course, modern machinery and computers have allowed us to build magnificent, and, in some cases, beautiful buildings, bridges, and houses. It's a pleasure to live in a house that is tightly made and energy-efficient. But is it necessary to lose the presence of the hand altogether? Can't we have both machine and human hand as signatures in the manufactured world we inhabit? Can't we keep those things of the past that were made by hand, rather than seeing them as an affront to our modern machine capabilities and disposing of them? Can't we honor both the future-loving spirit and the nostalgic soul romantically attached to the past?

Working with the hands also fulfills a need of the soul in a way that operating a complex machine simply cannot accomplish. The hand is not just a prehensile instrument, a materialistic appendage of the body, a machine itself made of pulleys and hinges. The hand is an apparition of the soul, and its work is an extension of the spirit breaking into ordinary life. What we do with our hands has immediate effect on our emotions and sense of self, and evokes deep aspirations and ancestral motifs.

It isn't enough that we have "meaningful" work. What is also required is work that satisfies the soul, not only through the remote channels of the mind but also through the immediacy of the hand. The cliché for workers of an industrialized world is that they are "cogs in a machine." When the hand isn't present, the worker may be treated in every way as a machine part. Eric Gill, the Catholic sculptor, stonecutter, and calligrapher, who worked with his hands all his life, once complained: "Industrial labor has for its end not the fulfillment of the personal vocation of the laborer, but the production of profit for those who employ him." In a world that considers a worker part of the machinery, this is an extraordinary statement, suggesting that in our labor practices we might make as our primary purpose the fulfillment of a worker's personal vocation, and in that goal we might see the satisfaction of the worker's hand.

We are called (Latin: *vocatus*) to our work more through our hands than through meaningful activity or profitable enterprise. The work we do with our hands satisfies the soul's vocation, whether or not it has anything to do with our making a living. Work at home, then, is as important as work at the job, and so-called hobbies may be more significant for the soul's vocation than the work we do for a living.

A painter's brush strokes on a canvas give us the supreme model of the hand's imprint in our work. In those personal marks we can almost see the fingers and hand at work and trace in imagination the artist struggling to transfer inner images into color and line. Looking at a painting from a distance, we may see its parts and colors come alive and become translucent, but up close we behold another kind of magic, the clear prints of a hand at work. Art reveals what is present everywhere in handcrafted work: the conjuring of the craftsperson's ghost, and in the presence of that ghost the work's enchantment.

The presence of the hand in objects animates and quickens the world in which we live. Comparisons between the efficiency of machines and the limits of handiwork are beside the point, because each method has a different purpose. One makes the world operate smoothly, the other makes the world mysteriously alive. Perhaps we need both, but our humanity certainly can't survive without the impressions of millions of hands in the things that fill our world and help us live.

Habitat

The wheel outside the door is just the moon.
Those objects hanging from the eaves,
just Autumn clouds.

LIANG LI (A.D. 850)

The Eternal House

*I*T'S CURIOUS THAT we talk about housing and homelessness as social issues, and yet our songs and poems show how soulful our sense of home is—Stephen Foster's traditional, plaintive "Old Folks at Home" and the song "Going Home," set to Dvořák's melancholy tune, and the phrase "Home, Sweet Home." No one talks about the sweetness of home these days, and yet sweetness is what pleases the soul.

To appreciate the enchantment that home can bring into a life, we have to shift attention from the literal house to the felt experience of home and realize that the sometimes bitter and tenacious longing for home many feel may not be satisfied by an expensive house or a mere shelter. Memories, fantasies, and desires for home are subtle and set deep in the heart. The longing for home may ask us for the kind of attention that is much less literal than housing, or that can be satisfied only by aesthetic, emotional, and memorial aspects of a house, and not its convenience and good functioning.

Home is an emotional state, a place in the imagination where feelings of security, belonging, placement, family, protection, memory, and personal history abide. Our dreams and fantasies of home may give us direction and calm our anxieties as we continually look for ways to satisfy our longings for home.

The Virtual House

In *The Poetics of Space,* the French philosopher Gaston Bachelard describes home poetically: "All really inhabited space," he writes, "bears the essence of the notion of home." We could be in a room anywhere, out in nature, in someone else's house, or at work, and still feel at home. All that is required, according to Bachelard, is truly to inhabit the space.

The word "inhabit" comes from a root that means to give and to receive. We inhabit a place when we give something to it and when we open ourselves to receive what it has to offer. Some places don't seem to have much to give, or what they have is not something we're inclined to receive, and so it may be difficult to inhabit them. But if we find the right place and enter into the give-and-take of homemaking, then we will have a good foundation for a life of enchantment, because few things in all of life are more enchanting than the feeling of really being at home.

Bachelard goes on to say that we "experience the house in its reality and its virtuality, in thought and in dreams." It's the virtual house that I'm interested in, a place that satisfies the heart and the imagination, a place that may or may not look like a house at all and yet evokes feelings and fantasies of home. This home may vary widely from person to person and from culture to culture. My wife feels at home sleeping under the stars, while I sometimes feel very much at home in a hotel.

We all have some Platonic "idea" of a house; maybe that's what we mean when we talk about our "dream house"—an imagined home that is not just projected into the future but also has a past, as though we're remembering in the Platonic sense the archetypal home set deep in our hearts the day we were born.

Except for fleeting moments in a dream, I have never seen my dream house clearly, and yet I know that it exists and that no house I've actually seen or lived in matches it exactly. This house of dream is not efficient, exquisite, grand, or huge, but it quiets my anxiety about home. It is my home in such a deeply personal sense that I can't describe it in detail, and yet I recognize parts of it when I see them here and there already existing in the world or pictured in a magazine.

Sometimes, when I'm visiting friends, I get the feeling that I have found a piece of this dream house. I notice a color, a ceiling treatment, a sink, a fireplace, and suddenly I feel profoundly at home. My first thought is that I could reproduce that piece of home in my own house, but then I remember that this house of the soul is a mystery. I don't know if I'll ever live in the house of my longing, because it's an eternal home that can take flesh only in pieces and in passing moments.

It's an illusion to think that we can build "the house" once and for all, and live in it, conscious of its dreaminess, for the rest of our lives. That expectation contradicts the rules of enchantment. The charm of feeling quite at home is often a momentary realization. It may come upon us like a spell in the most unexpected moment, or we may sense it intensely in the sad hours when we are moving to a new place, or leaving home for life's adventures, or visiting an old homestead after years of distance from it.

Most of us build our house of dreams day by day in imagination, as we fuss with our house or become enchanted with someone else's. Why else are we drawn to read magazine articles on the homes of celebrities and others? Choosing paint, fixing a door, mowing the lawn, adding a piece of furniture, cleaning the floors, changing a lightbulb, all take on at least two levels of significance: the literal need for attention and further inroads into this mystery of fabricating the Platonic idea of home.

Few things are more enchanting than a real home, even if that sense of home lasts only for minutes, or if it suddenly makes an epiphany when we're far from home. On my first trip to Italy, I found myself in Rome in heavy traffic, riding out to the highway that leads to Florence. We were driving during the rush hour in winter, and so the sun was setting, and the unique pastel colors of the eternal city made the old buildings come alive in the warming light. Suddenly I had the sensation that I had been on that street before and that I was recognizing those buildings and their extraordinary colors. For just a few seconds, on that particular unfamiliar street and for the duration of those few blocks, I felt exquisitely and enchantingly at home. Such enchanted moments can feed the soul for a lifetime.

The Magic of Homemaking

There is an art to finding and making a home, for evoking the eternal house in the eternal city unique to each person. For eons people around the world have turned to magic as they have selected a site for their dwelling, begun construction, initiated life there, and maintained their home. The building of foundations may begin when the moon is full or at the outset of spring, and precautions may be taken to be sure there are no bad spirits on the property. Once, people made human sacrifices to ensure a good life on the site and buried a human skull at the cornerstone.

Today builders may place a tree on top of a building or put a time capsule in the earth, but these rituals, carried out in a culture generally forgetful of enchantment, are often games and not serious rites. When our family had some stone steps laid in front of our house, leaving a large empty space in the earth beneath the top step, we placed a bottle with a note, photographs, and other mementos in the earthen room created by the dirt and rock, a gift for the spirits of the place. We imagined some future dweller discovering our buried hoard, but we were also aware of the tomb created by our steps, and the cold, dark shadow of home that our little rite evoked, and the knowledge that one day we would not be there in that house making it into a home.

In his book on dreams, James Hillman goes to great pains to say that the chthonic spirits, those associated with the earth, are not concerned with fertility and agriculture—the usual mythic connotations of earth—but are deeper and darker. As the magical traditions of people everywhere teach, it is a dangerous thing to build a home in the wrong place, at the wrong time, or in the wrong way. If we want our homes to be enchanted rather than haunted, we have to think deeply about what we're doing when we build and maintain them. If we think that in our sophistication we're beyond enchantment, then our homes will likely become haunted, as so many are, with the spirits of uncontained aggression and violence or with continuing failures in an attempt really to make a home. With or without a basement, a house is built in the earth, and if we forget the lower spirits of the house we may well find ourselves troubled by their complaints.

Traditions associated with building give us hints about making a home for the soul. The most emphatic warning we hear all over the world is to find out what kind of lives have been led on the site and in the building, and not to take a chance tangling with ghosts connected to evil acts.

The Genius of the House

Looking for a home or furnishing and decorating the home we have, we could make our decisions from deep intuition rather than from fashion or efficiency. When our family moved into our present home, we decided we would rather put money into a garden than into a garage, and so, with help from a local student landscaper, we made lovely patches of herbs and perennials and set up an arbor and a pond. When it came time for the bank to assess our property for remortgaging, we were told that our home was worth far less than we had calculated, because we had no garage or paved drive. Our gardens and gravel lane were too rustic and undeveloped to count. I learned from the bank that one's personal pursuit of enchantment often goes against the tide of current thinking and has its penalties, which I understand as partial fulfillment of the sacrifices that always have to be made to the spirits of a place.

The *genius loci*—genius of the place—reveals itself slowly and enigmatically, and yet it is the ultimate judge of how we are to make a home on our small patch of land. "Genius" derives from the same word that is in "generation"—it has a begetting and procreative function. From the *genius loci* flows abundant life, and so we are ill advised either to act counter to its nature or to neglect it.

Vegetation, climate, colors, animal life, contours of hills and valleys, stories about the place, its history—all of these hint at the nature of the place's genius. You can't go to a government office and ask to see the register of geniuses, but you can consult local people familiar with the personality of the place. You can also rely on your own intuitions and impressions, which can be educated and sharpened through practice. The genius lies deep within, and as Richard Onians suggests in his extraordinary book on Roman ideas about the soul, it can't be uncovered by conscious thought or explained by literal fact. It requires from us trust in our less rational ways of knowing and in whatever practices of magic we feel comfortable with and capable of performing.

When we look for a home, we can learn something about the neighborhood and the history of the place, and walk the perimeter of the land or the building, taking in as much of its spirit as possible. We could seek the help of a *feng shui* expert to guide us further in exploring the place, and on our own we could continue to become acquainted with the *genius loci*. Sometimes he or she—Onians says this spirit may be either male or female—needs a home in the form of a shrine, if only a pile of stones or a small grotto. It's a good idea to make some seat for the spirits of a place, beginning the process of enchantment with a simple rite of remembrance and acknowledgment, and then literally setting up for the spirit a chair or a stone ledge that is excluded from human use.

Some places are clearly more fertile than others, some more dangerous. Our homes, whether situated on acres of farmland or in the middle of a city, may have their gardens of Eden and their Golgothas, places of pleasure and tragedy. Like a diviner casting for water, we need a "nose" to detect the spirit of a place, because rational arguments won't take us there. Whatever method we use, we should not omit, in our homemaking, our survey of its spirits, learning from the place itself how to please them and, sometimes, how to appease them.

The Imperfect House

A home will never be perfect, for perfection is an idea and an ideal, and our home is always an approximation of our dream. I wouldn't want to live in a perfect home, because enchantment and perfection do not lie in the same order of things. If you're looking for perfection, you don't pursue enchantment, and vice versa. Enchantment pours out of cracks in shifting walls, tilting roofs, and not quite square corners. When we were looking for models for our house, we studied fifteenth-century Norman and Flemish farmhouses, and I wondered how in our new home we could make up for the slanting, rusting, and aging of those great buildings. Our builder said that his way was to avoid using a measuring tape and square whenever possible, instead relying on the eye, which is never perfect but always human.

Things sing only when they reach a certain degree of presence, and that point may come through design, placement, surroundings, neighborhood, age, or color. It may have nothing to do with cost. Some of the most enchanted buildings are the simplest. On a country road near my house, in a wide-open pasture of short grasses edged by a hill of exposed rock and trees, sits an old one-room schoolhouse, so picturesque that I've seen photographers and painters with their tripods and easels trying to capture its charm. Its roof curves low in the center like a slack rope, and its siding has been so weathered that it blends in perfectly with the changing colors of the grass.

An enchanting home is not an ideal home but is made for the people who live in it. We have small children, and our home has to allow noise, breakage, chaos, and much physical use. Our children enjoy leaping from couch to couch, running sharp objects across the wood floor, and swinging from banisters. A delicate house would not be home to us now, or perhaps ever. I like to fix things around the home, and yet my talent falls far short of my ambitions, and so my repairs are not even close to perfect. We are reconciled to the simple, imperfect house.

I learned much about houses and buildings from James Hillman, who in a lecture on architecture a number of years ago complained about modern ceilings being treated as functional spaces. We may lay expensive hardwood on our floors, but we let our ceilings go blank or stuff them with pipes and vents. It wasn't always so. In the past ceilings might be dressed with beams, paintings, moldings, chandeliers, and even religious and astrological motifs. In New England, you often see stenciled borders on or near the ceiling. Hillman did not advocate returning to these old ways of building, but he recommended preserving the tradition of "shapes in replication of the cosmos, where the roof over our heads brings imagination into our minds."

In general, we can cultivate enchantment by designing a deeper sense of home in all buildings. There is no reason why we couldn't evoke the cosmos, our great home, with a dome or an arch, or, like Shakespeare's Globe Theatre, make the stage of our home the whole world. Or we could design a public building in the image of a house or in tune with the architecture of the region or the history of the place. In Old Deerfield, Massachusetts, not far from where I live, visitors can walk through several eighteenth-century houses and find inspiration for giving their own houses the charm of this period. Of course, one can approach preservation and restoration in ways that are shallow and narcissistic, but old houses can also teach us how to go about enchanting our ordinary surroundings.

One of the most extraordinary houses I have lived in was the old family homestead in upstate New York, where my great-grandparents made a home when they came from Ireland. When I lived there, the house had three porches, a whitewashed cellar under the pantry, a large linoleum kitchen with a kerosene and wood-stoked great cooking stove, and an attached earthen-floor shed. Back past the kitchen, the living room, and the stairway was a parlor, which housed an old piano set against a wall, and beyond that was a bedroom. In my memory I can still smell the mustiness of the parlor, where I would spend hours playing simple tunes on the piano.

Now that the farmhouse is a ruin, nothing left but the stone foundation, I wonder what happened to the piano and to the old pitchers and basins that served us in my childhood in lieu of running water, and to the child's toilet seat that always looked strange to me — a dark wooden throne fitted with a deep floral basin.

The restfulness of finally finding home is not unrelated to the strange longing for death that rarely becomes explicit in the minds of most. I had an acquaintance, a psychoanalyst, who lived at the edge of a cemetery and continually talked about death and his longing for the ultimate rest. He loved to visit cemeteries, and when he spoke of them, I thought I detected a feeling of homesickness in his voice.

Home is not the only need of the soul, even though it is a primary one. We need to leave home, be away from home, find pieces of home in hotels and tents, and maybe move from house to house in quest of home. "An entire past comes to dwell in a new house," says Bachelard. Like turtles, we carry our homes with us as we move from place to place, all homes mobile, because home is ultimately located in a deep recess of the soul, a cornucopia that pours forth endless gifts.

Anyone entering therapy might first inquire into the state of his or her soul's homemaking, for this is the essential need, primary in time and primary in importance. We need make no judgments about homes that have failed or have been abandoned or lost, but can simply see the journey into home as one that takes a lifetime of experiment and piecing together. Once we appreciate its ultimate value, then we might focus all our attention on home and on the many satellites of home — family, community, neighborhood, nation.

Nothing is more intimate than home, and therefore nothing more proper to the soul. Whatever it takes to call forth the spirits of home, our own lares and penates—ancient Roman household spirits—is worth our effort and expense. It is always time to trim a plant, glaze a window, clean a rug, or write a poem about home, talk to relatives about the old days and the old homestead, and remember the failures and painful memories that took place at home. All of these go into the making of the soul's home, a daily work that prepares us for our death and gives our lives the intimate focus that is the primary gift of home.

Ruins and Memory

YOU DON'T HAVE to look far for ruins. As I gaze around my desk I find in a box old pens that don't work now and never worked well, and behind my New England house is an old stone wall, put there, my neighbors tell me, by ancestors who farmed this land. Today our few acres of living space are cut out from thick woods, but when you venture into the forest you find stone fences, no longer even or complete, now covered with the velvet green moss that makes nature's claim. One road over, in the very heart of a bucolic forest, is a five-acre junkyard filled with the remains of automobiles from many decades, while in town there is a church trying to become a ruin. Its steeple slants acutely to the south, while the church faces Main Street on the north—our own Tower of Pisa.

The presence of ruins, in spite of the ambivalent feelings we may have about them, does more for a community's soul than many a new edifice. Like the ill-placed junkyard, they may be an eyesore, and yet no one can deny their fascination. Children love to play in an abandoned car or an old box, and tourists are drawn to crumbling buildings and mysterious monuments. We have an old Iroquois fireplace down the road from us, which stands as the silent presence of another age and another people, and to visit it is to honor a neighborhood shrine.

Ruins are enchanting because the function these things once fulfilled has gone off like a bird flying away from its nest. We are left with objects that have a hollowness that we can fill with our own wonder and fantasy. Their role in the living community is also gone, and so they sometimes enchant the way graveyards do, or haunted

houses, which doubtless enrich a neighborhood and add a necessary unsettling theme for fantasy. Ruins conjure up the past, not
only with a historian's reckoning of calendar time but in a haunting
way that makes the past immediate. Ruins place us chillingly and
perhaps attractively in the world of ghosts, where the soul is as
much at home as it is among the living.

Ruins present us with an inescapable natural alchemy, a putrefaction and corruption of things we have made and that give us
pride. Indeed, the cool, impersonal soul hidden in our personal
achievement comes to the fore when we examine ruins from the
past; and so ruins play the important role of balancing the building
of culture that so occupies our spirit, with the unbuilding that
speaks to the soul. In a society feverish in its dedication to futurist
thinking and building, it takes courageous effort to protect artifacts. Even the past falls under the heavy tools of renovation and
restoration, and there's nothing worse than finding a ruin that has
been reconstructed for our education and enlightenment. William
Morris argued that ancient buildings are not tokens of the past but
part of our present lives, and he spoke often against the kind of
restoration that tries to improve on the past in the name of preservation.

The ruins of Rome, for instance, give so much enchantment to
that soulful city that it's impossible to imagine Rome without
them. When my wife and I visited the Vatican, the experience for
both of us, Catholics from before birth, was indescribably powerful,
but nothing in the magnificent Baroque upper church had any of
the enchantment of the lower crypts. Above, all was fine and elegant; below was death and ruins. In the upper vaulted halls our spirits soared and expanded, while below in the crypts our thoughts
turned inward to our own mysterious pasts as we walked meditatively, soaked in the silence of the deathly tombs.

Here is another clue to why we have lost the enchantment that
gives human life meaning and value: We are so intent upon building a well-oiled society—literally and figuratively—that ruins
clearly get in the way. They are an obstacle and a nuisance. They
represent a regressive movement rather than a forward one, the disabled past rather than the enabling future. Yet maybe our forward
progress needs to be disabled, now and then, simply to allow the

thoughts and feelings of the deep heart to emerge, providing a grounding of values and the essential element of mystery, without which our progress goes on unhindered and therefore dangerous.

Pieces and Fragments

What I enjoy most about ruins is their incompleteness. The lovely New England stone wall travels awhile along a road as though, like a good fence, it were serving some purpose, and then, long before its proper corner, it topples down and trails off in a cascade of loose stones. It offers no deterrent to escaping animals or land-hungry neighbors. These fences are not just beautiful, they're enchanting, because, like sculptures made by fairies and leprechauns, in their ruinousness they bear no mark of human art or intention. They sing of a presence that is not human, and that song is the essence of their enchantment. As I sometimes ask my children, "Who tore that fence apart? Is there any neighbor we can blame? Is it sufficient to explain the crime as the work of time?" Time doesn't have hands or even force. We have no option but to refer these scenes of natural, unobserved corruption to those invisible mischief makers Emily Dickinson, in a poem we've seen, called "Green People."

I have visited only a few castle ruins on my travels, but those that I remember—Corfe Castle in Dorset, England, and a small castle on the Dingle Peninsula in Ireland—buried themselves deep in my memory, along with the enchantment they performed. What is it about a castle, especially a ruined castle, that is so captivating? And why are children especially drawn to one? At a feast in a living, unruined castle in Ireland, my young stepson, five at the time, was intoxicated by the dagger set next to his plate in place of knives and forks. That dagger was fairly alive with images of Robin Hood, danger, excitement, and wildness, and he was eager to use it, while at home we have to remind him constantly to use a fork or a spoon. We seem to have forgotten, in our cool, metallic pragmatism, that romanticism can be a powerful motivating force toward a civilized life.

A castle also has a shape that evokes primitive emotions and fantasies, above all as a microcosm, a contained space in which all of life seems to take place, a world in itself. Games create such a space, whether Monopoly, chess, tennis, football, marbles, or "playing house." When we behold castle ruins, we are looking at old worlds, experiments in life that embrace the whole of human possibility, a chessboard in the form of broken historical remains. In the presence of tumbled rocks, decayed roofs, and staircases that end in midair, we are filled with imagination of lives not entirely unlike our own, and maybe we wish for the vitality and containment a castle gives image to.

Ruins also may give rise to reverence. When I was a young man studying in Ireland, I went with relatives to see the place where my great-grandparents lived before they left Ireland for America. We found a woman who remembered the family and the site of their house, and then we went down road to lane to path, coming finally to a house that was in ruins. Only the stone remained, but it felt like holy ground, and I was pleased, even in those young years, that the sacred font of the family was a ruin.

I don't share many of my colleagues' enthusiasm for wholeness. I like fragments and pieces, innuendoes and suggestions. I expect never to feel like a whole person, because I'm so aware of the fragmented nature of many of my emotions, the plans I have for my life, the elements of character that are never fully present or rounded off. In the same way, I like to see sculptures of a goddess with no head or arms, or just a piece of torso. Temple ruins and the remains of a civilization make much more sense in pieces than if we were to come across a ghost town intact except for the human citizenry.

Decay, corruption, falling apart, memory, traces of the past—these are all aspects of life that are with us every day. They may hint at failure, ignorance, or some other imperfection, but they are a significant dimension of all kinds of life, including our own interior experience. When I entertain memories, I see plenty of ruins—failed marriages, dead relatives, houses no longer in existence, careers ended in their prime. A melancholic mistiness may surround these memories, but that, too, is an important part of life.

Lifting the Repression of Ruins

We try to repress ruins, especially in America, probably because we have little appreciation for failure, ending, and the past. We tear down lovely old buildings without enough pangs of conscience to slow us down and consider what we're doing. We reconstruct past architecture, but we're not good at preserving ruins. There's a vast difference between allowing our cities to become ugly through inattention and economic neglect, and allowing ruins to stand in our midst.

Last year there was a terrible fire in a nearby town, which destroyed several old buildings that had stood on a corner for one hundred fifty years. Workers have removed all the rubble from the fire, but now we fear they'll build a charmless little shopping center there in exact duplication of other charmless little shopping centers that now serve the purely pragmatic shopping needs of towns all over America. I have been enjoying the burned timbers and tumbled stones and bricks for over a year, with compassion, of course, for the people who suffered the loss of their businesses and property, as the town officials argue over the economics of rebuilding.

Architects are among the most important curators of enchantment. If they don't appreciate a place of ruins and know how to preserve something of the past that a fire may configure, then we will continue to suffer a soul-parching loss of ruins. Corporations, as well, play a major role in dealing with ruins and replacement architecture, as they direct architects in their work; they, too, could realize that they have a responsibility to the soul of our communities and that they are in the business of enchantment. They could learn to preserve something of the ruined remains of a fire, or at least preserve their spirit in rebuilding, but it's difficult to imagine an office in a major corporation today dedicated to the protection of ruins!

Ghosts are among our primary enchanters. We say we "don't believe in" ghosts, but ghosts, like most elements of enchantment, are not a matter of belief. Ghosts can be real without being scientifically measurable or even observable, and even if we strongly disbelieve in them, we might still sense their presence on a lonely night walk through an ancient cemetery. Ghosts haunt the scene of a crime, an old family home, or a relic of our ancestors, and just as the Green People work at nature for our edification, ghosts keep our attention focused on past lives and the significant presence of death in all our lively activities.

Ruins are an endangered species today because in a materialistic worldview they don't appear to have any relevance; yet from a spiritual point of view, they are irreplaceable containers of the spirit of family, ancestors, and time itself. Get rid of ruins, and we lose the guidance offered by memory. We wander around untethered to the past and carried, anxious and unconscious, toward a floating future.

Today people ask why we seem to have lost a stabilizing and orienting sense of values, why the family doesn't hold together as it used to, and why aggression and anger cannot be contained, as they creep out in vandalism, crime, and ubiquitous signs of decadence. Why can't "those people"—meaning some other race or nationality, youth, the homeless, the emotionally unstable—live properly? we say moralistically. A more accurate question might be: What have we done in creating this modern culture that makes it difficult to live from deep values?

We have narrowed our values and sentimentalized them into slogan words that seem to be filled with value but soon reveal themselves to be dangerously inadequate: words like wholeness, progress, good functioning, forward looking—all terms that threaten the validity of ruins. We might consider some corrective alternates, like fragmentation, stasis, breakdown, memory, and imperfection.

Remnants of Traditional Piety

In spite of our century's fascination with the future, we are still drawn to the past. Thousands of people visit Stonehenge in England each year, many drawn by the lure of memory or by some mysterious promise of spirituality. Each generation is moved to profound wonder by the pyramids of Egypt. Visitors crowd the ruins of Machu Picchu in Peru, Mesa Verde in New Mexico, and the Maya temples of the Yucatán—not as tourists, but as modern pilgrims without a tradition, as did the thousands of pilgrims who in centuries past trekked to the Holy Land or to Santiago de Compostela. The modern pilgrim wanders in search of a nameless but clearly spiritual goal, hoping for some slight sensation of enchantment and for an experience that will feed the soul with a life's worth of spiritual vision.

Just outside the city of St. Louis, America has an extraordinary ruin in the Native American mound and relics of Cahokia. This ruin is not widely known, even though it has elements quite similar to Stonehenge—a circle of standing posts used for astronomical reckoning. We have many other places that preserve the memory of pre-European life and values, and these could become our own focal points of sacred memory, giving us an image of our land not as a mere stage for development and progress but as a terrain made sacred by the pious imagination of our ancestors. The kind of spirituality that comes from our national ruins is genuine and deep. It doesn't ask for belief or morals, and yet it offers a profound experience of and sensitivity to the sacred. You don't have to be a member of the community that produced the mounds, shrines, and other relics to let them feed your most personal and ardent spiritual life.

The aboriginal people in a nation hold much of its unleashed spirituality, which is rich food for the soul. Our maltreatment of Native Americans goes hand in hand with our single-minded pursuit of a secularistic society intent on building its own Tower of Babel. Frequently the spirituality that attends this project of future-building—churches and clergy trying to be modern and up-to-date, for example—colludes ingenuously with the secularism of the culture and itself is shallow, if not fraudulent. If we could entertain a fuller imagination of the spirit, we would come hungry and thirsty to our aboriginals for the soul food of the past they have preserved. Often it appears that our craving for fulfillment looks to some future achievement, whereas the deeper longing may be satisfied only by the past, by a rich inheritance that is usually ignored in our rush into the future.

Family ruins—whether people, relationships, homes, artifacts, or stories—are also good food for the soul. The futurist in us looks forward to the day when the family will be blissfully happy and content, whole and healthy; but the ruins that lie strewn in our path by family struggle and failure have their value.

I recently retrieved some stones from the foundation of the old family homestead, and I hope to use them in a house of my own, if only in a ritual and symbolic way. These stones call to mind stories of charming days and shining individuals, but they also resist the repression of family neuroses and tragic developments. They save me from the waxy sentimentality of futurism, instructing me that human life has its way of moving calamitously toward death, as a deep calm and resolution of conflicts gradually bring peace.

Towers of Defense

If there is anything in modern culture that stands as an antipode to the wisdom of ruins, it is the skyscraper, often named a tower. Like temples and steeples, these towers rise off the earth in direct expression of our desire for transcendence, and they sometimes stand narcissistically as troops of the ego, swelling high in their pride while mundane life carries on at their feet.

Literature has long considered the tower either a place of transcendent purity, a ladder to heaven, or else a dangerous fabrication of human ambition, like the Tower of Babel, which sowed confusion among the peoples of mankind. The celebrated mystical and moral story of the first or second century A.D., *The Shepherd of Hermas*, describes the building of an allegorical tower, made of stones carried by virgins. Throughout the story, Hermas asks the Shepherd to explain the tower that is being built:

"What does this tower mean?" Hermas asks.

"This tower is the Church," says the Shepherd.

"And these virgins, who are they?"

"They are holy spirits."

The Shepherd goes on to interpret the tower in terms of perfection, siding only with the pure virgins and warning against women who are "clothed in black, beautiful, with bare shoulders and disheveled hair." Allegorically, these black-clothed women include Unbelief, Incontinence, Disobedience, and Deceit, and their followers are anger, folly, and sorrow.

Without going into a discussion of the tendency of spiritual ambition to repress shadow emotional qualities by attaching them to Aphroditic imagery, we can see in this passage the idea that a tower is virtuous and embodies our hopes for purity. I would see our towers of commerce and habitation as coming from the same wish that separates us from aboriginal life and from the teachings of ruins. The tower keeps us ambitiously off the earth, beyond corruption, free of memory, and fully given over to the future.

I sometimes arrive at a hotel in a city and am given a room in the "tower." Without explanation, I ask if there is an alternative, knowing the dangers to the soul in towers. I'd rather risk the sight of the seductive women in black of whom the Shepherd of Hermas disapproves and preserve the ruin fantasies of my low-level soul.

The Luba people of Africa tell a wise story that might educate us further about the dangers of towers: Humanity originally lived in the same village as God. But the creator wearied of the constant quarreling in the village and exiled humanity to earth. There humans suffered hunger and cold and, for the first time, sickness and death. Following the advice of a diviner, who told them to go back to heaven to regain immortality, the people began building an enormous wooden tower, which after months of labor reached the sky. The workers at the top signaled their success by beating a drum and playing flutes, but God hated the noise and destroyed the tower, killing the musicians.

Our spiritual leaders—leaders in business, education, religion, and travel—seem to prefer towers and convince us to build them and then live and work in them. When I lived in Texas, where towers abound, I often heard the ambitious shibboleth "The sky's the limit." Yet it is also Texas that gives us the mythic story of a young man standing in a university tower, spraying the earth and its youth with bullets. As we rise high in our building of culture, we risk the vengeance of the gods with our noisy boasting and ambition to be better.

Both in the Bible and among the Luba, this ambition is the cause of humanity's dispersion; for in the tower we are cut off from our roots, from the land and the particulars of place, and from the ruins that would keep us piously intimate with our earthly home and with our past, which has been scoured of its ambitiousness. We build our towers, literal and figurative, and then we suffer the punishment of return to our particular place, our own language, and our need for food and warmth. There is nothing wrong with building high, but if we are to believe sacred literature, it is dangerous, and the higher we build, the more we may need our ruins to keep us close to home, where the soul is fed.

I don't see our towers as places of power as much as products of anxiety and battlements of fear, the shadow elements of our ambitions toward perfection. We are often afraid to live within the confines of human life: afraid to be limited to one mate, one place, one job, one lifetime. We are not at home with our place, and so we want to be as far as possible away from it or above it. To honor ruins would be to express our ties to the past and to acknowledge the wisdom of those who didn't enjoy our technologies and information.

Vincent Scully, the architectural historian and philosopher, makes an extraordinary point about Americans' feeling about their place. "In some strange way," he writes, "we tend to feel [the place] is threatened by us. We do not trust ourselves in relation to it." A similar feeling might keep us at a distance in love, as we realize in some subtle way that our ambitions could be dangerous for the person for whom we feel so much affection. We may have reason to worry about our plans for the land and the people of the land.

We are anxiously environmentalist and anxiously anti-environmentalist. We build and feel guilty about building, or we indulge in hubris. It isn't easy to find a comfortable relationship with land and place and time, and so coming to terms with ruins could offer us a way to peace of heart. We can build our culture forward with courage and an undisturbed heart only if we are at one with the past, giving it as much respect as we offer the future or, more basically, attending to death as much as to life.

We could also learn from the alchemists to appreciate processes of corruption and decay. As things become ruins, they go through a natural alchemy in which their soul is revealed, a falling apart and entropy as important to life as growth and expansion. Ruin and renovation are like yin and yang, an interweaving in which one thread affects and influences the other. In ruins we can celebrate life and find hope, while in new building and making we can from the very beginning sense inevitable decay and dilapidation—a word directly related to the cascading, moss-covered stone walls of New England. Every soulful moment and act requires this embrace of the living and the dying, and only an anxious heart is incapable of enjoying its dance.

A Garden Paradise

THE BIBLE TELLS us that paradise was a garden, but it also hints that a garden is paradise. I suspect that a good path to paradise is through a garden. The trick may be not to take gardens too literally but to allow the great variety of gardens to instruct us in garden poetry and spirituality.

Let me define a garden as the meeting of raw nature and the human imagination in which both seek the fulfillment of their beauty. Every sign indicates that nature wants us and wishes for collaboration with us, just as we long for nature to be fulfilled in us. If our original state was to live in a garden, as Adam and Eve did, then a garden signals our absolute origins as well as our continuing condition of eternity, while life outside the garden is time and temporality. I don't much care for interpretations of Eden that celebrate our parents' expulsion, as though Eden were infantile and our individuation could be found only in exile. I prefer to live both in time and in eternity, both in Eden and in New England, and find in the counterpoint of those two locales the fundamental rhythm of my humanity.

If, without heavy symbolism and metaphors, but relying on my own sensations, I make a connection between Eden and the garden outside my door, then I see that nothing in life is more important than the garden. Even the simplest garden then becomes something profoundly implicated in my origins and destiny.

A garden can't be defined adequately in plain physical terms, because a garden is a place in the imagination. We find it sometimes in a patch of vegetables or in an arrangement of plants, trees, and flowers, but not everything that goes by the name garden succeeds in evoking it in the imagination. The great gardens of the world may not conjure up the eternal Eden nearly as effectively as a small grouping of bushes and flowers in your own backyard.

Still, wondrous gardens all around the globe, expressing a multitude of philosophies and sensibilities, demonstrate that few products of human creativity have as much magic. Gardens work powerful enchantment as they take us body and soul out of the busyness of life and into a place set apart. It's tempting to describe the withdrawal and repose offered by a garden in terms of mere physical rest or even emotional restoration, but the effect of a garden lies much deeper. In Jung's view, a garden in its formality and structure represents a containment of the many meandering emotions and fantasies that crowd our interior lives. The garden creates an especially effective temenos, he says, an embracing perimeter, and even plays the role of a companion, an image of the deep self, as we go about our daily business.

Entering a garden is like passing through a mystical gate. Things are not the same on the other side, in the interior where nature has been arranged, whether formally or casually, to suggest to our senses and our subliminal imagination a midrealm somewhere between the conscious, known world of ordinary life and the less conscious, mystery world of the garden. All religions have used this power of the garden in service of their own designs in caring for the soul, as in the monk's or nun's cloister, or the Islamic fountain garden.

In a garden the soul finds its needed escape from life and its entry into a space where eternity is more evident than time and where the ritual arrangement of life is more important than the business of surviving and making progress. Time stands still or at least moves more slowly in the garden, and so even today the sundial seems more appropriate there than the clock.

The garden is a proper place of the soul, where concerns of the soul for beauty, contemplation, quiet, and observance take complete precedence over the busier concerns of daily life. There you will likely see the butterfly, an ancient image of the soul, and the bee, representing the kind of work the soul does—unheroic, hidden, mysterious, and sweet. The priestess of the ancient Greek goddess Artemis was called Melissa—bee or honey—and Love was once depicted as a wasp. The garden is full of mysteries.

Not long ago I had the opportunity to serve as the "anchor" for a film series on spirituality in everyday life. One of the segments told of a woman who had lost her daughter and whose life had come to a standstill in her grief. Inexplicably, one day she began to dig in the earth around her home, with no intention of making anything, but soon a garden appeared, and her grief grew roots and became creative, offering her unexpected solace.

I suspect—one never knows for sure about such mysterious things—that the garden helped because it addresses the soul so directly and gives it the things it needs much more plentifully than does the culture around us, which is so spirited, so bent on productivity and activity, that it has forgotten how to tend the soul. The garden might also help us survive the death of beloved friends and family members by keeping us in touch with eternal matters, the absolute fundamentals of earth, sun, and rain, and the absolute rhythms of birth, flowering, and death. A garden epitomizes the most rudimentary materials and timings of all life, including our own human elements and seasons.

The Garden of the Philosophers

I want to return to the theme of pleasure and the epicurean life. For centuries, Epicurus's philosophy of pleasure has been repudiated by moralists, but occasionally his central themes break through and are given at least momentary consideration—sensuality, pleasure, friendship, moderation—I think he has been neglected because there is so much soul in his philosophy, and it is not insignificant that his classes were held in an Athenian garden, a place where the soul is most at home. The garden of Epicurus invites us to reflect on the epicurean aspects of gardens, especially the sensual pleasures they provide.

In a disenchanted world, it's important to get somewhere and accomplish something, but the time spent in a garden gets us nowhere. A garden entices us to slow down and stop, an important dynamic in the soul, and even as we work laboriously in our gardens, for many of us the seasons change, frost arrives, and our work goes into hiding. One of the primary benefits of a garden is to relieve us of ambition, or at least transform our ambitions into the natural rhythms and cycles of the garden. Our philosophies of personal growth can be sublimated in the garden into the work of helping flowers grow.

A garden also asks us to open our senses wide, take in the green arc of a plant or the subtle sweet fragrance of an herb, and be unusually present to the physical world. An enchanted life finds its spiritual charm through an intensification of life in the body. Ancient magical charms are filled with recommendations for the body: eat your words, wear your amulets, burn incense, smear paint on your eyes. A garden is a sensual ritual in which the spiritual life emerges directly out of the dirt and the green and brilliant colorings of nature.

The garden reconciles human art and wild nature, hard work and deep pleasure, spiritual practice and the material world. It is a magical place because it is not divided. The many divisions and polarizations that terrorize a disenchanted world find peaceful accord among mossy rock walls, rough stone paths, and trimmed bushes. Maybe a garden sometimes seems fragile, for all its earth and labor, because it achieves such an extraordinary delicate balance of nature and human life, naturalness and artificiality. It has its own liminality, its point of balance between great extremes.

Gardens do not make these balances intellectually, but rather they take us in our senses *into* the liminality, a *mundus imaginalis*, a special place in the imagination that is neither wild nor cultivated, neither human nor otherworldly. This liminality, felt physically and emotionally as we walk in a garden, is analogous to temenos, and it, too, is a rare gift to the soul, because liminality presents a window onto eternity and offers epiphanies and deep sensations of transport that are of greatest importance to the soul.

One powerful convergence of spirituality and sensuality in a garden lies in the aromas and smells, first of the earth and then of flowering plants. The sense of smell not only conjures up memory, as is well known, a primary activity of the soul, but is intimately implicated in the spiritual life. The Magi give the infant Jesus the gift of incense, according to the biblical infancy narratives, and incense and perfumes have been used widely to accompany prayers, with the purpose of making prayers more pleasing and getting them into the spiritual realm quickly and directly.

But, of course, perfumes are also epicurean delights, and so once again we see the convergence of sensuality and spirituality. Chief Dan George prays:

> the fragrance of the grass
> speaks to me . . .
> and my heart soars

Here, as in many Native American prayers, we find the theme of enchantment—nature speaks, in this case through her fragrant grass. Aroma is utterance, the smell song in the ordinary grasses that are indigenous to the garden. What is sweeter than the aroma of curing hay or the passing scent of blossoms in a morning garden! This is the stuff of natural religion and the origins of enchantment.

The monk Thomas Merton, who spent much of his life in silence, was among many other things a nature mystic, who listened to the flight of birds and took note of the aromas of the fields surrounding his Kentucky abbey. In his journals, he wrote: "The completely irreligious mind is, it seems to me, the unreal mind, the tense, void, abstracted mind that does not even see the things that grow out of the earth or feel glad about them." Gardens help us leave abstractions behind and find joy in the simple presentations of nature, rather than truth in the complicated interpretations of human ingenuity.

Garden Dwellers

Merton offers another image of nature's voice linking the garden and the spirit: "At two-fifteen there are no sounds except in the monastery: the bells ring, the office begins. Outside, nothing, except perhaps a bullfrog saying 'Om' in the creek or in the guest-house pond. Some nights he is in Samadhi; there is not even 'Om.'" Nature's voices are inherently spiritual because they convey, without the mediation of analysis or purpose, the designs of God.

Around our home we have made gardens of various kinds, and it seems the invitations to creatures announcing an open house go out before we've completed our work. Along come frogs, snakes, unexpected flowers, unplanted vegetables, moss, crayfish, butterflies, dragonflies, minnows, toads, bees—a host of new dwellers and visitors. Some of them speak in chant, others in aromas and colors. The garden quickly becomes a compleat aesthetic experience—"aesthetic" in the early sense of perception through the senses.

A garden could teach us to live aesthetically, by sensation rather than thought, and immediately rather than by plan or projected analysis. This aesthetic life would not be unintelligent or unreflective, but it would be grounded in the daily sights and sounds of nature, like the diaries of Merton, which are punctuated over years by single-sentence observations of nature that give a Zen-like contemplative counterpoint to his personal thoughts and experiences. We could all live in this way, drawing the garden into our innermost life of soul—our language, ideas, and decisions. We could learn from the artist Claude Monet and build our professional lives around our home garden.

Enchantment can't be achieved in the abstract, any more than we can know what a garden is by looking it up in a dictionary. It must be concrete, green, earthly. It is always the work of one of the earth spirits, and you won't have such a spirit in the vicinity unless you inhabit the earth. More specifically, there is an enchantment that arises out of the garden spirit, which, for all the variety of gardens around the world, is unique. A farm is not a garden; neither is a park, a wood, or a golf course.

The genius of the garden is one of the protecting spirits, a guardian and companion, and so it is appropriate to have a garden near your home. This spirit will thrive in the country or in the city, both of which have their counterparts to the garden—farmland and pavement. It will be fully present in a grayish garden of rocks and sand, or in a lushly colorful garden of blossoms and ferns. It will be called forth like a genie from a bottle in a large garden in a great city, and from a miniature bonsai garden in a corner of a desk.

The Interior Life as a Garden

The many great gardens of the world, of literature and poetry, of painting and music, of religion and architecture, all make the point as clear as possible: The soul cannot thrive in the absence of a garden. If you don't want paradise, you are not human; and if you are not human, you don't have a soul.

The comic adventurer Candide roamed the world in search of the meaning of life and ended up sitting at home in his garden. We might take a lesson from him, save the time and money, and tend our garden. Its gift of repose and contemplation is the soul's treasure we seek under the pseudonyms of success and happiness. The meaningfulness of the garden, equal in all respects to its meaninglessness, is the goal in our quest for meaning.

Jung alludes several times in his alchemical writings to the medieval habit of describing the Virgin Mary as *hortus conclusus*— an enclosed garden—and she is sometimes depicted in such a garden in the company of a unicorn, a mythical animal often identified with Christ. Mary's holy virginity suggests the virginity of the soul, and the delicate, enclosed privacy of any garden also reflects our own delicate, enclosed hearts. They are easily disturbed, as we all know, and therefore require solid stone walls and a strong gate.

Everything in culture conspires to penetrate the garden of our innermost and most private hearts. We have to be vigilant, like a careful gardener, to keep out the pests and do regular weeding. This is a great mystery, as the theology of gardens implies: how the heart itself is stationed in delicate balance at a crucial point midway between nature and culture, between privacy and community.

People used to pray in great numbers before the image of Mary as *hortus conclusus,* but now we have few images of delicacy that inspire us to safeguard our hearts. We expose them daily to many things that probably should be kept outside the gate. We may have to learn again the mystery of the garden: how its external characteristics model the heart itself, and how the soul is a garden enclosed, our own perpetual paradise where we can be refreshed and restored.

Noise and Silence

WIND IN THE trees, thunder, flowing water, falling leaves, rain, animal voices, birdsong—we live amid a teeming polyphony of natural sounds. Add to these the sounds of human activity, from soft footsteps to pneumatic drills, from muted conversation to pounding trains, from jetting fountains to jet planes. Then, we have the articulate, measured, imagined sounds of art—all the many kinds of music, which so specifically and directly convey the spirit of a people. Our world is permeated with sounds, some calming the heart and mind, some keeping us frenetic and on edge.

It is almost impossible not to hear some sound, and so our notions of quiet and even silence have to include sound and not be imagined as removed from it. "Quiet" means rest, while silence is a toning down of sound, or the absence of expected sound, as in the silent rests in a piece of music or during a retreat deep in the woods.

Both quiet and silence are aids to enchantment, because they allow us to hear the "chant" of nature, the sounds of our interior lives, and music. The incessant and inescapable noise of modern life, standing in the way of an aural relationship with nature and making it nearly impossible to hear our own thoughts, blocks enchantment. To be susceptible to the spells of everyday life, we have at least to perceive nature, both inner and outer.

I live among trees in the woods partly because I need silence. I know that many people enjoy the sounds of the city and feel as uneasy in the quiet of the forest as I do on a busy street. As I consider silence, I know that I'm writing from a personal point of view.

Many people, of course, appreciate quiet, but admittedly I'm somewhat obsessed by it.

The excuse I sometimes give for my craving for silence is the fact that I have studied and played music all my life, but many musicians enjoy a noisy city or a raucous nightclub or a deafening rock concert. Maybe it's because of the years I spent in a religious community where silence was often the rule, but my colleagues didn't seem nearly as preoccupied with quiet as I was. My parents tell me I was a quiet child. In one story they often tell, a cousin, who was a good friend and also quiet, once sat with me in a car for twelve hours on a long vacation trip and, to the astonishment and discomfort of the adults, we remained quiet and untalkative. I sometimes think I took the vow of silence in the womb.

The key to finding enchantment through the doorway of silence is not to consider silence negatively. Silence is not an absence of sound but rather a shifting of attention toward sounds that speak to the soul. In a moment of silence you may feel your heartbeat or hear your breathing. Silence is a positive kind of hearing, which requires turning off the knob that tunes in to active, literal life and turning on the one that amplifies the movements of the soul. Nature can be very loud as you sit quietly on a rock overlooking the ocean. Anyone who has ever meditated knows, too, how loud your own thoughts, memories, and wishes can be as you seek a moment of interior stillness.

Listening in Silence

Silent listening is a particular way of being active, not passive, in the world. Over the years, I've spent hundreds of hours as a therapist listening to people's stories, emotions, and struggles, and for the most part I sat quietly. But I listened with great attention and intense focus, so that this quiet listening was perhaps the most active thing I've done in my life.

In silence we can hear subtle sounds that are usually drowned out by the cacophony generated by a technological culture. Find a quiet room in the middle of a city, and you begin to hear clocks tick or notice your own sighs as your emotions manifest themselves. A city park is as important for the quiet it offers as for its colorful flowers and open fields. Churches are temples to silence, wrapping themselves around a relatively few cubic feet of quiet. I can never get used to people talking in churches, or applauding during rituals. To me, the very point of a church and a liturgy is to invoke fruitful silence, and to disturb that special quiet is to fracture the ritual.

Noise is not expressive, as music and natural sounds are. We hear the bark of a dog, and nature is present to us. The howl of a wolf or coyote somewhere near the horizon contributes to the enchantment of a quiet night. Raindrops on a roof or a windowsill also put us in touch with nature and may lure us into reverie or reflection. But walk past a delivery truck just as the door is slammed shut, or pass a work crew breaking up concrete, or walk in front of a car when its dissonant horn blows intrusively, and you know the jarring effect of noise.

The priests of the Old Testament who performed divinitory readings of the rustling of oak leaves must have educated themselves in quiet. Silence is a requisite for personal divination, for living with a sense of direction. How are we to know where to go in life if we don't hear the daimonic voices saying, "No, not that way. Go here." These voices speak softly, as gently as the rustle of a leaf, and generally they don't repeat themselves.

If the world is enchanted, by definition it must have a voice, because a chant is made by a voice, and so for enchanted living we need to hear voices. Modern rationality blanches at the idea of taking "voices" seriously, and we diagnose people who hear voices as emotionally disturbed or mentally ill. I've worked with several people who have heard voices and other sounds, but the truth is, I have too. Once in a while I will be lying in bed and suddenly hear my name called out sharply. I may wake up and wonder who is there. Occasionally in waking life I'll hear a voice or a sound, and I won't be able to tell whether the sound was physical or "psychological."

I need silence to hear the intuitions that pass by, like angels on their vaporous footpath, making soft, barely perceptible sounds. Rarely does a new idea come along orchestrated for trumpets. The vibraphone is a good instrument for the soul, or panpipes, or the Celtic harp. The most important sounds in a person's life may be so quiet that they are easily missed. In the noise of life you may not notice an invitation to a new career or a marriage, and you may be distracted when out of the air a message comes that a new home is waiting for you.

Reading in silence and stillness invites these life-shaping intuitions. This is one way I understand the many old paintings and icons of the Virgin Mary sitting alone in a room, reading a book, as the angel Gabriel appears with his extraordinary message: "You are going to conceive something wondrous and divine!" I imagine all our important conceptions and concepts arriving with the announcement of an angel. But we don't always recognize the presence of angels, so subtle is their embodiment. Libraries offer an active kind of silence, and I would expect to find many angels like Gabriel in them, as in the scene from Wim Wenders's film *Wings of Desire* in which angels pay a visit to a modern library.

Saturn's Silence

In Renaissance medical texts, Saturn is presented as the patron of silence, and this appropriation makes me wonder if depression, such a problem in our time, is related to our poor relationship to silence. Is depression, the illness most closely connected to Saturn, to some extent a symptom arising out of our neglect of silence, Saturn's treasure? The writings of Ficino indicate that we need to cultivate the qualities favored by such a patron, so as not to suffer his symptoms.

In other books, following Ficino I have recommended bringing artful forms of Saturnine experience into our daily lives—by making dark corners in gardens where we can sit and brood, and rooms in office buildings where we can withdraw. In the same vein, we could imagine many other ways to shape daily life for Saturn's silence. A few moments of silence may be all the meditation we need at times. Our homes could have a little space for withdrawal and quiet, and even a small garden could offer some distance from noise. A screen or a wall could invite Saturn into an otherwise busy and noisy space, or we could take five minutes from a noisy schedule and devote it to Saturn's quiet. Silence calls for the artful practice of Saturnine virtues, using our imaginations to their fullest to design a life that honors quiet and solitude.

When we plan on moving our homes or businesses, we could

take silence and quiet into serious consideration, as my family did when we moved to the countryside. We were shown many homes in lovely settings, but they were not protected from the noise of nearby highways. When a business plans a move or a building project, it could give attention to the need for quiet among workers, if only in a small part of the plant, and for the community. We could take the time needed to evaluate soundproofing walls and arranging rooms so that quiet would be available where it is most appropriate.

We could be serious about lowering the levels of noise in our cities and in the workplace. Automobiles transgress not only our Artemisian need for fresh air but our Saturnine need for quiet as well. Airplanes taking off, landing, and passing low over inhabited areas shake the soul with their inhuman noise levels. I, for one, am undone by the presence of a noisy snowmobile during a blissfully quiet cross-country ski. I suspect that snowmobiles and similar machines might have an entirely different presence if they operated silently. The same is true of motorboats that zoom across small lakes where people are trying to find a retreat from the busyness and noise of everyday life. Laws and customs that allow such ubiquitous noise offend something deep in the soul that the ancients called Saturn, and I believe we are suffering the consequences of our transgression of this mystery in widespread soul maladies.

We have only a limited number of places where we can go to honor our Saturnine needs, and these are diminishing quickly as we ignore the soul and banish every opportunity for enchantment. I don't intend to moralize against these sports and machines, because obviously something valid in the human spirit craves the excitement of speed and powerful locomotion. I am simply suggesting that if we give everything to the spirit, the soul suffers. We are feeling the effects of modern soulless culture in the "mental" illnesses of cities, families, and individuals.

Maybe it's time to realize not only that "small is beautiful" but also that "quiet satisfies the soul." With an appreciation for the necessity of caring for the soul, we could venture into the cultivation of quiet just as creatively as we pursue power and speed. I'd rather take an extra hour to get somewhere in quiet than to sacrifice silence for a few extra minutes at the end of a trip.

Another violation of the soul's need for calming sound is the quality of loudspeakers in public places, such as trains, planes, transportation terminals, and government buildings. We have developed extremely sophisticated machines for music listening, including excellent compact speaker systems, and yet in public life one's ears are often acutely attacked by loud and piercing voices, static, assaulting electronic feedback, and unsettling white noise. It's unusual to hear a clear, soft voice on a public-address system, yet this would be an excellent way to join modern technology with care of the soul. In my definition of silence, which includes sound, a well-made loudspeaker could serve the soul's Saturnine requirements.

Sounds of Silence

While many sounds of modern life destroy all opportunity for silence, some sounds positively foster quiet. For twelve years of my life I sang Gregorian chant every day, and this ethereally calming music served meditation and helped create a contemplative mood. Chant is modal music, which means that it doesn't have the powerful drive that much of modern music has to arrive at a final harmonic destination. Modern harmony is sometimes called "functional harmony," because one chord serves a function in relation to all the others, offering either strong tension or definite repose.

The modal harmonies of chant have more subtle forms of tension and ease. Chant floats in space and proceeds unhurriedly and gracefully to endings that are soft and often tentative. Its rhythms and melodies, too, are gentle and rounded, so that even though it is a form of sound, it generates a spirit of quiet. We might learn from such chanting how to enjoy sounds in our environment without having them contribute to the anxiety of modern life.

Studies have been made noting the kinds of noises that disturb one culture in comparison to another. In Africa, bird and animal noises seem to be a problem, while in North America, air-conditioning, construction, and trucks top the list. My own list includes the telephone ringing at home, airplanes flying low overhead, and traffic noise on an expressway. Sirens on emergency vehicles seem to have grown louder and more piercing over the years, perhaps because of the increase in the general sound level.

We all make individual choices about sound too: blowing the car horn too often or in the wrong places, placing noisy "music" on telephone answering machines and "hold" periods, using loud machines inside and outside the house, violating the silence in parks and other nature retreats, allowing televisions and radios to be running all day, and playing music loudly late into the night in quiet neighborhoods and apartment buildings. Our family has a young dog that barks a good deal of the time when she is outside the house—our contribution to the noise of the neighborhood.

We could make and furnish a house that is as carefully designed for sound as for visual effect. A wind chime can be a bridge between the sounds of nature and the home. In my woodworking I don't use a router mainly because of the shattering sound it makes, frightening all children and animals in the vicinity. We have a Celtic harp in our home, and a large Native American drum, a lush harpsichord and a piano. Their sounds all add to the home environment and offer moments of enchantment.

In our own lives we can seek out experiences of sound that nourish the soul, like a hike to a quiet spot in nature or to a stream or waterfall, or a visit to a park that offers a retreat from city noise. The sounds of falling water and blowing winds make real music that enters the soul and gives it the aural nourishment it needs. People spend huge sums of money on stereo equipment, and they try to keep up-to-date with the latest formats, but I wonder if this attention to the technology of sound covers over a deeper need for a life lived every hour of every day with sufficient quiet and with sounds that nourish rather than wound.

The Ears: Portals of the Soul

Sound and the soul are poignantly intimate with each other. There are words I have heard in my life I wish I had never heard; they still send a shudder when I think of them, and even in memory they are still shattering. I've heard stories of atrocious acts I wish had never come into my ears. I sometimes wonder about Hamlet's father poisoned in the ear and feel my own sensitivity to themes carried on the airs of sound. In his enchanting poem "Peter Quince at the Clavier," filled with subtle references to sound and musical instruments, Wallace Stevens makes the point that music is always more than an aural experience:

> Music is feeling, then, not sound;
> And thus it is that what I feel,
> Here in this room, desiring you,
> Thinking of your blue-shadowed silk,
> Is music.

If our feelings are music, then the sounds we hear in our everyday environment are especially important to the soul, and we let them take an unconscious course to our own peril. As the best in music therapy demonstrates, sound is also positively healing.

Music is the sound of art, whether jazz, rock, or classical, but it's also the everyday sounds of nature and culture. Not only might we rid our environment of wounding sounds; we could go farther, placing our daily lives in a context of enriching mundane music. We could hire musicians to advise us in building and in all decisions that have to do with sound. Surely we could design pleasing doorbells for homes, ringers for telephones, chimes on computers, bells on elevators, and horns for automobiles. A sensitive musician could advise restaurateurs about the aural needs of patrons and the many creative possibilities for a pleasurable aural environment. We could have ear police protecting us from disturbing sounds in our neighborhoods. The result would be an advance toward enchantment, even in our cities, for the ears are the most intimate organs of the soul.

Sound is at least as intimate as smell, and clearly more intimate than vision. When I think of sounds that have lodged themselves charmingly in my memory, I recall the perfectly intoned opening chord of a magnificent student orchestra at the University of Michigan, a bell set ringing in a meditation room at a Zen center on the Pacific Ocean, my confreres in the religious community chanting litanies through the orchards and fields on a cool spring morning, and my daughter at three singing the alphabet song in inimitable child tonalities.

We know from formal religions the power of sound, whether from Tibetan monks each chanting chords, or the sound of OM drawing all beings into essential harmony, or the psalms of the Bible.

We know also from countless paintings of angels that there is a music that is truly heavenly, not of this world. Or could it be that music and soul-stirring sounds link our daily life to eternal things? Ficino said that music comes to us on air that has been tempered by sound, sets in motion the air spirit of the person, and then affects the heart and penetrates to the most intimate levels of the mind. And this music is directly tied to the music of the world, its rhythms and modalities. Ficino's sense of music was extraordinary and leads me to think that we will have soulful sounds in our environment when we finally discover the necessity not only of the artist but of the magus as well.

Sound is one of the most direct and simple means we have at our disposal for enchanting life and caring for the soul. There is no reason why we could not tune our world, keep it at pitch, and allow only the most forgiving dissonances. The soul would then be ready for joy and pleasure, and not be crimped into protective postures in absolute horror at the noise we allow to be characteristic of civilization.

World

Nothing happens for the first time.

NORMAN O. BROWN

The Spirituality of Politics

POLITICS MAY appear to be an unexpected place to look for enchantment, yet it deeply affects the lives of all citizens and has meaning far beyond any practical considerations. The greatest temptation, from the viewpoint of the soul, is to treat any aspect of life too literally, without seeing its depth, resonance, and transparency, and politics is so concerned with information, decisions, and actions that it may seem to be the most literal aspect of culture. But unless we gain an appreciation for the interiority of politics, it will continue to be a massive barrier to cultural enchantment.

The word "politics" comes from the Greek word *polis,* meaning city, and shares the same root with "police." Originally the word denoted a crowd, and only later a crowd formed into a city. We still have a few linguistic indications that politics has sacred connotations, as in the many crowds we call a metropolis—the mother city—originally the cathedral city where the archbishop held authority. A more recent word, "metroplex," refers to the "weaving" of several communities into one, and weaving is one of the chief attributes of the goddess Athena, the Greek archetype of citizenry and politics.

A crowd becomes a city, and therefore truly enters the realm of politics, when it develops an identity, a personality, and a spirit. All the major cities of the world are cathedral cities, not in the formal Christian sense but insofar as they perform the maternal functions of providing nourishment, comfort, protection, and family relatedness. We talk about our native city sometimes in maternal tones, when we ask each other not "Where do you live?" but "Where were you born?" and "Where do you come from?" suggesting origins in the motherland.

I live in the country and enjoy the charms of nature and small communities, but when I travel to cities, I find a different magic, a powerful manifestation of human life, business, and creativity. It doesn't seem to matter that almost all cities fail to work smoothly in providing services like transportation and garbage removal, for their incapacity is as enthralling as their ability to spawn endless forms of life. People's attachment to cities, even when they are full of problems, indicates that a city is a soul place and that people relate to it as family.

Politics as Care

Another word for city life, and close to "politics," is "civil." Its root is in the Indo-European *kei,* which means bed, rest, endearment, and is related to "cemetery." This word has strong soul qualities of intimacy and relatedness, and might give us direction in discovering the soul of politics. It suggests that the role of politics is to make a home for the dead, give us all a place where we can sleep, and foster a sense of mutual endearment.

These goals are all quite different from the more practical aims we usually consider appropriate for politicians: that they should be preoccupied with life, make the system work, govern, and administrate. Yet the root words surrounding politics imply work of the heart more than the brain, the caretaking of human life rather than an effort to keep the machine of society well oiled and operating. I doubt very much that John F. Kennedy's portrait hangs in the homes of so many people around the world because he was an efficient administrator. It may be telling that many who honor him now didn't agree with him during his lifetime, and most are not terribly interested in revisionist histories questioning his lifestyle or his administrative judgment. Criticisms of his actions don't seem to spoil the "heart" that he brought to civic life.

I take all these signs as indications that ultimately politics is not a matter of administration as much as care, and I'm tempted to think that politics could be re-enchanted if we could make the shift from the mechanics of the system to giving everyone a bed, maintaining the family of humankind, and tending our cemeteries. The process of politics often gets in the way of its essential vision and charge: the care of citizens. Politicians seem to believe that they should be tough-minded administrators and hide their emotions of empathy and care.

These alternative ideas about beds and cemeteries, too, should not be taken literally, but they do suggest an attitude that could be the foundation of political action. Our current idea of politics as bureaucracy, administration, and lawmaking is what Jungian psychology labels an *animus* activity, where thought, judgment, and heroics are central. Politics could also be imagined as work of the *anima*, with emphasis on imagination, caretaking, and depth of vision. Imagine, for example, a political science department in a university shifting its attention to soul issues, leaving behind its critical, argumentative, and analytical style, becoming interested in the myth and poetry of political language, the emotional needs of citizens, and the role of art and beauty in the life of the culture. The politician courageous enough to explore the soul of this activity might also discover its depth and spiritual dimensions.

The Religion of Politics

It's no accident that one of the principal roles of the politician is to be a representative at state funerals and memorial services. In many traditional societies, care of the dead is the primary duty we have toward one another, and funeral rites are usually elaborate and time-consuming. The leave-taking by death of a person from the community is felt as a major political act, and the period of mourning a necessary rite for dealing with the disturbing mystery of death.

Typical of modern times, we have *vestiges* of powerful funeral rites, like flying the flag half-staff across the country, proclaiming a holiday or holy day for the deceased person, and laying the body in state for visitation and contemplation. The funeral of John F. Kennedy was a rare instance when the nation became emotionally involved in highly symbolic and imagistic rites of a slain president, allowing business as usual to be temporarily forgotten.

Politicians are called to a certain kind of priesthood for the community, not only presiding at funeral rites but also gathering the people together for other civic religious rituals, such as receiving foreign heads of state with pageantry, giving speeches in parks and at parades on holidays, and even throwing out the first baseball of the season. These and other ritual roles are usually eclipsed by politicians' assumed administrative duties, but the soul is more directly addressed by them than by the running of bureaucracy.

In many traditional societies, the political head is also a spiritual leader, and in others the secular leader is limited by ancient religious teachings. We Americans pride ourselves on separating church and state, rightly worried that citizens may lose freedoms if politicians mix their religious beliefs with their political agendas. But as a result we have created a wholly secular state that can't truly govern a people, because its activities ignore the needs of the soul and play out as if a human community were a mere aggregate of inanimate bodies. How could we run a country according to the most recent reckoning of pollsters unless we considered citizens as mere numbers?

Maintaining a basic religious outlook on life with a corresponding set of values does not necessarily lead to the imposing of a belief system on others. If we could distinguish between a basic religious attitude and a system of beliefs, we might bring to our civic lives a spirit of reverence, an acknowledgment of mystery, and an appreciation for ritual, all in an atmosphere of tolerance. In our desire to preserve a secular state and freedom of worship, we often prohibit expressions of religion in public life, whereas it is the imposition of belief and not a religious sensibility in general that is a threat to freedom.

Quite properly we value the secular life, but we often confuse that, too, with its anxious, defensive, and generally neurotic relative, secularism. The religious life and the secular life go hand in hand; they support each other. Religion can teach us how to appreciate everyday life with depth and reverence, while commitment to a secular lifestyle can keep religious expression from excessively dominating daily life.

But secularism arises from a fear of religion. It's a defensive insistence that religion remain on the sidelines, if it is in the picture at all. In a secularistic world, we have few resources for values, vision, and civic order, while in a theocracy we haven't freedom to explore values and create a satisfying secular life. The alternative is to maintain a harmony of the secular and the religious, protecting society from the dangers of religious intolerance and the imposition of belief.

Political Narcissism

I recall attending a lecture given at the University of Chicago many years ago by a prominent historian and political adviser. The audience was an interdenominational group of theology students. We were stunned to hear the leitmotif of this man's talk—the "national interest." We asked him: "What about international interests? What about the legitimate needs of individuals?"

"Of course other countries have valid concerns, and we work with them and for them," he said, "but our representatives are elected to serve the national interest before all else."

Not a philosophy, but a *religion* of nationalism prevents some political leaders from seeing their role as caretakers of the family of humankind. From a psychological perspective, nationalism is an emotional complex, a whole set of feelings, thoughts, and attitudes that have not been woven into a person's thoughtful and dispassionate philosophy but rather operate autonomously, without a human, and therefore humane, context. We accept that the "national interest" is the prime directive of our politicians, without having examined the implications. What if I said that the great imperative of my life was my own interest, or my family's? The narcissism and immaturity in my position would be clear.

Link this self-focused attitude with the widespread problem of politicians serving their own constituencies at the price of others, falling into myriad forms of corruption on behalf of their own interests, and giving up basic forms of morality in order to preserve their positions, and we see to what extent narcissism interferes with "deep politics," or the soul aspects of the political enterprise.

Narcissism is always a failure in love, the inability to love oneself and one's immediate world. The comfort with oneself that is a prerequisite for any genuine service to others is symptomatically elusive and unattainable. Paradoxically, narcissism can be cured only when individuals find themselves in community, for the soul is incomplete when experienced only through an individual life. Care of the soul can be accomplished finally only through politics, and those many politicians who demonstrate the narcissistic neurosis in their behavior can find their true role only when their anxiety about caring for themselves is relieved by their full surrender to community.

When a politician has not been truly initiated into the role, or when his or her personal psychology lacks maturity, the necessary elements in the political process might well appear symptomatically. For instance, instead of having an honest sense of community, the politician may hide disingenuously behind claims of speaking for constituents. Or instead of narcissistic needs being fulfilled in a deep feeling of community service, they may be expressed in embezzlement—using the community's money and services for personal gain and comfort.

If we lived in an enchanted world, where we realized that the spirit of the community is the ultimate governor, then we would be less likely to confuse the power of the office with personal, narcissistic aggrandizement. It makes sense that a culture that grants personality only to human persons is going to personalize political positions and be corrupt from the outset. The ancient Greeks knew that they were held together as a community by a divine spirit, or by a number of spirits, but we think government is a human endeavor, and so of necessity we are plagued with narcissistic politics.

We are all politicians to some degree. We all live in community, and we all participate in the community's life. If our politics is ever to become re-enchanted, we all have to discover the holy, sacred, and spiritual dimensions of community life. When we give away the power to shape our communities to certain individuals we call politicians, and ourselves enjoy a life of vicarious politics, then we are contributing to the disenchantment of the world. Politics can work at a deep level only when all the people are engaged in its spirit and live fully aware that they are community beings. One reason politicians cannot bear the weight of their responsibility and privilege is that they carry too much of the political life of a city, county, or nation. Leaders lead, they don't do all the work themselves.

We all become political when we realize that our lives are not bounded by the perimeters of self, family, and home, and when we feel and act from that realization. A person is more than an individual, more than a self. A person is one whose vision and identity include various communities—neighborhood, town, region, nation, and world. Paradoxically, we may gain a stronger sense of self when we extend ourselves generously and courageously into our community, when we exercise our political nature. As anyone who has served community knows, that extension of oneself can be thrilling. Community makes the heart come alive and in that particular way brings charm and deep satisfaction to a person's life.

Not only can politics be enchanting—an almost absurd notion in modern life—it can be one of the most enchanting aspects of life. Recall the essence of enchantment as I have been attempting to define it: the transhuman voice or music rising from deep within nature or culture that seizes us with awe and spellbinding pleasure. Now recall moments in life when the community spirit was so strong that for a moment at least you felt utter belonging, a profound sense of home, a release from loneliness, and a reason for going on. This enchanting realization lies at the heart of politics.

Or recall a visit to a great city and the feeling of vitality and the variety of life that the place evoked. Visit an unfamiliar country and become absorbed in the ways people do things, the turns of phrase they use in daily speech, the food that is available in markets and restaurants, the sights to see. Politics involves the care and tending of all this rich soul life, and in a certain way a politician is the therapist of a community—"therapist" meaning one who offers care and tending.

Why does a person feel called to be a politician? Ideally such a call comes from a sensitivity to the rich gifts and potentialities of a region or a nation and to the citizens who for one reason or another are deprived of those gifts and potentialities. In all forms of care, we give attention both to sustaining the good life that lies before us and doing what we can to give it to everyone.

By definition, a politician's life is dedicated wholly to community, and his or her calling to community bears signs of soul in its eccentricity and exaggeratedness. Gandhi is an example of a supreme politician who found himself—his destiny, his gifts, and his powers—as he entered more fully into community. Martin Luther King, Jr., is sometimes criticized for personal deviations, yet he gave us a rare example of how to be political by becoming increasingly identified with community and increasingly expressive as an individual. Of course, he had the advantage of having a spiritual understanding of his political life.

Ecological Politics

Our very words "civil" and "political" invite us through their histories to imagine politics as dealing with death as much as life, home as well as the world, and so the political life is essentially an ecological one—eliciting and caring for a profound sense of home. It is not primarily a materialistic role, although politicians easily become caught up in finance and projects. Nor is it a moralistic role, but rather a moral one. Politicians have great power to set the ethical and visionary tone of a people, and so it is clear that a real politician would have to have both deep wisdom and the skill to get things done in the world. As the Chinese philosopher ChuangTzu says of a good ruler: "In tranquillity he becomes a sage, and in activity he becomes a king."

Enchanted politics requires both practical skill and personal wisdom. We think a person is ready and qualified to be a political leader when he or she has received a high level of education, often a law degree, and has had experience in various government positions. But we have no way of educating for "tranquillity" and sagacity. The ways of the Tibetans, for instance, seem strange to us. They look for signs indicating a child who might be the reincarnated Dalai Lama. Their method is an enchanted one and speaks to the need for an eternal dimension in serious political leadership. The Hopi have a similar method. It was known to the people before he was born that their great leader Lololma would be a certain boy ordained to become a chief. His name as chief means Many Beautiful Colors—his godmother was a member of the Butterfly clan. Such rites and "illogical" ways of finding political leadership evoke the element of enchantment, which takes politics out of the purely pragmatic, materialistic realm, to speak to the soul of a community.

Of course, modern societies are never going to go looking for obscure signs of future reincarnated leaders, but the gulf between the traditional and modern approaches tells us how far we have strayed from an enchanted way of being in community, and I believe it gives us a hint as to why our political systems are so often ineffective: They have no inherent, deeply spiritual dimension. We would have to have a radical change of attitude to move closer to the Tibetan and Hopi ways of spiritualizing politics, but if we do not think too literally about such things, there may be ways consonant with what we consider intelligent and practical to re-enchant politics along these lines.

One way, the usual first step in any soul care, would be to take a long look at things that now stand in the way of enchantment. We might reflect on our philosophy of life that divides the sacred and the secular so starkly. We might re-evaluate the place of rituals, old buildings, and our use of public language. We might seriously think about our own collective psychology: our tendency to be defensive, narcissistic, and controlling in our public posture. And we might rediscover the importance of beauty at all levels of public life. Is it too much to expect the *polis* person, the politician, to safeguard the soul's need for beauty?

The rare politician who can be filled with enthusiasm and personality without getting caught in the neurosis of self-aggrandizement, the person of genuine wisdom and tranquillity of heart, will stand far above colleagues in stature and achievement and enjoy the deserved honor of the people. Just by being a public person with honesty and sagacity, this individual in his or her own person would contribute greatly to the re-enchantment of community life; a public person can be overwhelmingly enchanting, and maybe our current "cult of celebrity" is our way of reaching for this kind of enchantment and expresses our need for political leadership in enchantment.

When we all, leaders and participants in community, discover the sheer joy of creating a way of life that serves families, ennobles work, and fosters genuine communal spirit, then we will begin to touch upon the sacredness that lies in the simple word *polis,* which is not just a city defined in square miles, income, or population, but a spirit that arises when people live together creatively.

The Business of Enchantment

WHILE IT TAKES an effort of imagination to find enchantment in politics, it may be almost impossible to conceive of business and work as enchanted. We tend to think of business as entirely pragmatic and therefore literal; fantasy, charm, and other qualities of enchantment would seem to have no place there. We know, too, that business can involve a great deal of labor and pain, and daily we are reminded that it is highly susceptible to corruption. Enchantment, in contrast, seems to require pleasure and ease, and a relatively shadowless role in life.

On the other hand, it's clear that money can cast a spell on just about anyone, and even those few ascetics who disclaim money as a primary value and live a life of voluntary poverty seem enchanted with their own posture toward it. Building a business can provide the primary thrill in a life, and finding the right work often appears to be the panacea that will finally make life worth living.

The Medici family in fifteenth-century Florence conducted business with great seriousness and success, and at the same time they were intensely interested in matters of theology, philosophy, and the arts. They did more than support the arts—Lorenzo de' Medici was a poet of considerable talent, and his grandfather Cosimo could carry on a conversation with the best of philosophers. As patrons, they knew what they were supporting and took a genuine and educated interest in the work of their protégés. As businesspeople they played a crucial role in the extraordinary phenomenon that we know as the European Renaissance. This was a brief period when money, work, civic life, the arts, and religion came together to vivify a community, and in spite of political upheaval, widespread disease, and other problems, the culture came close to establishing an enchanted, soul-centered way of life, in many respects a good model for us as we search for a way to re-enchant society today.

Our words often tell a deeper story about the subject we're dealing with, and in this case they betray a deep spiritual element in business. As we have seen, the words "commerce" and "merchandise" contain the Latin *merx*, which can be traced directly to the Roman god Mercury, who was widely known as the divine patron of commerce, especially connected with accounts and the exchange of money, to say nothing of money's shadow—deceit, trickery, and outright thievery.

It may be difficult for a modern person to imagine a society in which business is considered a sacred endeavor, or that one could pray to a patron saint of commerce. If it is difficult to do so, then maybe the problem is not with the audacity of some other culture to find business holy but with us, who have secularized most of life, including and especially anything having to do with money and goods.

The idea that business is holy and that a polytheistic culture like that of the Romans honored a god of commerce hints that what goes on in business truly has deep roots and that what we typically consider a purely secular matter, to be taken literally and pragmatically, is a matter of far-reaching dimensions. Business reaches so far into the concerns of the heart that perhaps we should investigate the soul of commerce and the state of the soul in the workplace.

What is business about? Buying, selling, working for pay, paying for work, lending, making, marketing, saving. These are all activities of major importance to every person, and for this reason alone they affect the soul, but more than that, they are activities full of fantasy and meaning as well. Money in the bank may relieve our anxiety about security and living a meaningful life, and it may also contribute to a strong feeling of personal worth. Shopping and buying are "therapeutic," people often say, and there is no doubt that consumerism has a strong emotional component and is directly related to a sense of well-being or, in the other direction, an obsession that betrays some psychic disturbance. In either case, the soul is involved.

For most of us, a career is largely a matter of business, and so the thing that gives us our very identity and offers a profound sense of meaning and purpose in life is in large part business. When we meet someone, we say, "What do you do?" Or, more directly, "What's your business?" These questions suggest that what we do in life is the most important factor in expressing our individuality. Our business life and the work we do reveal our values, family vision, longings and desires, ethical sensitivity, and passions—the greater part of our soul.

Our life in community is also largely lived out through business, as when we take in the mail, hop on a bus, go to the grocery store, purchase a pair of shoes, go out to dinner, buy a newspaper, and certainly as we spend eight or more hours a day at work. Economics is the law of life, and in fact this word also has deep meaning, coming from *oikos,* Greek for home or temple, as we have seen, and *nomos,* meaning custom, management, and law. The word has misty historical origins in the pasturing of sheep and offers another hint as to how fundamental business is to getting along in life. Business involves all aspects of managing our home, whether the family house or the planet, and therefore has to do with survival, fulfillment, community, and meaning.

It's no accident that when men and women gather in monasteries to intensify the communal aspect of life, they take an economic vow, the vow of poverty, promising each other common ownership of all property, even the most commonplace and personal. They follow an exceptionally vivid "law of the house"—eco-nomics—and find a doorway to intense community through that particular law. Marriage, too, has a similar, significant economic dimension, where two people blend love and business into the most soulful of living arrangements.

Business, then, clearly touches on many matters of genuine importance to the soul, but how is it involved with enchantment, and can there be such a thing as enchanted work and enchanted commercialism? One way to imagine enchanted business is to examine several aspects of business life and determine how they might have soul, how they might stir fantasy and increase the interchange between the life of things and the life of humans.

Family Business

Home, as we have seen several times, is one of the primary needs of the soul—not mere physical shelter but a deeply felt sense of being at home. Business, of course, allows us to have a home: to be able to afford a house, furnish it, and buy food. This is the absolutely fundamental role of business: to allow each of us to satisfy our primary needs, not only of the body, but of the soul too.

But business can provide home in other ways. The workplace, where most of us spend a third of our lives at least, is, for good or ill, a kind of home. Business could recognize its role of providing the soul with a home and not make a sharp division between home and work. A home provides shelter, safety, family, food, and basic bodily needs. If a business overlooks any one of these things, then it isn't even providing the fundamentals of enchantment.

More than physical safety and comfort, the workplace can provide a felt sense of home. When possible, we need the freedom to make our work space our own, with pictures, colors, furnishings, and clothing. Go into a workplace where workers can make a home for their eight hours of labor, and you may sense the enchantment of the place, especially in expressions of individuality and family. Workers don't have to be taught to put a flower on their desk or keep photographs of the family in sight; they automatically do these things from the heart, provided they aren't hindered by rules and regulations.

Related to home is the soul's need for family wherever and whenever it can find it. Employers may treat workers as if they didn't have families, demanding, for example, that they move from place to place, or they may not include the families in other decisions that affect them. This blindness to family betrays a serious neglect of soul and at the same time offers a relatively simple way to deepen and humanize the activity of a company. When employers do see their workers as members of families, the workplace itself can find soul and even enchantment through a genuine and concrete honoring of family life.

One of my current jobs is to travel from city to city, speaking in bookstores, churches, and universities. I have found that when I travel with my wife and children, I'm treated differently from when I'm alone. People pay attention to my children and are aware that they require time and tending. I think they see me as a rooted, ordinary, entangled person rather than as some angelic figure flying from city to city as if I had no place on earth. They observe my own efforts to deal with the irrational emotions and needs of the children, and they know firsthand that I live all the complexities of marriage. There is an infinite difference between enchantment and idealism, the former keeping us charmed as we live our ordinary earthly lives, the latter focusing our attention away from the ordinary and the human.

Family has its own brand of enchantment. A publisher calls me on a weekend afternoon, and my wife tells him I'm giving my three-year-old daughter a bath. When I talk to him, he is full of fantasy about the charms of fatherhood and imagines his own enchanted life as the father of a little girl. This is not mere sentimentality, or if it is, it's the kind that borders enchantment. Of course, this publisher may have an unrealistic view of what it means to have a child, but those enchanting moments of deep love and meaning give soul to parenthood.

I can imagine businesspeople sitting around a conference table discussing the impact on everyone's family, including the managers' and CEO's, of their decision to move their offices or operations to a new locale. It's clear how far we as a society have moved away from soul values when it seems radical to include the family in all our business and social decisions. Those who speak so freely about "family values" might deepen their agenda by offering concrete ways we can care for the family as we move ahead socially and technologically.

Why not find ways to help families know the workplace where a father, mother, or in some cases a child spends so many hours of the day? Why not acknowledge the fact that no person is alone, and include the family in every aspect of business life—at least giving it a modicum of consideration. The fantasy of the unattached worker who has no family ties and no community context may be a useful one for employers, who want to be able to make quick and clean business decisions, but it is unrealistic and slices away the soul that could profoundly help the business in the long run.

Some employers and workers, extending the idea of family, proudly proclaim that their business is one big, happy family. Since the family the soul needs is not a literal entity, the family spirit one occasionally finds on the job is of great importance. Soul is fed by this spirit, which enchants the workday and helps heal the breach between work and home.

These days, many of the metaphors we use for business organization are structural and abstract—the pyramid, for example. Family and home would be more soulful images for business, more organic and intimate, and might help us imagine work and commerce in more enchanting ways.

Many of us lament the passing of the "mom and pop" corner grocery store. When I was a child, on the east side of Detroit, we lived on a block with such a store at the corner, and the family nature of that business helped the neighborhood hold together. The woman who owned the store knew me, knew my parents, and gave us the precious soul gifts of safety and understanding.

Our society has suffered from the disappearance of family businesses and the spread of impersonal, massive, anonymously owned and operated supermarkets and other kinds of stores. These changes in social patterns suck the soul from everyday life, ounce by ounce, and we're not aware of the impact of the change until we see crime increase or the neighborhood become lifeless or decayed. Think back on any family business in your past, then think of the same service or shop that is now a chain operation. Somewhere in the differences you can detect a loss of enchantment.

I'm not saying that we have to turn back progress entirely, or that large companies can't sustain a soulful business, but it is clear that one immediate way to keep enchantment in our business lives would be to run and patronize businesses that are family owned and managed. Large corporations could find ways to keep an authentic family spirit and support values connected to that spirit at all levels of their operations.

I once had an enlightening conversation with a man who owns

an office supply store in my town. He has a small storefront on the main street, in an old building that gives much to the spirit of the town, and I go out of my way to buy from him almost all the supplies I need. He and his family take turns minding the shop. Across the street is a chain drugstore, staffed with college students who are putting in their time for a small salary.

"Every time I put a sale price on some small item," he told me, "the chain lowers their price on that very item. They have tons of business, and I don't understand why they have to compete so nervously and aggressively with my little store."

One day I noticed that a national office supply chain was opening yet another store at the edge of our town. That store shows absolutely no sign of New England in its architecture, and it stands there narcissistic and anxious in bold, unnatural red and absolute white against beautiful green forest land. Whoever decided on the shape and color of these molded stores had no idea of the importance of keeping friendship with nature as we go about our business, or of becoming part of a tradition and a community. The town, of course, for financial reasons welcomes the business and seems to be unaware that loss of soul brings crime, family breakdown, school chaos, and political malaise—all problems this little town discusses without solution month after month, even as it continues thoughtlessly to license disenchanting businesses and fails to support the few family enterprises that remain.

There are thousands of ways to bring the spirit and values of family into business. We can each do it in our own way, whether as proprietors or as employees and customers. No human activity should lack the family spirit, because without including family we automatically exclude one of the cornerstones of our humanity. Most of us know, too, that for all its imperfections, family can be profoundly enchanting, and that family brings to any activity a magic that can't be explained by any social theory. It's that magic and enchantment that business needs and can find, if it could only imagine family intelligently, deeply, and poetically.

Friendship

Next to family, perhaps the most important value of the soul is friendship, and so, in search of the soul of business, we can examine the condition of friendship in the marketplace and the workplace. "The only reason I come to work every morning," a radio producer told me, "is because of my friends there." But the owner of a large furniture business confessed, "We're afraid that if we encourage friendship among our employees, productivity will go down. In management it's all right, but not among the workers."

It's true that values of the soul sometimes stand at odds with other values: speed versus a slow pace, efficiency versus quality, function versus imagination, and productivity versus creativity. We will have to change our ways as a society if we want a soulful life and if we really want solutions to our so-called social problems. We may have to slow down, live a somewhat less efficient and less convenient style of life, shake loose the dominant philosophy of functionality, and not give productivity such a high place in our priorities. Once, at the end of a flight the pilot said goodbye to us passengers and wished us a "productive" day. I thought to myself, I hope my day isn't too productive; I'd rather see some moments of surprise, rest, and creativity.

I can't promise that if a company supports friendship among its employees it will be more productive. It might well become less productive, but I can confidently predict that the company will have better morale with the increase in soul and may well find fewer problems that come from its neglect. If in business we keep an anxious eye only on the profit margin and productivity curve, we may succeed in the eyes of our fellow neurotic associates, but we may have missed the opportunity to satisfy our soul during the workday.

One of the problems one faces in dealing with business is its own brand of fundamentalism: certain values are absolute and unquestioned, like productivity and profit. The soul has its own, different rewards, which are deeply satisfying but are not necessarily compatible with typical business absolutes. Employees may love their work, enjoy each other's company, and feel loyal to the company, but the price for these happy outcomes may be a shift in priorities that represents a radical reorientation of business wisdom. It seems obvious to me that a small company with good morale, a beautiful environment, just and altruistic practices, a positive place in the community, and products that contribute to a full life is more valuable and more worth developing than a company without those qualities whose profits are always growing. Small can be beautiful even in the business world.

I wonder how much longer anyone will be willing to be a cog in the business machine. As I speak to people in every part of the world about soul, they talk ecstatically about their gardening, writing poetry, traveling, making a home, caring for children, and looking for a modest occupation that will feed their souls if not their wallets. I imagine the whole edifice of inhuman business collapsing from lack of interest among the "work force"—a telling phrase in itself. Some people will always want to be makers, doers, and achievers, but many are now looking for more intimate values like friendship and beauty, family and ethical satisfaction.

When a business shows signs of failing, the worst response might be to intensify those very things that wound the souls of workers, consumers, neighboring community, and the business leaders themselves. Increasing productivity, raising the anxiety level about profit, cutting programs that serve the soul, instigating less humane organization and authority patterns—each of these common practices places a business deeper in trouble, because it eats away at the human elements that ground and fortify the workplace. It might be better to refresh the imagination of business radically, placing enchantment high on the list of priorities.

The soul hungers for friendship just as ardently as the body hungers for nutritious food, and something as simple as friendship can make a workplace enchanting. A factory or an office can hum with the thoughts of good conversation and empathetic fellowship, with fantasy about fellow workers and longing for their company. When people stand next to each other at work and have no fantasy about each other, no stories on which to dwell, and no history of interaction, then they are inanimate—not animated, not ensouled—as frigid as the machines that labor metallically around them.

Annoying and sometimes debilitating office romances may be a sign that eros is not woven into the fabric of the business and so floats autonomously and dangerously like a virus in search of a victim. I doubt that business leaders recognize how effectively and deeply friendship can satisfy, humanize, and contextualize the need for love and thereby keep eros relatively contained.

Material

Enchanted business requires another kind of intimacy, too: closeness with the matter at hand, the materials and objects that are made, sold, shipped, and tallied. Things can enchant. I once went in search of a harpsichord in Manhattan, walking down the noisy streets full of people and taxis. Eventually I found the door I was looking for, a simple door on an old, unimpressive building, and walked into the plain room filled with the fine, delicate instruments. It was like coming across an oasis in the Sahara, a respite from the busy streets, but more than that, a house of animated things, things of beauty that made wonderful sounds and had such presence as to take your breath away.

I'll always remember my father, when I was a child, showing me pictures of buildings under construction. He would look at a certain arrangement of pipes and fall into an aesthetic reverie that no art expert could match. Most people involved in the manufacture and sale of products appreciate the beauty of good materials and construction, but it seems that to a large extent we have lost this important source of enchantment. We think that our abstract goals and objectives are more important than the satisfying materials at hand.

If we ship all our plans and materials to other places for assembly and manufacture, we will be denuded of real things just as we risk becoming denuded of trees and wilderness, and yet things are as much a source of soul as waterfalls and shady groves. Or, if we discover through chemistry that all natural things can be duplicated in synthetics, we will have preserved the shell of things and lost their matter; then, without a genuine interior, they will have no capacity for enchantment. Perhaps the threat to health in synthetic foods is the fact, lost on contemporary chemists, that whole food has a soul that can't be put into a chemically processed substitute.

Today we can remain in close contact with real things simply by making and buying cotton, wool, linen, and silk; by refusing "oak

finishes" made of petroleum on our furniture and polyurethane var-
nishes that shield us from sensual contact with real material; by listening to live music and by going out of our way to buy fish freshly
caught; by reading a poem instead of watching a television program, and by reading a story to the family and playing the piano
and going for a walk together. Some businesses support these
choices, and in so doing they contribute to the re-enchantment of
everyday life, but for the most part business remains, perhaps with
politics, one of the greatest obstacles we have toward a soulful social
life.

The workplace, too, could be less artificial, providing workers
with fresh air, natural light, a human schedule and pace, signs of
nature, and things of beauty. As with all things, enchantment usually asks for only a small libation poured in its honor: a lovely
antique, a well-crafted chair, an artist's painting, a colored wall, a
remarkable door, a lamp with personality, some hand-worked clay,
intimate lighting, a view of a landscape, a pleasing pot, a wondrous
plant, a vase of fresh flowers, access to a park, flowing water, a few
inches of wood. We may need to pry ourselves loose from the
clutches of function, profit, authority, and productivity, which keep
soul and work, enchantment and the commercial life, at odds.

The new romantic basis of cultural life that I am describing as
enchantment may seem soft and effete compared to the hard realities we usually associate with business and other parameters of society, but for all its softness, it is a radical proposal, asking for nothing
less than an inversion of many of our social values. But I see no
other way to bring soul to a soulless world, sacredness to a secularistic enterprise, or enchantment to a disenchanted situation than to
summon the courage to do things differently. It's clear to me that it
is the romantics in our history who have sustained a vision of the
humane life, who have nurtured the deep virtues of natural religion
and piety, and who have cared for our souls when others have tried
to convince us we have no soul to care for.

Mystic Transport

WHEN I WAS nineteen and still a member of a religious order, I sailed the *Queen Mary* to Ireland to study philosophy in a Catholic priory. I remember well the day we departed from New York: the crowds of people cheering us into the brilliant, sparkling ocean and the air of festivity thick on the many decks, cabins, and hallways. The ship was built and furnished with warm woods and shiny brass, and the British staff took care of our every wish. This was my first venture into the big world beyond the midwestern United States, and most of the time it felt like a thrilling dream. There were a few nightmare feelings as well, as when I would sit in a lounge watching the ship rock back and forth and pitch to and fro, and sense my landlubber stomach begging for a return to *terra firma;* and the anxiety, too, of leaving home for my first taste of other countries.

After several days of pampering and near seasickness, I looked out our porthole, which must have been down close to the waterline, since it was open only during calm seas, and beheld the French town of Cherbourg. When the ship docked for the day, I walked through the colorful market and into the inviting countryside, a charming respite on my journey from Chicago to the village of Benburb in Northern Ireland. What a difference it made in travel—compared to going by air these days—to eat in style, to pass through time zones one hour each day, and to make a daylong stopover in a place filled with charm. The very fantasy of travel lacked the drivenness and goal-directedness inherent in today's efforts to save mere minutes whenever possible.

If I were in charge of transportation, I would place enchantment far above efficiency in my design of cars, trains, planes, roadways, gas stations, and airports, for transportation doesn't have to be considered as a utilitarian service only; it also can be an experience of beauty and fascination. If we imagine transportation as the process of getting from point A to point B, we are reducing it to absolute and unadorned pragmatism, whereas it can be an exciting sensual and emotional experience in itself.

Sometimes the difference between practical transport and pleasing travel depends on a simple decision to care for the soul. As a writer and lecturer, I travel a great deal. I recall once being picked up by an airport limousine service near my home, and the driver suggested we take the "scenic route" to the airport. We bypassed the interstate highway, the usual and the most direct route, and instead rode through lovely countryside, taking in fresh air and the sight of green fields, and still arrived at the airport early. I flew to Washington, D.C., that day, and coincidentally, when my host picked me up at the Washington airport, she said, "Let's take the scenic route." Once again I found myself on beautiful roads where nature was plentiful even in the city, and I was able to get to work in an unusual state of calm and relaxation. Now I always try to take the scenic route.

From the soul point of view, travel is not primarily concerned with transportation. The word "travel," older than "transportation," is closely related to "travail," which, not a pleasure word, derives from the Latin *tripalium*, a three-pronged instrument of torture; most of us who have traveled have felt the prick of that instrument on occasion. Sometimes arduous and taxing, travel is often a kind of birth labor too, affording us new visions and experiences. The very idea of travel, in contrast to transportation, is to be en route, to be away from home and on the road, in strange lands and among unfamiliar people. Travel is a state of being and a particular mode of imagination occasioned by but not identical with the process of transport.

An American, you may find yourself in Asia, surrounded by unfamiliar languages, customs, food, and sights. Or you may "travel" only to a nearby town and still find yourself in territory that is not home, and this travel, too, can be travail, the work of birthing the soul even farther into the world and away from your mother's body and the comfort of home.

Regardless of its dimensions, travel is not just an activity; it's a mystery in the fullest sense of the word. In a section on walking in *Love's Body*, Norman O. Brown hints at the paradox and mystery of travel: "Movement is in space; and space, as Plato says in the *Timaeus*, is a receptacle, a vessel; a matrix; as it were the mother or nurse of all becoming." It is as if in travel we were exploring the mother's womb, for the world is also our mother, in which we are contained and held. Travel is a discovery of the world soul of which we are a part and which mysteriously is also the matrix of our own identity.

One benefit of travel is the opportunity to see the world's soul in the concrete and discover the many ways life can be lived out. If we reduce travel to transportation, we withhold soul from our movements, and then, for all our moving around and getting from place to place, the soul goes unfed. Travel is a profound mystery, but for it to speak to the soul, we have to go about it with care, especially inviting the soul to share in the experience.

And so it may be good if we choose to walk to a place rather than drive; to go by ship rather than air; to drive indirectly rather than by the shortest route; to dally rather than rush; to experience foreigners, whether the inhabitants of another country or simply of another suburb; to eat their food, and not our own; and, above all, to allow other places to be themselves and not to impose our own values and manners on them. In our economic efforts to Westernize the globe, we are diminishing our own resources for enchantment, and I fear that in the future, wherever we go, we will find only ourselves.

Transports of Dream

One indication of the soul's role in transportation is the fact that we dream so often about cars, airplanes, trains, and roads. Dreams reveal the poetry embedded in the ordinary things of life and hint that travel is meaningful to the soul and leaves deep impressions. The soul recognizes the automobile, for example, which, like the body, has to move about independently at times. It's familiar with a bus, because it, too, travels in crowds along certain ordained routes. It certainly knows airplanes, for it has long been described as having wings and can move through the air. Neoplatonists, like Ficino, often wrote about the soul's "vehicles."

A woman once told me she dreamed she was in the back seat of a car that was being driven by a shadowy man. She was deathly afraid of him and felt uncomfortable sitting in the back. But then she found that she had been driven to see her family, whom she hadn't visited in years, and as the dream ended, she was overwhelmed with gratitude.

One nightmarish feeling that sometimes comes up in dreams is the sense that you don't know what's going on and that you have no control. You're being taken somewhere, and you'd like to know from the beginning where you're going. Not only in dreams but also in life, we all like to be "in the driver's seat," and it isn't irrelevant to the dream that we use that expression.

Travel has rich metaphoric value and leaves impressions that influence the way we experience other aspects of daily life. I will never be the same for having spent some time in Ireland in my youth, and in Italy later on. I traveled physically to these two places and can describe my travel, but my soul was transported too, and it went through an initiation in each case, leaving me changed for life. We could all tell stories of being affected by travel.

Transports of Mysticism

Modern improvements in transportation also lead to new emotional challenges. I feel frustrated at not having a home in the many places where I have made friends. How can I not live in Italy, where so much life and friendship were revealed to me? How can I not live in California, where I feel so many elements of home and where I have so much potential for life? How can I not live where I used to in the Massachusetts Berkshires, where I felt enchantment more than any other place? How can I not settle in Ireland, where my heart feels so comforted and where I feel connected to my family? How can I not be a resident of Michigan, where I grew up and where so many family members live? How can I stand not spending time in the Finger Lakes region of upstate New York, where my family roots are strongest and memories of childhood sweet?

Having traveled so much, I'm led to the very heart of Neoplatonism, to the longing for a bodiless home for the soul and a way to be in all these places at once. Travel gives rise to its own kind of spirituality: to a grand appreciation for community, to a passionate love of this earth, to an urgent longing for transcendence, and even to a sweet foretaste of death. Shakespeare uses the word "transport" to refer to taking leave of this life. Just as the philosopher prepares for death by working out thoughts and ideas that transcend the body, the traveler, too, builds a mystical ship of death, the ultimate form of transportation D. H. Lawrence describes in his late poetry:

> Oh, build your ship of death, be building it now
> With dim, calm thoughts and quiet hands
> Putting its timbers together in the dusk,
> Rigging its mast with the silent, invisible sail
> That will spread in death to the breeze
> Of the kindness of the cosmos, that will waft
> The little ship with its soul to the wonder-goal.

Religious traditions around the world have emphasized the image of travel as central to the soul, especially with boats used to ferry souls to the land of the dead. In the Babylonian *Epic of Gilgamesh*, the hero makes every effort to reach Utnapishtim to obtain the plant of immortality. He crosses the waters of death in a boat equipped with 120 punting poles, each of which he can use only once, since a human can't come in contact with the otherworldly water.

The Greeks placed a coin in the mouth of the dead person in payment to Charon, the ugly ferryman, who would pilot the soul across the river of the underworld to the gates of Hades. Egyptians buried their dead with replicas of boats that were often elaborate vessels, complete with cabins and crews. Celtic legend is full of stories of sea journeys by the dead to such places as the Land Beneath the Waves and the Island of Laughter. The *Navigation of St. Brendan* is the most famous of these stories, and Brendan's crucial voyage is depicted everywhere in traditional Irish art. In Buddhism one makes the journey of the soul by means of the raft of religion.

What is so enchanting about setting out on a canoe, a small rowboat, a sailing vessel, or a great ship? We sail not just for the physical sensations but also because the soul has its own fantasies on water and on a boat. In some deep way, we are living out a ritual that has strong ties to Jesus in the boat with his apostles, the Buddhist on the raft of religion, and Odysseus on his sea voyage home. Enchantment arises sometimes when myth and ordinary experience come together, as when we engage in some apparently innocent pastime, like a canoe ride, and are surprised to find that we're sailing on mythical water.

The teaching career of Jesus consisted of a long journey from Galilee to Jerusalem, a tortuous movement of the soul that ended in another mystical journey, the Way of the Cross. The story of the journey of Odysseus is a sacred tale about the travels and travails of the soul, where the emphasis is on fateful turns, blocks, enticements, and the will of the gods. In Christianity the believer is a pilgrim on earth, and in the Gnostic "Hymn of the Pearl" the soul is a sojourner in this world, an alien whose true home is far away in another land.

Leonard Cohen's melancholic song "Suzanne," alluding to one of Jesus' great miracles, adds another dimension to the image of travel—magic:

> And Jesus was a sailor
> When He walked upon the water
>
> And you want to travel with Him,
> And you want to travel blind.

Enchantment demands that we blend realism with imagination, that we move beyond the laws and expectations of natural science and discover the magic of travel. Physically, travel is full of practical and logistical challenges, but for the heart and soul it always requires real magic: one has to find ways to arrive fully, body and soul, in a new place, and how to make the getting there a voyage of enchantment.

The enchanted life is not without fear and the existential anxieties associated with abandonment to fate, but it entails an Odyssean surrender to storm and calm seas and a Buddhist setting out from the shore, a Moses march out of captivity, and even a Christ-like walk upon the waters. Every day we may have to take a step and keep the journey going. The soul needs an endless tableau of visions and sights that can be seen only as we travel, both literally and in the way we live, for according to one of the commonest and truest clichés, "Life itself is a journey."

In our prudence we tend to value such stationary attitudes as stability and security. People who don't show these virtues we label unstable and insecure. But in our desire for enchantment we might consider other virtues, such as the capacity to wander and the ability not to become too established in any place. Jesus was born in a makeshift shelter on an anxious trip to Egypt, and the Buddha found enlightenment only after leaving the safety and comfort of home.

I have been a traveler all my life, ever since I left home at thirteen. I've lived in eight states and two countries, I've had several professions, and my mind is always moving from one attachment to another. Some say that moving from place to place is the problematical result of modern living, where there is little anchoring and settling. I prefer to think of the conflict of mobility and stability as a yin and yang, which varies in style and degree from person to person, depending in great measure on the vicissitudes of fate. People in remote ages traveled and moved their homes, engaged in pious journeys of pilgrimage, and ventured into new lands and lives. As much as the soul loves a real home, it also loves to wander. It holds familiar places and things dear, and yet it craves novel sights and new belongings. We don't have to moralize against instability, to take sides in this ancient dilemma of whether to stay put or set out. We can live both of these archetypal necessities in one life, in a variety of styles, more or less metaphoric, more or less literal. Enchantment lies buried beneath the moralism that chooses one or the other as good and healthy, and it is released when we find ways to invite both travel and settling into a life shaped by responsiveness to our own destiny.

Emily Dickinson rarely ventured far from her home and garden in Amherst, and Marsilio Ficino never left Tuscany. Yet these two lovers of the world traveled as far as any adventurer. They teach us that the soul's journeys may or may not coincide with actual travel, but they require an Odyssean spirit of abandon, guided by love and eager for delight.

Enchanted Travel

The mystical dimensions of travel I've been charting here are not unrelated to the everyday details of getting from place to place. Although we rarely think of mystical travel, it is implicated in so common a thing as public transportation, in getting our car started in the morning, in catching a bus. In an enchanted world, myth and ordinary life come together, so that in our experience of something as ordinary as a bicycle, we might notice and feel ancient themes of mythology and religion.

Imagine if we designed all aspects of travel with the soul in mind—schedules, seating, pace, routes, machines, and terminals. The soul has certain needs that generally are quite different from the needs of the body alone, like comfort, space, conviviality, quiet, and things of interest to look at. Why do we devour magazines on trains and planes, unless our souls are hungry for thoughts and images? Why do we talk so much about the quality of food on airplanes and in places we visit, unless those simple pleasures are important to the soul?

In the past few years of my life, I have spent more time on airplanes than ever before, and I've had time to think about the soul's role in all that travel. When I fly from Boston to San Francisco I arrive with the excitement of being in a place I love, but I always feel some shock and considerable fatigue. Experts explain jet lag in physical terms, but to me it's the result of the soul not traveling as fast as the body. I'm halfway across the country, jetting toward the West Coast, but my soul is just leaving Boston. My memories, feelings, and even my breakfast are bound to New England, even though the plane has taken my body two thousand miles. On a ship, I could watch the passing of time zones, but in the plane they zoom by unnoticed. On the plane, we might stop at Chicago's airport, but we don't have a day to stroll through the city.

I'm not complaining about air travel, because we're all caught up in the modern style of living, but I want to speak on behalf of the soul in travel. Only once in my flying experience were passengers allowed to board the plane over an hour's time, at our leisure. What a difference it made not to be filing numerically into a cabin, falling over each other, getting in each other's way. The soul was served by that simple change in routine.

I often wonder what is in the minds of those who design planes when they crowd people and force them into inhumanly narrow seats. Especially when traveling, the soul needs physical comfort and room for conviviality, yet the aisles are usually too narrow and busy with service to allow roaming and conversation. If I'm going to speak somewhere, I know I shouldn't talk to my seatmate because, owing to the noise of the engine, I may not have a voice left when we land. Having a few empty seats on a plane gives my soul room to breathe, and yet the airlines have found clever ways to make almost every flight full. The only conclusion I can come to is that those who design air travel either don't understand that the soul has its requirements, which are every bit as important as those of the body, or, like our culture in general, they think there's no harm in overriding those concerns.

These basic needs of the soul form a ground for enchantment, but for really charmed travel we would need much more. Terminals for buses, planes, and trains could be places of genuine oasis. Now they are typically filled with uninviting chain stores and coffee shops, but is there any reason why there couldn't be a fine, affordable restaurant and shops that offer local products? Good shopping is a major element in enchanted travel.

Once in an airport I came across a very small bookstand run by a man who thought air travelers should have access to excellent literature. I was surprised at the quality of classic and modern books in his small selection. He explained that he felt he had a niche to fill, since airport bookstores cater only to what they imagine to be popular tastes. He knew that a bookstore can be remarkably individual in its offerings, and he thought travelers read mediocre books and magazines simply because that's all they can find. A good book can make all the difference, and in some cities fine bookstores are establishing branches at airports, making a significant contribution to enchanted travel.

The soul has so many other needs in travel that one wishes travel companies would hire someone to oversee these special soul requirements—a vice president of enchantment. The soul, and not just the body, craves good food, a pleasing sound environment, and appropriate places to say goodbye to loved ones. Compare old movies showing people running after trains, their lovers and relatives hanging out the windows, to a modern scene of families being held back at checkpoints because they are not ticketed passengers. It's not the same, saying goodbye at a security station.

Hotels, too, can be merely utilitarian or merely pampering, but sometimes they surprise with special delights for the soul. I recall a lovely old hotel in Indianapolis with a window in the bathroom, a Japanese hotel in San Francisco with beautifully simple furnishings, and my favorite hotel in the Los Angeles area—by the ocean, having an enormous, inviting ancient tree at its entrance. It's always easier, but not necessarily automatic, for an old hotel to comfort the soul, but even new ones can do it, with, say, real paintings in the rooms and hallways. I often wonder why, with so many artists in need of commissions, we don't find original art wherever we travel. Some new hotel rooms are spacious enough to allow the guest to make a temporary home in them, and some offer a variety of fresh food, instead of the standard heavy, meaty, and fatty menus.

If I had my own soul-oriented travel agency, I would focus on certain qualities—individuality, pace, pleasure, comfort, family. If I owned a hotel, I'd find some way to allow people to check in early and leave late. I'd make certain children were invited and given a proper environment, for families and children bring more soul to a place than individuals whose goal is efficient, businesslike, and quick travel.

Transportation can be profoundly enchanting. The air industry began with dreaming inventors, Kitty Hawk, daredevil barnstormers, Lindbergh and Earhart, all culminating a long history in which people dreamed of flying. In experience and in literature, trains are full of romance, and even a bus can provide opportunities for genuine adventure. But there is a trend in modern life to render everything, including transportation, merely efficient. The soul suffers considerably in this shift toward pragmatism in travel and away from beauty and the needs of the heart. Still, there is no reason why transportation can't be re-enchanted, restored to its full capacity for fantasy.

The Particularity of Place

SOMETIMES THE spirit of a place is so strong you may think you see its face and glimpse it gamboling over a field or peeking out of a forest, but at other times you struggle for words to describe it. San Francisco's spirit looks you in the eye, but the genius of the Finger Lakes Region of New York sleeps shyly in the thick of its rolling hills and tranquil waters. This spirit we sense in each locality would once have been described as the scintilla, or spark, of its soul, the pearl in the oyster. It accounts for the magic of a region, and without it, an acute sense of place dissipates into a vague and lazy feeling of nowhere.

Many people have found ways to honor the *genius loci*, the spirit of a place, the presiding and protective presence. The great god Pan of the Greeks was known to roam the mountains, and Artemis could be felt deep in the seclusion of the forest; on the American plains, a corn spirit, a genius of flatlands and grains, haunts the area, while in the Rocky Mountains a very different spirit, of high and vertical terrain, fills the hearts of those who live there and visit. When we speak of the "atmosphere" of a place, we're probably reaching for its genius, although we don't have the descriptive language our ancestors had for such presences.

There is a tendency in modern life to water down the particulars of life into generalizations and abstractions, but abstractions don't have much of an inner voice, because there is nobody at home in them—no scintilla and no pearl, no face and no voice. We do the same with places: we forget that a place has its own character, and turning it into an abstract spot on a map, we use it for anything we can think of and force its own spirit underground.

Sometimes the spirit lies in the history of a place. A piece of country property may seem entirely ordinary and abstract to the real estate agent making calculations, but to the person whose grandfather settled the land, a family spirit is vividly present, transforming that characterless space into a real, haunting place. Enchantment requires that the particular spirit of a place be honored; we could go a long way toward bringing charm into modern life by revering local spirits and protecting their haunts.

Not long ago I was walking the streets of a charming New England town, when suddenly I looked up and saw a looming verdigris gargoyle climbing up over the roof of one of the buildings— a good example, I thought, of giving body to the spirit that haunts a street of shops. And when I walk the streets of Manhattan, I recognize a particular spirit in the buildings, the traffic, and even in the faces of people I pass, and as in the small town, I find that spirit given form in the rooftops of the city—in the filigree of finely forged parapets and in ornate cornices and dormers.

Enchantment can't be achieved in the abstract; we need strong physical images to capture and embody the spirits that populate our towns and wilderness. The streets of many Italian cities are filled with figures large and small, from the great anthropomorphic sculpted rivers of the Piazza Navona in Rome, to small bees and flowers carved into bridges and doorways everywhere. In a strange way, the more we invite the nonhuman spirit world into our environment, the more human our world becomes.

Particular Places

A peculiarly modern way of violating a place is to construct homes and businesses without regard for traditional local forms of building and decorating. Some architect working in an abstract building on an abstract street comes up with an efficient plan, and then the plan is copied all over the world. In the "Xeroxed" landscape, where all people and places look alike, we can't find our way, but worse, we have no signs indicating the spirits that give a place its soul. We patronize cloned restaurants and clothing stores, but the individual shop with an independent owner perhaps speaks more fully to the soul. If a place doesn't have its own spirit, we can't enter into dialogue with it, and so we treat it as a lifeless object, and it treats us, too, as an abstraction—one customer among many, a subject, a number.

In an enchanted world you are surrounded by "real," individual things, not imitations. You honor the particular qualities that make a place unique, or at least take them as a starting point for imagination. I once asked a highly successful architect how he would build a modern house in New England. "I'd probably use the saltbox shape in the design," he said, "without making literal copies of old saltboxes." Cloning the past can sometimes be as heartless as making multiple copies of a fresh design, but inviting the local spirit into our new building connects our life and work not only to the past but also to the spiritual influences that account for the particularity of the place.

Perhaps the most typical American example of disenchantment is the "strip" of chain restaurants and stores that lines highways going in and out of towns all over the country. The primary impression these strips make on me is of emptiness. They seem to be hollow, void of the genius that resides in real things and particular places. They make one town look like another, whereas the genius of a place gives a town a strong sense of identity and individuality.

Marsilio Ficino's writings on enchantment give lessons that are quite different from those used in the building of chain stores. A visit to his hometown of Florence might demonstrate definitively how to make a place unique and how to entice its spirit to come out and bless its residents. Ficino says we should draw spirit and soul down *into* a thing, not away from it. In what could be a definition of enchantment, he says, "Everywhere the world is alive and breathes, and we can absorb its spirit." This statement could be a test of the enchantment quotient of a place: Is it alive? Does it breathe? Can we, and do we want to, take in its spirit? Does it have a spirit to take in?

If the world is indeed everywhere alive and breathing, then each place is unique, with personality and character, not a dead space waiting to receive whatever personality we choose to paste onto it. If we do our part by being open to the enchantment, it can waken our souls, and we may feel charmed and deeply stirred simply by making ourselves present to it. Ficino's philosophy emphasizes the magic in such enchantment, involving intentional, artful means of translating the local spirits into laws, customs, festivals, color, architecture, home-building, and decoration.

Travel and visit places that are rich in soul, he advises. Honor local spirits—not only your own but your neighbors' and those most foreign to yours. The worst traveler is the one who expects faraway places to be like his home and wants the comforts and conveniences he's used to. Travel for enchantment requires a "beginner's mind," a cultivated naïveté, because a jaded attitude toward new places sets up a barrier against the possibility of being charmed, and in fact one wonders if the cynical attitude some travelers bring with them is a defense against being enchanted.

Arriving home from a journey, we can "translate" the spirit of a place to our own homes in a number of familiar ways: bringing things home from faraway places—crafts, arts, food, clothing— and taking care of photographs, journals, and notes we might have made on the trip. One of my great pleasures in traveling is to watch my wife take out her sketchbook on a beach or on a mountaintop and "capture"—a technical term in magic—the spirit of the place. Of course, we do these things anyway, but a philosophy of enchantment might inspire us to travel without a defensive attitude and annoying judgments, and with real appreciation for the simple things that hold the spirit of a place and that can sometimes be brought home for our continuing enchantment.

Ficino also recommends playing the music of a place, a powerful way, he says, to attract a local spirit to your own home. My neighbors occasionally have a "session" of Irish music, when twenty men and women gather together, with all kinds of instruments, to conjure up the spirit of Ireland; other neighbors meet regularly to perform and dance to African music. The spirit given to the neighborhood by these two different kinds of music is entirely distinct and touches different parts of the body and the soul. These simple communal activities keep the soul of a neighborhood rich and full, brimming with fantasy, memory, emotion, rhythm, and a haunting connection to other cultures and ways.

Taste is another good way to keep spirits, both local and foreign, alive and well. I treasure recipes for "Tex-Mex" food I brought to New England with me from Texas when I moved north. A library of good cookbooks is like the scriptorium of a Renaissance magician—a storehouse of spells and formulas guaranteed to work wonders. Cooking regional food is a culinary form of magic, in the strict sense of the word, because it's an effective way to give body to local spirits. Some chefs, we say, perform magic in the kitchen, but anyone can become expert in this homely form of enchantment.

The basic requirement for a magic based on local spirits is an appreciation for their existence and their value. We may not need a collection of exotic foods or clothing, although this would be one way to make magic at home; our magic may be no more than a trunk of heirlooms or remembered recipes handed down through the family over generations, or a life shaped by local seasons, foods, and customs. It's when we lose a vivid sense of region and locality that the spirits crawl back into hiding, and human life becomes pale with the loss.

Civilization and Its Anxieties

If we continue to transform all nations of the world into homogenized high-tech, no-image, all-function cultures of disenchantment, we will have few unique spirits left to nourish our souls. We will be a people without ghosts and without things to house those ghosts, a people so bereft of spirituality in everyday things that we will turn, as many already have, to outrageous otherworldly venues for our spiritual experiences. This truly will be a dangerous time, because human community and civility are not, as some would say, humanistic achievements; they are the work of the ghosts of memory and the spirits of place, of the genius in things and the soul of culture.

The collective emotional complex that drives us to homogenize the planet, to make every place comfortably predictable and controllable, seems to derive from a deep insecurity, the kind that motivates us sometimes to demand that everyone share our precise and narrowly defined beliefs. We may be disturbed when we don't find a convenience store in the jungle and may want everyone to speak the same language. This xenophobia isn't really a fear of strangers; it's rather a fear of the strange and the unfamiliar in the broadest terms, and therefore a fear of life and vitality. It stems from a cultural fundamentalism that is uncomfortable with all forms of "otherness" and therefore strives to make everything one.

Enchantment flows out of the unique presence. Certainly the desire to update, civilize, and gentrify a place is valid, and it does no good to moralize against it. The local genius is not necessarily served by preserving the past, but the desire to develop a place commercially may well arise from motives that work against it. A corporation wishing simply to expand or to experiment with new markets might easily tread over local customs and unconsciously quash the spirit and destroy the natural religion of an area. We have become so accustomed to this kind of development that we don't seem to realize the dire harm that comes from the loss of the local genius.

Modern development also seems to be antagonistic toward all that is pristine and raw, or old and falling apart. Undeveloped nature appears as an affront to our civilizing efforts, and we may pave it over or build insensitively on it out of anger. In the right hands, a bulldozer can be a sculptor's scalpel, but often it's a weapon of rage. As we become increasingly sophisticated technologically, we seem to be more and more cut off from our own wildness, our own uncivilized natures, so that taming nature seems to be an effort to tame our own feral desires and fears. We hold on to our civilized natures anxiously, as though they could easily be lost.

When I first became a therapist, I was surprised to hear people speak anxiously about the intensity of their passions and emotions. The worst thing that could happen to them, it seemed, would be to lose their control or, worse, the persona they had painstakingly put together of a civilized, well-adapted individual. Our technical manuals of emotional disorders could be seen as compendiums of defenses against the natural soul. For many of the people I worked with, marriage was not a passionate, unique engagement with another person but a social arrangement, and success in life was measured not by faithfulness to their own spirit but by allegiance to a widely accepted norm. At the same time, raw desire or aggression might be erupting in them, and they rushed to therapy as a means of keeping it all within acceptable boundaries.

The wildness of nature in the forests and on the plains is the same wildness we feel when a strong desire comes upon us and throws our hard-won living arrangements into question or threatens the moral principles that have remained fixed for years. I've heard dreams of tornadoes from many people over the years, tornadoes threatening their homes and persons, or actually destroying them. These dreams show that the soul's inner passions and nature's outer turbulence lie in the same sphere. When we treat one, we may be trying to deal with the other. We could develop our interior selves and our personal lives with care for the wilderness in them, even as we do the same with the outer world around us. I would expect success in one realm to have an effect on the other.

There is also a strain of narcissism in our efforts to remain civilized. We're in love with our own achievements and jealous of nature's ways of being creative. We like to brag about our inventions and discoveries, but we don't often express the important companion sentiments of respect and honor toward nature's creativity. Compare the Promethean boasts of modern developers and politicians with the more humble sentiments of the ancient sages. The *Tao Te Ching* says:

> Man models himself on the Earth;
> The Earth models itself on Heaven;
> Heaven models itself on the Way;
> And the Way models itself on that which is so on its own.

We could model ourselves on earth and find a kind of humility that in no way contradicts or interferes with our creativity but instead puts valuable limits on growth and development.

For many, the enchanted life remains elusive because of deep feelings of insecurity. The theologian Paul Tillich often wrote about this cultural anxiety as an aspect of being itself: "This anxiety is aroused by the loss of a spiritual center, of an answer, however symbolic and indirect, to the question of the meaning of existence." I myself have long felt the dilemma of looking for meaning, and therefore relief from the cultural anxiety, either in a mental understanding of life and culture or in plain emotion. But now I formulate the issue differently: the fundamental anxiety can be relieved more by a *meaningful* life than by any quest for meaning, and life itself becomes meaningful when we discover its interiority, its soul, its capacity to entrance and enchant.

Xenophobia, the fear of strangers, is an infection of the soul particularly virulent in our times, but it is not a fear only of foreign people. It's a deeply disturbing anxiety that affects everything we do. At its root is a fear of "the strange," which is nothing other than nature, nature inside and nature outside. Overdevelopment of natural resources in the external world parallels overdevelopment of natural resources in the interior life. We seem to be always reaching for an elusive goal, rather than loving the world in front of our eyes, just as we put anxious effort into becoming a new person, instead of loving and living the life we've always had and always will have.

If we could really love the place where we were born and the place where we live, and let its history, geography, and genius enter our lives and affect them in every aspect, then we might not be so fearful when we meet people who love their place and its own ways, and more positively, we might find the security we need in the ground under our feet.

Our xenophobic anxiety is rooted in our failure to be in place, to be conduits of the *genius loci*, not subjective and independent, but representative of our region. In his great poem "Esthétique du Mal," Wallace Stevens writes: "The greatest poverty is not to live/In a physical world." In another remarkable poem, "Asides on the Oboe," more directly to our theme, he describes the poet, or perhaps any of us living with imagination:

> He is the transparence of the place in which
> He is and in his poems we find peace.

We are the "transparence of place" when the spirit of our ground concretely influences what we do and the way we live. Secure in that place, we need not fear strangers who are more familiar with other places. The religion of place, so grounded and so intimately linked to nature, climate, and geography, is rarely defensive. It enjoys the calm where meaningful life emerges out of intimacy with the place. It doesn't suffer the spiritual neurosis that seeks relief in knowing that the entire world shares its belief and even its place. For that universal place is really no place at all but is absent of geography, history, limit, and the enchanting songs of local nature and local culture.

Psyche

*If he stays inside himself, if he is contained
within his nature as he is participant in the
larger force, he will be able to listen, and his
hearing through himself will give him secrets
objects share.*

CHARLES OLSON

Sex and the Soul

I HAVE NEVER imagined Jesus or the Buddha or Moses or any other great religious figure as asexual or as speaking against sex. Nor, having lived the monastic life for many years as a young man, do I think that spiritual dedication, even to the extent of taking a vow of celibacy, is necessarily a statement against sex or precludes a sexual life. The only way such assumptions could be entertained would be if sex were understood in purely biological terms—materialistically. If we allow sex any meaning at all beyond the literal and biological, then the monk and Jesus and other spiritual figures may be perceived as fully sexual beings and the life of the spirit in full accord with sexuality.

Followers of many religions, of course, often see a conflict between the spirit and the body, and they assume that the renunciation of intercourse implies a judgment against sex. For several years I ate in a monastic refectory beneath a painting that showed Jesus naked without genitals. Apparently this unnatural presentation was preferable to the image of the human body as God created it.

In this anxious warfare between spirituality and sex, the spiritual inclination is to strive for a life without sex, or with sex subdued— witness the many stories of those who became saints by successfully overcoming the temptations of the flesh. But this imbalance may create a tormenting preoccupation with sex, making sex the focus of all that is not spiritual. Then sex becomes the chief target of moralism, which, from a certain point of view, is nothing but spirituality trying vehemently to be disconnected from body and soul, to deny the desires and needs that press from within and without as though they were merely biological and therefore to be transcended. We try to diminish the role of sex, and in doing so make it the biggest thing in life. And then sex, of all things, becomes disenchanted.

Sex and Carnival

If we turn to religion to find models of enchantment, we discover several curious ways that sex enters ritual and daily religious life. In some traditions, for example, certain days are set aside for complete release from all sexual inhibitions and loyalties. The resulting orgies provide divine power to the participants, who are believed to be engaged in a truly holy act.

A more restrained yet still carnival re-visioning of sexual practices took place in the communal marriage of the Oneida Community of upstate New York. In the early nineteenth century, John Humphrey Noyes led this community of about four hundred people in a "complex" marriage in which any community member might have sex with another member, provided they sought the mediation of a third party. In the Oneida Community it was considered scandalous for two people to be emotionally involved with each other in any exclusive way, and if found out, they were separated and sent off to satellite homes.

These religious practices correspond to sentiments that many people express as a desire for anonymous sex or release from the limitations of marriage vows. Over half the American population, according to some studies, engage in extramarital sex, and so one is tempted to conclude that something in the most dedicated people desires sex outside marriage. Pornography often shows a similar interest in group sex, so that sexually explicit magazines echo certain ancient religious practices, and pornography casts its spell as carnival too, a release from the constraints of civilized mores.

The most common response to these fantasies of sexual liberation takes the form of moralism: "How can we keep these desires in check?" the moralist asks. "How can we free ourselves from the shackles of traditional mores?" the libertine asks. An alternative would be to explore the mystery of traditional practices of carnival and its modern traces in pornography and personal fantasies, without being limited by either the moralistic way of repression or the unreflective way of acting out.

Many people entertain two competing desires: one for the security and comfort of a marriage, and the other for nonmarital pleasures. The old religious practices of carnival suggest that there is some real power to be found in breaking away from the socially approved patterns of marriage, and yet religion has also been the chief source for the protection of marriage vows.

The only way I can imagine affirming both carnival and vow is by not taking either in plain, literal terms. Religious orgies take place in the context of ritual, which is a heightened form of imagination. Nothing in ritual is to be taken at a plain, literal level. Indeed, in these rituals ceremonial intercourse takes place between the human person and a divine figure, and the fertility sought is not personal but is rather the well-being of the farm or the family. Sex is not to be understood only as two individuals expressing their love; the community and the cosmos are involved as well.

These ancient religious practices, combined with current sexual problems, offer two hints as to how we might re-enchant sex in our own lives: one, pay more attention to ritual, and two, find ways to "sexualize" our community and the culture at large. A prerequisite for both of these approaches is a rejection of materialistic, biological, and behaviorist attitudes toward sex, and the return of sex as magic.

A ritual is an act that is performed primarily for its symbolic and imagistic import and for its effect on the soul. I grab a quick sandwich one day, but another day I go to a special restaurant to celebrate an anniversary. The meal at the restaurant probably will have more of a ritual quality than the sandwich, although even that could be a simple ritual. Discussions about sex often focus on its parallel with hunger, and we tend to speak of it in biological terms, stressing the physical aspects of sex and moral issues of responsibility and mutuality.

But sex is a ritual, too, and as such speaks for the needs and desires of the soul. As we make sex mainly a medical and moral issue, we lose track of its soul, because any human act stripped of its ritual aspects becomes materialistic and therefore problematical. We might expect that as we neglect the soul in sex, we will force it into exaggerated forms that will be difficult to reconcile with morality and community. We will also force it out of marriage and stable relationships, as it seeks its necessary carnival expression.

To counter the tendency to keep sex under the rubric of hygiene, we could find ways to keep imagination alive in all sexual matters. Without rushing to judgment, we could consider the fantasies we and others entertain about sex. We could have some empathy for those caught between their monogamous ideals and their polygamous passions, and recognize that an individual's sexual problems are often a reflection of society's failures. We could acknowledge that sex is a great mystery and, in spite of all the studies available on the subject, we don't know how deep its roots lie in the soul or what its ultimate place in life is. We could turn to writers and artists and to the world's religions for insight, but most of all for images of sex that present it to us for our contemplation, rather than for moralizing and medicalizing.

Sacred Sex

In Homer's *Odyssey,* Odysseus describes how he made the bed for himself and Penelope from a living olive tree, which became the bedpost, and decorated it with gold, silver, and ivory. "Then I lashed it with thongs of oxhide, dyed bright with purple." This detailed aesthetic attention to the bed, presented at the crucial point where Odysseus is finally united with his wife after years of wandering, indicates the mystery, as well as the cosmic and ritual elements, of their sexual love. Odysseus builds their bed from and around the cosmic tree, showing the mysterious and infinite dimensions of their sexuality. In a related way, Augustine refers to another aspect of the cosmic tree, when he describes the cross of Jesus as a marriage bed, an allusion that Jung takes note of in his exploration of the mystery of conjunction, the challenging and elusive reconciliation of opposites. These obscure references lead us to think of sex in much more embracing terms than we usually do.

In modern life, we have gone a long way in just the opposite direction: rather than focusing on the ritual and holy aspects of this great mystery, we reduce sex materialistically to the body and interpersonal relationships. As Augustine suggests, what goes on in the marriage bed is a union of great consequence to the world. We tend to see marital problems as caused by the fast pace of the modern world, but we might also understand that the marriage bed is what makes culture. If we could live a holy sex life, we might be able to live together with nature and in community, a goal anthropologists describe as the essence of many sexual rituals.

Jung offers further insight into sex in his essay "On Psychic Energy." He tells an anthropological story, about the Wachandi people of Australia. In their ritual they dig a hole in the ground, oval in shape and edged with bushes to look like female genitalia. The men dance around this hole with spears in their hands held to look like erect penises. During the ceremony they aren't allowed to look at a woman, so that, as Jung comments, they won't be distracted from the illusion that the hole is actually a sexual orifice. In Jung's explanation, this ritual is a "magical act for the purpose of transferring libido to the earth, whereby the earth acquires a special psychic value and becomes an object of expectation." He goes on to describe a farmer having intercourse with his wife on a spring night in the fields of his farm. "The instinctual energy becomes closely associated with the field, so that the cultivation of it acquires the value of a sexual act."

One often reads about such rituals carried out to ensure the fertility of the fields, but Jung adds some insight into the nature of the ritual, highlighting the directing of libido or interest to the fields, so that farmer and field will have a relationship of desire and fruitfulness. I'm interested in extending the idea to suggest a "sexualization" of daily life, whereby our sexual lives at home would spill over into our work and community activity, which then would be carried out with "libido," with desire and pleasure. In a philosophy of enchantment, these are central ingredients in every act, because there is a close connection between eros and enchantment. Just as we might be enchanted with another person and be filled with desire and pleasure, so we might experience a parallel interaction with nature and culture.

The World Is a Sex Object

The pink plastic toys sold in sex shops and the overt sexual designs of bottles and other products may not just increase personal pleasure but also sexualize the plastic. Just as traditional people shape the earth to look like a sexual organ, and the earth is thereby made fertile and sexual, so when we take plastic and shape it erotically, we may be trying to give our plastic world some sexual energy. The more plastic our culture becomes, the less sexual interest it has, because sensuality and real material go hand in hand.

Just as the farmer and his wife bring desire to the fields with their love and pleasure, we could take our sexual feelings into the world and live a more sensuous, more intimate life. The eroticization of work was the goal of William Morris, who time after time in his lectures advocated what might sound like a utopian view. A factory, for instance, "besides turning out goods useful to the community will provide for its own workers work light in duration, and not oppressive in kind, . . . amusing relaxation . . . leisure . . . beauty of surroundings, and the power of producing beauty." There is no reason why a workplace should not be a place of beauty, intimacy, pleasure, and desire—sexual values. Our homes and cities, too, could take on some of the qualities of the marriage bed, becoming "bedroom communities" in a sexual sense.

I often find myself sitting on an uncomfortable public bench or wandering in the labyrinth of a vast public building, wondering if the makers of these places had ever heard of the human body. I was struck by a scene in a film on Glenn Gould in which the Canadian pianist stands on a modernistic angular glass skyway and says: "This is craziness." Does an architect ever ask the question: "Will this foyer be sensual? Will it give its visitors pleasure?" The pleasure question is an important one and could be the most direct route to enchantment, because the line between sex and enchantment is thin.

If we don't live in a sexual world, then we place all our sexual expectations on a personal lover, and sexual love simply can't thrive in such a loaded and desexualized context. Time after time in therapy I listen to people trying to sort out their feelings of desire and sensuality in terms of their spouse or lover. They rarely consider the sexual nature of their work, their homes, or their experience of nature. In their sacred dance, the Wachandi honor a profound mystery: the fact that the earth has sex organs. They reveal that the earth itself is sexual, and that the human experience of sex embraces both persons and the world.

Those who work the earth in their gardens or on their farms, who take daily walks deep in the forests while doing their jobs, who fish in the sea and know intimately the taste of the brine and the smell of fish, who cut and shape wood by the feel of their fingers and the aroma of sap—these people have a sexual relationship to the earth that transcends in its own way the abstract knowledge of books and quantitative studies, as well as hyperproductive factories and cool offices. Whenever I pass a field of hay or grass that has just been cut, especially in the cool sunset of the evening, I am taken out of time and filled with a pleasure that brings my childhood directly into the present and for a moment erases all concern for current problems and preoccupations. This is enchantment, and it is largely a sexual experience, involving aromas, memories, and sensations.

If we live in this world with a body that we love and honor, refusing to chastise it from too exalted a spiritual position, then we may discover how sex gives enchantment its foundation. We may learn that there is a wide spectrum of sexual experience, from the courtesan to the nun, from the man sowing his oats to the monk. We may discover in this expansive sense of sexuality that the forms sex takes differ remarkably from individual to individual and from one time in life to another. If we live in daily intimacy with the world around us, we may be less anxious in setting limits around everyone else's sexual odysseys and learn to tolerate this mystery that, as the Jungian analyst Adolf Guggenbühl-Craig says with saving stubbornness, has no discernible meaning or limits.

When it is carried out without effortful intentions, power struggles, and obsession, sex can be an exploration of the soul. Imperfections will always be present to some degree—I want to keep in mind Guggenbühl-Craig's advice that sex offers no easy explanations—but we could find a way out of disenchanted sex, where vulgarity has replaced beauty and pragmatism stands in the way of pleasure.

The Imagination of Sex

The Greeks saw all of the gods and goddesses as sexual and therefore all sex as holy in a variety of ways. The Greek imagination
could teach us how to imagine our own sexuality through, for
example, the image of Aphrodite. In mythology, Aphrodite trea-
sures the accoutrements of sex: perfume, clothing, beds, jewelry,
and private places of rendezvous. Aphrodite renders them sacred
and full of imagination, in contrast to our tendency to find something immoral or inconsequential in them. When all the details are
right, her daimonic presence is summoned, a spell is cast, and the
temenos of sexual pleasure is established. If the details are not right,
and the context and materials of sex have been reduced to moralism
or biology, Aphrodite surely will not appear; and yet without her,
sex is impossible, or becomes disenchanted. This common condition inspires a wide range of sex problems and therapies, but I can
imagine an approach to sex therapy based entirely on the mythology of Aphrodite and primarily concerned with technologies of
enchantment.

Many different spirits set the tone under which sex can play
itself out. The myth of Aphrodite appeals to me most, but I appreciate the lure in Jesus, the Buddha, and Krishna as well. Jesus especially brings a spirit of unlimited tolerance (the woman caught in
adultery), sensuous ritual (the wedding at Cana), and gentle, intimate love (his beatitudes)—excellent virtues in developing the soul
of a sexual life. The Buddha sees the spiritual deeply embedded in
ordinary life and easily finds holiness in sex. Krishna is honored
regularly in erotic settings and receives the love of his followers, the
gopis, with grace and beauty.

If we aim only at a sentimental imagination of sex, we will lose
its soul there as well. Sex takes us not only to the green meadows of
Krishna but also to the dank underworld haunts of Hades and
Persephone. Other fruitful and enchanting images of sex are not so
sweet, like those I explore in my book *Dark Eros*—the rituals of
power, dominance, and impersonal pleasure.

Sex is one of the most powerful and fruitful sources of enchantment available to us, and maybe that is why we are so driven to its

moments of ecstasy, a rare time when we can lose ourselves, allow ourselves to be caught in a spell and become fully enchanted. Loss of consciousness and intention is a state the soul longs for, and this is why, perhaps, mystics so often compare their religious ecstasy to the enchantment of sex. But if we wish to keep the enchantments of sex in our lives, we may have to rebuff those influences in modern life that reduce sex to personalistic or mechanistic explanations. We may have to go to extremes to surround our sexuality with poetry, delights of dress and color, and all forms of imagination. These are ways foreign to a world soberly focused on its medicine and morals, but close to the spirits that give sex its vitality and enchantment.

Mars and Aggression

*T*HERE IS NO denying that violence and aggression can cast a spell. Movies have taken advantage of the powerful lure of violence, giving us colorful images of tough detectives, rough cowboys, and mean villains, and in recent years they have taken advantage of new technologies to make scenes bloodier and more horrifying than ever. Few things in our day are as captivating as violence, whether on the streets or on celluloid, and the level of violence in both places is overwhelming.

When I travel in the United States, I typically ask where it is safe to walk at night, and I notice that every local newspaper contains at least one lurid narrative of violence and tragedy. Whether the statistics show violence going up or down, and whether violence is any worse now than it has ever been in history, we are surrounded by it and deeply affected by it. The news of violence in wars, on the streets, or at home penetrates deeply into the emotions and imagination, where we know, like animals alert for predators, how vulnerable we are.

Some, of course, see a link between increasingly graphic images of violence in the movies and the unusual degree of violation on the streets. It's assumed that if people are exposed to images of violence, they will act them out. But there are problems with this kind of thinking, for it's obvious that millions of people watch violent scenes in movies without ever having the slightest impulse to act on them, and that those who patronize violent movies are not there to learn how to be more violent. The lure for most lies elsewhere.

The enchanting quality of violence in the typical action movie hints at a powerful spirit that has a role in the economy of the psyche. Violence is not only demonic but also daimonic. A demon is a fully negative spirit, but a daimon is in classical terms a nameless spirit that can be good or bad. To call something daimonic is to point out a power within it that is not entirely personal and yet undeniably present, giving it a sense of strong compulsion or overpowering influence.

The Spirit of Mars

James Hillman's spirited treatment of aggression takes as its theme Mars, the Roman god of aggression and strength, and offers insight into the roots of violence. Mars is prominent in Hillman's style, and when he speaks of Mars you sense the influence of this daimon. My style, on the other hand, is dominated by Venus, and so when I write about Mars or violence, I tend to understate and soften this hot, raging figure. Both ways are valid. Hillman's may be more directly evocative of the daimonic than mine, and yet we may find hidden elements in aggression by entering from the side of Venus, who in classical literature is sometimes linked amorously to Mars, suggesting complicity of a sort between her mysteries and aggression.

Hillman has long been interested in the accoutrements of warfare, the style with which generals and admirals have fought their wars and lived their lives, the uniforms they have worn and the strategies they have conjured up in the midst of battle. He does not approach war from the perspective of the innocent, idealizing advocate of peace, but says that we can find our way to the heart of violence only by approaching its mysterious core. "To know war we must enter its love," he writes. "No psychic phenomenon can be truly dislodged from its fixity unless we first move the imagination into its heart."

In his essay on Mars, Hillman explores many facets of aggression: our love of war, America's denial of its war spirit, differences between Mars at war and nuclear warfare, and the necessity of the Mars spirit. These are not easy subjects, but our streets may be dangerous precisely because we have not looked into our hearts and honestly appraised our attraction to violence. Our sense of our own virtuousness may conceal insights into the lure of aggression and the appeal of viciousness, and, as is often the case, until we examine our own hearts we may not appreciate what is happening in the world outside us.

It's undeniable that Mars has played a major role in the establishment of civilization. I remember once in college approaching a history professor and asking him if there was any way I could study the history of ordinary life through the ages. I felt I had spent years learning about battles, generals, emperors, and genocide, concluding that history is nothing but a long list of bloody victories and exchanges of brutal power. I had little dedication to Mars, and with Venus in tow, I tried to find a way out of the battle zone. I was told, not without some Mars-like authoritarianism, to go back and learn my lessons as they were taught.

On the other hand, I confess that I share with many people a fascination for World War II, which was still raging when I was a child. Both documentary and fictional movies of the war have considerable attraction, in part, I'm sure, because they evoke the historical period that coincided with the childhood of my generation, an era that carries the strong scent of nostalgia. Yet the attraction also has to do with the drama of that horrible war: the emotional parting of soldiers from their families and sweethearts, the menacing consolidation of evil in fascism, the uncertainty of victory up to the last, heroism everywhere among both combatants and civilians, and the whole world as a theater of land, sea, and air battles. This is the war of the documentary film and the World War II genre Hollywood movie.

Revisionist historians are now making us acutely aware of the shadow side of that war, as though we didn't know already that it was sadistic and brutal. America still enjoys the taste of victory, witnessed by anniversaries that are congratulatory and in which the deaths of hundreds of thousands are sentimentalized, but it is only beginning to face the awesome responsibility of its atomic attacks on Japan and recognize its quick tendency toward racial and ethnic oppression by the incarceration of Japanese Americans. Fifty years after the war's end, Congress can suppress the showing of the bomb's violent impact on Japanese civilians, and the victims of American bigotry have different nationalities but still suffer the same prejudice and degradation. Not only have we not learned from the war, but we have not presented ourselves for initiation into the mysteries of Mars. One can at least wonder if our attitude toward recent wars, our bravado and self-congratulations that shield us from the lessons of war, are not implicated in the violence of our cities and towns.

The Necessity of Aggression

What is the enchantment in wars and weaponry? The answer for me lies in old, obscure, esoteric ideas about spirits and planets and the transformations of sulfur, and in ancient astrological and alchemical texts that explore the basic substances and processes of life. From the Greek philosopher Heraclitus I learn that the soul lies deeper than we can ever imagine, and in the magus Ficino I read that the soul plays out its destiny and takes form through the influence of a variety of spirits pictured in the traditional images of the planets, including Mars.

These old traditions say that we need the spirit of Mars every day and in everything we do, for Mars gives life its flare and fire, while accounting for the impetus that makes life dramatic. Jung's alchemical writings highlight the role of aggressive factors in the alchemical process that is human life, where mortification, putrefaction, and separation are all-important processes. We tend to identify ourselves as victims of these processes and immediately imagine being mortified, enduring the rotting of relationships, ideas, and careers, and being the victims of separations of many kinds, from leaving home to divorce to suffering the death of loved ones. But these processes have perpetrators as well, a spirit that corrupts, kills off, and separates, and a spirit that lives through us, using our muscle and imagination, accounting for both our creativity and our destructiveness.

The alchemical sword, says Jung, quoting alchemical writers, "is that which kills and vivifies." We know this secret in the simple idea that life is creative and productive only if it is also destructive in some way, and that new life requires the end of old ways. In our innocence we often enjoy victimhood and look for someone outside our own ranks as the aggressor. But in that masochism we lose sight of the fact that every person needs to be aggressive, to express himself or herself as an individual, to make a mark no matter how great or small, and that these efforts at self-expression are positive examples of aggression. Mars deserves as much honor as any other spirit, and if we don't give him his due, we are risking the rampage of his repressed but necessary force. War and street violence are literalizations of his spirit, but he can be honored in ways that are not literally dangerous.

From alchemy we learn that the spirit of Mars reddens and hardens, heats and tempers. The first sign in the zodiac, Ares, identified with Mars, is the force that begins the process, allowing us to get over the heavy inertia that precedes all beginnings, keeps us content with the status quo, or idealizes and sentimentalizes the past. Inertia and contentment are deathlike states, which keep us from entering a living process that Mars quickens and vivifies, like the sentiments of death sung by the Sirens to distract Odysseus from his work of homecoming. Even in the midst of fanatical productivity, a disenchanted world is threatened most by the lure to remain lifeless and essentially uncreative. Feverish productivity may look like vitality and yet lack the hot spirit of Mars and paradoxically serve the death principle, as it reproduces, imitates, clones, and mass-produces a world of things that show none of the quickening Mars bestows even on objects.

A Dutch alchemical painting of 1675 shows a boy holding a sword representing sulfur, the burning element essential in any creative process. The boy suggests beginnings, the puer spirit of ambition, and the sword and sulfur the aggression and fire needed to get things going. It is the young masculine spirit that takes initiative, and it is the young male who carries the symptoms of his society's dishonoring of Mars. Violence on the streets is a symptomatic sign that we've lost all initiative to live lives of dedication and fire, and instead content ourselves with numbing work and numbing entertainments.

Sulfur, a key ingredient of gunpowder, and iron, a metal long associated with Mars, and Marsian fire can all be found in the modern gun. We might understand the alchemical sword as the *subtle* weapon needed to be a creative and vital individual or community, while actual weapons are mere symptomatic fetishes of that Mars spirit and the alchemical sword. As such, although they give the illusion of Mars, they are dangerous and ineffective in the realm of the soul.

In the past, weapons were meticulously decorated, often with precious stones and ornate engravings, and might be given elaborate and beautiful sheaths, boxes, and cabinets. Even today collectors treat guns with loving attention and seem to appreciate the association of Mars with Venus. Instruments of aggression do, in fact, excite the imagination and spark the soul's aesthetic impulse. They are attractive, as a strong person might be, for their potential power and their Marsian aesthetic qualities, and, of course, they hold in symbolic form the strength and power we need in daily life.

This alchemical boy, sword in hand, brandishing the sign of sulfur, an emblem of manhood, we see in the young gang member identified closely with his weapons, and in the young soldier whose attention is focused on the gun lying on his shoulder. But soldiers and gang members disregard the enchantments of nature and culture, blasting away at lovely buildings and treasured artifacts, running over forests and polluting rivers, transforming a city's enchantment into an atmosphere of fear and danger. In spite of their aggressiveness, they fail to bring the exciting spirit of Mars to a community, replacing it with fear and victimhood.

At the same time, these gun-wielding young men portray a spirit desperately needed in a disenchanted culture, a spirit that could provide ardor, passion, strength, endurance, initiative, courage, daring, and enterprise if it were not literalized in plain aggression. Whenever a person or a society becomes disenchanted, these virtues turn into dangerous caricatures of themselves—brute muscle, unbridled energy, misanthropic organizations, criminal economies, and unconscionable violence.

Crime in the streets invites us to study ourselves and ask: How can we create a society in which everyone can be an expressive individual, feel personal power and dignity, carve out a place and leave a mark, shine like the gleaming steel of a weapon? Are we a people on fire with creativity, or are we defeated and numbed by the demands of productivity? Is there still some element of the venturesome knight in us, or has it been forgotten and buried? Does Joan of Arc or the armed Diana still offer daring and strength to our notions of what is female and feminine, or do we fear the spirit of Mars in women as well?

What could be more enchanting than King Arthur's Round Table, full of magic, romance, and courageous acts? There is no reason why modern life can't be a Round Table of beauty and daring, but to bring back the ideals of knighthood we would have to free men and women from the excessively productive life that now consumes our energy. Not only the gleaming rifle but also the deafening shiny steel machine serves as a fetish of the Mars spirit.

A Venusian Tonic for Mars Unleashed

In Greek and Roman mythology, Mars and Venus were lovers. The art historian Edgar Wind points out that many have seen in this union an echo of Empedocles' teaching that Love and Strife are the building blocks of existence. According to Pico della Mirandola, "Venus was placed in the centre of heaven next to Mars, because she must tame his impulse which is by nature destructive and corrupting." Pico resolves the relationship poetically in the kind of oxymoron Renaissance humanists loved, as "amicable enmity and concordant discord." For us, this might mean living in a marriage, a family, or a nation where Love and Strife are neither diluted nor divided from each other and people can thrive as forceful individuals and yet also with a deep appreciation of community.

Venus civilizes the Mars impulse by deconstructing it and deliteralizing it. As goddess of beauty, art, ornament, and poetic language, she also shows us a way to keep the spirit of aggression without forcing it into violent forms of expression. In so doing, she also restores its capacity to enchant. A person with courage, a community with a stout heart, and a people with conviction and confidence are all enchanting, and they show how we bury the spirit of Mars when we hide behind the mask of victimhood or allow our lives to be uncreative.

Our challenge, then, is not to suppress violence but to fulfill it and, once it has been liberated from its repression, to discover its charms. Leaving a mark on this world is an aggressive act; standing firm as an individual, man or woman, is an expression of Mars' virility; and letting our spirit and soul creatively loose upon life is an act of reverence to the spirit that makes life vital.

Young men willingly joining gangs and entering armies may well be in search of the special, enlivening enchantment that is born in the presence of Mars. But they may be disillusioned as they painfully discover that a weapon is a mere fetish and a tough manner nothing more than an affectation. Mars is set deep in the heart, or he is not present at all, and if he is not present, we will continue to be plagued by violent movies and violent streets, signs of our disenchantment.

An Education in Dreams

*D*URING THE twenty years that I practiced psychotherapy, every day I found myself drawn into the dreams of those who consulted me, and every day I grew to appreciate the mystery of dreams, finally giving up any attempt to make them clearly intelligible. At the beginning of an hour I would ask for a dream, and after listening to it closely I'd let it drift into the background as we talked about the life problem of the moment. During the conversation I'd watch for signs of the dream either embedded in the story being told or evoked by it, and by the end of the hour I would note how the dream had informed or influenced our conversation. This was my way of following Jung's advice of "dreaming the dream onwards," not getting tied down to rationalistic interpretations and yet being affected and educated by the dream.

Dreams are the purest form of enchantment. In a dream we find ourselves captivated by personalities, locales, events, moods, magical events, and terrors. As we wake from a dream, we gradually become aware that we have been enchanted and are now re-entering the world of the everyday. For centuries, people have understood that the enchantment of dreams is not unrelated to daily experience, and indeed that dreams offer guidance and understanding in actual life. Enchantment is valuable not only for its own sake and for the pleasures and dread it can inspire but also because it takes us away from ordinary, habitual ways of seeing. It allows us to stand outside life and then return to it with a fresh perspective and with precious knowledge that is not available in ordinary states of awareness.

People may not understand dreams, but they have many opinions about them. They think that certain dreams are more important than others—the "big" dreams and "little" dreams. They think that some dreams are meaningful and that others aren't. They think there is something wrong if the dream they remember isn't a complete story. They think a good dream is one that has a happy outcome. They think it's an achievement to know within the dream that they're dreaming, and that it's even better if they can manipulate a happy ending.

Some people talk about "decoding" a dream, assuming that a dream is a scrambled message from the "unconscious." Freud had a strong influence in this regard with his suggestion that the obscurity of dreams, covering over deep and disturbing messages, allows us to sleep well. Generally we assume, in the case of art as well as dreams, that obscure imagery begs for interpretation and "decoding."

After long experience with dreams and influenced by the writings of James Hillman, I find that rather than extract meaning from dreams, I want to remain susceptible to their enchantment. To put it another way, many of the modern attitudes to dreams I've just listed appear to be subtle ways to keep our lives disenchanted by maintaining our control and insisting on the dreamer's and analyst's point of view over that of the dream itself. It is an irreligious position, and therefore by definition contrary to enchantment.

Initiating Dreams

Over the years, I've examined many theories about dreaming, from Freud to Fritz Perls to C. G. Jung to James Hillman, and, as in most things psychological, I have been most influenced by Hillman and consider his "dream book," *The Dream and the Underworld,* the most intelligent and convincing approach to dreams in modern times. He describes the place of dreaming as a world related to but apart from our ordinary realm of experience, and says it's up to us to become familiar with the values and expressions of that world. He begs us not to force the underworld of dreams to be interpreted and made relevant to the conscious realm we know so well.

In Hillman's view, there is no need to take a heroic posture and try to conquer a dream, "break" its "code," and exploit it as a way of improving one's personal life situation. Just the opposite, in his view dreams invite us down into a place where values and events are similar to but at the same time different from those of waking life. The soul is at home in that deep place, but consciousness often sees it as too dark and misty. We may be tempted to shine the light of understanding in its dark corners, but we could also treat our dreams as altars of initiation, where attitudes may be deepened and perspectives broadened.

I've spent many years trying to adjust myself to the world of images by becoming familiar with them in painting, dance, music, architecture, and religion. I don't understand dreams and other kinds of imagery as "the language of the unconscious" or as a "forgotten language." This imagery isn't a language at all, at least not in the sense that each image could be defined conceptually and thereby rendered intelligible and applicable.

I prefer the approach contained in seed form in the writing of Ficino: art objects are lures attracting certain spirits, and they're containers for that spirit. Our task is not to explain images but to expose ourselves to them and have our thinking and feeling affected by them. Images are inherently and necessarily mysterious. They invite us to enjoy a life where mystery deepens the level of our thought and experience. As Hillman suggests, going against many approaches intended to help us get along in life, we don't have to treat images as though they were psychological aids to healthy living. A reverential attitude toward the life we've been given is more important than living that life correctly, successfully, or healthfully.

The idea that the very purpose of life is to become more healthy and achieve a higher level of consciousness seems so embedded in modern thought that it's rarely questioned. I once heard a medical researcher say that we should all remain close to our families because studies have shown that people who stay near their families live longer. At first this idea may sound reasonable, but why justify family intimacy as a way of living a long life. Why not appreciate the inherent values of family and give up the narcissism that places value on a thing only when it serves our own personal purposes?

In a similar way we could enter the mystery world of dreams without *doing* anything to them and without bettering ourselves by them. We could be quite active as we engage with them—tracking down images and symbols, talking about them with friends, discussing them in therapy or in a dream group—but we don't have to exploit them for our own purposes, no matter how humanitarian and enlightened those purposes might be. Tending our dreams, we might live from a deeper place, know ourselves better without necessarily understanding ourselves, and appreciate more the many mysteries that surround us in life. A sensitive approach to dreams could provide a foundation for a religious attitude and open the way for other forms of religious practice. Dreams offer an excellent model for the life of the soul, a model that is not dependent on our subjective choices and experiences.

When we finally give up the project of making an enlightened self, then gates are opened. As Shunryu Suzuki Roshi says in one of his talks, "When a frog becomes a frog, Zen becomes Zen. When you understand a frog, through and through, you attain enlightenment; you are Buddha. And you are good for others, too: husband or wife or son or daughter." This understanding of a frog is achieved not by a biological analysis but by observing how a frog is a frog, and perhaps getting an inkling of how you are a frog, and then how you are you. The same could be said of dreams: As we are educated in the way a dream plays itself out, we discover our innermost and outermost natures.

I can be affected by mere observation of the dream: as I tell it to my wife, as I remember it during the day, as I write it down in a special book of dreams, and as I recall it many days, months, and years later. My dream is an intimation of my mystery, not the solution to my problems. My dreams teach me constantly that whatever it is that makes me a person is both the stuff of which I am made and stuff that has nothing to do with me. My dreams are me, and not me. They are mine in a certain sense, and yet they possess me more than I possess them.

The Enchanting Power of Dreams

Dreams also teach us that enchantment is a state of being, and not a message. They show that we can live in various states and that we can withdraw from this world of normal and ordinary living so completely as to "forget"the realm in which life takes place. Some mystics have called this retreat to an alternative place of being *vacatio*, an emptying of ordinary life, which affords the opportunity for a different kind of seeing and experiencing. Dreams also empty ordinary life and usher in a world that is almost completely different, except that it has echoes of daily life. Many are tempted to conclude that dreams are *about* daily life, messages from the unconscious, but we could also see them as taking daily life to another dimension, revealing an interiority proper to daily existence, which is usually hidden by the literal and practical concerns that keep us focused on the surface details.

Dreams can initiate us into a stereophonic existence, in tune with surfaces and depths, literal reality and images, meaning and mystery. Dreams can help us "pan" from left to right, as in a stereo system where you can hear from either speaker at the turn of a knob. This kind of life, I admit, can appear irrational to those who believe in the practical world alone, and at times it can be somewhat disorienting, but it also satisfies the soul's hunger for meaningfulness and depth.

The word "dream" is related to the Anglo-Saxon *drëam*, which meant joy, music, and minstrelsy, and to words for "ghost." When we have a radio playing music as we work, we are straddling the literal realm of life and the enchanted world of art. We are doing what is most pleasing and necessary: living in the two realms at once. With the radio playing, we may be hard at our literal work and yet at the same time tuned in to a realm of charm. When we dream and consider our dreams in waking life, we are similarly keeping our attention focused in two places, the world of practical living and the realm of ghosts.

If we resist the temptation to rationalize dreams and, in the project of building a successful self, to enslave them, then we may discover that life plays itself out not only on the stage of conscious life but on many other stages as well, and that there are many realities, each with its own rules, stories, values, and personalities. We are multiple, multilayered, many-mythed, and many-lived.

This accommodation to dreams that I am recommending is a path to enchantment as well, for enchantment is the spell that spirits us away from familiar reality defined in one-dimensional terms.

The practice of tending to dreams doesn't interfere in any way with the practical life, and yet it fills out experience to include the events of dream that are mysteriously relevant. Even if it can't be understood precisely, a dream can give unexpected resonance to everyday life.

Instructions for a Noninterpretive Approach to Dreams

From these many sources and against the background of my years of work with dreams, I have a few simple recommendations, not for interpreting, but for living with dreams:

1. We can entertain those dreams that we remember, in whole or part, not demanding that they take a story form and surrendering our desire to understand exactly what they mean. By simply giving our dreams serious, intelligent consideration, we may take a small step away from the controlling rationalism that is the hallmark of the modern world.

2. We can keep a record of our dreams, so that our dream journals or logs serve as a personal sacred text, a compilation, much like sacred literature, of mysteries that have special relevance to our own lives and fate. It isn't necessary to tell a dream as if it were a story; a poem, incomplete sentences, or a sequence of nouns and adjectives will do. A more subtle way to give dreams a place might be to weave their themes into our creative work or into the everyday design of our lives.

3. We can tell our dreams to someone close, someone who will receive them with respect. The very telling is a form of art and offers a way to preserve the dream, if only momentarily. Conversations about dreams, when carried out with respect for the imagery, can also bring people close to each other because of the inherent intimacy of a dream. The telling of a dream is a special form of discourse, a revelation of the soul that requires unusual conditions of intimacy and trust.

4. We can review and recall our dreams over a period of months and years, noticing the often unexpected progress one senses from dream to dream. Certain themes and figures may appear over and over as the years go by, and these figures and themes may change significantly. Too often we measure our lives by

outward events, ignoring very important inner developments signaled by dreams.

5. We can follow the example of many artists and find or make art objects or write poetry that will "keep" the dream and give it a home. If we were to find visible expression for our dreams with regularity, our entire culture could be transformed, becoming less divided between the inner and the outer life. We might discover that dreams are a significant source of an appreciation for sacred motifs in everyday life.

I consider all readings of a dream provisional, so that I'm always ready to consider an alternative slant on the same imagery. The best model of interpretation is the kind done in music, where a pianist or violinist "interprets" a composition of Bach or Mozart. The musician's reading of the piece is meant to draw out fresh nuances and subtle aspects of the music, rather than to drift away from the original composition. The interpreter's role is to become so intimate with the music that it sings more clearly than ever through the interpretation and yet is always ready for the next interpreter. These qualities would help us keep our dreams intact, even as we draw out their implications.

The most valuable gift of dreams is not specific insights or meanings—most of us have too many ideas about ourselves—but rather the development of an attitude toward life that appreciates the importance of imagery, mystery, and interior experience. Dreams teach us how to live an enchanted life: how to glimpse underworld themes and characters in daily life, how to look at and listen to the arts, how to reflect deeply on relationships, and how to see the soul in our work.

As we become more at home with dream imagery, we may discover the importance of the arts and of the rituals and icons of religion. There is a sense in which all of life and art can be perceived as a dream, but since the prevailing attitude of modern culture favors facts and interpretation, this dream sense is largely lost. Yet it's quite clear that every personal problem and every social conflict has a deep story or theme, its own dream, that accounts for the particular quality of its power. Being sensitive to the dream within our problems places us at a level where our responses count and have an effect. Dreams afford an immediate and pure avenue to enchantment; they ask only that we treat them carefully.

The value of dreams lies in their power to enchant, to give us glimpses of the murky, seething life that forms the inner vitality of everyday events. If we remain disenchanted, we will be tempted to take life on the terms that are presented, whereas dreams teach us that nothing is simple, nothing is without its poetry, and nothing that truly affects us is void of an inner dream core.

Circe's Dreams

In the story of Odysseus, there is a celebrated episode where he encounters the enchantress Circe, who casts a spell on his companions and turns them into pigs, while he himself is protected by a gift from Hermes, the plant moly. Over the centuries, this spell has been seen as a warning not to fall into ignorance or sin, and moly has been read as education, virtue, and faith—means of overcoming the darkness of enchantment.

In the spirit of this book, we may want to celebrate Circe and her power to enchant, regardless of the possibility of our becoming piglike. Sometimes in our odysseys we lose our rationality and take on an inhuman point of view, find our powers of speech stolen and our civilized ways lost.

Homer makes the point that Odysseus's men took on the appearance and voice of pigs, but their minds remained human. Dreams often make us feel ignorant, like pigs, but they don't take away our intelligence. They resist all our efforts to make sense of them, but they offer lessons in a different kind of intelligence. As Circe's power lay in her song, dreams, too, have a Circean quality, seizing consciousness and casting a spell. Rather than search desperately for ways to be rid of our neuroses and dense, piglike ignorance, it might be better to surrender to the enchantment and take time out from the heroic pursuit of meaning and success in ordinary life.

It was Circe, the enchantress, who gave Odysseus the gift of a necessary initiation and ultimately allowed him to return to civilization. In our dreams we find ourselves afloat on our own mysterious odysseys, as though the dream were a hiatus on our life journey, an interruption that paradoxically allows us to continue. If we insist on forcing dreams into our preconceptions and categorical ways of thinking, placing them in the service of our ambitions for the meaningful and healthy life, then we will have lost yet another valuable gateway to mystery and to the soul. But if we surrender to dream enchantment, we may discover such intimacy with the roots of our being that worry about health and anxiety over correct understanding may fade into the distance, and in their place we may find the kind of fulfillment glimpsed by mystics and visionaries. We may find that dreams offer a way toward a level more satisfying than meaning and infinitely more pleasurable and fulfilling than adjustment, correctness, and personal success.

The Therapist's Chair

*I*F YOU TRACE the word "therapy" back far enough, you find that "chair" hides in the word's history. This pleases me, because I've often thought that the most important instrument in therapy, both as something to sit on and as a symbol of the work, is the chair. Sitting is one of the most valuable things you can do for the soul, freeing the imagination to wonder, converse, or engage in fruitful reverie. The Buddha attained enlightenment just by sitting beneath the bodhi tree, and the very essence of Zen is sitting. Chuang Tzu, in a famous statement, called his method "sitting down and forgetting everything." That's a good summary of my approach to therapy: sit down and forget everything you know. Be present. Don't try to achieve anything. A Zen poem says:

> When sitting, just sit,
> Above all, don't wobble.

I couldn't express my goal as a therapist more exactly—to sit without wobbling. The people who come to me, like myself in my own life, are wobbling, and I know it will do no good for me to lose my grip and wobble with them. So as firmly as I can, I sit in my chair, the sign of the office of therapist, and offer a chair to the other person, with all the implications of the idea of the chair. I don't think it is my job to do anything to the person—not teach him, not cure him, not make him healthy, not even help him. Of course, one's general intention is always to help, but I believe that if I have the specific intention of helping, our work will be ruined from the start.

I can't presume to know how to help anyone. What I have learned as a therapist, something I didn't know before I began this work, is that each person is a mystery never to be fully understood. The so-called problems people bring to therapy aren't problems at all; they're mysteries, and the response to a mystery should be entirely different from that to a problem. A mystery is something not to be solved, but only to be honored, appreciated, contemplated, and revered. I can best do my job by offering a chair, week after week, and a space free of ambitious intentions and heroics. I have to wash my hands, the way a priest ritually washes his or her hands before the holiest part of the rite, as an image representing purity of intention. I have to free myself of any salvational fantasies—any need on my part to save this person from fate or destiny, from the pain that is part of the initiatory progress of life, and from whatever demons he or she may describe in the hours of conversation.

The chair represents a "nothing doing" attitude, a phrase I love and have picked up from Samuel Beckett. In Beckett's novel *Murphy*, the title character spends hours each day tied by seven scarves to his rocking chair, an allusion perhaps to the gnostic view of human life as an exile from our proper home beyond the seven planets. According to the Egyptian Gnostic Basilides, in its descent into human life the soul is garmented in and limited by the various complexities of each planet, and so a human life is bound to the many influences, interior and exterior, that motivate it. Sitting and doing nothing heroic is, for me the therapist, a way to perceive the soul and glimpse what drama is taking place in the guise of a life problem.

I sit with men and women in our chairs, discussing our human condition, our own seven scarves, the limitations and challenges we each have as we try to find our way through the maze of emotions, relationships, moods, and obstacles that give life its tonality and tension. I try to invite the soul in, give it a place where it can reveal itself without any threat of adjustment, normality, or even propriety. The work isn't amoral at all; rather it is supremely moral, as we search for signs of moral claim, wondering how to be responsible in the face of seemingly impossible challenges.

My early training was influenced heavily by Carl Rogers's philosophy of unconditional regard. I read everything that I could find by Abraham Maslow and Fritz Perls and their cohorts, and I had teachers imbued with the spirit of "client-centered" active listening. I liked the unintrusive approach of these "hands-off" practitioners, but its mechanics came truly to fruition for me when I studied the work of C. G. Jung and James Hillman, who gave profound theory to the method. Hillman especially showed me how to respect the apparent twistedness of the soul and not get in its way, a deepening of Rogers's method of letting the client reveal himself freely. Theory and literature helped me have confidence as I sat in my chair and listened to painful stories from the person in the other chair, even though in sitting I tried to take Chuang Tzu's advice and forget everything.

The Human Comedy

As I see it now, this studied and practiced sitting without judgment and with deep appreciation for all expressions of soul laid the foundations for enchantment. When you stop thinking moralistically about the soul, it begins to reveal its charm, even in its dark moments. When you're not trying to make the heart into something you think is proper, it showers you with its magic, and even in the midst of pain it can offer moments of rapture.

During sometimes tense hours of therapy I laugh frequently. Laughter is a common response because, through being charmed by the mysterious ways of the soul, especially as it outwits both me and my "clients," I often discover the absurdity of my own efforts at understanding and manipulation.

I have always enjoyed the jokes of Zen Buddhism, and I've long thought that the greatest therapists and true spiritual teachers are comedians, advocates of a comic sense of life, who break open our serious efforts to arrange life as we think best. In therapy I am often reminded of the Laurel and Hardy movie in which they're professional piano movers. Every time they get the piano to the top of a three-story stairway, it falls back to the bottom. This modern comic version of Sisyphus gives me courage as I listen to people describing their failed attempts to make a decision about a career, establish harmony with a mother or father, decide to get married or divorced, lose weight, or stop smoking.

Nobility and true innocence emerge as we live out our comic

natures in the face of the greater forces of fate and destiny. Avoiding the embarrassment of failure, ignorance, and foolishness only keeps us ignoble, humorless, and bound in our secularism, because deep humor arises out of genuine piety, from a bighearted acknowledgment that life cannot be circumscribed within the perimeters of our knowledge and intentions, no matter how enlightened and well intentioned these may be. This humor is a sign of religious faith, not necessarily belief in any one story or leader but the faith that comes from standing on the edge of your own existence, and in the face of absurdity, courageously and humorously allowing life to happen.

Creative Failures

And so over the years I have sat week after week, using all my wits, all my knowledge, and any skills I picked up in school or from experience, knowing that often they would be sacrificed in this process of therapy, eventually to be exploded, proven wrong, or invalidated by events or by next week's wisdom. People sometimes come to me now as an expert on dream analysis, but the truth is that after years of working with dreams, I am now fully at their mercy. All my theories and methods have been shown to be inadequate, and now I can only resort to truisms and clichés: write your dreams, tell them to somebody close, make waking life more dreamlike. I have no ideas, no tricks, no expertise whatsoever.

The shedding of heroics in the process of therapy allows for unexpected enchantment. Dreams uninterpreted and unexploited remain in memory like jewels whose sparkle and beauty give life charm, and charm is so much more valuable than understanding. Impossible knots of relationship and decision making unfold themselves over the years, and former clients teach me that the hours of therapy we endured solved no puzzles but accomplished necessary loosening that was not even our intention and that lay entirely beyond our vision at the time. Never forget that "analysis" means loosening, and that "psyche" means butterfly, a beautiful but elusive being that should be glimpsed in flight but never pinned down. Quite literally, psychoanalysis means "letting the butterfly go free."

During all the years that I have practiced therapy I have had a plaque, given to me by a friend at the start of this career, of the Greek god Asklepios, the founder of medicine and the archetypal dream healer. On my plaque he was portrayed with his staff, and a single snake curled along its shaft. To be cured in the healing temples of Asklepios, you had to dream of a snake. I tried to keep that snake's presence felt in my work, by keeping my sights low, by always looking to the underground of what was being presented, by noting elements of sex and evil in all matters, and by recalling the snake of Eden, who tempted our parents into the complexities and suffering of human life in the first place. I also imagined change, that golden idol wished for at the beginning of most therapy courses, along the lines of the snake shedding its old skin—as organic renewal rather than forced transformation.

Another image of Asklepios shows him sitting in a chair, his dog at his side, and I feel further supported in my notion that therapy is mostly about chairs and sitting and the unheroic conversation they inspire. It is more "therapeutic" to be enchanted by the soul than puzzled by it. Puzzles lead to energetic solving, conquering, and decoding, while enchantment leads us deeper into life with the promise of pleasure.

I don't mean to sound unrealistic about therapy. It's full of tears and struggle on everyone's part, but pain is not incommensurate with enchantment, and in fact life's charm is revealed only through the initiation of suffering. Without struggle and even hopelessness, enchantment becomes nothing but another kind of sentimentality. I felt little sentimentality in those years of doing therapy, and I have no intention now of presenting enchantment as a sentimental ideal.

Therapy as Service to the Soul

In therapy, the fence that keeps enchantment out is made up of many different elements: theories, expectations, demands, moralisms, great teachers, methods, training, authority, academic degrees and professional certifications, licenses, catalogs of disorders, pathologizing language, sweet sentimentalities, workshops, books, professional papers, studies, diagnoses, treatment plans, insurance requirements, offices, and, above all, our own need to cure. Most of these procedures can be revealed as "defenses," to use a therapist's term, against the soul and its power to cast a spell.

"Therapy" is from the Greek word meaning servant or nurse, and yet the discipline we have established as therapy doesn't always serve the soul but often works against it as it tries hard to explain and heal. If our job as therapists is to serve the soul, to be its sacristan, as Plato recommends, then it's the soul that is master. We follow it, we don't demand that it conform to our expectations and standards. We are its servant; it is not ours. As Jung said, "the psyche is a world in which the ego is contained." "Esse in anima—to be in the soul," he said, quoting Thomas Aquinas. The soul is not in us or contained by us, nor is it ours to do with as we please; if anything, we are its toy for amusement, its clay to be shaped according to its wishes.

In a condition of enchantment, we stop talking and the soul speaks, we stop doing and the soul acts, we stop interpreting and the soul is revealed. But stopping is not easy, especially in the face of suffering or when you feel that your profession requires you to act. My clients have done many things over the years that I might have stopped out of professional propriety: they brought me gifts, shut themselves in closets, covered themselves with curtains, crawled under chairs, sang songs, switched chairs with me, arranged late-night appointments, fell asleep in the middle of conversations, ate and drank, came in disguise, used fictitious names, flirted, got angry, quit, started again, gave up, and became close friends.

This kind of work, allowing the soul to have room to play itself out, is captivating, and the soul teaches and initiates, performs the therapy we're looking for as our dreams interpret our lives and our conversations give rise to theory and principle. In a real sense, we are interpreted by our dreams, we are healed by our illnesses, and our theories and ideas are born from our suffering.

Therapy as care of the soul doesn't take place only in a clinic or consulting room; it happens every time we do anything that nourishes the breath of life, whether that breath is calm and secure in our homes and families or excited in panic, anger, fear, or confusion. Therapy takes place whenever and wherever we allow the soul to assume the lead and when we tend its needs. When I was still a teacher, I once spoke to a group of university professors about education as therapy, and in unison they scorned the idea, because they couldn't see beyond the notion that therapy is a program of personalistic problem solving. Yet in education as in formal therapy, the soul requires only some attention, some shift in our practice that takes it into account.

Therapy of the World

I first studied therapy not to become a therapist but to give depth to my teaching. As a student I had the idea that therapy is more than formal analysis or counseling; it can be an ingredient in everything we do. For me, a car mechanic who is honest, who knows what he or she is doing, who makes my car run smoothly and reliably, is caring for the soul. I have found piano tuners to be sensitive to the soul. They, too, have been honest, sensitive people who show their love of the instruments they work on and establish a relationship to each particular one. This close relatedness and attention to the individual object are signs of soul, and there is nothing as enchanting as listening to a delicate tuning taking place, hearing the mysterious clear harmonics as metal strings gradually come back into sharp resonance.

One of James Hillman's most significant contributions is his reading of the ancient idea of *anima mundi*, the soul of the world. This important phrase can be taken in a structural, abstract sense, so that mentally we conceive of the notion that the world has a soul. Or we can bring a purely spiritual sensibility to it and imagine it as an Over-Soul, as in Emerson, or some pinnacle of spiritual progress. Hillman leads us down into a vision of the world's soul as that which makes every single object of nature and culture alive with personality and subjectivity.

Therapy as care of this mundane soul becomes a daily, value-led attention to every aspect of daily life, and so it is a necessary component of enchantment. To speak of enchantment is to consider a certain aspect of the world's soul, and when therapy focuses on the world instead of only on the interior emotions, and when it brings to the fore its otherwise concealed work with magic, harmonics, images, rituals, and dreams, then it becomes a primary means of enchantment. When we get over our narcissism—a valid goal of therapy—and stop living in a world in which we are the center and all activity neurotically serves our need to be at the top of the hierarchy of beings, then the world can sing and we can enjoy its song.

But this kind of therapy looks quite different from the usual kind, because it isn't concerned with helping people adjust to a disenchanted world. It may invite us into eccentricity, so that we do not fit snugly into a world that systematically and universally neglects the soul. It encourages us to build enchanting homes, raise enchanting children, do enchanting work, and live enchanting lives—not exactly a way to keep up with the Joneses.

The essence of therapy is service, and specifically, as Socrates says, service of the gods, and one of its ancient meanings, as we have seen, is "nurse." So whenever we nurse life along, truly serve it when we see it faltering, we are doing therapy. If we nursed our neighborhoods every day, in every area in which they are suffering, we would be doing therapy for the soul of that neighborhood. If our politicians could imagine their work as therapy, they might tend the soul with a degree of subtlety, and we would see some alleviation of human suffering, because soul-centered therapy really works. Genuine, ongoing attention to suffering and failing has an effect, while repression of the symptoms only makes matters worse.

If transportation has lost its capacity to enchant, then something is wrong, and we will suffer this loss. If there are no enchanting restaurants or shops in a town, then something is seriously weak in the life of the place. If there are no enchanting streets down which to stroll, then it's time to call in the therapists of the town to take a look. Ordinarily we think our task is to fix what is broken, but the soul asks for a different kind of attention, because its role is not to "work" but to enchant.

If something in a town isn't working, but the place does have enchantment, then the brokenness is not so serious and may not even need attention. An enchanting house may not have running water, an enchanting city may not have an efficient bus system, and an enchanting person may be out of work or lying in a hospital bed. Good functioning is not the primary value in a soulful life.

The Therapy of Enchantment

The therapy of enchantment has a different set of concerns compared to our usual notion of therapy. It aims at letting the soul sing, show itself, create a beautiful life. The most enchanting places on earth are especially subject to bad weather, earthquakes, and extreme temperatures. The same is true of the enchanting person and city: they, too, may be perforated with problems and yet retain their capacity to charm.

When we tell stories of the past, do we emphasize efficiency or charm? Do we ride the Orient Express because we know it will arrive on time? Do we visit Antarctica because the accommodations are so comfortable? Do we try to imitate Grandma's cooking because it was so low in fat?

Ultimately, what most satisfies the soul is that which is captivating, spellbinding, and full of charm. A pragmatic person or society may explicitly place these values low on the list of priorities, and yet as individuals we seek these experiences and talk about them all our lives. What is healthy may not be as important in the long run as that which is enchanting, and so we could imagine a therapy of the person and the world that serves enchantment and aims at charm.

In the examples of enchantment I've mentioned, the charm of a place or an experience gives it its value and makes it desirable. Yes, there is a lightness about the idea of charm, but maybe our usual notions of therapy are much too heavy. I have often thought in my practice that tense moments in therapy, as when a client might call to say she was seriously considering suicide, were asking for a measure of lightness. We speak of the results of therapy as "relief," a word that means lift. What better way to be relieved than to have a weight lifted, allowing the soul to soar. Relief is in the many figures from alchemy showing the soul flying up and away from its containment in water or sludge, and how many times do we go to a therapist or take a therapeutic walk just to get a "lift"?

I am not worried about the lightness in enchantment and charm, goals of the therapy I'm sketching here. Therapy sometimes carries a subtle moralism, which is a weight even to those who appreciate its effectiveness. At the very least, we can add the goal of enchantment to all kinds of therapy, noticing what the soul longs for, what thrills it and gives it reason for going on.

As several poets have lamented, the gods have departed, and we live in a time when God and Adam no longer walk together in the cool of the evening. Or as Jung said, the gods now appear as our diseases. When a sense of the sacred leaves a people, enchantment disappears as well, for enchantment is really the nymph song within our music, the fairy voices within our speech, and the little people laboring within our work. When we are convinced by experts to take our lives too seriously and literally, losing fantasy and dream to pragmatism and the obsessive struggles of "personal growth," then the very powers that can fulfill our goals go into eclipse. Our medicine kills us, and our philosophies of change prevent us from being transformed.

The sacred gives everything we do a powerful and expressive resonance. Without that holy reverberation, we suffer a sad, deprived, one-dimensional life. We experience this lack of dimension as personal problems and social disarray, and we respond with personal and social agendas. But what is called for is a genuine Socratic therapy of service to those elements, easily recognized, that foster enchantment. They promise a return of soul and the restoration of a sacred way of life—ultimately the only therapy that works.

Art

*I have nothing to say
and I am saying it
and that is poetry*

JOHN CAGE

Archetypes and Mysteries

NOTHING SEEMS immune from the disenchanted philosophy that has shaped the twentieth century, as even the arts sometimes share the exaggerated personalism of the age with an emphasis on self-expression or dedicate themselves to a technological advancement in music, architecture, dance, and theater. A re-enchanted art would once again use materials and craft as a way of housing spirits that are irreducible to an artist's intellectual or emotional life, or to ideas and ideologies. Once again archetypal themes, eternal and universal, might widely enter the arts, and through the arts audiences might again have the opportunity to contemplate the mysteries that stir in their own hearts.

As used by early Greek and Roman philosophers, the word "archetype" meant origin, model, or even, as an adjective, old-fashioned, in the sense of copying the ancients. The pre-Socratics were concerned with the *archai*, the fundamental building blocks of human life: Were they water, air, fire, flow, attraction? We may ask a similar question about our own ordinary experience. Are there fundamental ways human life shapes itself that are reproduced in each individual human life, and are there raw materials out of which a person's life is made?

Throughout his writings Jung used the word "archetype" psychologically to describe deep patterns that lie, for the most part unconsciously, at the very base of our being. He compared them to instinctive patterns in animals, like a bird building a nest or an insect making its home. In some recent spiritual literature and even in some Jungian studies, one gets the impression that there are a few grand archetypes like Mother, Father, Child, Wise Old Man, and Anima, which have a significant impact on our actions. Jung himself provides a much broader notion of archetype, as in an interview with Richard I. Evans, a professor of psychology in Houston, where he gives the unusual example of the archetype of a ford through a river.

Suppose, he says, you're wading through the shallows of a river. There is an ambush, or a water animal. You sense danger and wonder if you can escape. "This whole situation makes an archetype," he says. You are seized by an emotion or a spell, and you behave according to that seizure.

Jung's example of the river is a strong one, illustrating emotions of fear, wonder, and confusion, but any life situation can be imagined to have an archetypal dimension. As I write, I'm doing something that is not foreign to human experience, not a purely individual act. It has its archetypal roots, and to a large extent I am moved unconsciously into certain emotions and behaviors that are not intentional or even entirely individual. A reader, too, as she reads falls into a pattern that is not limited to the variations in her own personality but has deeper roots.

Archetypal Images

In his writings on archetypes, Jung says that only through archetypal images can we know the archetypes that seize us or subtly shape our behavior and thoughts. Such images are especially important, as they allow us to glimpse the source of our feelings and even our thoughts. As a writer, for instance, I like to read the reflections of other writers on their experience at work. They talk of blocks to creativity, work habits, settings, and attitudes toward their writing, and as I read them I get to know the archetype better. I realize that I'm an individual and that my experience of this writer archetype will be my own, and yet by comparing my experience to that of others I can appreciate some of the deep sources of my work.

We need images that effectively give us insight into the archetypal depths of our life experience; otherwise, we are left with surface explanations that remain on the purely personal, social, and physical levels. Psychoanalysis, from Freud to contemporary Freudians and from Jung to modern Jungian studies, has made a wide range of archetypal studies, searching out the deep "spells" that draw us into marriage, incline us toward a career, or even entice us to travel. But most of the studies done these days in professional and academic circles rely on research methods and assumptions that don't reach down to the level of the archetype, and so our thinking on any subject is often insufficiently profound and imaginative.

Even when psychology attempts to trace the archetypes that underlie human experience, it is often tempted to shrink those archetypes to a certain number and to develop interpretations and methods of exploiting them. If we know all about the archetype of the shadow, for instance, it's assumed we won't be caught in problems of the shadow. But as Jung often said, archetypes can never be known, but only glimpsed. The purpose in glimpsing them is not to explain them away and then have control over them, but rather to be guided by them toward our own instinctive way of life, to feel the very roots of our identity, and so be able to live in intimate relation to our own soul.

In the interview mentioned, Jung talks about primitives who educate their young by telling stories: "Our ancestors have done so and so, and this is your model," he summarizes. A certain kind of storytelling can be an education in the archetypal foundations of our own experiences and is especially important in modern life, where we get the impression that we live from the surfaces and are left to suffer the depths in our emotional turbulence. The stories we hear, read, and see in the movies may be thrilling and stimulating, but rarely are they numinous—a common quality of archetypal images—and rarely do they draw us deeper into our own mysteries; yet we need "models" of that more profound life that forms the bedrock of the soul.

Jung also describes the saints in religion and figures in mythology as archetypal models of behavior. When I was a child, I learned about many saints, men and women of a far distant past, figures of myth as well as historical time, whose stories crept deep into my imagination. Later, as a friar in a religious community, I lived a calendar year that was largely based on saints' days, so that most days of the year I would automatically read about and meditate on the story of a saint.

One saint in particular stands out and for me serves as an archetype in a vivid and meaningful way—Thomas More of England. It was common in Renaissance times, including the period in which More lived, to find meaning in the name fate had given you. I've been drawn to Thomas More since childhood, charmed at first by his good humor, wit, and full life, and later by the "coincidence" that he was instrumental to a degree in introducing Italian Platonic humanism into England, just as I am using the same sources for a renewal of psychology and religion. He translated into English a biography of Pico della Mirandola, friend and colleague of Marsilio Ficino, and much of his life was defined by the religious, humanist values of Ficino and his circle.

I find myself translating Ficino into twentieth-century language, while trying to live out and write about a religious, humanist, soul-centered way of life. Reading Thomas More's letters especially, I feel as though I'm looking into a deep mirror that possesses secrets about myself that are unknown to me. As an archetype, More is not a mental category but a deep mystery that I can't and never will understand, and it is just this kind of mystery that the artist is open to glimpsing and can portray in sufficient measure for our meditation and edification.

Archetypes and the Arts

The arts can do a better job than psychology of educating us in the archetypal realm, because the arts can portray the mysterious import of the archetype without reducing it to an explanation or a method. A good movie showing a scene of Western settlers, for instance, caught in the ford of a river and surrounded by an attacking enemy, could impress upon our imaginations the emotions, thoughts, and meanings attached to that archetypal situation better than an abstract theory of entrapment. We may find ourselves in such a "ford" one day, in a shallow passage through a career or a relationship, with similar emotions and dilemmas, and we may be guided by the movie scene not to get out of our predicament, but to remain trusting and confident in the challenge.

Psychology generally tries to give us relief from the emotions stirred up by an archetypal seizure, whereas the arts intensify the emotions while giving them the sharp definition that comes from increased imagination. Just as the so-called primitive is educated into ancient patterns of behavior through story and ritual, so the arts offer us a way through our predicaments with the tempered light of imagination instead of the blazing lamp of enlightenment.

The arts provide a viewpoint fundamentally different from the one that shapes most modern psychology. Through the artistic imagination we are liberated more by entering into our experiences than by being led out of them. The arts show us our souls, and therefore they are often deeply moving or sometimes profoundly disturbing. Unlike modern allopathic therapies, which tend to numb us to the pain in our predicaments, the arts sharpen the emotion and intensify the crisis of meaning. Psychology may talk abstractly about decision making and change, but a good film places us with all our senses and emotions in the ford of a river, bullets flying, horses falling, water rampaging.

Jung uses the word "seizure" to describe the experience of an archetype. The fear that falls upon us in that ford of decision making puts us under a spell, and the spell, according to Jung, is a sign that something archetypal is at play. I see my daughter hurt her finger, and I rush to her in a seizure of empathy that is part of the spell of fatherhood. I'm told that my books have failed in a certain way, and I feel a crushing sensation—not a mere personal problem but a setback in the deep story of writing and publishing that I'm living.

By presenting us with a ritual-like exposure to the archetypes that shape our lives and seize our emotions, the arts contribute powerfully to the enchantment of everyday life. We live in a culture dominated by logical and quantitative analysis, one that has forgotten the many alternative means of dealing with experience—ritual, story, sacrament, sacrifice, icon, temple, sculpture, and dance. More than ever, we seem to be living a cerebral life, a preciously cultivated one in which our primitivity, which we've never really lost, comes out in savage crime, warfare, and camouflaged embattlement in business and politics. The arts speak to the primary imagination, in a sense to our primitive natures, and so address the archetypal dimension of our thoughts and emotions.

Medieval theologians described philosophy as the servant (*ancilla*) of theology—analysis comes after enchanted imagination. The artist works out of her seizure, and the powerful images that arise out of that altered state retain qualities of emotion and meaning that are proper to the spell. Emily Dickinson wrote: "Nature is a haunted house, but art a house that wants to be haunted." We might apply that same dictum to ordinary life and culture: Nature is an enchanted place, but human culture an effort to evoke and sustain enchantment. We know that we can make a world that works efficiently, but the soul craves charm and fascination. Its natural emotions are longing, desire, interest, attachment, surprise, and pleasure, as well as darker feelings of melancholy, fear, loss, envy, jealousy, and anger. A well-functioning machine or organization can provide certain satisfactions, but the soul feeds on deeper pleasures, and it needs to contemplate its emotions and not just suffer them in the raw.

The arts allow us to contemplate our experiences and therefore invite soul into the picture. They sustain the emotions the soul feeds on and retain the complexity of meaning that is proper to its realm. The mind appreciates the reduction of meaning to logic and classification, but the soul finds more to chew on in diversity, density, and subtlety.

The soul is always searching for itself, and it takes great pleasure when it finds itself mirrored in the material world. When we look at a stunning sunrise, we are seeing the beauty of our own body, for in the mystery of birth we have risen out of this earth. Sunrise offers us a new day and a hopeful glimpse of renewal and resurrection.

If we see ourselves as a puzzle to be solved, then we will be satisfied with rational explanations, but if we see ourselves as made up of unfathomable mysteries, then we will need images that are not excessively reductive. A good artistic presentation may well lead us deeper into confusion and help us feel the chaos of life more vividly than ever. The truth in art is diffuse and largely ineffable, but at the same time it offers a degree of honesty and certainty not found elsewhere.

The Mysteries

Mystery is not a vague unknown; it is a specific unknowable. Our lives are built on a wide variety of themes that can never be compressed into an intelligible formula: birth, illness, love, marriage, work, longing, failure—these are all common experiences and yet at the same time they are mysteries.

The point in the arts is not to make these mysteries conscious—for that approach would encourage us to live only from the mind—but rather to educate and initiate us in these mysteries through contemplation. It's an illusion to think that we discover freedom when we have been disconnected from our instinctual roots. On the contrary, we may feel freer and more engaged with life as we live from a profound engagement that resists rational analysis and can be found only through powerful images.

Without art, we are like Jung's "primitives" deprived of the traditional stories that initiate them into human life and community. Lacking that deep education in the archetypal imagination, the individual is nothing but a collection of passions, without focus and deprived of containment and direction. Contemporary Western life is often split into frenetic passions and emotions that break out destructively on city streets and in family homes, and an endless supply of explanations, interpretations, and solutions is offered. What is missing here is the soul, evoked by an archetypal imagination in which the passions and the imagination combine in an alchemy that generates our humanity.

Museum

A museum or a gallery is truly a temple in which the mysteries that I have to deal with every day are presented for my reflection and deep education. The museum is the workplace of the Muses, those inspiring figures of Greek piety that sing the eternal themes. The poet Hesiod tells us that they were the daughters of Zeus, father of the gods, and Mnemosyne, memory, and that they bring forgetfulness of sorrows and rest from anxiety. Desire and the Graces, he says, always accompany them. "They sing of all the laws and all the gracious customs of the immortals," he writes.

Museums evoke the Muses, filling us with desire and pleasure and giving us images of immortal realities. Above all, museums are palaces of memories, not only personal but immortal ones, the stories and images of humanity that come to us from the eons. With good reason, many museums give their visitors—I'd rather say pilgrims—imposing entrances, long stairways, vaults and high ceilings, stone walls, and gardens, all creating an air of the eternal and placing art in its proper mystery context.

In its origins the museum was a place of lectures, discussions, symposia (with eating and drinking), and meditation. Learning certainly has an important place, but keeping in mind that a museum's mother is Memory, the most important activity carried out in a museum is simple, quiet, prolonged, undisturbed meditation. Some believe that museums are mausoleums, where dead art is housed in a deathly way. I prefer to understand the quiet and the stony timelessness of the museum as its strength. The opportunity to soak oneself in grand memory is becoming rare. Memory doesn't appear out of the blue; it requires a temple atmosphere carefully built and maintained.

When I find myself in a city, for a lecture or other business, and have a free hour, I always try to visit an art museum or gallery. I do this not only because I'm interested in art but because I work with the soul and I live a human life; I have a family and I get sick and have thoughts of mortality. I visit a museum to find myself. On the prowl for art, I'm like the Egyptian Isis, who sought all over the world for the pieces of her dismembered brother and husband, Osiris.

A piece of my soul might be encased in a gallery in Seattle or Rome or Brussels. In fact, I have found lost portions of my soul in these very places. I remember walking up a curving stairway in the magnificent art museum in Brussels and discovering a great piece of my identity in the twelfth-century stone reliefs I saw there. I suspected before but never knew so palpably that I have some kind of life in that century, or that it has a place in mine. I have no doubt that the experience that day was one of remembering, for it had all the emotions of recognition, not of discovery.

A museum is not a building or a social institution; we can have a museum in our own homes and towns. In my writing studio I have a museum that is about four square inches in area, where a small bronze idol stands and overlooks my work, reminding me of the spirits that fill every home and room. It helps me to remember and invites mystery into my room. Clearly, the idol helps enchant what could be a merely utilitarian space, and it especially invokes the spirit of deep memory—the chief role of the muse in her museum.

The Many-Storied Life

A single image, such as a simple painting of Krishna and his gopis, or the Virgin in conversation with the angel, or a Van Gogh haystack, is a window into an infinite mystery, whereas an abstract category is a narrowing of vision. Art teaches us that we are made up not of many parts, as though we were mechanical objects, but rather of an infinite number of stories. We are not "mechanical beetles," to use a phrase from Wallace Stevens, but rather polyfabulous persons—many-storied beings always living out the plot of some inscrutable tale.

When we make our pilgrimage to the museum, we find images showing what the soul is made of, what *my* soul is made of. We celebrate those artists who powerfully and beautifully paint the secret sources of our lives. The images, so carefully made, educate our imagination in the precision, depth, range, and focus of human life. In a museum we see more of our souls than we could find through any means of introspective analysis.

This gaining of intimacy with our soul through art may be seen as a kind of therapy or catharsis, for if we are living from a deep place, we will probably feel a decrease in alienation and anxiety. The catharsis comes not only from understanding what we're going through but from a sophistication of our imagination. Anxiety is the result of too limited an imagination of human life and our own situations, and so it follows that a true education in imagination has strong therapeutic value.

The picture of the crucifixion of Jesus, for example, has long given Christians and others a powerful image through which to ponder their own suffering. I remember being moved while listening to an interview David Frost conducted with Billy Graham, as the Reverend Graham spoke about his personal appropriation of the image of Jesus crucified. This kind of thing can be done in a sentimental way, but he talked as though his life had been profoundly enchanted and formed by this particular image, and although Graham may not appreciate the language of enchantment and archetype, I felt that he knew the power of images to guide and instruct the far reaches of the soul.

As it puts us in touch with mystery, art can also play a role in our healing. According to the art historian Andrée Hayum, the famous Grünewald crucifixion was placed in the chapel of a hospital and surrounded with traditional motifs in such a way that patients could relate the crucifixion directly to their illness. Sickness is not a problem to be solved by medical science alone; it's a mystery that requires the deepest imagination, forged by the combined work of art and theology. The potential role of art in the medical world is profoundly underappreciated in our time, and yet the meeting of these two areas promises to be one of the most important areas for re-enchantment.

With immense power to profoundly affect our imagination of every aspect of life, the arts play a crucial role in the enchantment of ordinary life. They can be called upon in all sorts of endeavors— religion, medicine, education, business, transportation, politics, homemaking—to evoke the mysteries that underlie our many daily concerns. Decoration can magically transform a door from a functional entry into an initiatory rite. An animal motif on a machine can give defining fantasy to what would otherwise be a simple functioning device. The painting hanging in my writing studio, a multilayered figure of a woman painted by my wife, invites an infinite, invigorating, ever-changing, inspiring spirit into my workplace, and I wouldn't want to write without it.

"Remembering the mysteries" is a good definition of enchantment, and it's a simple statement that hides just beneath the surface of art words like muse, music, and museum. If we first realized the absolute importance of honoring the mysteries that shape our lives, and then recognized that nothing presents those mysteries to us as powerfully as the arts do, then we might accomplish a miracle that seems to have happened briefly in the period of Western history known as the Renaissance: the recovery of soul and the enchantment of ordinary life through the arts. There is no reason why we can't have our own renaissance, but that deep renewal would require a radical reorientation of values, in which we would appreciate all spheres of life for their mysteriousness and the arts would be brought in from the margins of culture to capture and dispense those mysteries for the benefit of us all.

Objects of Art

MORE THAN TWENTY years ago I was struck by an idea in *Giordano Bruno and the Hermetic Tradition,* a remarkably lucid and graceful book on magic and the art of memory by Frances Yates, the widely respected historian of Renaissance esoteric culture. She is discussing the astral natural magic of Marsilio Ficino and, in passing, comments on Botticelli's famous painting *La Primavera.* In the context of Ficino's magic, she writes, "the picture begins to be seen as a practical application of that magic, as a complex talisman [of] Alma Venus . . . whose function is to draw down Venereal spirit from the star and to transmit it to the wearer or beholder of her lovely image."

When I first read that passage, I thought: If Botticelli's much-loved painting could be seen as a talisman, why not all paintings and, for that matter, all works of art? Of course, there are complications with this direction of thinking. Many artists, if not most, don't see their work as magic, and some would be offended by the idea. Most ideas about art focus on self-expression, creativity, cultural criticism, and the evolution of styles. On the other side, there are those who intentionally make talismans and amulets, but serious artists might not consider their work true art.

In my view, all art has magical power that may be infused into a work by the artist and enjoyed by the beholder. Art can be merely aesthetically pleasing, philosophically meaningful, and personally expressive, or it can have the special power to evoke and transmit a particular spirit to those who come in contact with it. Many traditions teach that our lives could be enriched, made spiritually alive, and even healed through the magical power of art.

Frances Yates bases her idea on Ficino's theories on the power of images. Ficino was a priest, a magus, a physician's son, a professional sage, and a therapist, and his philosophy and personal way of life, bringing together all these arts and pursuits, offer a basis for imagining art as having an absolute, serious, and primary place in the lives of everyone and in the work of culture.

My book *The Planets Within* summarizes Ficino's approach to magic. A brief outline of that summary might help us see the role of magic in art and in that way glimpse art's capacity to enchant. Scholars study many facets of Ficino's career, some emphasizing his philosophy and others his place in history, whereas I'm drawn to Ficino the magus, who places soul at the very heart of his worldview and treats ordinary life as having power and effectiveness through the daily practice of natural magic.

Natural Magic and Worldly Radiance

In Ficino's story of the cosmos, the planets, including sun and moon, each contain a particular kind of spirit, a quality that emanates as rays pouring out of their bright presence in the sky. Human life requires a mixture of these various qualities, and when the planets' rays fall to earth and are drawn into the different natural and artificial objects in the world, we can absorb them by exposing ourselves to objects rich in a certain quality. This radiance of the stars is not scattered around the world randomly but is sorted out among objects according to patterns of resemblance. Venusian radiance, for instance, will inhabit Venusian objects, such as gardens, flowers, beautiful clothes, certain green objects, and sensual and sexual things.

In magic, things that contain a certain spirit can offer that spirit to us. Ficino says, for example, that clever monkeys and dogs contain the spirit of Mercury, a figure known for his trickiness and mental acumen, but glass and agate also are mercurial, perhaps because of their shine. Sapphire and sugar contain the spirit of Jupiter because of traditional interpretations and because they contribute to a feeling of joviality.

In this magical approach to life, a person could use certain objects, natural and human made, for their planetary properties or their characteristic spirit. We could wear a sapphire ring to keep our spirits jovial, or a green shirt to invite the mood of Venus. Ficino's system of magic allows us to sort out and classify various qualities in human life and then find ways to intensify those qualities in our homes and persons. We do something similar in a modern way when we name the various emotions, disorders, and temperaments. In the twentieth century, we have been especially creative in making lists of human qualities, from Freud's anal-retentive personality to Jung's introverted personality type, and in developing therapeutic modalities based on our classifications.

The advantage of Ficino's charting of the soul is that it is imagistic and is rooted in ancient traditions. It's less rational than modern theories, and that, of course, might make it appear more esoteric and exotic than it really is. Ficino's early followers kept the astrological, planetary nature of his archetypes, but today his approach to magic could be practiced in broader ways.

It isn't necessary to use Ficino's myth of the stars literally; we could apply his theory to all images. We might ask, What is the spirit in Monet's paintings of his gardens? We could speak of a "garden spirit" in general, or the spirit of Monet's personal view of flowers. Even here, of course, we're close to the ethos of the *La Primavera*. It wouldn't be difficult to determine the Venusian elements in Monet's work, but we could also delineate a "Monet spirit" and incorporate that spirit into our homes and environment.

It's the next step in Ficino's system that's crucial—our way of making and "using" art. In Ficino's view, all of life is an art; every day we choose what clothes to wear, where to walk or travel, which foods to eat, and how to spend our time. We have conversations, meet friends, live a family life, go to work, write letters, and do many other things that draw particular kinds of spirit into our souls. Some of these activities may be nourishing, some may be detrimental. In any case, we can make an art of daily life by diagnosing what the soul needs and determining how everyday activities could satisfy those needs. The title of his book suggests an artistic approach to ordinary life: *How to Design Life in Accord with the Sky*.

In Ficino's philosophy, everything contains some kind of spirit, so whether or not we design our world artfully and magically, we will nevertheless be exposed to certain deep influences. Better to bring art to our design of life than to be affected randomly. As a doctor, he advises diagnosing our personal lives and our world for certain imbalances and excesses of one spirit or another. As a magus, he teaches how to sort out every aspect of life according to qualities that the soul needs, and suggests ways to have magical effect as we go about creating a life rich in a wide variety of spirit.

The dominance of a particular spirit or the absence of a much-needed one may adversely affect the condition of the soul and the quality of life in general. The lack may be felt either as a certain kind of emptiness or as a symptomatic preoccupation with some quality felt as missing. Either way, we would benefit from an enrichment of the missing element.

It's in this spirit that I have recommended in my other books to treat depression with the arts of Saturn. If you're depressed, you might be lacking in saturnine spirit, and so you might try one of the traditional cures, such as wearing black, withdrawing from life, putting on a broad-brimmed hat, reading some melancholic poems, or listening to sad music. To keep Saturn constellated in life, I've recommended the traditional practice of creating a saturnine place of withdrawal in a garden, park, or home. The art of bringing saturnine spirit into life could help heal a person or even a nation that has lost sight of the value of certain things like solitude, grief, sadness, and reflection.

In this context, it isn't difficult to see a role for the artist in tending the soul life of a community by giving it powerful images of needed spirit in music, dance, food, painting, and architecture—in all the arts. We might also expand our notion of therapy and see that in presenting objects full of certain spirit for a community's absorption and consideration, the artist is a therapist and a magus in the Platonic sense. The artist's work not only is beautiful but has considerable healing power and is essential to the soul of the community.

Through a magical, spiritual use of images, the arts nourish the soul, creating a richly varied atmosphere, an environment that is not only practical but spiritually nutritious. In this way, the arts also might enjoy a central role in the life of a community and would not be made marginal, as is the case almost by definition in a disenchanted culture. As Ficino says in great detail, to thrive the soul needs a wide variety of qualities, and so the soul's vitality depends on its exposure to strong and well-executed images.

Amulets

Among the many magical objects Ficino recommends in the artful tempering of everyday life are amulets and talismans. An amulet is an object chosen for its particular constituent material. A ring or pendant made of a simple stone worn every day or on certain occasions can be the stuff of natural magic, but the idea of "amulet" can be extended to apply as well to the rest of our material existence. As we select fabrics for clothing and home furnishing, for example, we could use a magician's eye and be aware of the spirit that is invited by a particular material.

If we choose to wear polyester shirts because of their convenience, we might realize that they bring a certain spirit into life, as is also the case with cotton or linen. A store or catalog of simple, natural clothing conveys a spirit quite different from that of traditional utilitarian styles or sexy and silky materials. They each have a place, perhaps, just as each planet is unique, but each one brings a different kind of magic into life. As artists of our own lives, we can choose the materials and fabrics that create the spirit we need or desire.

All choices of material, from children's clothes to a public building, could be seen as a magician's work with amulets. Amulets were first used in history to keep infants from an early death, and in an extended sense they still keep us from death of soul created by lifeless buildings and spiritless furnishings. Everyone knows that a bland environment generates a bland spirit. We don't think about ordinary things as amulets, as objects of magic, but we make choices of them every day as we inspect the leather in a walking shoe or feel the texture of a shirt or blouse.

Careful selection of materials in building our cities, bridges, roads, factories, and offices could go a long way toward the re-enchantment of culture, but it would entail a craftsperson's eye for building and an artist's sensitivity to color, shade, hue, texture, and shape in everything we make. Nothing is too practical, nothing too small or large, to be considered for its role as an amulet. We don't hang buildings around our necks, but we do live with them around our families and communities every day and are deeply affected by their presence.

A book on Japanese carpentry and the rebuilding of an ancient temple says: "Temple carpenters must be well versed in Buddhist theology and ritual, and are treated as members of the clergy on certain ceremonial occasions." I look forward to the day when in the Western world, too, we will have discovered the secrets of enchantment and appreciate the theological skills required in building a home, and when carpenters will imagine themselves as engaged in a sacred activity. Today our work and the things we build suffer the burden of secularism: work doesn't arise from a place in the worker deep enough to grant sufficient satisfaction, and our buildings have lost their temple nature—every building is a temple to something. The Japanese temple builder, initiated into the ancient traditions, works religiously and magically: "One should take as much time as necessary. One must concentrate completely all the while, and be in good spirits, because a craftsman's frame of mind permeates every aspect of his work, and the work will bear the imprint of its creator as long as it exists."

A maker of things is not only a person of craft but a magician as well. If we disregard the spiritual nature of materials when we make things for the home, objects as simple as bowls, plates, and utensils, we are diminishing the spiritual lives of those who use the things. It makes a difference whether a platter is ceramic or plastic, whether we stir our stew with a wooden spoon or a rubber spatula. We have to make our own decisions about which material is appropriate and valuable, and must constantly assess the impact of our physical environment on our souls. Often the less expensive object has more magic, precisely because of its simplicity and the material from which it's made, but sometimes we may want to make an unusual expenditure for the sake of our souls.

Another area where materials are significant is jewelry. During the early European Renaissance, when magic, humanism, and religion enjoyed a delicate balance and a fruitful association, it was a common practice to cast special rings, medallions, and other forms of jewelry that captured the essence of a person, family, or city. The banker Lorenzo di Pierfrancesco de' Medici used an emblem of a coiled serpent, and the artist Alberti a winged eye.

The sparkle and shine of jewelry pleases something deep in the heart. As we have seen, Ficino taught that a sparkle on earth echoes and reflects the twinkling of the stars, so that wearing a radiant diamond is like having a planet on your finger. Earthly sparkle also suggests the ancient notion of the scintilla or spark that is the inner luminescence of the soul. Solar gold, lunar silver, and the red and green stones of Venus common in jewelry animate a person and make her life especially potent. What is the feeling you get when you wear a brilliant diamond or a simple string of beads? I believe it's the sensation of magic, of being empowered through the vitality and potency that lie in the stuff of nature. This is the secret of the amulet: it keeps death at a distance and makes life scintillating and powerful.

The amulet also embodies the raw material out of which our identity is sculpted. Think of Isadora Duncan with her flowing robes, Oscar Wilde in his velvet suits, Marilyn Monroe with her sparkling dresses. The material in our lives is part of who we are, and attention to clothes and adornment need not be narcissistic. Indeed, the magical practice of objectifying our individuality and personality in clothing and jewelry can be a way of refining and diminishing our narcissism by giving our heart the attention it craves.

Among the layers of personality Jungian psychology has defined lies the "persona," usually described without much appreciation as a shell we wear like a suit of clothes: our job, our station in life, our style and manner. Sometimes this persona is judged to be superficial and only skin deep. In his *Vision Seminars,* Jung complains about the negative side of the persona: "If you have nothing but the ego consciousness, the very next thing you will do will be to buy a pair of new shoes and a suit of clothes and a becoming hat and look like a gentleman, so that everyone will look at you and think: is he not a nice man? You buy a persona as soon as possible because you are nothing else." We all know that it's possible to use clothes and status as an empty way of trying to be somebody, but that is not the whole story of persona. Clothes, job, and home furnishings can be a vital and valid part of the soulful life. In an enchanted world, sur-

faces count, and the underappreciated persona can be more important than the deep, inner, celebrated Self.

The emphasis in some psychologies on the hidden, interior, true
substance of a person may be a reflection of the disenchanted world
in which we live. If we don't value nature, materials, things, and
appearances, then we will look for substance in some deep interior
place. It may be time to drop the word "self" altogether because it
gives the illusion of an invisible life detached from the world of
things and because it contains an inescapable element of narcissism, which is inimical to enchantment.

It's interesting that in the story of Narcissus, he himself is narcissistic until the moment when he stops to look at nature, a pool of
water, and finds himself there. Then he becomes nature, as he is
transformed into a daffodil. In the same way, we could heal our narcissism by discovering the enchantment of the world, realizing that
the world is me. I'm as much a flower as I'm a human being, because
I am of the same natural world. I'm not only animal, which we all
seem to admit, but plant too. There is a secret to my identity lying
in the surface textures and colors of a daffodil, or in my particular
flower that I have to find as I'm driven by my afflictions toward a
fruitful contemplation of nature.

Talismans

As potent as materials are, objects may take on even further magical power when they are imprinted with an image and thereby
become talismans. In the strict sense and in some usages, a talisman is an amulet that has been stamped or painted with a design or
with words. In Ficino's magic, cosmic imagery was particularly
appropriate—sun, moon, and planets. Wallis Budge, an archaeolo-
gist of magic at the turn of the century, studied traditional Christian objects of piety as amulets and talismans: the cross; relics; biblical texts printed on leather, parchment, stones, and paper.

Images, whether painted, sculpted, drawn, or photographed,
have great power, in the Ficinian sense, to bring specific kinds of
spirit into daily life. For several months, while working at my desk,
I have been staring at postcards picturing a twelfth-century French
monastery, and I have no doubt that these small black-and-white

pictures, sent to me by a friend, have kept alive for me the spirit of monasticism and the medieval world as I have been writing about magic and enchantment.

The way amulets and talismans are used, of course, has much to do with their magical power. If we treat paintings as mere self-expressions of the artist, then their capacity to draw power and spirit into our lives may be diminished, but if we treat them as power objects, as icons and talismans, then we might have a fundamentally different appreciation for the role of art in life, and we might "relate" to art in a very different fashion.

A few years ago my wife and I visited Santissima Annunziata, an old church in Florence that just happens to have been the birthplace of the religious order I was in for many years, and there we witnessed a special ritual honoring a painting of the Virgin Mary. The painting is usually covered and out of sight, but at certain times it is mechanically raised into its ornate shrine so that people can not only inspect it but give it reverence. Such a ritualizing of the art object could be a step toward the re-enchantment of art. In his book on art as icon, Hans Belting speaks of art having "a magic rooted in the object itself," and he describes many ways icons and other works of art have been honored.

Not long ago I visited the relatively new art museum in Dallas. I remembered that years earlier, before the current impressive museum was built, the collection of pre-Columbian art was housed in a few small, dark rooms, and the visitor examined the many objects, large and small, as though they were in storage. Now, in the massive new museum, pieces are displayed dramatically, with attention to lighting, room dimensions, space, color, and placement. This attention to the presence of the object, almost making altars of the display areas, helps move closer to the idea of art as magic rather than as mere aesthetics, and then, too, the museum becomes a place of enchantment rather than dead history or merely technical study.

An appreciation for the power of talismans might help us understand many things in our ordinary world, such as glass sauce jars that have letters stamped into them. In my house, we have a difficult time throwing away jars like these, and I suspect it is because of the subtle talismanic quality of the lettering. Graffiti is a very complicated phenomenon, but maybe it, too, is a form of talismanic illustration, etching potent images onto buildings that have lost their enchantment in cities that have failed to charm their inhabitants. I was once walking through the narrow streets and piazzas of Rome, when I came upon an alarming piece of graffiti. Across the wall of a very old building was the chalked-in word "Beatrice." The name may well have referred to some young man's girlfriend, but to me it had strong echoes of Dante, the love of his life, and his poetry.

For the soul, it isn't merely pleasing to have pictures in the home and the workplace; it's necessary, because the soul can work in our lives only through magic, and talismans are the tools of that magic. Once, people seemed to know this talismanic secret, as they carved images into furniture, tools, doors. Today we have grown accustomed to an imageless world of boxy computers, boxy office buildings, and boxy homes, smooth in line and texture, unhindered by gargoyles, filigree, ornament, and natural motif. We may call this style "modern," but from a magician's point of view, it is simply void of talismanic power, yet another sign of our failure to maintain enchantment in everyday life.

There is a spirit in human beings that seeks purity, and this spirit can become iconoclastic, railing against images. It's an impulse that has appeared in most religions, as in the late fifteenth century when the fiery monk Savonarola incited people to his "bonfire of the vanities," destroying books and works of art. It has appeared in communism, in businesses that disallow images in the workplace, and among architects whose aesthetics do not include image and reference. It can appear in any person's life as a passing fascination or as a philosophy of life. It is profoundly anti-pagan, anti-magic, and anti-imagination. It may be mind wanting to be free of body, spirit wishing for liberation from soul, thought wanting release from the heart. Since, as the ancients taught, soul is what makes us human, this spirit is a dehumanizing force, often finding relief from the burden of humanity in purity and self-righteousness.

To restore magic to art, then, we may have to learn to appreciate a lowlier spirituality and a humbler approach to daily living. Perfection and purity are not the goals of a soul-centered life. The soul craves ordinary pleasures, depth of feeling and relatedness, worldly delight that is not inimical to a spiritual practice, human scale in the making of culture, and exposure to the magic that lies just beneath the surface of familiar things.

The soul cannot be present without its contaminants—imperfection, impurity, worldliness, ordinariness, and humanity. Once we acknowledge this "unfortunate" condition, we might embrace art intimately and enthusiastically, and judge it not as a threat to our intelligence and virtue but as an instrument in soul-making.

Musica Humana

TOWARD THE beginning of the sixth century, Roman statesman, philosopher, and theologian Anicius Manlius Severinus Boethius (480–524) wrote an essay called "De institutione musica." He is also the author of *The Consolation of Philosophy*, a widely read meditation of comfort written in prison shortly before his execution for his supposed participation in a plot of treason. His book on music became immensely influential in the later Middle Ages— almost all authors then writing about music cite it—and for a few centuries, at least, it helped prevent music from becoming a wholly technical art.

Briefly, Boethius mentions that there are three kinds of music: *musica mundana*, cosmic music, recognized in the harmony of the different celestial bodies as they move through the sky and in the blending of the four elements, earth, air, fire, and water, throughout nature; *musica humana*, the harmony that unites the spiritual with the physical in the human person, the parts of the soul, such as the rational and the irrational, and the parts of the body; and finally, *musica instrumentalis*, the music we hear with our ears.

Thirty years ago, when I first read about Boethius and his approach to music, I was deeply taken by his ideas, and as a college student I wrote essays about the music of the spheres and its psychological implications. One of my early publications was an essay in the journal *Spring*, edited by James Hillman, entitled "Musical Therapy." I didn't write about what we usually understand as "music therapy," using song and instruments as an aid in dealing with emotional problems, but rather therapy itself as musical, in the Boethian sense. I wrote about harmonies and dissonances in the soul, with no violins or trumpets: "The psychotherapist as *musicus*, as musician, must have an ear for the temperament and harmony which resonate deep with the melodic (personal) events of life."

I had written these ideas in a paper presented earlier at a conference on archetypal psychology, a paper I had submitted first to James Hillman, whom I had not yet met but who was already becoming the major influence in my intellectual life. He flew in from Zurich for the gathering in Dallas, and when he approached me, his words of greeting were: "Hello. You're right. Music, but no violins."

That remark has stayed with me over the years, because it recognizes that nothing need be taken only literally. Even music is not so plainly physical as the music we hear on our radios and stereo systems. From the beginning, I understood Boethius as saying not that the music we hear is a metaphor for what goes on in the soul, but that the music we create with the voice or on instruments is an expression or representation of the essential music of nature and the human being. In our very constitution we are musical, as is the world itself. If anything, the music we listen to is a metaphor for human nature.

Boethius's definition of music, drawn from many classical sources, adds a helpful element to a philosophy of enchantment, as it offers an aesthetic image for the world and for human life. We are not only an amalgamation of chemicals and electrical charges, we are music; and the world is not only a construct of atoms and molecules, it is an artistic work.

The Music of the Soul

In therapy, I often listen to the stories of my clients with a musical ear, musical in this sense I'm describing. When someone is trying to resolve two or more pressing themes in life, like the need to be a serious student in school and at the same time a playful and free individual, I might see the situation as a problem in counterpoint, the aspect of music composition where two or more melodies play independently and yet harmonize with each other. Often we approach life as a logical problem and try to decide which alternative is correct and makes sense. A musical approach looks for ways to combine many different themes, without logical solutions and without allowing any one theme to dominate.

As a therapist, I also sometimes consider the common musical structure found in hundreds of classical sonatas, concertos, and symphonies, where there is the initial presentation of material—themes and counterthemes, harmonies, and figures—then the intricate dissolving and free "development" of that material, and finally the recapitulation, when the material is again presented in its clear and cohesive shape. Life often takes the sonata form.

The clearest example of living a sonata in my own life is my experience of religion. At first, for twenty-five years of my life, I found religion clearly packaged and quite beautifully presented in the institution of the church, but then I made a marked and radical break, spending years in wonder, questioning, confusion, and experiment. Only recently have I noticed a recapitulation, not as a literal return to my former condition, but, as in music, a return with significant twists and alterations, which I see as a profound deepening of the original material. The recapitulation always shows signs of the process of development and is usually presented in slightly different tonalities.

This recapitulation of Catholicism and religion in my life is a deeply satisfying development, as it reconnects me with my past. If I felt that life should always be moving ahead on a straight, evolutionary path, then I might overlook this other more musical structure; but thinking musically, I can appreciate many different ways life arranges itself.

Another musical form I find useful in therapy is called an episode. In a piece of music, minor passages sometimes link major themes to each other. They pass quickly and rarely take on major significance. The word literally means side road, as it contains the interesting Greek word for road, *hodos*. I often think of certain life themes, though weighty and bothersome when they appear, as mere episodes, not likely to last long and become significant in themselves, but contributing in a small way to grander issues and developments. I can weather a tough time if I perceive that what is disturbing me at the moment is a musical episode and not a lengthy development.

This musical view of the soul accepts rhythms, harmonies, dissonances, and developments, and so it is tolerant of the many different kinds of figurations that make up a life. Thinking musically, we can ask not what is the right way to go, but rather what is the form here? Is this depression caused by some mistake I'm making in daily life, or is it a tonality of the soul, a mood that will take its place among the many other tonalities? Is this new job the end point of my longing for a career, or could it be a "deceptive cadence," a minor pause that seems like a grand conclusion?

Boethius encourages us to see that the soul, the very core of personality, is expressive. Today we are taught to think that whatever happens to us internally is the result of some external decision or experience, but premodern philosophers saw the soul as a world unto itself and not a mere reflection of external events or a reaction to them. One of the reasons we lack enchantment in daily life is that we think too much in terms of cause and effect, instead of acknowledging the autonomous expressions of the soul and thus allowing our very depths to have subjectivity. With a musician's sensitivity, we could observe our personal lives with a degree of enchantment, appreciating the mysterious ways our own soul expresses and manifests itself.

Harmonies and Counterpoints

The musical nature of reality and of the soul entails the coming together of differences. To a great extent, the art of music is a process of "arranging" different themes, pitches, rhythms, and timbres, and in a musical psychology, our various moods and traits each could find their place in an emotional harmony and counterpoint. Thinking psychologically, we often try to eliminate inner conflicts and competing desires and longings, but thinking musically, we may be able to find a way to appreciate the many elements that make us up and allow them to be independent and yet in tune with one another.

I use the word "harmony" with some reservations, since the word is often used sentimentally. For instance, we talk about world harmony as a sweet unreachable goal rather than as a tough ongoing task, or about marital harmony as the absence of conflict. But in the field of music, harmony is not sentimental by nature. It's a way of joining many different tones not only so they sound good together but also so they can then progress to the next set of tones in a meaningful and creative way. Musicians talk about "harmonic progression" and "chord changes," referring to this unfolding of harmonic relationships, and they often try to come up with new and fresh ways of letting one chord lead to another. The musician tries to develop a good ear for the inherent implications and directions of a harmonious chord or unresolved interval.

Living musically involves an appreciation for the dynamics inherent in our own soul and in the shapes life takes. The jazz piano player listens to a flatted ninth chord, a rich and complex set of tones his fingers have found, and then tries to sense where this chord, in context with many others, wants to go. The worst players are those who force a harmonic progression in an easy or obvious direction, or in a series that they have learned abstractly as a rule or typical pattern. This kind of jazz is dull and uncreative, and so, too, is a life that is not in tune with the possibilities inherent in one's situation. It's as though each life condition were a dynamic chord leaning in a certain direction—a job that offers new vitality, a marriage that exhibits new possibilities for each of the partners, a child who opens up new experiences of life, a home that invites new friendships and activities.

The beauty of music lies in its organic unfolding, in the creative use of all materials at hand, no matter how unusual or apparently meaningless. If you were to analyze the harmonic developments in a simple Bach fugue, you would be astonished at the composer's ability to see implications for fresh sounds in every musical situation, from the most commonplace to the most unusual. I've often thought how fruitful it would be to teach a psychology course using the preludes and fugues of Bach as the only textbook.

A Pythagorean Way of Life

Boethius recounts an old story about Pythagoras, the Greek philosopher known for his musical philosophy and his community of followers. One day, passing a smithy, he heard several men pounding iron with their hammers, and he detected consonant harmonies ringing out from their shop. He investigated and found that each had a hammer of a different weight, and the various weights lined up in a proportionate series that he later concluded was the proportion that holds the whole world together.

In the Pythagorean worldview, certain consonances are built into nature or in things made by humans, and these consonances have special resonance. They sing the fundamentals of human life. In the seventeenth century, Robert Fludd, another musical philosopher, illustrated one of his books with the image of the "Temple of Music," which includes a drawing of Pythagoras at the smithy. In Fludd's philosophy too, care of the soul is rooted in a profound relationship between human life and the eternal themes or elements that are beyond human making, and Fludd refers to these relationships in the musical terms of octaves, fifths, and fourths, and in the imagery of musical instruments and their tunings.

Many take the Pythagorean viewpoint and develop a highly numerical and symbolic approach to life, but I prefer to hear the story of the smiths more broadly, as having to do with life lived in consonance with one's own deepest nature and with the ways of the natural world outside us. My interest in this kind of music lies not in intellectually clever and remarkable correspondences but in the deep resonance one sometimes senses in everyday living. I often imagine mythology, the arts, and philosophy as creating a resonating chamber, like the body of a guitar or violin, allowing ordinary actions to have increased sonority and intensity.

A musician has to have a good ear. I remember that when I first seriously studied orchestration, learning about all the instruments—their timbres, ranges, and fingerings—I was shocked to discover that within a short time it was as though someone had performed surgery on my ears. I could hear things that previously were completely mute to me. Literally, a world of sound opened up, and I was astonished at what I heard for the first time.

I think we can achieve the same tuning of our inner ears, the subtle organs that detect the counterpoints and harmonic tensions of the soul. When we are busy putting our theories into practice, we may not listen with real care and hear the music of the heart, and when we are attached to familiar understandings and unconsciously involved in the culture around us, we may not hear the music of our own souls. Rather than being musicians of the psyche, we are truckdrivers, putting our muscle into getting the job done and getting somewhere on time. As musicians of the soul, we could be unusually sensitive to the heart's music and care for it with all the attentiveness of a jazz piano player working out a new riff.

Musicians of the Everyday

Our view of the world and our own lives is always guided by some basic metaphor. Some see the soul as a set of problems, as an object of moral concern, or as the sum of external influences in life. Some psychologists see it as a mass of behavior patterns or chemical interactions, or as the arena of personal history. To Aristotelians, a human being is a rational animal; to a magus, we might be an incarnated star.

We could follow Boethius and imagine the soul as music, and as musicians of the everyday we could be more attentive to the ways of nature and our own emotions. We could bring an artist's sensitivity to all issues of daily living, instead of wanting always to doctor the soul, or teach it, or get it into moral alignment. Instead of always trying to make the healthy or morally correct choice, we could make life decisions with art and with a sense of the beautiful and the harmonic.

The moralistic person tends to be wary of the artist, perhaps because of the freedom and individuality that art inspires. But the way of art can be the most moral of all, if it is lived with honesty and in a transparent search for images that reveal the figures and patterns of life. Too often we look at the arts and focus our attention on the pictures or on the aural or visual patterns in their technical brilliance. But these pictures are only the tools of the artist who surrenders a lifetime to the work of evoking the most spiritual and moral themes through arrangements of matter.

A typical musician takes the art seriously and often devotes unlimited energy to its study and performance, but this devotion is usually rooted in love and pleasure. In the same way, a musical approach to everyday life could be serious and dedicated without being grounded in anxiety. As musicians of our own lives, we could enjoy the harmonies, counterpoints, fugues, sonatas, concertos, quartets, and simple tunes that give shape to our lives, we could appreciate the aesthetics of events rather than their truth and correctness. There is no essential conflict between morality and aesthetics; in fact, they serve each other well when each has subtlety and depth. But in a literalistic age, we tend to emphasize the morality of events and neglect their aesthetics.

The *art* of life is quite different in tone from the *project* of life. The freedom granted by an artistic attitude allows us to take pleasure in the responsibility we have to shape a life and a society according to its soul. As musicians in the broadest sense, we might be able to fashion a world and a life that are beautiful and enchanting rather than merely effective and productive, and that distinction could make all the difference.

Furniture Music

ONE LOVELY SUNDAY morning in spring, my wife and I were walking through the streets of London on the way to the Tate Gallery, when we happened to pass by the entrance to Westminster Abbey. We are always in search of a beautiful liturgy, of whatever denomination or religion, and so, in spite of crowds of tourists at the doors, we decided to go in.

As we entered, the well-trained choir was singing sixteenth-century polyphony, music certainly written to be sung by angels. If the soaring vaults of the church didn't snatch our spirits out of time and into eternity, then the music certainly did. I had no awareness of the many visitors standing behind us as we sat in the nave, not able to see the choir but fully taken up into its magic.

As the liturgy came to an end, the organist played a recessional that was modern in tonality and figuration and that perfectly accompanied the swift, no-nonsense exit of the clergy, choir, and attendants. The firm, perfectly voiced diapasons of the organ stirred me deeply, as I remembered for the first time in years that when I was a young man the pipe organ was the focus of my life. I had taken lessons first in Chicago with René Dosogne, the man who introduced me formally to music and who from the beginning set my sense of musicianship and taste. Hearing this organ in Westminster, I knew that René would have loved both the instrument and the well-articulated technique of the organist.

I remembered, too, Eddy LeGreve, a singer and organist from Belgium, who had been invited to the post of organist at the small church in Detroit where I grew up. He was a musician of extraordinary talent, and he found at our humble church a pipe organ that was the antithesis of the Westminster gem, an instrument that gasped and screeched as he did his best to make music on it.

I remember the first time I heard Eddy play at Mass. I was in high school and had had a few years of lessons with René. When I heard Eddy's Bach on that calliope of an organ, I couldn't believe it was the same church in which I had spent hundreds of hours, maybe thousands, as a child. The building and the service were both transformed by Eddy's spirited performance of Bach and other Baroque and contemporary composers, music that conjured up a strong, intelligent piety and made the heart and imagination come alive.

I took lessons with Eddy for a summer, but he developed cancer and within a short time died. He taught me, as René had done, how to find the firm, stonelike soul of the organ, and during those two summers I discovered something about the mystery that resides in music. I remember at my last lesson asking a question that clearly came from my youthful innocence: What could I do to remember all my life the approach to performance I had just begun to explore and taste? How could I stay on the right track? I knew that I had a sentimental streak in me, which could pull me away from the solid music I had glimpsed through Eddy LeGreve. He told me, in the last words I ever exchanged with him and in a conversation that took place almost forty years ago now, in the quiet shadows of open organ pipes in a high church balcony, simply to relax, trust my intuition, and build on what I had been doing.

I knew even then Boethius's ideas about music, that it, more than all the arts, has a powerful effect on a person's life and moral sensibility. I learned this lesson when I was in my teens, in those hours of practice when I tried to find the animated but noble tones of the organ, and curiously it seems I was also getting lessons that would serve me in later life as a psychotherapist.

Music and Character

I grew up on Bach and Bartók, but I think the mysteries I was exploring in them can be found in any kind of music, from any part of the world, and in any style, from jazz to country to rock. As Plato knew so well, music is an education that forms the character of a person and a people, and as he warned, we should be careful in selecting the kinds of music that accompany our lives.

If we have no music in our upbringing, then we will have suffered an unimaginable loss. Some people think the breakdown in morals that we sense around us has to do with the failure of religion or with the decadence of culture. Yet when financial circumstances become tight, those same people are willing and sometimes eager to cut music programs from school curricula. As we approach a new century and a changing international economic climate, we think that scientific and technological education should be our highest priority, and yet these fields, at least the way they are practiced today, only tangentially affect the heart and soul, where morality and values are rooted, while music goes right to the heart.

In the third book of the *Republic,* Plato poses a question about education: Is it right to think of gymnastics as training for the body and music for the soul? His answer would surprise some readers: Both, he says, are for the soul. Gymnastics, he says, derives from the "high-spirited element in our nature," and if it is carried out in conjunction with music, it educates a person in courage. But if music is lacking, gymnastics makes a person hard and harsh. On the other hand, if you learn music but not gymnastics, you become too soft, you "melt and liquefy until your spirit dissolves away."

He goes on to say that without music, the soul becomes "feeble, deaf, and blind." "A stranger to the muses achieves all purposes like a beast through violence and savagery and lives a life of disharmony and gracelessness."

Studying music, one learns about talent, thought, work, expression, beauty, technique, collaboration, aesthetic judgment, inspiration, taste, and a host of other elements that shape life in all its aspects. As we learn to control our fingers, lips, and breath in making music, subliminally music is shaping us, making us people of sensitivity and judgment. At the same time, music brings the soul further into life.

Music, like all the arts, affects us deeply, touches our soul directly, and so brings out fantasy, individuality, and imagination. In music school, the chairman of our department often walked the halls lost in musical cyberspace, humming and setting his eyes on some remote planet of notes and instrumentation that no one else could see or hear. Mental studies make a person controlled and controlling, logical, focused on the literal here and now, and so to this kind of person a musician might appear lost in inner space and dangerously unconscious. From a musician's viewpoint, the soberness and focus of a rational person might look odd. I would expect that an increased appreciation for the muses in our culture might result in a more poetic style of life generally.

I'm intrigued by the general point in Plato's discussion of music—intense concern about the place of the soul in education. As a culture, we seem to have lost sight of the soul in learning, while we focus on gathering information and acquiring skills. We wonder why character seems to be disappearing in adults and young people, and yet we find many reasons for ignoring education for the soul. The very consideration of the dangers in becoming too brutal or too liquid would make an excellent beginning in the project of restoring soul to its central place in learning.

Musical Accompaniments

If the choir at Westminster Abbey had exited the sanctuary without musical accompaniment, they would have appeared odd. One of the primary functions of music is to provide accompaniment to many things that we do. Accompaniment may sound like something of little significance, but music can breathe soul into whatever we're doing, even if it's only in the background. Enchantment itself could be imagined as a kind of accompaniment—not the central focus of our activity, a transformative yet ancillary facet.

Except in concert halls and stadiums, music is almost always an accompaniment of some sort, whether it is a radio playing country music in a pickup truck rolling down a dusty road, or a Baroque quintet playing French delicacies at a luncheon in a museum courtyard. As I write my books, I take a few minutes each day to play some Mozart or Bach, and I'm convinced that this little bit of musical accompaniment contributes significantly to my work.

The eccentric French composer Erik Satie approached music with whimsy and humor, stressing some of its otherwise hidden aspects in ordinary situations. In 1920, he composed and performed what he called *Musique d'ameublement,* furniture music. He instructed that this music be "a part of the surrounding noises and take them into account. . . . Furniture music for law offices, banks, etc. Do not enter a house that does not have furniture music." He wrote music that he intended for performance between the acts of a play, but he couldn't convince the audience to leave the theater for the lobby, to talk and carry on while the music was playing.

Today Satie might be called a performance artist. His works are based on a philosophy similar to that of William Morris: The arts are for the people, for everyday life, and they give that ordinary life civility and beauty. "Nothing can be a work of art," he wrote, "which is not useful, . . . which does not amuse, soothe, or elevate."

Through the invention of the radio, the phonograph, and all their rapidly developing forms, we have discovered that any music can be used as "furniture" music. We hunger for the company of a muse, and we get that companionship simply by turning on the radio or wearing a portable tape player and earphones as we walk, run, or exercise, and when we "pipe" music into the workplace. Imagine a new car without a radio—it would still be a useful contraption, but sorely missing the presence of the muse.

Whether music is performed live in a clean, resonant concert hall or is transmitted on a tiny radio in the greasy bay of a mechanic's garage, it is at all times educating us, to a greater or lesser extent, in civility. For again as Boethius taught, we are made up of music. The soul itself is fundamentally musical, complete with tonalities, moods (modes), rhythms, counterpoints, harmonies, and dissonances. Not all music is uplifting. Sometimes it echoes our sadness, at other times it teases us into lasciviousness. It always corresponds to some feeling or thought, and when we listen to music, if only as accompaniment, we are led to sensations that dispel the literalness of daily living, along with all its dangers and illusions.

In one of his most famous poems, "The Man with the Blue Guitar," Wallace Stevens writes: "Things as they are / Are changed upon the blue guitar." I'm sure Stevens is referring to the arts in general and maybe even to the imagination itself, implying that an aesthetic sense gives new dimension to ordinary things, but his words could apply directly to music. Music profoundly transforms whatever we are doing, and it affects us deeply, shaping our character and giving our lives dimension.

Like anything else, music of any style can be of excellent quality or thoughtlessly and unskillfully composed, arranged, and performed. It can be well recorded and produced, or it can be carelessly slapped together. Like all art, it can serve a person's personal or political agenda, or it can reflect a true artist's honest exploration of the nature of things. We might thank both Bach and Hank Williams for the egolessness of their art.

How extraordinary it is that something full of pleasure can be the very thing that most effectively guides and educates the soul and enchants everything we do, and how sad that we have largely forgotten the value of such things as live performance, music in the home, and quality in our "furniture music." It is a problem, though, that is easy to correct, for we have many unemployed musicians and music teachers waiting for us to rediscover a Platonic approach to education and a Satie-like re-enchantment of culture.

The ancient Orphic hymn to the Muses hints at the deep power the arts, and especially music, have to provide ordinary life with beauty and poetry. It states, as directly and as powerfully as one could wish, a lesson we badly need in a time of uninspired pragmatism—the absolute need of the soul for constant interaction with the muses:

> In all forms of learning, you give birth to pure strength of
>   character.
> You feed the soul.
> You make understanding true.
> You guide and govern the powers of knowledge.

Word

_Those who are in a frenzy utter many wonderful
things, which a little later, when their frenzy has
abated, they themselves do not really understand, as if
they had not spoken them, but God had sounded
through them as though through trumpets._

MARSILIO FICINO

Everyday Mythologies

THE WORD "MYTH," it is sometimes said, derives from the Greek word *muo*, meaning to close your eyes and shut your mouth, and is related to "mute." This etymology is questionable, but it does offer a good beginning as we consider the role of myth in the enchantment of ordinary living. Myth also means story, and so I ask myself, What is the story I behold when I shut my eyes, and what is the story I speak when I close my mouth?

The answer to the first riddle is "dream." I have to shut my eyes before I can dream, and the fragments of story I experience in dream are much like myth; for myth is not just a story to be told and heard but a story in which in some mysterious way I participate. A myth is no ordinary story; it's the kind you can believe in and give your life to. The story that some other person believes in wholeheartedly may be only a myth to you, and the story that literally means the world to you may be a mere myth to another person. But myth itself has the power to shape a person's life and vision.

Oddly, depending on your point of view, the word "myth" may be full of meaning, or it may be empty. Religion scholars treat mythologies around the world as life-shaping, sacred stories. Joseph Campbell taught that myth makes the cosmos meaningful, helps a society find an identity, guides the individual toward a life of value, and establishes for all a sense of religion. This is no small achievement for fanciful stories. On the other hand, in daily conversation, when we call something a myth, we mean that it has been shown to be false: It's a myth that living together before getting married prevents divorce.

Anyone who has studied religions closely may be dismayed to hear the word "myth" used disdainfully as a sign of falsehood. And yet there is an element in even the most profound, life-shaping myth that is not true in any ordinary, worldly sense. Mythology describes a level of experience so deep within or so transcendently beyond that it is rife with impossible feats and extraordinary characters, including monsters, heroes, gods, goddesses, angels, and devils.

If I wanted to tell a story about love in my life, I could describe particular persons, events, and times, or I could tell of feelings, intuitions, fears, and fateful developments. I might tell this deeper story in larger images, perhaps describing love, as the Greeks did, as a young male with great wings and an indomitable spirit, or I might color it in softer hues as the work of Venus, goddess of beauty and natural growth.

It's typical of the twentieth century to depict human events in purely personal terms. To get a larger picture, we take polls and do quantified studies. Compared to sums and percentages, myth may appear wildly irrelevant and unreliable, and so to appreciate it we may have to step outside the modern spirit that wraps itself in numbers, and find truth and insight of the highest order sometimes in profound stories that have no obvious relationship to the world of fact.

The quantification of life takes us away from the limited experience of the individual to a more general sense of the facts, but myth takes us even farther with its own kind of reliability. Once we realize that the stories of myth accurately depict the invisible and eternally valid structures of ordinary life, then we can appreciate not only their validity but also their absolute importance.

Many people study myth in school but never consider the stories as having any relevance to their own lives. I myself don't remember being taught much mythology in school, and I didn't take a real interest until graduate studies, when, with the help of the writings of scholars, I was able to see how helpful mythology can be in taking us beneath and beyond surface appearances.

Other problems, too, block a modern appreciation for mythology. Some get the impression when reading Jung, Hillman, and others that you have to know mythology to know the soul. Some just don't have a taste for myth, and so they give up on the whole idea of looking at the soul. Others become so absorbed in the details of the stories that they become myth experts and fail to look closely at the soul as described by the stories. My view is that mythology is one useful source among many for tracing the patterns life takes at a very deep level, and so I like to mix myth, dream, poetry and all the arts, occult studies such as alchemy and the tarot, and traditions of magic, as I look for ways to make sense of the subtle and various ways life presents itself.

The second riddle: What story do you tell when you shut your mouth? Many stories lie buried in our daily actions and behind the facade of our ordinary words. There is always a story within each story, a deep story that can be felt like a drum in an orchestra—not much melody, but plenty of rhythm and pulse. Sometimes you can glimpse a traditional myth or fairy tale in the simple story you tell about some ordinary event of the day.

These days, for example, I have a strong desire to protect my young daughter from the world. I imagine keeping her from school and teaching her at home. I realize, even as I entertain these thoughts, that I'm like the father of Siddhartha Gautama, who tried keeping his son within the confinement of his palace, and I know that Siddhartha became the Buddha only after he found his way out of the palace and saw for himself that suffering and death are part of life. Knowing the myth doesn't stop me from having my protective feelings, but it gives me insight and a way both to accept my feelings and not be too attached to them. Myth always provides both affirmation and distance, giving us insight and ideas about the ineffable patterns human life assumes.

As long as the stories we tell are personal and mundane, we will feel distant from our experience, and that distance may translate into disenchantment. Mythology is a special tool for enchantment, because it brings to mind the world of invisibles—the spirits, thoughts, and emotions that crowd our imaginations and yet are untraceable by personal or mechanical methods of detection. Mythology keeps our imaginations at a level where emotion and meaning have a home but where rational analysis has no entry.

One of the purposes of mythology is to transport our imagination to a level beyond the factual, giving full articulation to matters that can't be measured—things like love, hate, death, fear, and evil—and noticing themes that underlie surface events and understandings. The mythology of Venus, for instance, teaches me the importance of beauty, flowers, gardens, sensuality, and color in everyday life. The mythology of Mars reminds me that aggression has a place in every minute of the day and that my anger doesn't always have to be expressed or acted out blindly.

Mythology also leads us deeper into the complexities of our emotions and personalities. One of the first pieces of writing I ever published was an essay on Narcissus that explored the phenomenon of self-love through the subtle images of the myth. In many pieces I've written since then, including this book, I have returned to that story and have found there further nuances in the mystery of self-discovery. Certain stories, like the tales of Tristan, Nasrudin, Hamlet, Daphne, and the Virgin Mary, get a hold on me and don't let go. I'm charmed by them, and they become my teachers, revealing secrets about the outside world or about the inner life that would remain hidden without them.

Among mythological figures, I've been attracted especially to Artemis, the Greek goddess of integrity, virginity, and remote nature. The attraction seems to be deep-seated. Something urged me at an early age to withdraw from the world and live a celibate life in a religious order dedicated to the Virgin Mary. Interestingly, in some Artemis stories, the goddess is implicated with young men, the Jungian puer types. In those early years and even now, both enjoying and suffering her patronage, I feel a special attraction to the side of human life that Artemis prizes. I have been her Actaeon and Orion and Hippolytus, young male devotees of the goddess, hunting the world at large with a certain innocence and purity of intention.

I'm also drawn in quite a different direction to the gorgon Medusa, the fear-inspiring ruler who petrifies with her gaze but who is also pregnant with the winged horse, Pegasus, who springs from her body when Perseus finally reaches her protected lair and decapitates her. In my dreams I often find myself petrified, standing like stone in the presence of dire threats, and in life I sometimes feel frozen, unable to make a move or come to life.

Myth and Mythology

Myth is not exactly the same as mythology. Mythology is a collection of stories that range far beyond the limitations of nature and the personal details of human life. Myth is the living of those stories. Life may be moving along at a quick pace, when suddenly we find ourselves caught in a myth, stirring such deep feelings that we are shaken to our very foundations. Frequently as a therapist I felt that a disturbing problem was really the advent of a deep story or a mythic theme announcing its arrival. One's sense of meaning is shaken by the new presence, and the implications of a new narrative direction in life can be extraordinarily threatening, as well as promising.

Day by day we live emotions and themes that have deep roots, but our reflection on these experiences tends to be superficial. Instead of imagining with Plato that in disturbing moments we may be seized by a madness of soul, we talk about right-brain thinking, a far more materialistic and bland description, or we look for explanations in childhood and trauma. Mythology is not the mere depiction of various facets of human life; it reaches deep roots of feeling and conjures up the terrors and absolute delights that motivate life and make it passionate. To live with a myth-tuned imagination is to see the world and one's own life as enchanted and to have increased possibilities for a deeply based, passionate, and individual life.

Not only are our reflections often insufficient to account for intense feelings, but we may be living from a place that is too rational and dispassionate. Rainer Maria Rilke advises the young poet to "go deep into yourself and see how deep the place is from which your life flows." We could all take that advice, go deep into ourselves and discover how deep is the source of our everyday lives, and there we would find the environment of myth and begin to crave mythology as a suitable expression of our emotions.

Our modern tendency is to numb ourselves to the intensity of myth or to reduce it to psychological symbolism. The unconscious is a fabrication of modern thought that demythicizes our experience of life, rationalizing it by creating the illusion that grand pleasures and terrible torments are mere products of a field of sensation wholly psychological and therefore only tangentially, if at all, real. The modern person has a difficult time finding a place in life for dreaming and reflecting on dreams, because this is all unconscious material, of certain psychoanalytical interest but otherwise irrelevant. It's all symbolic, or coded, and it requires a good decoder if it is to find a place in the orderly life. Our very interior lives have become disenchanted by this rationalization of the soul's milieu.

Sensitive to myth and mythology, we might see that our dreams are real, taking place in a land both wild and civilized, in which our soul works out its destiny alongside life. We might appreciate the arts as offering us an indispensable mirror to that world of myth and dream, which is in some measure more important to the soul than any daily life event. And we might even see the work of psychotherapy and psychoanalysis as a serious guided entry into the landscape of myth, where our emotions are grown and cooked, our thoughts seeded and cultivated, and our life stories spun.

We could follow Rilke's advice even more radically by living every day from the deepest possible place, with full-blooded emotion and bold individual thoughts. We could love and hate, be angry and sympathetic in ways that would shape our lives into dramatic form, and then, of course, our very lives would become mythic. There would be a diminishing of the gulf between deep feeling and action and between profound motivation and behavior, and that passionate life would feel intoxicating.

The stories we would tell of those passionate moments of love, death, illness, and struggle would be our mythology, not because they would conform to some literary category but because they spring from our living of myth. *Fides quaerens intellectum*—Faith seeks understanding. We live the dimension of myth in faith, because that deep level teems with mystery and resists rational categorization. Only after we have been caressed and pummeled by the rawness of that life can we seek an understanding of it, and then, if we wish to preserve its intensity in the telling of it, we need stories that are grand in scope and expansive in language, imagery, and plot.

When we live a passionate life and with courage have touched the level of myth in our experience, we may have a pressing desire to tell the stories of that courage and of our occasional foolishness. We become storytellers and storylisteners, compelled in both directions, and we may feel outrage at the paucity of stories around us, demanding a real mythology that embraces both the eternal and the temporal sides of human experience.

Anthropologists tell of communities in which elders pass on traditional stories to the young as a piece of their initiation into the community and into life itself. But we, too, have both our stories and young people who need to hear our stories. This exchange of stories, when done with full intensity and seriousness, can bring myth into the lives of the young, who with myth in their imaginations are ready to deal with all the discrete, unpredictable challenges that life will present. It is only when we have an uneducated imagination that we are completely thrown by events and are made mute in confusion, addiction, and a hunger for meaning. Myth is an initiating story, an experience of the emotions and the imagination in which we make a significant shift from one level of awareness to another.

The Initiating Role of Myth

My father is unusually sensitive to the need for initiation in young people, maybe because he was a fine teacher all his life. Once, when I was just a boy, he had designed a plumbing fixture for the county morgue in our city. One afternoon he had to go to inspect the installation, some kind of vacuum breaker on an autopsy table, and he invited me to join him. When we arrived at the morgue, an official there gave us a tour, leaving the autopsy rooms for the very end. My mother didn't feel comfortable about exposing me to this side of life—once again the theme of the Buddha's father—but she let me go.

In our current world, where death and violence are so prominent and are depicted so graphically in the movies, it may not seem like much of an event to visit the morgue, but in those more innocent days it was an extraordinary thing to do. I still have strong images from that day, and I believe that my father succeeded in giving his son a small initiatory experience. It was a mythic visit to the realm of the dead, not unlike the descent of Odysseus into Hades, where he observed with a chilling sense of recognition those who had passed on.

Some mythic experiences are sexual: the first kiss or the first lovemaking. Some are rooted in fear: a near accident or a serious illness. Others might involve a discovery of the world: a first trip overseas, a visit to a big city, or the first experience of being in a place where another language is spoken. These experiences change a person forever, and in that way they are true initiations.

Myth gives a person the sense of living in a meaningful story, the feeling that one's life makes sense and has value, and these sensations are the basis for self-confidence and stability, purpose and poise. Without myth, life has to be proven valuable every day and is lived from profound anxiety; but with the awareness that one's life is grounded in eternal stories and motifs, one's own personal story begins to feel enchanted, and this feeling gives rise to a love of one's own life that is the cure for narcissism, insecurity, and self-doubt.

In these ways, myth is strong medicine in a time of personal anxiety and a tonic for a society used to living too close to the surface, too tamely, and insufficiently acquainted with the winged spirits, passionate deities, and terrifying demons that populate the imagination.

When a great story touches our heart, or when a mythic moment seizes us passionately, we feel caught in a spell—a sign of having been enchanted. Myth takes us deeper into our world and into ourselves, where we can live beyond meaning, led by an intensity the Greeks, with their extreme mythological sensitivity, called Dionysus. Myth is built on the paradox by which we find ourselves most fully in those moments of ecstasy—literally standing outside ourselves—when we give up self-consciousness and let the human story be told through our very lives.

Stories Imperfect and Impossible

THE MODERN AGE has its own magicians—not only advertisers, who can use language and pictures to charm people into buying their products, but television programmers too, who can cast a spell and make us sit in a chair for hours, staring at commercials and programs that we admit annoy or bore us. People sometimes confess that they're susceptible to television because they live such busy lives and feel a strong need to become, in the words of a remarkable modern metaphor that harks back to medieval notions of a vegetable soul, a couch potato. I have a different explanation for the mesmerizing effect of television: We are a people in desperate need of stories, so needy that we don't care much about the value of the story, as long as it absorbs our attention and stirs our emotions.

We watch the news, and we are given more or less true stories in abbreviated form, but stories nonetheless. We watch a television movie or a situation comedy, and we are drawn into stories that captivate even if we know them to be weak and poorly written or acted. We see interviews with celebrities or panels discussing politics or ordinary persons revealing their private lives, and we are invited into stories that may be either important to the community or of no relevance. The stories we see may be inspiring or pathetic, extraordinary or commonplace; regardless, we are enticed and entranced by the narrative.

Some stories have the special power of uniting an entire nation in common conversation: a Senate hearing, a celebrity murder trial, a natural disaster. Few things can draw millions of people to a common focus as well as a story that casts a spell and keeps the listener riveted. The country has been captivated by the trial of a celebrity accused of murder, the investigation of a president, and hearings to impanel a Supreme Court justice. An insurance company in a neighboring town recently bought a new television set and bolted it to the office ceiling so clerks could watch the current court drama. Such is the power of a mesmerizing story.

A newsperson is supposed to gather the facts of an event, but the real genius lies in writing the narrative. We read a newspaper for information, and yet we know that a reporter is someone who can follow up on a good story. Something in us pursues information and data with some passion, but the soul is always eager to hear another story.

Information is simply data to be stored for use, but a story stirs our deepest curiosity, usually about the plots, characters, settings, and tensions that give human life its texture. Every story seems to hold a clue as to who we are and what our lives are about. But maybe this is simply a fantasy about stories, one possibility among many. Maybe we enjoy some stories because they tell of lives entirely different from our own and have nothing to do with issues that concern us deeply.

Some stories take us away from ordinary experience, spirit us to a different time and place, and connect us emotionally to people who may exist only in imagination. A story may so seize our attention that we neglect our work or shorten our sleep just to remain close to it. Stories, so often enchanting and captivating, cast a spell, setting aside the concerns of practical life so the soul can be served. Some complain that the stories that appeal are escapist, but maybe we need to escape, to live, as Ficino would say, only partly in this temporal life, leaving a portion for some other time. *In illo tempore,* Mircea Eliade said: in that other time.

Stories offer a powerful way for the soul to find a space for itself and to have some relief from the pressure of just getting along in daily life. Stories allow us to reflect on our experience without being too rational, or to leave the limits of our own personal landscape altogether, offering the soul another of its most prized experiences—pleasure.

All these thoughts about stories may sound familiar and obvious, and yet our disenchanted culture doesn't seem to recognize how serious our need for stories is. We have plenty of sources of story—television, movies, magazines, books, church—and yet we don't always treat them well.

The Soul of a Story

Stories of substance usually revolve around the familiar soul themes: love, death, family, friendship, loss, community. The classic story of Oedipus, though filled with violence, focuses on conscience, ignorance, family emotions, and fate. The tale of Tristan and Isolde takes us painfully through the crossed intentions, complexities, and difficulties of love. *Hamlet* leads us into the dark fantasies of a disturbed young man as he tries to sort through the vagaries of his extraordinary destiny, and the story never really leads us out.

We talk about themes in stories as though they were fragments of a narrative cleverly fabricated by their author, but if we reflect more deeply on them, we might see that a theme is an aspect of being that emerges from some wrinkle in a life's unfolding and is not a mere literary construct. When fate or some other intentionality enters a life and has its effect, a theme arises. A story may begin with a person's birth, a wrinkle if there ever was one, a divine gift of life and personality. More ominously, it may begin, like Euripides *Bacchai*, with smoke rising on the horizon.

Our everyday stories may focus on a new job or a divorce or an accident we read about in the newspaper. These themes mark the intersection of human intentionality or understanding with grand or slight turns of fate. *A Slight Ache*, Harold Pinter's remarkably simple play, holds our attention on the foreboding presence in the neighborhood of a match seller. Like many people who can get stirred up by illness and surgeries, I'm sometimes tempted into telling the story of my appendicitis, a wrinkle that appeared thirty years ago.

Themes are interventions of providence that make an opening through which life can be born again and again, and the many stories with their many themes keep us aware of the liminality of everyday experience, the threshold where the human and the divine converse, or where closed human understanding is pried open by fate. It is at this very point of convergence that enchantment is born, for our stories grasp and contain the mystery of that wonder of divine incarnation that gives our lives purpose, meaning, and value beyond all personal, human capacity.

Wounded Stories

It isn't always easy to tell the difference between an enchanting story and a compulsive one. People who are defensive about a sacred story that gives their lives meaning may not be enchanted by it as much as cursed. For all the sentimentality sometimes poured onto stories, they can put a spell on people that freezes their humanity. We may be attracted powerfully to a story, even a personal story of abuse or victimization, and yet the story may serve only to cement our neurotic, petrifying fear and to rationalize the status quo.

Stories themselves are often deprived of enchantment, as when, on television and in the movies, they follow a proven formula, the zigzag pattern in which first the good characters succeed, then the evil ones dominate, then the good characters thrive, and then the evil ones return, and so on. Sometimes producers try various endings of a film on audiences and then select the most popular one based on careful demographic analysis. Years ago I had the idea of writing a film script, and so I sought out some books for guidance. I found they presented foolproof formulas of plot and character, and listed film after film exemplifying the given pattern.

The formula story is not really a story, because a genuine story has its own soul, its character, plot, and outcome, none of which is within the full control of the author. The word "author" comes from the Latin word *augere*, to increase, and is related to "augment." This is an accurate description of what storymakers do: They unfold, increase, swell out the characters and story lines that come to them. They assist in the birth of a story, which then has its own life.

Not everything that presents itself as a story is really a story. In a real story, the characters have lives of their own, and the manipulating intentions of the author are invisible. The novelist William Kennedy has said, "If I knew at the beginning how the book was going to end, I would probably never finish. I knew that Legs

Diamond was going to die at the end of the book, so I killed him on page one." Real characters can't survive in an atmosphere of formula, cliché, and emotional exploitation of the viewer or reader. In a real story, we are not distracted by the writer's cleverness from meeting characters who live outside the writer's purposes. A good writer introduces us to characters and their predicaments but doesn't truly create them.

If storytelling is going to play a major role in the re-enchantment of our society, we will have to be more careful in the way we treat stories. We could demand more artistry from the people who make movies. They not only often literalize subtle elements of eros and aggression into blunt pictures of sex and violence; they also present propaganda espousing certain prized values, instead of offering stories that give root to a moral sensibility. A good story may throw us into a quandary about what is right and wrong and who is on the side of good, and the resulting reflection may flower into genuine moral insight.

As a therapist, I have listened to many stories and believe that if a person can find a deeper story to tell, one less familiar and worn, less useful in maintaining the status quo, then something might happen that we call change. I have sometimes challenged a detail that doesn't ring true or have remarked on an emotional response I felt toward some theme or twist, all aimed at getting to the story within the story, or the story that wants to be told but is obstructed by the storyteller's intentions.

We are all bundles of stories that are interlaced, embedded in each other, and connected to stories of greater scope. One story, even an autobiographical one, only hints at other stories that could be told, and in that we are like an onion: peel off one story, and another appears, until it is no longer possible to tell a story.

On Not Being Able to Tell a Story

Modern academic interest in stories and the new popular enthusiasm for storytelling sometimes lead to sentimentalizing. Storytelling feeds community spirit and family intimacy, but it can also be painful and challenging, as when a person finds it impossible to tell the story of a childhood trauma or of an adult tragedy.

The stories we tell with good intentions and with as much honesty as we can muster may be incomplete, like a statue of Venus without arms or a nose. We may be tempted to make up for the lack by adding plastic parts, unnatural and anachronistic, but ruins of statues are often more beautiful than the originals. Our partial stories may be complete in their imperfection and their refusal to be brought to an end or to have all the necessary and required parts.

Twenty years ago my colleague Ted Estess published a fresh and challenging essay on stories, called "The Inenarrable Contraption," a strong defense of the story that refuses to be told. "We can get carried away," he says, "in our enthusiasm for stories and overlook the many ways life simply won't fit into a story. Writers sometimes give the impression that life is like a well-integrated plot. It may be that life is more often like a loose-leaf novel."

One problem with stories is that they sometimes have too much ego. A person might tell the story of her life as a way of defending her values or her understanding. As a way of explaining my fear of water, I sometimes tell the story of how I almost drowned as a child, but I don't think that conclusion is entirely true. I'm muscling the story to fit my present purposes, as does any adult who uses a story of the past to justify feelings of victimhood.

The more subtle idea that Ted Estess offers is that life is not a story but rather a collection of pieces waiting to be told as a story. A Beckett specialist, he mentions Samuel Beckett's idea that it would be satisfying to be able to tell the story of our lives, but it can never really be done. In his novel *The Unnamable*, Beckett writes: "there were three things, the inability to speak, the inability to be silent, and solitude." These are three things we don't allow much in modern life, which demands not only that we tell all but also that we analyze all that we've told.

My interest in inenarrability, the impossibility of telling some stories, lies in an acceptance of those moments in life when we must say something but a full story is not possible. We may have to speak in incomplete sentences, telling a story that trails off unfinished or moves in many directions at once. This nonstory told in incapacity is a valid expression of the soul and perhaps paints its condition more faithfully than an artificially well-rounded story that has only half its honesty. As Ted Estess remarks, "A hasty imposition of the story-form can undermine the attitude of wonder toward the relatively chaotic flow of life experiences."

Besides, there are modes of expression unrelated to the story form that speak well for the fragments of experience: journal entries, songs, poems, notes, letters, dream logs, diaries. It is sometimes more revealing to read a writer's letters than his or her essays and books, because fragments and pieces betray the soul, while a story may hide it as it serves the purposes of the ego.

A good story, of course, doesn't have to have an ego problem. It can be honest in conveying the provisional and fragmentary nature of experience. The stories we tell in our daily interactions can share the quality of honesty, ending where they will and taking their directions from the deep imagination rather than from intentionality and defense. Our stories can be excellent in their telling and yet imperfect in their completeness and their insight.

Perhaps because stories can reveal the soul in all its paradoxical splendor, industries are created whose intention is to bind the power of stories. We disenchant stories, for example, when we explain them away. A preacher can silence the song in a good Christian parable by reducing the story to a moral. A psychoanalyst can disenchant one's precious life story by explaining it according to theory. We can disenchant a movie or a poem by going first to a critic to find out what the story means, if it is good or bad, and where it fits in the current vogue of criticism.

If I were a critic, I'd try to probe deeply into the evolution of a movie or novel, inquiring into the fantasy of the producer or writer. What was he trying to accomplish? What kind of problems did she run up against, and how do these problems connect to the mystery of the project? Do the imperfections reveal something about the theme? If our criticism is nothing more than judgment on technical details, our very reflections will contribute to the disenchantment of our storytelling, but if our criticism has depth, it could add valuable elements to our constant search for good stories.

Eros and Aggression

Like the soul itself, a good story runs the gamut of emotions and experiences: love, death, harm, fear, sexual passion, and violence.

When these elements are deeply rooted, they give stories vitality and emotional power. And, when a story is not preoccupied with any single factor, they can coexist.

One reason sex and violence dominate our current stories is that these passions are not easily integrated into daily life. Sex is not fully woven into our regular life structures; instead it appears in unwanted pregnancy, in affairs that tear apart marriages and careers, and as an obsessive presence in films and other popular media. A powerful erotic story may tell us about romantic passion and sexual desire without itself being confused about the role of sex in life.

Sexually explicit stories may present the physical dimension of sex without its heart and soul, and then they only stimulate the imagination unfruitfully, leaving us hungry for more. They fail to satisfy the honest desire of the soul for eroticism. Supporters of pornography sometimes point to the lusty stories of the Bible as justification for their own tastes, but the biblical stories, like the sexy stories of myth and Greek drama, place sex within a context and not isolated as a physical phenomenon without a soul.

Some object to pornography because it presents sex as impersonal, but a soulful story is not always personal. The sex in mythology, in the world's religions, and in much great literature is not personal, yet it plants sex deep in the human quest for value, experience, and vision. The adolescents ogling adult magazines and the men and women who buy explicit videos and watch strip shows all represent our community's search for eros, an element we need more than any other. We need images of sex and violence just as we need portraits of families, romances, and mysteries, but the best images come in real stories, stories that don't merely conjure up our fearful complexes but give us a vision, a point of view, a taste of the story's theme, which remove us from the actual life problem while giving us an insight into its truth.

A story is not *about* anything; it is a world in itself. We need to get away from actual things and events to perceive the story that lies within them, and in that sense a story is always false, a departure from reality and an entry into the realm of imagination that forms the interiority of all facts and events. If people sometimes act on stories they have read, especially of sex and violence, the problem is not the dangerousness of stories but the folly of confusing fact with fiction.

The mystery evoked by a story is its heart and value, and our reflections on our stories, as well as the way we tell them, read them, and perform them, should be consonant with their mystery. Explanations and final interpretations, canonical collections and standard performances, are all inimical to the nature of stories. They all inhibit the power of stories to enchant, and it is enchantment that is a story's greatest gift.

Stories enchant not by allowing us an escape from the human condition but by taking us to a place of meeting where our personal lives and all that is beyond them meet. Stories enchant by opening up our vision to include the marvelous, the mysterious, and even the inhumanly evil. If we avoid the dark stories, we are avoiding real enchantment and self-protectively seeking refuge in sentimentality. If we are obsessed with the dark in our movies and novels, then maybe we have yet to discover the full reality of evil, and when we do, our stories may find their soul.

The enchantment of a story lies in its capacity to take us away from the rules, expectations, physical laws, and moral requirements of actual life, and that is why the best stories usually betray an influence of mythology, fairy tale, sacred parable, or some form of magic. A good story is like a wand brushing against the mind, sending it into trance, teaching it lessons from another land, beyond East and West, or from a golden time before and outside this realm of fact and history.

Books and Calligraphies

M Y THREE-YEAR-OLD daughter, who often watches me sign books at stores, likes to put her autograph on books too. She writes her name in zigzag lines, imitating adult script, and from the way she writes, it's clear that she doesn't have the slightest intention of spelling her name. When adults sign checks and other legal documents, they don't write legibly either, because a signature is not so much an expressive form of writing as a magical one.

Both signing books and a child's attempt at handwriting are magical acts of writing, because the purpose in each case is not to convey a meaning but to make letters for the sake of letters. A book has special value when the author's hand is visible, whether in handwritten draft, notes, or an autograph. My daughter's little mountains of script look more like exotic calligraphy and runes than communicative handwriting, and so when I autograph a book I try to remember that magic and put a runic spirit into the signature.

An autograph is not the only way to render a book magical. In many traditions, a sacred guild makes holy books, copies them, and illustrates them with elaborate care and imagination. *The Book of Kells* and the *Lindisfarne Gospels* are outstanding European examples, but the range of calligraphies, book designs, materials, and theories about books, alphabets, reading, and recitation around the world is vast.

Jewish literature pays special attention to the symbolic meaning of letters and words and their numerological values. Islamic care for the recitation and writing of the Qur'an culminates in the teaching that the calligrapher who can translate the word of God into beautiful letters will certainly go to paradise. In Islam, the first letter, alif, symbolizes Allah, and to write it is to represent the shaping of Adam after the form of God. For the Sufi, a dot in the calligraphy is equivalent to the primordial dot from which everything that has been created unfolds. Religion teaches us what pragmatic linguistics has forgotten: the very letters, sounds, and punctuations of words have considerable power.

If we want a real spirit to settle into our books and words, we could present them with care, art, and magic. Shortly after my book *Care of the Soul* was published, a woman told me how she read passages from it to her husband over a two-week period as he lay dying. Another woman wrote to tell the story of her miscarriage: her husband read to her aloud from one of my books during her long wait in the "post-op" area of the hospital. These are among the most moving of the many stories I've heard of the recitation, study, and artistic presentation of these books, and other authors tell me similar tales about the ritual use of their books. I have learned from stories like these that people do indeed understand the magic of words. If our culture at large daily violates the sacredness of language, these transgressions are made up for by the sensitivities of people who read to each other, keep elaborate and beautiful journals, and find myriad ways to preserve letters, books, notes, and scribblings.

Tibetans have preserved their scriptures on long oblong blocks; the Chinese on silk scrolls; Christian monks on colorful illuminated pages of vellum and parchment. Perhaps the most widely known illuminated religious book in Christianity, the *Très Riches Heures of Jean, Duke of Berry,* a beautiful collection of images, depicts hours and days, astrology and sanctity, and sacred stories and psalms, in a florid blend of letters and pictures. Today artists and owners of small presses sometimes publish extraordinary books in limited editions, but with rare exceptions we have lost a living tradition of the illuminated page, and with that loss has gone some appreciation of the magic associated with books.

Worldwide traditions honoring books, words, texts, letters, and reading remind us that each of these elements can be rendered in a way that is filled with art, piety, and reverence. In illuminated manuscripts and other books of beauty, it is impossible to separate art, religion, and magic, for all three work together to make these ordinary acts—reading and writing—truly enchanting. Maybe if we could realize again that books are primarily objects of magic, and only secondarily sources of instruction and ideas, we might manufacture them differently and allow them to make their considerable contribution to the re-enchantment of everyday life.

I still remember vividly the first time I saw the *Book of Kells* at Trinity College in Dublin. I was twenty and didn't know much about the history of books, but I had become an altar boy at ten and had spent years in the company of great leatherbound liturgical books, and each monastery I had lived in had kept beautiful libraries. I was familiar with leather covers, colorful ribbons, and textured endpapers. The *Book of Kells*, of course, raised the precious book to new levels of magic, and I stood there for a long time mesmerized by its intricate designs and extravagant calligraphy. This book was filled with musical script that could not be restrained in its improvisations on words and letters.

What if each person possessed just one such book, handmade, precious, full of beauty, and learned from it the magical potential in all books and all forms of writing and reading! Of course, the great painted books are too expensive for all but the wealthy to own, but there are still a few dedicated bookbinders making extraordinary volumes at affordable prices, and large publishing houses sometimes produce books of scintillating beauty. If nothing else, as individuals we could make one book for ourselves, or cover a prized volume with our own crafted fabric and design. The secret is to find enchantment in extraordinary instances where it exists, and learn how to bring that magic into our personal lives.

The Book Beyond and Within the Book

In many cultures sacred books are understood to be earthly versions of "heavenly books," like the divinely inscribed tablets containing the Commandments of Judaism and Christianity, or like the Qur'an, given to Mohammed by the angel Gabriel. Medieval monks said that the world itself is a book, *liber mundi*, to be read, studied, and enjoyed. In light of these religious ideas, we could reassess our view of books and apply the teachings of religion to our ordinary experience of reading.

When we write books, make them, sell them, and read them, we're engaged in a process that has its own deep mystery. When people profess heartfelt faith in the Bible or the Qur'an, they know intuitively that life is guided and shaped according to a "Book," and even when we make the small purchase of a new psychology book or a new novel at a local bookstore, we, too, are engaging in that mystery of the heavenly book. We may be filled with fantasy as we open such books, hoping to find a thread of understanding and a hint at the mystery of our own lives. Turning to the first page of any book is a ritual act, like going through the door of a cathedral or walking into a concert hall.

All books are variations on the books of wisdom we find in traditional religions, or the books that record our deeds on earth, or the book of our days. In some traditions, the story is told how as each person is born, the days of her life are written on a leaf that falls from the great Tree of Life. Beneath and beyond the facts and information offered in a book lies its mystery, its echo of sacred books, and it is in this hidden resonance that the book finds its enchantment. The heavenly book held so reverently in the hands of angels can be seen in any book, provided you have the eyes for it.

The Autonomy of Books

My house is filled with books, and each time I've moved during my life, the most difficult part has been the packing and lifting of those books. I have a small library compared to the collections of friends who have never had the attack of monkish simplicity that has overtaken me two or three times in my life, inspiring me to thin the ranks of my books. Now I wish I had all the books I have ever owned, because I'm beginning to see that any book might offer just one thread in the tapestry of understanding, and that one thought or image is worth the poundage and price of a book. Nor is meaning enough to explain the preciousness of a single book, for there is something about the mere existence of a book on the shelf that makes it a treasure and helps enchant one's life and home.

During a bookstore lecture I was once asked for suggestions of books to read. My recommendation, not to be taken literally, was to spend a year or two just looking at books, surrounding yourself with beautiful books, and only then return to reading them. We could restore an appreciation of the book as a holy object, forgetting for a while the meaning of its words, and perhaps evoke once again the special enchantment that attaches to books.

Many years ago I bought a manual of home bookbinding, purchased some red leather, and stitched together and covered a large book of empty pages for writing my dreams. I've never looked at a book in the same way since that little project. Knowing a book from the inside and being its maker was an initiation for me into a dimension of books that I would never find in any other way. It was another means of discovering personally that a book is an object full of mysteries and its making the work of magic.

There are several books on my shelves that I love to see there for their sheer company, although I have no intention of ever reading them. In some cases, I have several editions of a book, not because of variations in translation but because of different bindings and typographies. A book is a book, and in these times in particular, when information is becoming available in many different formats, especially on computers, it may be important to remember that a book is more than its text. It has a presence, and in that presence lies its magic.

We moderns make the mistake of giving too much praise and criticism to the author and not enough to the book itself. I have been shocked to discover how a book I write goes out into the world on its own, independent of my intentions. Many people have a significant role in its production, and I have no control over its lifeline or over the way it's read or treated. It has its own life, and to a degree I never would have imagined, I can only watch the book find its way in life, like a child separating from its parents.

The current tendency to shrink thought to information and analysis, to present data as though it were reflection, and to make books that lack the special soul that a book can have, is contributing significantly to the disenchantment of modern life. There is something narcissistic about information-gathering, as though the purpose in reading were to become a merely informed person or to acquire personal power through information. This kind of narcissism is what old texts used to warn against as "black magic"—the use of words for personal gain. Without art and magic, it's impossible to make a real book, and yet once a true book comes into existence and the narcissistic elements surrounding it are transcended, it is there to work its magic for millennia.

The Magic of Bookstores

If we are not magicians of the word, then our words make their own black magic and will haunt us and suck the life out of us. One of the reasons I gave away many precious books during one of my more ambitious moves was that I had accumulated a number that I thought were superfluous, and when it came time to sort them out, I made many serious mistakes, losing some books that I have now discovered are irreplaceable.

Bookstores sometimes make a similar mistake when they supply great quantities of books that are current and popular and yet don't offer books of weight, which would give their stores substance and interest. Recently I walked into a mammoth bookstore that was carefully mapped and posted, complete with comfortable chairs and many harried salespeople, but when I asked for a book on the arts and crafts movement in nineteenth-century England, I was directed to the single shelf the store had dedicated to all of art history. Next to this shelf I saw three long, heavily stocked aisles of cookbooks. A good cookbook is a real treasure, but here the imbalance of cooking over other categories gave the impression of shallow commercialism.

Even the children's section in this store was filled with commercial and artless stories, or new condensed, flat versions of great old stories. There is nothing more enchanting than a good children's book, but it's often difficult to find one in the midst of sentimental and poorly written volumes that are published in the tens of thousands.

The magic of a bookstore stems in part from the depth of literature it contains, its surprises and mysteries. If bookstores shelve only the best-sellers, the obvious classics, the most recent editions, and popular paraphernalia surrounding books, then the stores will all be alike. A magical store has its own character and spirit, and the browser gets the impression that the store will never reveal all its mysteries. To me, a bookstore should be more like a haunting castle than a government information center.

Extraordinary books of the world, like the illuminated books of the Middle Ages, exist either in single copies or in very limited editions. We probably publish too many books. If we published fewer, we might give them more attention and treat them with special reverence. With so many books around us, we take them for granted and forget the book within the book, the book that numbers our days and records our mysteries. We give attention to unworthy books or to volumes that lack the magic of a real book. Yet we could each find, purchase, and treat our books as if they are unique and deserving of honor. We could be highly selective in the books we allow into our homes and into our minds, and then we might resist the cultural trend toward the disenchantment of the word, keeping the magic alive in our own idiosyncratic ways.

Spiritual Reading and Spiritual Writing

When I was still living in a monastery, a fellow monk gave me lessons in calligraphy. I didn't pursue the art seriously or for a long time, but I learned enough to make me sensitive to letters, books, papers, and especially the artistic process of writing by hand. I don't expect everyone interested in re-enchanting their lives to turn to calligraphy as a necessary art, but it does offer lessons that extend far beyond the limits of a page.

In China and Japan, to name just two examples, calligraphy, which means "beautiful writing," is more than a fine art; it is a spiritual exercise. Alan Watts, the extraordinary writer on things religious and especially on the spiritual arts of China and Japan, emphasizes two lessons one can learn from calligraphy, an art that he practiced with devotion. The first is the patience and sense of time required to make a beautiful page. When I write at my word processor, I hope to produce a page in about an hour, but a calligrapher may take weeks and months, if not longer. The second lesson is to abandon the typical Western attitude that art is a means of conquering nature or materials. As Watts says, in the spirit of the East: "when you climb it is the mountain as much as your own legs which lifts you upwards, and when you paint it is the brush, ink, and paper which determine the result as much as your own hand."

The art of writing can be a means by which you learn lessons in the spiritual life. For my part, when people ask me what meditation practices I pursue, I feel at a loss because I know they hope that I have studied with a teacher from India or Tibet and that I have much ceremony and tradition around my practice. The fact is that I consider my primary contemplative exercise to be my writing, my daily work of putting words on a page and even enjoying the playfulness and graphic capacities of my computer. For me, play, work, and spiritual practice come together in the activity by which I make my daily bread.

I work in solitude, although the children often play just outside my door without excessive concern for quiet. I enter a contemplative state, focused, concentrated, open to influence. I have a Buddha, a bell, an idol, and a candle near me as I write, and a piano keyboard is within reach for moments when I feel the need to turn from words to music.

My desk is rarely neat—books and papers surround me—although for years I have imagined that one day everything will be in order. Nevertheless, in this state of writing, time changes character, so that the words that appear on the screen come from a different time zone. I try to put into practice further words of Alan Watts on the art of writing: "Thus the aimless life is the constant theme of Zen art of every kind, expressing the artist's own inner state of going nowhere in a timeless moment."

Reading is a similar exercise of "going nowhere in a timeless moment." In the monastic life, I learned to practice "spiritual reading." For years, fifteen minutes of a busy daily schedule were given to this practice—a way of reading in which information-gathering has no place but where you read for the edification of your heart and spirit. If you're doing "spiritual reading," you search for books and articles that feed contemplation, books that you may wish to read slowly, and more than once. I also found that reading in other languages helped slow the act and encourage special attention to the color of words.

As I write this book, I read pieces from many books in my own library. Frequently I withdraw to another room and take down a

volume from the collected works of Jung, or from the opulent encyclopedia of religion developed by Mircea Eliade. I'm always ready
to search through the writings of James Hillman, and when I need
inspiration I usually draw upon Rainer Maria Rilke, Wallace Stevens, Nicholas of Cusa, Emily Dickinson, or one of the several
intriguing Christian women mystics, Julian of Norwich, Teresa of
Avila, or Hildegard of Bingen. I'm drawn to Sufi stories and poems,
and I love the songs and poetry of Africa and Native America.

This reading in small pieces focused on the theme of the
moment I find deeply satisfying and meditative. Usually one book
or passage leads to another, and so my day is marked by moments of
spiritual reading in which the books, like the mountain, help me
climb. We could each learn from the world masters of writing and
reading how to allow these arts into our daily lives to work their
enchantment. For most people, the monastic practice of fifteen
minutes a day given to spiritual reading is easily within reach—on
a train or plane, in bed before sleep, even on a cassette in a car.

We could also practice "spiritual writing," whether in journals,
poetry, books, pamphlets, or letters. Writing out words gives them
body, and then they can speak to us in an enchanted way. A Chinese
priest said of the Buddhist scriptures, "If you do not understand,
write the sutra. Then you will see its inner meaning." Writing letters and journal entries is not just a way to communicate or to keep
a record; primarily it's a form of contemplation, while the act of
writing gives body, sensation, and beauty to our thoughts. Letters
were once written both as ways of being in touch with others and
for eventual publication. We might see all our writing in a similar
way: it has its immediate purpose, but it also exists as a "body" of
thought for other generations, or perhaps merely for its own incarnated, immortal existence as letters, words, and books.

One of the fundamental mistakes of modern times is to confuse the
mental life with the interior life. All that is interior is not mental,
not rational. As we read our books and write our letters and journals, we might realize that though we are using words, we are not
necessarily engaged in a mental exercise. Reason may be irrelevant
to the task at hand. The purpose may not be to be informed, educated, trained, enlightened, or taught. The magic of books and

words may bypass the mind altogether and affect the soul, whose interests focus more around eros and mystery.

The style of modern writing often ignores possibilities for enchantment, as when it attempts to be explanatory, self-expressive, and authoritative. Even business and scientific writing doesn't have to be wooden. I get the impression sometimes that technical writers are so focused on information that they don't give a thought to style, and so the volumes they produce hardly qualify as real books but are compilations of data disguised as books. As a result, our very fantasy of science and technology is weak in soul; the way these fields are presented suggests a world of dense fact and mechanics, hiding the rich imagination they had at one time and that is still waiting to be revealed.

Once we get away from the idea that the purpose in reading and writing is to exchange information, then we may discover the enchantment power of letters and books, and then, too, we may have an entirely different appreciation for all the paraphernalia of books and writing—libraries, bookstores, pens, computers, paper, illustration, typography, calligraphy, bindings, and scripts. We might become magicians of the page, learning both how to enchant others and how to be enchanted through the magic of words.

Sense in Nonsense

*T*O THE MAGUS, a word is precious when it makes no sense, when its power flows from its sound, its letters, and its physical presence. This potent magic in words may appear strange to us, who treat words as encoded meanings and use them freely for our own purposes. We grab a word as though it were a tool rather than an object having its own personality and life, but the magician shows that a word doesn't have to make sense and doesn't have to be used for expression but, as a precious thing in itself, can serve as a vehicle of enchantment.

Some of our most common phrases are terms of magic rather than meaning: "Thank you," "I love you," "You're under arrest," "Yuk." Obscene words have considerable power that can't derive from a mere mental definition. Freud's colleague Sandor Ferenczi was particularly interested in the psychology of obscenity, and he concluded that obscene words have power in part because they compel the hearer to imagine the object as though it were present. The words of poets have a similar immediacy; reading poetry in a language you don't know can have a powerful effect.

Words of prayer, holy words from various traditions—God, Allah, Yahweh—and words of damnation and curse all take power from a source other than meaning, and they show that letters and sounds can be not only expressive but efficacious. In the Catholic Church, the words of consecration at the Mass have the power, it is believed, to transform the bread and wine into the body and blood of Christ. Traditional words of absolution can free a person from guilt in the eyes of God.

On the other side of this picture is language that has lost its holiness and power. The words we use in daily life are often highly abstract and distant from our emotions, like the psychological jargon we sometimes employ for our most precious feelings and experiences. Once, in therapy, a man said to me, "I'm addicted to sex." I was taken aback by the language, since my clichés tend to be not quite up-to-date. I tried to imagine what he meant by addiction in this case—probably that he felt a compulsion about sex, that he was repeating behavior that didn't have much meaning to him and in which he had little will. But his word was interesting to me, not just because it was a current piece of jargon that didn't express clearly what this individual was going through but also because of the word itself. "Addiction" comes from the Latin *dicere*, to speak, but originally it meant a sentencing. Maybe this man felt sentenced to empty and repetitious sex; his addiction may have seemed like being imprisoned or in bondage.

The widespread use of the word "addiction" may suggest that as a culture we feel sentenced and compelled toward many things, as though we've been cursed. It may also be relevant that people seriously troubled with compulsions often report that they hear voices ordering them to perform certain repeated actions. I've worked with people who hear voices of instruction from the back seats of their cars and from the walls of their homes. In our compulsions and addictions lie words of power, and yet in day-to-day living our speech seems to have lost much of its expressiveness and effectiveness.

As always, we can be guided by our symptoms back to a life of soul. In this case, we could take greater care with our words, avoiding jargon, abstractions, and other empty language, recovering habits of speech and writing that are close to experience, that come from a place deep in the heart or are connected to a living and vibrant imagination. Words have considerable power to enchant, but they can also disenchant and contribute to the "de-souling" of society.

When I write, I try to invite onto the page words that well up from a deep place in me, close to my own private thoughts and not disconnected from my passions and emotions. I look for soul words rather than abstractions, and I don't care if I am less clear or even slightly off-center in meaning, provided the words have the power of their deep origins.

Whenever possible, I think of the history of a word as a good portion of its soul, and I may use a word in a way that is outdated and yet etymologically rich. A word has a family and a childhood, and these relationships give body to a word in a way that eludes a dictionary definition. We might find more enchantment and charm in our words if we paid less attention to their meaning and more to their personality, tending less to sense and more to the nonsense element in all language.

I remember a difficult conversation I once had with a friend. I couldn't understand why he had been talking in such an angry and unsympathetic way. When he went away without saying goodbye, I knew something was really wrong. I wasn't bothered by the meaning of the words that went unsaid, "God be with you," but by his withholding of the courtesy. "Goodbye" is one of those ordinary words that bless rather than mean.

The magical power of words is sometimes difficult to distinguish from the potency of words in prayer, a potency that is sometimes referred to as "performance power." We can learn from prayer, from common expressions of blessing and curse, and from the play of children, that words invite spirit into life.

I'm still entranced each time my daughter calls me "Da-Da," those primal sounds of intimacy, filled with sentiment and preciousness. We may be losing some of that enchantment as we continue to make our social relationships less formal. It may help the soul to call each other mister, doctor, aunt, uncle, and miss, and our politicians at least by their full first names instead of Tom, Bill, and Dick. Formality can be heartless and superficial, but it can also arise from a sensitivity to enchantment, because a title evokes a fantasy about a person that transcends the individual. I appreciate my lawyer referring to himself and his colleagues as "Attorney So-and-so." I notice in courtrooms that attorneys sometimes are uncomfortable addressing the judge as "Your Honor," and I won't be surprised if before long we disenchant this last remnant of potent civic ritual and reduce it to a bureaucratic procedure.

Enchanting Language

In traditional magic, there are several ways to render a word magical. Its sheer length, for instance, may liberate a word from the constraints of meaning, as in the incantation "ablanathanablanamacharamaracharamarach..." One wonders if medicine doesn't practice a form of magic by using long words difficult for the average person to pronounce. Lawyers, of course, are notorious practitioners of black word magic, and psychologists are not far behind them. The American Psychiatric Association's manual of disorders lists "multi-infarct dementia," characterized by "extensor plantar responses and dysarthria."

The traditional distinction between black magic and natural magic lies in whether a person uses magic for personal gain or as a benefit for the other or the community. The distinction applies to our way with words. By using an arcane vocabulary, is the physician jealously trying to keep the profession intact as a closed society, or is this language particularly potent, descriptive, and helpful to patients? What is the difference between using Latin words in church and in medicine?

In psychotherapy, I have always believed that finding good words to describe a problem might be more important than coming up with explanations and solutions. I am careful to distinguish melancholy, grief, sadness, loss, and heaviness; or love, attachment, desire, longing, wish, and dependency—each of these words has an emotional and definitional aura as well as a meaning. A story, dreams, and drawings might suggest still other words to describe interior sensations. A person may describe herself as being "lost," while her dream may show her driving off a main highway onto a small dirt road—a more specific image for the feeling. As we move closer to the emotion, language may fall apart, and all that's left are sobs, shrieks, or silence, as sense deepens into nonsense.

Poetry and Magic

Poets know well the magical power of words, and they focus on that potency, sometimes at the expense of meaning. Rhythm, assonance, rhyme, and other typical poetic devices can give words magical effect. A medieval recipe for the cure of sciatica reads: "Dialanga dracumino diazinsebri, equally much," while a cerebral poet like Wallace Stevens, who delighted in the sounds and rhythms of words, could write the following lines:

> Under the eglantine
> The fretful concubine
> Said, "Phooey! Phoo!"
> She whispered, "Pfui!"

Magical language is often playful, and yet at the same time it may have a portentous ring to it—magicians and poets are usually deadly serious in their play.

Nonsense may appear to limit the power of language by inhibiting meaning, but it may also express sentiments for which ordinary language is inadequate. In 1759, Samuel Butler expressed this idea, adding to "nonsense" the qualifier "learned": "For learned Nonsense has a deeper Sound, Than easy Sense, and goes far more profound."

The magician, the musician, and the poet all know how to circumvent the expressive nature of language to do other things with it, and so their nonsense is often sophisticated. For them, nonsense is not the absence of meaning but a positive quality that emerges when meaning is allowed to recede into the background.

Children's books often appeal to a child's appreciation of magic and simply disregard meaning. One of my favorite examples is Mimi Otey's *Blue Moon Soup Spoon:*

> Blue.
> Blue moon.
> Blue moon spoon.

And in the true spirit of magic, she provides a remarkable recipe that calls upon sea, sky, water, and earth for its ingredients:

> Moonbeams
> Sunny dreams
> Swallow feather fluff
> Salty seas Bayou reeds
> Dandelion tufts . . .

In a spirit similar to that of Samuel Butler, Hawthorne said: "I am writing nonsense, but it is because no sense within my mind will answer the purpose." Sometimes we're led into nonsense when we arrive at the limits of language to say what we think and feel. As a therapist, I never try to force a person to be clear in expressing feelings or saying what is troubling him or her. Especially in times of strong emotion, when the soul is virtually bursting out from a person's heart, I trust nonsense much more than intelligent statements. Whenever I find it impossible to express myself in words, whether with other people or in my writing, I turn to music or some other art where the meaning is muted and the pure power of the words intensified.

Sylvia Plath apparently knew something of the power of words to render aggressive feelings potent and effective. "Fury jams the gullet," she wrote, "and spreads poison, but as soon as I start to write, dissipates, flows out into the figure of the letters: writing as therapy." Perhaps what she is describing is therapy from the point of view of the writer, but the letters themselves find magical power from the fury that is pressed into them. Or perhaps the therapy lies in the transformation of emotion into magic.

Persons intimate with each other know that certain words "press their buttons," as they sometimes say, meaning that the words have special emotional impact, toward either love or anger. As a therapist working with couples, I sometimes have had the feeling that the two people with me were speaking their own language, and I had to discover their magical vocabulary to know what they were really saying to each other. I remember in particular one session with a couple when a shouting spree developed after one of them used a word that obviously touched them both like fire but had no meaning whatsoever to me.

When we explore language for its magic more than for its meaning, words can become enchanting. Poetry and song, of course, make good use of this power of language, but we might discover that even ordinary speech and letter writing open the soul when the boundaries of meaning are relaxed. We could talk to each other less directly but more expressively, being less clear and yet more evocative and effective. When we write letters we could give attention to the elements more important to the letter's magic than to its sense—in the choice of paper, letterhead, seal, envelope, handwriting or typography, image (remembering Ficino's emphasis on solar spirit, I use a simple child's ink stamp to place a sun on some of my letters), heading, greeting, and language. I find that letters offer a good opportunity to bend language in personal directions, and so I sometimes make up my own words and syntax when I write a letter and happily stretch the rules of grammar, hoping to elicit a degree of glamour.

Words as Objects

Magical language makes good use of the physical presence of words and letters. A letter or word on a doorpost may have magical properties, or words written in special script, or runes that comprise both a practical alphabet and magical lettering. Words may be chanted, kept in a special language, written in color, carved, baked into a cake, or hidden in a sacred code.

The widespread historical use of phylacteries, or pouches filled with words and worn around the head or some other part of the body, rings inscribed with magical letters and words, and potions made from written words suggest that there are alternatives to reading and speaking words and that these other ways may be more enchanting than the typical use of words for clear expression. Children love to see their name sweetly inscribed on a birthday cake, and adults, too, could take care not to lose the practice of inscribing rings, watches, and other adornments. If the original magic in such inscriptions has been reduced to empty formality or fussiness, we could restore the magic rather than lose the practice altogether.

Especially in our day, when millions of people are going "online" and doing their reading at a computer screen, we have to make a special effort to recall that words are objects and as such have magical power. Beautiful books and elegant libraries honor words as things, not as mere conveyors of meaning, and as anyone knows who spends time in libraries, they are not mere storage places for ideas. They truly are temples of the word, and their long wooden shelves, catalogs, reading lamps, and heavy tables all participate in the magic of the place.

I go to libraries not only to look up information but also to be inspired in my writing and to have an experience of sacred language. Some libraries are strikingly enchanting with their grand staircases and ornately framed oil portraits of local citizens, while others are quite simple and yet still magical. The tiny library in the town where I live is not without its magic, even though it doesn't have classical columns or encircling balconies. I can only conclude that the books themselves, gathered together and ritually placed on shelves, have sufficient magic and don't require another level of technical preparation.

Special inscriptions on public buildings offer real magic. The great letters carved into the facades of the Post Office and the Public Library in New York, the Lincoln and the Vietnam Veterans memorials in Washington hark back to a time when this aspect of word magic was widely appreciated. Someone in my nearby town had the imagination to place on many public buildings beautifully designed, colorful plaques on which are inscribed lines from local writers. Jung, one of the outstanding magicians of our time, had an incantation in Latin cut into the doorway of his house: *Vocatus atque non vocatus deus aderit*—Summoned or not, a god will be present. Two strong advocates of enchantment in England, William Morris and Eric Gill, showed in their work how overwhelmingly beautiful letters can be, whether they are cut in stone or printed carefully in a crafted book.

Liquid Language

Some magical recipes call for the eating of words. Arnold of Villanova, at the beginning of the fourteenth century, describes an exorcism in which the opening verses from the Gospel of St. John are placed in a liquid, sometimes holy water, and then drunk. Language can be used as a potion, taken in without passing the portals of the mind and the interpreting intellect. We can ingest words, make them part of ourselves, without necessarily understanding them. Memorizing poems is a form of language ingestion, and the recital of a poem "by heart," as we say, has a special magic.

It's curious that magical recipes call for soaking words in liquid so that they can be ingested. Our words often need liquefying, for they tend to become rigid and brittle. I have had my lifetime's quota of dry books, and now I'm in search of only "juicy" volumes. Imagine soaking the many prescriptions you learned as a child in a liquid imagination that would render them flexible and digestible. This is one way to accomplish the alchemical *solutio* that Jung presents in his writings as a necessary stage in which the hardness of the heart is softened in the liquidity of various baptisms.

Our daily language, too, could be less dry and more liquid. The language of business, government, and law is filled with rigid, brittle, indigestible words whose value stems only from the dictionary or the personal manipulative intentions of their users. How many ordinary people can comfortably fill out an income tax form, or sign a lease, or contract to buy a home? These words we use daily are formal but not enchanting, and they all beg for some moist magic to make them palatable to the average person. A good poet shows us how formality serves enchantment, and I see no reason why our ordinary legal documents can't be more like the Declaration of Independence, a good blend of legality and stirring, liquid language.

The alchemical *solutio* offers a good way to imagine living a liquid life. In the alchemical process, *solutio* comes early and serves the important function of breaking up into parts what has been fixed and perhaps too tightly packed. In therapy one usually senses an important phase of *solutio,* a time for allowing intransigent problems and issues to soak in the liquid thoughts of therapeutic conversation. The purpose in that stage is not to get somewhere or to achieve an insight or arrive at a conclusion, but simply to liquefy our questions, assumptions, and intentions.

Discussion, conversation, journal writing, sketching, walking meditatively—these are but a few of the practices anyone can incorporate into daily life that offer a watery solution in which our problems can dissolve and break into manageable pieces. The magic in these methods does not lie in logical conclusions we may arrive at, but in the less conscious developments that arise out of the talking, walking, and sitting. An enchanted few minutes of heartfelt conversation may have more effect than hours of analysis.

Beyond Functional Language

Several years ago James Hillman published an essay on language, in the journal *Corona,* produced by my friends Lynda and Michael Sexson. In it, he talks about the kinds of stories we need especially in our time, and as the essay goes on, it moves toward an appreciation of a certain kind of nonsense. The stories we need, he says, are useless ones, in which we might be "trotting out old words and obsolescent structures, implanting the ditty and bits of nonsense rhyme." He argues against plain and simple language, which he says is appropriate for "prose that tells you how to assemble a camp bed."

We may evoke the magic in words by their placement, capitalization, rhyme, assonance, intonation, emphasis, and, as Hillman suggests, historical context. When my wife and I were married, we knew we didn't want to make up our own language for the ceremony, because we felt that old and antiquated language has the weight and magic of another era and is not limited by current and passing tastes. We expected that there might be more magic in the musty atmosphere and the archaic tonalities of tradition. We wanted some "thee"s and "thou"s to give those important words weight and to set them apart from the vocabulary we might use to assemble a camp bed.

The Catholic Church's decision to stop using Latin in the liturgy may have helped people understand the ritual texts, but at the cost of some degree of magic. I grew up hearing words like *Kyrie* and *Dominus Vobiscum,* and until I studied to be an altar boy I didn't know what they meant. Yet the magic in these words was powerful. I remember serving at a solemn Mass when I was eleven years old, holding the hefty red Missal, the book of prayers and rubrics used for the ritual, on my head, while the priest chanted words from it. There was no lack of "performance power" in those words and in that reverence toward a book.

The spirit of our times tends toward pragmatism in language. We like typography without serifs, nouns, as Hillman says, without too many adjectives, and clear argument rather than the ornate exploration of an idea. Our newspapers shrink the size of their columns annually, and one wonders what they will look like in fifty years: perhaps a sentence for each item, or maybe not even that much.

We are also surrounded by acronyms and abbreviations, which are not magical nonsense but rather hyperlogical, symbolic shorthand for strings of bloodless vocabulary. An internet guide teaches that TCP stands for Transmission Control Protocol and may be used as a verb—"to TCP." If ever a phrase needed soaking overnight in a big tub of water, this is one.

The magic implicit in language, known to be powerful in prayers and enchantments, is being lost at a shocking rate. At the same time that dry technical language is entering ordinary conversation, the old explosive words of curse, damnation, and sexual allusion are being tamed and used as simple punctuation in daily speech. There is little left for our emotional explosions except to turn to physical violence.

The magus knows well how to curse and knows that words and letters of curse need not, and perhaps should not, make sense. The *Picatrix,* an old compilation of magical formulas and theory that was influential in the development of Renaissance magic, gives some good examples of cursing. The following is one of its many colorful spells:

"To make a place unlucky when you don't want it to be inhabited: Make these figures on a lead amulet with the brain of a pig on the day and in the hour of Saturn, when the second part of Capricorn is ascending and Saturn is present there. Put the amulet in the place that you want to remain uninhabited. Then the evil power of Saturn will flood into it, and no one will live there as long as the amulet stays."

If the figures described are to have powerful effect, they have to be written in pig's brain and at the proper dark hour. Timing and choice of medium are important in language and could make our daily vocabularies more enchanting and less technical. I find words like "codependent," "dysfunctional," and "wellness"—current and popular words in the psychology field—either too technical or too sentimental. Words get some of their blood from resonance of the past, while newly fabricated words often feel thin and brittle in comparison. We need every opportunity available to get blood (and pig's brain) back into our language in order to recover enchantment in the way we talk to each other intimately or in public life. If a word has soul, it will be powerful in daily use, but if it has no soul, it will be manipulated by those who want to exploit it for their own purposes.

The return of soul and enchantment to language is not a difficult task—a little flourish, some grace and color, and a love of language go a long way—but we have to be careful not to let the great hollow language of bureaucracy and technology creep into our daily intimacies. Many of our personal problems stem from the loss of individuality, expressiveness, intimacy, and power, and potent, spellbinding language can help us keep and restore those important qualities. The magicians of the past teach us that language is not a code for meaning; it is a powerful thing in itself that has its own color, passion, and magic.

Sacred

I was raised by the song
Of the murmuring grove
And loving I learned
Among Flowers.

FRIEDRICH HÖLDERLIN (*tr. T. Cole*)

The Holy Well

MY DAUGHTER WAS one and a half years old and my stepson four when, one July, we went looking for St. John's Well, in the west of Ireland. Taking seriously St. Anselm's theorem *Fides quaerens intellectum*—Faith seeks understanding, my family lives primarily by intuition. First, we place faith in our inspirations, and then we find out if there is any good way to understand what we have done. My wife had the intuition that we should go to County Kerry, and so without much ado we found ourselves on the self-proclaimed westernmost coast in the world, in a pasture that a small guidebook assured us housed a holy well.

If you had asked us before the trip why we were making the expensive and arduous voyage to Ireland with two small children, we would have answered: "We need to see a holy well." That is all the motivation we needed, and yet I felt a special weight, and not just my daughter in my arms, the day we roamed the ruins of an old castle, accompanied by sheep who roamed the grounds like owners, dispassionately chewing their grass and keeping their eyes on us as we moved from one excited discovery to the next.

"Walk down from the castle to the old coast guard boathouse," said the guidebook. And so we did. "Then go back one hundred yards to the gate of a pasture." I didn't know why we had to go first down the hill and then back up, especially with my daughter adding to the exercise of the climb, but, good Catholics all, we followed directions and did what we were told. We traced the line of a dilapidated fence and then discovered the holy pagan hawthorn tree that guarded the sacred spot. As we descended into the area around the well, our feet got wet to the ankles, but we were all impressed and moved to behold the gravelike oblong of water, edged with stone, at the base of the broad sheltering tree.

The children blessed themselves unselfconsciously without urging, and then they leaped into the water. My wife and I took the holy water on our fingers and blessed first the children and then each other. We all appreciated the mixture of pagan and Christian spirits that clearly haunted the place, and we knew without discussion that the trip had been worth the effort. We also discovered new meaning in the word "enchantment," because we knew then and there that this brief visit would stay with us all our lives.

This was a vernacular trip, because Ireland plays a major role in each of our lives. My wife's grandparents are buried in lovely Connemara, and my family has its roots in Cork and Tipperary. For two years I lived in Ireland as a friar in the Servite Order and visited relatives whose charm assured me of the value of my heritage. As a perceptive therapist once told me, Ireland is not just a place in my memory; it's a geography of my soul.

Pilgrimage or Tourism

What is it that inspires a people to discover and then to enshrine a holy well? Imagine such a thing happening in modern America, in a city or even in the countryside. Where are our holy wells? Apparently we think we can live without them, and without our own sacred places and elemental grottoes. Yet the preservation of holiness is a fundamental and life-enchancing skill that may take generations to develop and preserve. The loss of that skill may be a threat more serious than any failure to keep technology developing at a rapid pace or to pave our land with highways.

An enchanted experience can be renewed and preserved by enshrining it in some tangible form to serve memory and contain the spirit of the original event. At one time long ago someone came upon a nymph, fairy, or holy spirit at that spring in Ireland and had the presence of mind to enshrine it in stone and protect it from profanation. This technology of enchantment—knowing how to preserve the possibility of magic—is one that we have largely lost, owing to our present obsession with less sacred forms of technology.

In the modern world, *techne* is focused on machinery, and power is aimed at a material product, but there are other kinds of technology, which work with materials, with the purpose of giving something to the soul. Cathedral builders were engaged in this kind of technology, as are shamans who know about pipes, drums, and stones. Probably the closest we come to a soul technician is the artist, but even our artists often lose sight of their role as enchanters and play into the dominant cultural values, either focusing in on their own technical concerns, or reacting to technology by emphasizing personal expression. Whenever we make something for the soul, we are engaging in a magical technology that assures us a degree of enchantment.

Visiting Sacred Places

The secularization of culture manifests itself not just in business that is run on purely pragmatic grounds or in government that is rooted in eighteenth-century rationalism but also in the lack of sacred places of pilgrimage. Imagine someone from another country coming to the United States on a pilgrimage in search of holiness. We do have our sacred places, chiefly ruins from the Native American culture that was in place before Europeans and African Americans arrived, but they are not as ubiquitous as in other places.

Our version of a holy well is an inn where George Washington slept or John Kennedy's grave site. These are true sacred places, but they are based in recent memory and are related to persons, not to figures of pure, holy imagination, like St. John or the Buddha. We travel to the Grand Canyon, to Niagara Falls, and to other wonders of nature that bless our land, but it's a question whether these visits are truly pilgrimages to places of exceptional holiness, or whether we are visiting mere extraordinary sights.

Niagara Falls is a good example of a once sacred site turned into a tourist attraction. The native people offered their crops, game, weapons, and ornaments to the Niagara River and its falls, and even, according to their stories, made human sacrifice. A moving tale is told of the annual rite in which a young woman was sacrificed to appease the spirit of the thundering waters. She was placed in a white canoe filled with flowers and fruit, and wore white flowers on her head. She would herself guide the canoe toward the falls, and her sacrifice, it was believed, assured her a place in heaven. The last young woman to give herself to the rite was the daughter of a famous chief, who, overcome with grief, followed her to his death in his own canoe. According to the story, the chief and his daughter, the Maid of the Mist, still dwell in a crystal cave under the falls.

The Irish poet Thomas Moore visited Niagara Falls in July of 1804 and wrote to his mother about the impression they made on him, and his language, though too florid perhaps for current tastes, uses words that I use in this book as signals of enchantment: "I felt as if approaching the very residence of the Deity; the tears started into my eyes; and I remained, for moments after we had lost sight of the scene, in that delicious absorption which pious enthusiasm alone can produce." Later in the letter he goes on: "My whole heart and soul ascended towards the Divinity in a swell of devout admiration, which I never before experienced. Oh! bring the atheist here, and he cannot return an atheist!" If we don't take this last sentiment argumentatively and philosophically, it suggests that the falls offer religious transformation and an encounter with the numinous — no small achievement in a society short on numinosities.

Contrast Moore's emotional letter with a recent article in the *New York Times* indicating that merchants at Niagara Falls are in favor of instituting gambling there because the attraction of the falls isn't enough to draw tourists. Once we lose real enchantment, we come up with spurious ways to fill the gap.

Wells, springs, fountains, and pools come forth from beyond the sphere of human life, from deep in the mysterious earth, and so they convey a special spirit. The little spring in Ireland in which my children waded was not unlike the one Ezechiel saw in his vision [47:1]: "The man made me cross the water which came up to my ankles." Ezechiel was told that the eastward-flowing brook that streamed from the Temple would provide fish in its fresh waters, fruit from its overhanging trees, and healing from its plants — an enchanted cornucopia. Springs like the one in Ireland have similarly been honored as places of healing, oracle, renewal, and rejuvenation. Clearly, we need all these gifts but have forgotten that they are available in the simple holy places nature provides and enter our lives through honest piety and the tending of sacred places.

Today we look for healing and renewal in the offices of p
cians and therapists, when we could be out looking for holy wells
and enchanted groves that fortify the soul with their natural mysteries. The holy well is to the well-being of the soul as natural foods
are to the health of the body. Without natural religion, the soul
shrinks and fails, and all our problem solving offers only a small
portion of the nutrition it needs.

We have churches and temples, some would argue, and we don't
need pagan nature rites. The problem with churches and temples as
the only places of religion is that they tend to be merely spiritual,
and they don't speak directly to the soul. Why do people flock for
their soul needs to psychotherapy rather than to church? Because
church has become either so transcendent and mental, or conversely, so uncontained in its emotionalism, that the soul is not
served. Religion has adopted the dualistic philosophy of the times,
falling into the common divisions of mind/body, intellect/emo-
tion, right brain/left brain, and moralistic belief/amoral behavior.
Throughout history the soul has been discussed in a trinitarian
context where mind and body find their humanity in a third place,
the soul, where behavior and belief are deepened in imagination,
and where emotion and mind join in intelligent, deeply felt values.

Standing at St. John's Well, I thought long and hard about the
blend of pagan and Christian sensibilities that the place represented.
I knew that historically and even now the very mention of paganism sends a chill up the moral spines of many religious people. Yet I
not only see no necessary enmity between these two basic postures
in life; I see one needing the other. My prayer at that moment was
for an ecumenical spirit that is not much discussed: a reconciliation
of differing life philosophies and not just churches, of religions great
and small, and a renewed appreciation for neglected and despised
paganism. I don't expect to see this ecumenical wish understood or
fulfilled in my lifetime, but I have some hope for the future of the
soul's natural religion.

Reclaiming Paganism

When I lived on the farm in New York State during my childhood
summers, we didn't have running water. Water for washing and

general cleaning we gathered by a pail tied to a leather strap and dropped down into a cement cistern filled with rainwater behind the kitchen. Drinking water we got from a spring a hundred feet up the hill behind the house. On the hottest days of August, this spring had cool, fresh water, and after a day of taking in hay from fields across the road, this water was pure delight. But the spring was always mysterious to me. Only certain adults approached it and drew out water. I had the impression it was so deep that a child could fall into it and never be seen again.

Where I live now we have a dedicated spiritual community down the road a mile, and on their land they have a deep circular pit lined with stones, a hole they say was dug and walled by Native Americans who knows how long ago. It's twenty feet deep and looks even deeper, a dry well now, but one that lets you know that such things touch a chord of awe in the imagination.

Maybe it takes a pagan sensibility to see the potential religion in a grove of trees or a bubbling spring. St. John's Well is dedicated to a Christian saint, but like so many Irish antiquities, it has a pagan background. It isn't unusual in Ireland to find stones written in pagan Ogam script that at a time in distant history was partially scratched out and replaced with a cross. When I use the word "pagan," I'm thinking of a spirit or attitude, a fundamental way of imagining life, rather than a doctrine, beliefs, or a set of morals—a religion rather than a church. In essence, it sees spirituality in infinite variety and in all aspects of nature and culture.

The well behind the family farmhouse was a source of pagan piety. Recently, when with family members, amateur archaeologists in search of family remains, I sorted through the ruins of the farmhouse, we became preoccupied with finding that mysterious well, and I believe our obsession with it was due to deep pagan reverence.

Etymologically, "pagan" refers to a country person or an outlying villager, in contrast to the city dweller. The pagan is closer to nature, less caught up in the activities of city life, perhaps more prone to superstition, natural magic, and the spirits associated with trees, waters, and stones. The sophisticated city dweller has long felt superior to the country bumpkin, and perhaps there is some of that superiority in our distrust of paganism, but the division between the two runs, I'm sure, even deeper.

The *American Heritage Dictionary* describes a pagan, first, as one who is not a Christian, a Muslim, or a Jew; second, as a heathen, someone who has no religion; and third, as a hedonist. According to the first definition, the Dalai Lama is a pagan, as are many millions of people all over the world who piously and with many fervent traditional rituals and prayers praise God.

The second definition recalls the etymology, because a heathen is someone who lives on the heath, in the outskirts, someone whom the dictionary explains as having no religion. Here the bias is toward the city dweller, who is above rituals and myths that are intimately connected with nature. From the sophisticated city dweller's point of view, such rites are not even considered religion.

The third definition, paganism as hedonism, the philosophy or advocacy of pleasure, betrays further bias against paganism and our problems with it. Our culture distrusts pleasure in many ways, even though it often translates the pursuit of happiness as the opportunity to live a pleasurable life, and even though the modern person works long hours to afford a pleasure cruise or to have the latest conveniences and the plushest automobile. Our stated values and deeply felt longings in this area are often in conflict, and as a result modern life often falls into guilt and hypocrisy over pleasure. Certainly, this theme plays a role in our difficulties with sex, and indeed the long history of our belligerent encounter with paganism centers on matters of sex.

Just recently I was presented with a book on the Old Testament that was touted as an insightful reading of its ancient wisdom and applicable to all. The book did in fact begin with a measured and insightful reading of the ancient texts, but then it picked up the old theme that the God of the Old Testament is superior to the pagan gods and goddesses because they were described as always engaging in war or making love. This polemical theme you find scattered throughout the writings of early Christian theologians, from whom, oddly, we get much of our knowledge about Greek and Roman paganism.

Our culture's anxiety about paganism reflects an archetypal tension. Deep within each of us, a battle takes place between the transcendent longing for moral purity and the more mundane desire for full participation in life. The latter often presents itself as an invitation to pleasure, accompanied by the complexities that such an affirmation of life entails. We sometimes shy away from complexity, hiding in moral certitudes, and sometimes, perhaps in compensation, we let ourselves sink into immediate pleasures so that we don't have to deal with the principles, ideas, and transcendent elements in our own philosophy and vision.

Spiritual values and a willingness to live a full life together create passion and vision. But for some reason we have kept passion and principle divided, feeling the conflict in personal struggles and social tensions. We often assert values of transcendent principle and belief, while searching desperately for passion, and for this splitting of life we pay the price in personal guilt and social intolerance.

These tensions came to a point for me in the enchanting moment when with my family I literally stumbled across St. John's Well. That water was both pagan and Christian, and I profoundly appreciated the baptism and blessing it offered. I felt determined in that moment to find other such wells, to live by waters so holy, to live in a land that can still "see" the spirits that veritably arise out of nature's springs and caves, and to be blessed with a daily life that is thoroughly pagan without any corrosive effect on my fated and cherished Catholicism.

Everyday Shrines and Tabernacles

WHEN I WAS in elementary school I served as an altar boy in the parish church, and I'm certain that the experience of being so close to the life of the priest and to the holy objects of ritual had much to do with my decision at thirteen to enter a seminary with the idea of becoming a priest.

I remember being awed by the mystery of the Eucharist—the priest consecrating the bread and wine, revealing it solemnly to the people in attendance, eating and drinking the sacred substances himself, and then distributing them to the people. After communion was finished, the priest would gather up the remainder of the bread and place it in the tabernacle, a precious box with a secure door, covered with an ornate mantle of satin.

When Mass was over, the tabernacle was still the focus of reverence, and a sanctuary lamp burned red and steady whenever it held consecrated bread, the body of Christ. One would genuflect whenever one passed the tabernacle, and when the lamp was lighted, one would never speak above a whisper in its presence.

This was my first formal experience of a remarkable "technology" that religion has practiced for ages all over the world: the making and tending of shrines. The word "shrine" is from the Latin *scrinium*, a box or container, and the idea of shrine lies at the very heart of the religious impulse. It is also a primary means of sustaining an enchanted world.

Above all, a shrine gives presence to a felt but not always visible sentiment or realization. Significant intuitions and emotions about finding a place for the holy urge themselves toward some kind of expression, and a shrine comes into being. The shrine may be something quite ordinary, as when you visit a remarkable place, take some photographs, and then come home and hang a framed photograph of the place on the wall. That photograph is not only a reminder of a past experience; it also *captures* the spirit of the place and translates it to your own home. I use the word "translate" intentionally, recalling the traditional religious practice of moving the body of a saint from one place to another—the "translation" of a holy person. Translation is a form of the word "transfer," and a shrine does indeed transfer the holiness of faith and whatever spirit is captured by sacred imagination to a particular place for memory and honor.

My personal photographic shrines include a picture of the Arno River in Florence taken on a rainy day. The Ponte Vecchio stretches across the river in the center of this photograph, and a lone sailor rows his long, narrow boat on one side. Another photograph I've placed in a special wooden frame was taken in Rome at the Capitoline Museum. I was there on a crowded day, but no one stopped to look at the object of my search, a second-century sculpture of Eros and Psyche, Love and the Soul, embracing each other. Both of these photographs are shrines that capture certain elusive and eternal themes I found in Italy.

Spirituality's Place

One of my shrines, as I've mentioned, is a six-inch soapstone statue of the laughing Buddha. Little monks crawl all over his massive body, like children around a father. This statue, usually surrounded by stones I have found here and there, holds a spirit that I cherish, something to do with spirituality and humor, children and play. And yet the statue is not sentimental at all, but rather full of dignity and divinity.

To an extent, shrines like this one represent the art of memory, an ancient practice described affectionately in the writings of Frances Yates. Memory, she reminds us, is not only personal. We can remember not only the events that have taken place in our lives or in our collective history but also enduring and eternal realities. In the spirit of Plato, who said that all genuine knowledge is remembering, we can keep calling to mind the secrets of human life, nature, and existence itself. My laughing Buddha remembers the cosmic humor that undergirds all experience, both suffering and joy.

Modern people trust abstractions, and so they might prefer to read books about humor and religion, keeping the ideas in their mental storehouse. But non-modern people remember in a more concrete manner, building shrines and making all kinds of other religious art as a means of maintaining awareness of the eternal things. A by-product, perhaps, of that concrete form of memory is the opportunity for enchantment, because objects that encase eternal spirits themselves are given honor, and the spirit of the shrine permeates the place and the people who come into its presence. Catholics genuflect at the sight of the warm-burning sanctuary lamp, and they hold their tongues, aware of what they call the "real presence."

A spirit tends toward diffusion and so sometimes needs condensation. Ficino described the comet or star that guided the Magi to Bethlehem and the birth of Jesus as the condensed light of angelic intelligence. In a similar way, the spirit of a place or many other kinds of spirit can be focused and compacted into a shrine, where we can sense its intensity and recognize its personality.

Jung's Bollingen stone is an example of such a shrine. This is the stone, intended to be the cornerstone of a building, that was delivered to him by mistake, and yet he saw a more mysterious use for it than was originally planned. It was a cube on which to carve words and images. "I began to see on the front face, in the natural structure of the stone, a small circle, a sort of eye, which looked at me. I chiseled it into the stone, and in the center made a tiny homunculus."

This homunculus, or little man, is the spirit of the stone urging itself into fuller manifestation in Jung's carving, and that spirit has been present in Jung's psychology and is present long after his death. The shrine of Bollingen is now available to us all, and as pilgrims we can travel to that place just to be in the presence of Jung's spirit. Some complain about the worship of Jung—I myself have complained in print about making Jung into a saint—but maybe he is a saint. Certainly the spirit that animated his writing is enshrined in the Bollingen stone and has at least the rudiments of a personality etched there.

It may appear eccentric of Jung to insist on keeping a stone that had been brought to him by mistake, then to carve obscure sayings and images into it, but in a world where the pressure to be normal and adjusted is heavy, enchantment may require eccentricities of many kinds. We could all discover the importance of making our environment teem with images that sustain the soul. Everyone should have at least one Bollingen stone or its equivalent near one's home—each person is drawn to a particular fund of images and to special ways of capturing those images.

Black Elk, the Oglala Sioux who recorded his experience of visions, described how his images were painted on tepees and on his shirt, how they were sung and danced by his people. Ficino recommended painting images on ceilings and walls, and it is said his academy walls were filled with images that reminded his circle of its own vision. Stephen Huyler describes women's practice in India of painting ephemeral images in rice pigments on the walls of their houses and on their streets, as an invitation to the gods and goddess to make a home among them and to bless them.

By giving concrete expression to our interior imagery and sentiment, whether good or evil, at the very least we break down the barrier between inner and outer, to the point that discussion in these terms appears irrelevant. Once again, this is not a mental resolution of the problem of opposites but rather a concrete one, which leads us to define enchantment precisely as the reconciliation of inner and outer. We look out into our world and see dream, and, with Emerson and a host of artists and philosophers, we look at the literal world and behold signs, indications, metaphors, and poetry. "The lover of nature is he whose inward and outward senses are still truly adjusted to each other," says Emerson in his essay on nature.

Focusing and Compacting Our Spirituality

Not all art is a shrine. An object of art becomes a shrine when we make it a box, a container of spirits rather than an expression of human imagination, and then when we honor that box as a locus of spiritual attention. A special frame, an extraordinary location, and the invitation to ritual can transform an ordinary painting into an authentic shrine.

The Uffizi in Florence is, at least to me, a shrine rather than a museum. When I first beheld Botticelli's *La Primavera*, a large painting resting on a long table rather than pinned on a wall, I felt as though I was in the presence of a tabernacle of sorts. When with friends I was guided down the very long *corridoio*, a narrow passage that extends across the Ponte Vecchio and houses a great many self-portraits of artists from across the ages, I felt strangely misplaced. Eventually I realized that I was not in a museum, a place for the storage and viewing of art pieces, but in a temple that was designed and is still presented, to whoever will address it as such, as a place of pilgrimage rather than study. And the slight shift in attitude necessary to make this place a shrine gives it the enchantment a museum might not otherwise have.

As is the case with so many things of the soul, an object or a place may serve as a shrine for one person or community and not others. St. Peter's church in the Vatican is an interesting and beautiful church to some; to Catholics it's a shrine. The farm where I grew up in upstate New York is a shrine to me, an overgrown piece of real estate to others. To my friend Pat, an abandoned kiva in a remote part of New Mexico is a place of reverent personal ceremony and ritual; to everyone else it's a hole in the ground. The graves of my grandparents in a suburb of Detroit are two among millions of grave sites to the eyes of almost everyone else, but to me they are shrines, and every visit there a true pilgrimage.

In the passage on inner and outer nature, Emerson notes that the reconciliation of these fundamental dimensions of experience is natural to a child. My children make shrines almost every day. The painting stuck on the refrigerator door may be a shrine. When he was four, my stepson painted an astoundingly sophisticated picture of a bicycle, and we framed it and put it high near the ceiling in the most frequented room of the house. Height may be a sign of a shrine, like the photographs of ancestors sometimes placed high around the walls of the homes of people from the Far East, or pagodas that lift your attention in stages from earth to heaven. A shrine can be exceedingly formal and holy, like Mecca to the world's Muslims, or it can be a child's simple bowl of dandelions serving as a vase of flowers in honor of a treasured doll.

Shrines are characterized, as almost all matters of religion are, by their extraordinary worldly uselessness, as are the pyramids of Egypt or the great Indian statues of the Buddha. Yet to create a world of enchantment, these mammoth projects of religion are the most useful objects in the world. We can imagine people of strong religious persuasion dedicating their lives to the building and preserving of great shrines, like the Buddhas and the cathedrals, and yet we might also consider spending some of our own precious modern time on such activities, to bring enchantment to our own individual lives and to the culture around us, which suffers keenly from the lack of charm.

If you examine the many books that discuss psychological disorders, trying to account for the emotional and "mental" suffering of many people in our modern world, you will not find what I consider to be among the most devastating disorders around us—the absence of shrines. Of course, we are not without our important national shrines, like the various monuments and buildings dedicated to patriotic memory, and as followers of particular beliefs we also make significant shrines, such as the Mormon temple in Salt Lake City. But we lack the kind of thorough appreciation for holiness in all of life that would find expression in ubiquitous shrines representing a religious sensibility not restricted to institutions, whether religious or civic.

It was said of the Vietnamese during their war with America that when a family was threatened with bombardment, they would run from their homes carrying only their shrines. What would we carry from our homes? The most expensive items, those that aren't insured? Emphasis on financial value can sometimes indicate the loss of a deeper sense of life's value, so that the absence of shrines on our landscape may betray a loss in our daily experience of everyday religion or a quotidian piety that is not only equal in importance to any institutional observance but also the root and base of all formal religious activity.

We do, in fact, have many ordinary personal shrines in our

homes and throughout our culture, from jewelry boxes to precious heirlooms and antiques, but as a people we seem to be losing a communal realization of ubiquitous spirituality, and a tour of the modern world would convey the sense of almost total secularization. Our children make pilgrimages now to Disneyland, where they behold caricatures of the animal spirits that have inspired religious people for millennia. There may be vestiges of sacred elephants and eloquent birds in our cartoon figures, and a raucous carnival is certainly a piece of genuine religious piety, but at the very least we have shrunk those ancient animal avatars to figures we can control, who offer us some of the charm of the realm of spirits but without its necessary awesomeness.

The theme parks that are being built around the world have what a Jungian analyst might call a marked puer quality. They are playful and attractive, and certainly shrines are a form of sacred play, but the unfortunate side of a puer construction is its lack of seriousness. The way to restore seriousness to our shrines would be not to make Disneyland serious but to build as well shrines to the spirits of our rivers and streams, our mountains and valleys, and our deserts and prairies; to find ways to enshrine the spirits of our homes, neighborhoods, and cities; and to create places, as the ancients did, where oracles are genuine and the center of the earth does indeed make itself known.

Religion is always serious play and playful seriousness, and so one would expect to feel real joy and vivacity in the precinct of a genuine shrine. In many cultures today, people place flowers and food at the base of a shrine or even around and on top of the holy figures, knowing, as people have recognized for millennia, that a shrine is a real abode and that the spirits who inhabit the shrine are real.

The plaster-of-paris statues of the Virgin Mary that Catholics sometimes enshrine in their backyards, as well as the plastic Jesus that sticks to the dashboard of a car or truck and the sparkling shrines Indian taxi drivers sometimes fix to their cabs, may be sentimental and not aesthetically sophisticated, but still they represent the urge toward shrine making that is more fundamental to the religious spirit than are dogmas and moral prescriptions. Shrines make a spirit palpably present; they celebrate rather than explain and generate intimacy between the human and the more than human.

If we had more shrines, built from a deep feeling of piety and tended with seriousness and playfulness, we wouldn't live in a culture that looks so secular. We would be reminded continually that there is more to life than meets the naked eye; for a shrine is a means of making visible that which is invisible and for evoking a presence that is otherwise only vaguely sensed.

If I were the curator of an art museum or gallery, I would treat installations and exhibits as shrines. If I were a city planner, I would make sure that the city had its share of shrines in every neighborhood. If I were an architect, I would build shrines into the homes and workplaces I designed.

It makes little difference if no one else understands or appreciates them, because usually shrines are an aspect of intimate religion. Often our spirituality is abstract and public, but a shrine brings it close to home. We can garland our shrines simply and honor them in the passing moments of every day. We can keep them private, or invite friends and guests to enjoy them as well. They may be expressions of our church attachment, or they may house spirits of the earth, the family, or one's own memory.

Shrines can take many forms, but however they appear, they have extraordinary power to restore enchantment to the most ordinary places and occasions. They speak equally to children and adults, to believers and unbelievers, to scholars and ordinary folk.

A shrine is merely a box, but it is a box in which a spirit may take up residence. It's a box where we may find the interior world, the microcosm, that we are all looking for. It's a simple box for holding a thousand clowns and a million spirits, whose gift to us is a life of value and meaning. If we make these boxes right, we will attract a spirit, and our religious quest will find a home, an enchanted home because it is the dwelling of a spirit.

In her extraordinary book on "found religion," *Ordinarily Sacred*, Lynda Sexson writes: "Moving to a new house, giving birth, or going into battle might endanger the soul; and so, for safekeeping, it could be placed in a horn, the metal of a knife, a stone, a bag, until the danger was past." Loss of soul is an ever-present danger for all of us; we need numerous ways of sheltering the soul and housing spirits so that they will not disappear from loss of memory or sheer evaporation in the plethora of things and events that blow through our lives. All that is required is the homely art of keeping and caring, an art available to anyone who takes the time and gives attention to the spirits that preserve natural religion—life-giving piety in a world too often given to impieties and forgetfulness.

Temenos and Sanctuary

*W*E HAVE SEEN many ways the re-enchantment of culture requires the rediscovery of skills that once flourished but have been lost or forgotten. We focus so much attention on bringing ourselves into the future that we lose sight of the equally important work of keeping the wisdom of the past. One such lost skill that we may still glimpse in children's play and in sports is the making of temenos— setting aside a certain area as a special or even sacred precinct.

When we choose a seat or standing area on a bus or train, when we arrange space in an office or workplace, when we decide where to put a garden, or chairs on a porch, where to sit on the riverbank to have lunch, where to play with the children—all of these decisions have to do with temenos, marking out a space appropriate for a certain spirit that breathes life into our activity.

Without the ability to make temenos, we find ourselves in spaces that are purely functional and give us no more than an empty arena in which to work. For the ancient Greeks, temenos was the precinct of a god, a goddess, or another spirit that could have a beneficial effect on human life. Sometimes a temple or many temples would be erected within the temenos, but the essential thing was to mark out a special space for ritual and memory. The noted religion scholar Walter Berckert points out that the temenos was not determined by the natural qualities of a site but was essentially the walled separation of the space from the profane world around it. It's one thing to find a natural place that is home to a special spirit; it's another to set aside certain dimensions in any space to increase the possibility of enchantment.

The Borders of Our Lives

Berckert mentions that one had to be careful in ancient Greece not to pollute the temenos but to keep it pure for the sacred work done there. When we, too, wish to live in enchanted places, it may be necessary to keep certain spaces protected and dedicated for special activities. When I lived in Ireland, I was once walking toward a grove of trees, when an old man with thick white hair shouted to me. "Stay away!" he said. "That's a fairy circle." He approached me and told me sternly not to go near that place, because fairies danced around those trees. He knew the law concerning the transgression of place, but we seem to have forgotten it, and as a result we often find ourselves in lifeless space that keeps our work effortful and strenuous.

Although it is not entirely correct etymologically, "sacred work" is a good definition of "liturgy." All work can be sacred, and so it would be helpful to have a temenos for each of the various lesser liturgies we perform in daily life—not just a place where our work will go along smoothly but one where the spirit is conducive to the activity carried out there. Dedicated to enchantment, we could decide in the simplest situations never to do the right thing in the wrong place.

To a large extent, my writing is an expression of the place where I write. Like many writers who admit that they are not in full control of their words, I feel more like the instrumental cause of my books rather than the executive author; nor is the author simply a spirit within me, or an interior muse who seizes and inspires me. A visitor from England once told me that he found my ideas and language quintessentially New England, an interesting observation since I've lived in New England for only ten years now. Yet I do think the spirit of this part of the country has settled deep in me and speaks through my words, just as the spirit of place speaks through us all, even when we think we're independent of it.

The spirit in the *room* in which I write also has a powerful influence. Sometimes temenos is nothing more than a room—walls, ceiling, floor, color, and furnishings. Henry David Thoreau's simple cabin on Walden Pond, now reconstructed at the site, is a potent temenos. Looking at it, you immediately sense the spirit of his essays and diaries, and the same is true of Emily Dickinson's home in Amherst, where you can gain insight into her poetry just by walking through her house and garden.

Dickinson's garden is now relatively small, though the homestead in her time covered fourteen acres, and like many small gardens, it takes some of its magic from the strength of its perimeters, which are marked by tall bushes and closely planted trees. You feel held by the borders of the garden, and then you think about Dickinson, her life so contained within the walls of her house and the edges of her yard, creating a full, mystical microcosm, a world small and yet complete within the range of her vision. You remember her words:

> Eden is that old-fashioned House
> We dwell in every day
> Without suspecting our abode
> Until we drive away.

Resident Spirits

An enchanted place is one that is inhabited by nonhuman figures who perform the enchantment, who sing and speak and make their presence felt. When we are trying to make a place conducive to work, play, or just being at home, we might try to be receptive to the spirits that inhabit nature, geography, and even architecture. A friend once showed me the studio in which he did carpentry and sculpture. He was careful not to call it a shed, he said, because he wanted to work in a place that would foster his art, and a shed is not a place, either in name or design, that nurtures the artistic spirit. He pointed out to me how, with the door open, he could hear and see the nearby pond and watch his garden of wildflowers. This is a man whose sense of temenos is unusually acute and who dedicates an unusual amount of time and attention to his "environment."

If we were generally more skilled at creating temenos, we might not have to stuff our rooms with so many things. The ancient Greek temenos could be empty and yet still fill its visitors with its resident spirit. The spirit of a place inhabits it like a real dweller, and so when we are open to its presence, we feel the fullness of the space. We may not be driven then to fill the apparent void with things, but can instead discover the spiritual richness of simplicity. Often, the emptier a place is, the more it reeks of spiritual presences.

You can't force simplicity, but you can invite it in by finding as much richness as possible in the few things at hand. Simplicity doesn't mean meagerness but rather a certain kind of richness, the fullness that appears when we stop stuffing the world with things. This is my ideal in building a house: make it with genuine materials and don't hide those materials behind excessive paint and plastic. Let us feel the textures and see the colors, and then we won't need so many things in the place to make it nurturing. Certain spirits, of course, require more decoration than others, but still the maker of temenos has to come to a point of saturation and then stop.

Temenos and Liminality

The essential ingredient in a temenos is the perimeter that marks out the space, whether a wall, a fence, a hedge of flowers and bushes, or some rocks that only imply the full perimeter. Having crossed the border, we find ourselves in a special place where certain things happen and other things do not. A good door, whether light and permeable or heavy and secure, can serve temenos. Even carefully placed lighting can mark borders and create the kind of perimeter you need to keep the proper spirits housed.

Hospital psychiatric wards are sometimes sealed off with elaborate security systems, locks, cameras, and even laser beams—all aimed at keeping patients within the defined space. But one wonders if such extreme means are not excessive, betraying in their exaggeration and literalism a failure of temenos. Maybe what we need in hospitals are more symbolic and imagistic signs of liminality, a strong image of "threshold." In ordinary life, you know the difference between being in a supermarket and sitting in your living room, but in a hospital the sense of place may be determined only by function, and so to keep people in their place we go to extremes. But if a hospital room effectively conjured up the spirits of bedroom, we would know intuitively and surely when we were crossing the threshold into the public corridor or the nurses' station or the X-ray room. No one needs to be taught how to recognize the spirit of bedroom; in fact, we all probably know the exact point where bedroom stops and some other spirit takes over.

Since homes are such sacred places, it isn't surprising that temenos is an important element in their construction and maintenance. Doors, stone walls, fences, curbs, sidewalks, hedges, trellises, porches, driveways, and house numbers can all play an important role in creating the home temenos. Thieves breaking and entering not only steal and vandalize, they pollute the temenos of the home, and victims often report that they feel that violation more than the loss of property.

Temenos may take subtle forms. I have a friend who travels frequently, and he describes how important it is for him on a plane to establish his space so that he can work. I travel frequently too, and I notice that hotel life is keenly sensitive to temenos. I may have my room for only a night or two, but for that period it is mine, and in sensitive hotels the staff respects that space, entering only with permission and acting with great care while they are there. I establish the temenos by checking the perimeters carefully, discovering where the weak places are, where sound penetrates, how secure the sliding doors are. This check is not just for security but for the sensation that the space is now prepared for my habitation. I try to stay as often as possible at the same hotels, so that knowing the perimeters and the spirits of the place, I can feel comfortably contained and at home.

At home, every night, when everyone else is in bed, I walk through the house checking the outside doors to see that they're locked and the inside doors to keep the dog from eating toys and measuring the light going into children's bedrooms. This little rite is not just a practical check; it's a way of fine-tuning the temenos of the home, and the pleasure I get from it comes as much from the making of my home as from keeping it secure.

Games, music, dining, conversation—most of life can take place only where a temenos has been created. I remember once listening to the pianist Rudolf Serkin playing a Beethoven sonata in a small auditorium near Chicago. He was already in the second movement when a piercing alarm went off. He tried to play through the alarm, but he gave up, left the stage, and returned to start from the very beginning. He had to create the temenos of the piece and establish the aural temenos of the place by starting over.

Perimeters of the Soul

Sometimes temenos is established emotionally and ritually. Restaurant owners are usually good at creating temenos for their patrons, with colors and other aspects of decor, the arrangement of tables and chairs, rituals of entry and exit, music and dress. Physicians often pay close attention to temenos with the walls, doors, counters, windows, and furnishings of their suites. I always feel the magic of the examining room and have no trouble distinguishing the spirit there from the one in the waiting room.

In a culture given to functionalism and practicality, attention to temenos easily suffers, and then enchantment becomes impossible. All space becomes democratically functional, and there may be no real gateways and entrances, no real thresholds that lead the soul in and out. We can do anything in such spaces, and we can do nothing, because there is no clearly defined sense of place. We are always half present in what we're doing, and yet never fully absent. A threshold is a border that lets us know where we are and where we are not. When liminality has been lost, then we may not know where we are and may feel in several places at once.

The disorientation typical of modern life is often due to a failure in creating temenos. Our thoughts and emotions float too easily, and then behavior has no limits. A teacher knows how important it is to create a sharp sense of temenos in a classroom, or else the students will quickly fall into anarchy, and all is lost. My stepson's teacher meets his students every morning at the door of the classroom and shakes their hands—an effective way to establish the temenos of learning each day.

Windows, too, may create a much-needed temenos. For me, small panes in windows create a valuable tension between inside and outside by allowing me to see the outdoors while at the same time keeping me securely indoors. The architect Christopher Alexander recommends small panes because of the interesting views they present while keeping us contained indoors, in contrast to the plate-glass window, which tries to put us outside. Windows, he says, should also "give you a sense of protection and shelter from the outside."

An automobile, too, can provide soothing temenos with its quiet and containment. Sometimes when you drive, you want to be open to the world around you yet at the same time fully contained in the car; at other times you may want to roll up the windows and feel a higher degree of emotional security, the womblike enclosure that cars offer.

Automobiles give us space, but not much of it, and their limited dimensions may account for their effectiveness at emotional containment. Sometimes the spirit of a place seems to require modest dimensions. My wife found an extremely attractive old building where she thought she could paint, but in a short time she discovered that the space was too large, and it took her a long time just to get started with her work. Christopher Alexander mentions that our houses could be smaller and narrower, provided the distance between different elements is great enough. He recommends long, thin rectangles, branched shapes, and narrow towers. Enchanting department stores like Macy's in New York and Harrods in London owe their magic in part to the ingenious ways they make strong temenos in large indoor areas. For all their square footage, you never find yourself in a large, empty hall, but at every turn there is a different kind of border and a unique spirit.

We need thresholds in our daily lives, so that we clearly move from one sphere of life to another. The soul needs a variety of places where it can retreat and disappear from life. Parks, clubs, restaurants, beaches, trails, and chapels on the material level are of great importance, as are meditation, contemplation, daydreaming, night dreams, distraction, memory, and many things that fit in the category of rapture, on the spiritual level. Each requires a temenos that is created with imagination and protected fiercely and aggressively if necessary.

The Christian mystic Teresa of Avila described the soul as an "interior castle," and the Renaissance magus Giulio Camillo created a "memory theater," a small building, as Frances Yates describes it, full of little boxes containing images representing the many chambers of the soul. We ourselves have our interior spaces and places marked out by an interior system of temenos, corresponding to an outer life of demarcations and departments. These systems are not abstract, not grids for the mind, but rooms and gardens of the heart. If we would tend these borders carefully, resisting the modern tendency to live and work in undifferentiated space or in places built and arranged without sensitivity to the resident spirit, we would find a mysterious enrichment of the heart and a means for holding life together.

Numinosity and Luminescence

I REMEMBER THE first time I saw the Pacific Ocean sparkling in the bright sunshine as I rode with a friend up a narrow, winding, hilly road north of San Francisco many years ago. The water virtually pulsated and breathed in its quiet scintillation, overwhelming me with its beauty and the immensity of its power. It truly cast a spell on me, and even today I feel that one place I could make a home on this earth is on the western coast of the United States. The charm of that first sight of the ocean was more than a moment's rapture; it was a meeting that would have many repercussions in the years following, and the essence of its charm lay in the *numen* of that ocean.

In English, the word "numen" is obscure, as is its slightly more familiar adjective form, "numinous." The word comes from Latin *nuo*, nod, once used to describe the divine will or a decree of the emperor. Eventually, as the *Oxford English Dictionary* notes, the word came to identify "the presiding power or spirit." The dictionary cites a 1650 use associating it with the lightning and thunder of Jupiter, and indeed, the feeling one has seconds after a loud crack of lightning and the deep roll of thunder is closely akin to what I understand to be the numinous.

In his influential book of 1917, *The Idea of the Holy*, the German scholar Rudolf Otto defined religion in terms of the numinous and the holy. He had traveled widely and had many experiences of "presiding spirits" around the world, and he had also been influenced by another German scholar, Friedrich Schleiermacher, who defined religion as a "feeling of dependence." Otto said that becoming aware of the numinous is an extraordinary sensation, not a common one, and it stretches our idea of the nature of religion beyond ethics and belief to include a vivid appreciation of the holy.

Life is full of cracks, windows, and doorways that allow us to glimpse the eternal that lies hidden behind the surfaces of the temporal. These glimpses may be momentary epiphanies, rare sensations of awe that come along unexpectedly. Often they're associated with nature, which can inspire awe in a thousand ways and at almost every turn in the road. But sometimes the numinous also appears in human art.

One of the great epiphanies in my life took place when I was seventeen. Throughout my childhood my father had taken me to band concerts at the Michigan state fairgrounds or at Belle Isle on the Detroit River, but one day he bought tickets for a concert at Ford Auditorium, the home of the Detroit Symphony. We sat in the seventh row, and I was spellbound as Glenn Gould performed Bach and Mozart with the orchestra in one of his rare early concert appearances. I had never heard such beauty, and watching it pour out of the young man wearing a formal suit much too large for him, sitting at the piano in a way I was sure my teacher would never approve, was a transformative experience for me. Even now, I associate eternity with Gould's playing of Bach's *Goldberg Variations,* and I understand completely why this recording was played at his funeral.

Schleiermacher's "feeling of dependence" became in Otto the sense of our *creatureliness,* an awareness that comes upon us when we have a momentary sensation of divinity. I certainly felt like a fully human and ordinary creature in the presence of Glenn Gould's talent. The sense of being a creature is close to what I have been describing as the essence of enchantment—the recognition that the world is infinitely more vast and mysterious than we can imagine when we regard it only scientifically, and that a voice, music, or some other kind of utterance emerges from it, providing an opportunity for us to be related to it and profoundly affected by it. The sensation of creatureliness implies an attitude of genuine humility, another requirement for enchantment, allowing us to be entranced and stunned, as we are receptive to the revelatory influxes and transformative alchemies of life.

On Not Knowing Everything

In a journal entry from 1965, Mircea Eliade makes a subtle but important point: "When something sacred manifests itself (hierophany), at the same time something 'occults' itself, becomes cryptic. Therein is the true dialectic of the sacred: by the mere fact of *showing* itself, the sacred *hides* itself."

A disenchanted culture demands that the world reveal itself fully. We expect no remainder in our investigations of nature or of the human psyche and feel a sense of failure if we have not fully exposed whatever it is we're studying. But Eliade offers a key insight into the numinous when he warns that the divine hides itself even as it is revealed. From a distance, lightning and thunder may be fair game for scientific discussion, and we may come to the point where we think we fully understand them, but in those seconds right after a bolt has struck nearby, when our heart is still beating fast and our blood racing, we know lightning and thunder more intimately than we can with our mere minds. A hot and disturbing encounter with the numinous gives us lessons that can't be learned in the cool hours of study.

One reason why in modern life we may find it difficult to include the numinous in our experience is that we are not prepared to honor the hidden and the invisible. We know how to deal with what is plainly in front of us, but we have forgotten technologies of reverence that once were commonplace. Once, people knew of nature's reticence to be seen and known fully. The Greeks told stories of the nature goddess Artemis, who punished anyone who came too close and transformed those who, like Acteon, dared to invade her privacy.

Living in the presence of the numinous calls for methods and attitudes quite different from those that get us through ordinary days. We are generally proud of our attempts to master nature, and yet nature may ask us to acknowledge its power and immensity with prayers of praise, thanks, petition, and expiation. Our characteristic ambition and self-congratulations may occlude all sensation of numinosity, and yet without an appreciation for the numinous, there may be no soul in our relation to nature.

Otto's deep appreciation for numinosity led him to define religion in the celebrated words *mysterium tremendum et fascinans,* a mystery awesome and entrancing, a description that captures the odd contradiction we feel in the presence of the divine. A bolt of lightning may send a shiver down the spine, and yet in that shock we may perceive something of nature's beauty and learn the importance of filling our lives with the numinous. Glimpsing a world that transcends our mental universe of data and logic may produce within us a powerful longing to live in that transcendent state. Living with the numinous that surrounds us is like fulfilling the mystic's longing to come close to the eternal presence felt in moments of visionary ecstasy. Too often we place mystical experience outside the range of the ordinary person, and yet we can each have our daily moments of awe and enchantment.

With unusual beauty of language, Otto uses the imagery of the sea to describe the appearance of the numinous: "The feeling of it may at times come sweeping like a gentle tide, pervading the mind with a tranquil mood of deepest worship. It may pass over into a more set and lasting attitude of the soul, continuing, as it were, thrillingly vibrant and resonant, until at last it dies away and the soul resumes its 'profane,' non-religious mood of everyday experience."

The opportunity to have such experiences of the numinous is part of the enchanted life, but it requires an attitude that values an occasional seizure by the beautiful or the immense. With its emphasis on efficiency and practicality, modern life works against sustained appreciation of the numinous, although at times nature overwhelms us so that in spite of ourselves we have to consider it seriously, as when an earthquake, flood, or eclipse of the sun stirs us out of our forgetfulness. Even then our response may be to search for better machines for controlling nature, rather than to search our hearts for ways of living with the numinous and to acknowledge the limits of our creatureliness.

In the aftermath of a natural disaster, we gather to express our thanks for survival and to console one another in our mutual discovery of mortality. We tell our stories, express our emotions, pray from our creatureliness, and create a memorial that would effectively contain our strong feelings and realizations. We discover how ritual and holy language flow naturally from the depths of emotion stirred up by nature's powerful manifestations, and as pristine religion emerges from the encounter with nature's might.

In an essay written shortly before his death, Jung warned against our loss of appreciation for the numinous, citing the example of primitive societies that fall apart when the numinous disappears: "They lose their raison d'être, the order of their social organizations, and then they dissolve and decay. . . . We are now in the same condition. We have lost something we have never properly understood. . . . We have stripped all things of their mystery and numinosity; nothing is holy any longer."

Often when we talk about the loss of holiness or a sense of the sacred, we express vague thoughts about it and are often left without any idea how to fill the emptiness. More specifically we might acknowledge our own primitivity, without questioning our grand achievements. Disenchanted people fear primitivity as inferior and try at all costs to remain civilized, but "primitive" means "primary," not necessarily undeveloped, and from our primary, uninterpreted sensations we may detect the holy.

The Luminous and the Numinous

In a talk he gave as an Eranos lecture in 1946, one I find myself returning to again and again in my reading and writing, Jung helps us further to appreciate the numinous. He observes that a person usually appears to have more than one will. Jung is tempted to talk about a second ego but then considers that this secondary personality is really many personalities, lying somewhere between consciousness and unconsciousness. Finally, he settles on the idea that our conscious life is surrounded by a great many minor luminosities. From alchemical writings he draws the image of sparks, seeds of light lying in the chaos of life's fullness, which have "a certain effulgence or quasi-consciousness," and these lights are closely related to the numinous.

Then he quotes Paracelsus, the great sixteenth-century physician, alchemist, and philosopher, who said that just as a person can't exist without the divine numen, so one can't exist without the natural lumen. "A person is made perfect by numen and lumen and these two alone. Everything springs from these two, and these two are in human beings, but without them a person is nothing, though they can exist without human beings." This somewhat obscure but fascinating passage directs our attention to a certain brilliance in things that is close to the divinity in natural objects.

Jung discusses these lights and numinosities within nature and the human person in the language of archetypes and the ego, but I would rather consider them as felt realities. Light is not only a physical sensation but also an intuitive perception we might enjoy as something in nature or culture attracts and charms us. By living in an enchanted world and by sensing a deep significance in things everywhere, we live with added intelligence but not necessarily with added rationality. Our thoughts lie deeper, though they may not be easy to articulate and to express in words.

It may be difficult for modern people to appreciate the importance of interiority and intimacy in our relation to the world. We tend to see only the hard surfaces. Assuming that human beings alone have an interior life, we relate to things coldly. But once we allow the world itself to have a soul and an interior life, then enchantment begins to stir. Sensing the world's inner life, we are affected emotionally and may find a basis for a deeper connection.

The numinous is the unexplained, the world kept rich and complex, and therefore more like human life. We say lightly that a house has character or a car has personality, but we don't take our words seriously. Maybe things do indeed have more complexity and depth than our modern ways of thought allow us to appreciate, and maybe if we allowed ourselves to become intimate with the things around us, we might understand how they could have a soul and how our own lives might be profoundly enriched in an ensouled world.

The numen is the divine nod, not the human nod. It is not to be found at the pinnacle of the self-improvement road or at the zenith of moral conscientiousness. On the contrary, the numinous seems most accessible to the "beginner's mind," to the child's attitude of wonder and lack of ambition. It appears once our striving for it has diminished and once we simply open our eyes without concern for high spiritual achievement, discovering that the numinous is as commonplace as the sun setting behind a cloud or the moon casting blue shadows on a snowy scene.

As Paracelsus taught, whether we know it or not the numen is present in the world of things. To live an enchanted life, we may have to sharpen our perceptions so we can see the spark of divinity in the most ordinary thing. An education in numinosity would involve a shedding of the modern attitude that wants to explain everything in materialistic terms. We'd have to cultivate ways of honoring the "presiding presence" in the world around us.

Most of the suggestions I make in this book have to do with honoring the numen—allowing the spirit of a river to show itself powerfully, not leveling off all our mountains and hills for development, making things with strong imagination and handiwork, living in houses that truly are temples of natural piety, doing work that contributes to humanity and doesn't sacrifice others for personal gain—an ethical life can be as numinous as an awe-inspiring waterfall.

Appreciating the numinous, we don't accept any reductionistic explanations for human experience or the workings of the natural world. Nothing is stripped of its inherent spirituality, because, as theologians around the world have taught, divinity resides in all things. Every person, place, and object elicits reverence from us because of its numinosity—even the dilapidated building, the empty lot, and the criminal on death row. If there is any exception or reservation in our perception of the numinous, then we haven't shed our secularism. We are still attached to the disenchanted values of a culture that has forgotten its creatureliness and lost its capacity for unconditional reverence.

Ritual

Shall I tell you again the new word,
the new word of the unborn day?
It is Resurrection.
The Resurrection of the flesh.

For our flesh is dead
only egoistically we assert ourselves.

And the new word means nothing to us,
it is such an old word,
till we admit how dead we are,
till we actually feel as blank as we really are.

D. H. LAWRENCE

Theology of the World

"As I stand along the surface of the Earth she says child to me, she says grandchild to me,"goes a Navajo prayer. Ask a typical modern person what happens when he stands along the surface of the earth: "I see stores and roads that have sprung up here in the past few years," or, "There's some land that could be developed." In an enchanted world, one automatically thinks theologically rather than pragmatically about the world, and this enchanted theology is not rigid dogma but a natural, relaxed brand of piety.

The simple Navajo prayer expresses two fundamental aspects of enchantment: hearing the voice of the earth and being in a family relationship to the world. How would we moderns have to change to be able to say, "The earth says child to me"? Whatever that change may be is our direct path to enchantment.

Modern sciences, both social and physical, do not usually foster a real dialogue between nature and human life. In the sciences, so influential in establishing our worldview, we are the subjects and the world is an object. Only theology grants subjectivity and power to nature, and therefore only theology can speak adequately about the soul. Yet even theology has serious limits when it colludes with the disenchanted thought of the culture at large. The theology I imagine is much broader in scope and bolder in vision, a fundamental, life-informing mode of understanding that takes the infinite, the mysterious, and the spiritual into full account as it seeks to formulate our imagination of human events.

At present we try to respond to ultimate questions in the language of the sciences, physical and social, but this language and the vision it contains is profoundly inadequate in the face of life's deepest mysteries. We are in serious need of a discipline of theology that is nonsectarian and yet considers the many issues of ordinary life that involve mystery. We need the specialist who has no need to defend his or her own beliefs but who can speak intelligently and reflectively on how to live ritually, how to deal with death, and how to find deeply rooted attitudes toward marriage, illness, work, and community.

A Personal Theological Confession

I was trained early on to reflect theologically on my life. Some of the theology I learned in my Catholic grade school from the nuns and priests might have made Thomas Aquinas squirm and the Roman Inquisition turn livid, but it nonetheless was theological reflection. I knew in early childhood that the world was made in six days, that the bread I saw on the altar was the body and blood of Jesus, and that if I played with my rosary it would turn into a snake. Later, after passing through a few years of Aquinas, I was inspired by the words of Teilhard de Chardin, the priest-theologian who tried to blend theology and science into a fruitful marriage of old and visionary thought.

Today, as I continue to search for inspiring theological reflection, I am continually disappointed to see the most recent and brilliant writers assuming that "theology" means Christian thought. There may be ecumenical largesse in the language and spirit of this "new" theology, but to me it falls far short of what I imagine to be appropriate for our age. I love Christian theology and hope that it prospers—it has had extraordinary representatives in the twentieth century—but we are heading into a new century, and I see few signs that theology as a field is adjusting to this new world.

In my view, a theology for our time has to be not only interdenominational but nondenominational as well. It isn't enough to be Christian or Jewish and open-minded, tolerant of other misguided but honest ways of dealing with mystery. It isn't enough to stay within the limits of the Western ethos. It isn't enough to shape a theology out of the *major* traditions of the world, for the smallest religion has something of value to contribute. Nor is it sufficient or appropriate to look for some intellectual amalgamation of all religious views, the idea that all religions say the same thing or point in the same direction.

We need language and expertise for dealing with the truly profound mysteries that challenge individuals and society. Aside from the churches, we have no positive, adequate means for dealing with death, accident, meaning, nature, intuitions, rites of passage, sacredness, holy places, ethics and values, and education. The list of theological issues that inform daily life is long and filled with matters of great concern.

Without an adequate and timely theology, we are left with secularistic language and categories of thinking that fail us as we try to deal with questions of ultimate concern and spiritual import. Without theology, marriage becomes a social contract and divorce the failure of the contract, murder becomes a signal of social neglect rather than a moral and communal pollution, as one finds it in Greek tragedy. We assume that insanity and neurosis are caused by parental mistake or abuse rather than by spiritual neglect, and we exploit such personalistic psychologies to shield ourselves from communal self-reflection. In Euripides' play *Hippolytus,* the gracious wife and mother Phaedra is suddenly seized with a physical and mental disturbance, and the chorus asks:

> Mistress, is your mind suddenly possessed
> because Pan floods it with madness?
> Is this Hekate's fury at work?
> Should we accuse those holy Korybantes
> or the Great Mother of beasts
> glowering in her mountains?
> Did you forget to provide
> a smooth honeyed sacrifice, and that lapse
> offends the huntress—
> Artemis!—who sickens you,
> spiriting your vigor away?

I know of few passages in sacred literature that so clearly teach us which questions to ask and what kind of piety to seek when human life becomes afflicted with serious illness—how to reflect theologically on what has happened. Is there the slightest reason not to read this passage of Greek theology for a pious reflection on current disturbance? Would that offend any commitments and convictions we might have for our inherited tradition? Could not a Catholic or a Jew or an atheist meditate on this passage and gain theological insight and guidance?

The theology I'm looking for is not a blend of all traditions but rather a style of thought that takes spiritual matters into account as we try to deal with daily challenges. I imagine it as a foundation for those who wish to maintain church commitments and an adequate source of theology for those who wish to live outside a particular tradition. It's a theology that can derive insight from any community in the world and in all kinds of art and literature. Finally, it's a theology that is individual and unique, conforming to the vision and tastes of the person it serves.

My own theological thinking stems from many sources: my Catholic upbringing and education; my studies in Christian theology, especially the writings of Teilhard de Chardin, Paul Tillich, and Dietrich Bonhoeffer; my studies in world religions, especially the writings of Mircea Eliade and Karl Kerenyi; my reading of Western literature, especially Wallace Stevens, Rainer Maria Rilke, Emily Dickinson, and Samuel Beckett; my reading in Eastern literature, especially Chuang Tzu, Lao-tzu, Buddhism, and Zen; Sufi poets and storytellers from Islam; Native American prayers and stories; African songs and stories.

I don't think all these sources are saying the same thing or pointing to the same God with different names. These are radically individual visions of meaning, value, and the nature of things. I don't have to put them all into a blender to use them in the shaping of my own theology, and yet they do become mine as I arrange them in my own way in my own theology. As the great Renaissance theologian Nicholas of Cusa said in his letter to Giuliano: "All things Giulianize in you." He was describing the way in which the paradox of many worldviews coalesce in an individual, without any loss of their integrity.

Theology: The Discipline of Enchantment

Thinking theologically in a way that is not narcissistic or defensive, not obsessive and jealous, allows us to live in an enchanted world, close to the mysteries that give life depth and value. There we find ways of thinking intelligently about nature as alive and full of spirit. We find there, too, a way to imagine our own personal lives without blaming our childhood, our parents, or early traumas for our misfortunes. Most of all, we can find in theological reflection an adequate language for developing our own character, values, and sensibilities. Without a living theology, our interpretations and solutions don't reach nearly deep enough. What we perceive as a psychological and sociological problem may be a spiritual crisis, requiring a special way of thinking and responding that reaches into the mysteries that underlie human life.

A reporter once asked me what, if I could see into the future, I would like to know about the world fifty years hence. I could wonder about a thousand things, of course, but I answered: "I'd like to know the state of religion in another fifty or one hundred years." As we get to know the cultures of the world more intimately, we are going to be affected in our religious views, and it may become more difficult to remain provincial in our theology. This difficulty could, of course, generate a backlash, and some people may become even more defensive about their own beliefs. But there may be a more creative response as well, an appreciation of the spiritual and the sacred, irrespective of parochial beliefs and commitments.

I expect and hope that we will return theology to its proper place as the very pinnacle of education and thought—it was once the queen of sciences. This is a medieval view, but I'm not asking for the restoration of Christendom. I look forward to a rediscovery of the great philosophers and theologians from around the world: not just the outstanding thinkers of Judaism, Islam, and Christianity in the West but spiritual philosophers of India, China, Japan, Africa, South America, and many other parts of the world.

We are now seeing some renewed interest in mysticism, East and West, and this, too, is an important development in the restoration of a theology of enchantment. Mystical writers provide many necessary elements for such a theology, including a profound appreciation for dialogue with divinity, for the limits of human knowledge in the face of mystery, and for emptying our language and ideas about the divine so that we can live with an attitude of utter openness to fate, nature, and destiny. The failure to develop these theological capacities results, in my opinion, in the insanity of crime and the political and commercial corruption that makes community impossible. To put it somewhat differently, secularistic disciplines and methods force us to live in a closed system, while theology opens up our possibilities infinitely.

In the relationship between human and divine, mystics emphasize love over law and intimacy over understanding. They seem to use the accidentals of church and theology to reach the precincts of divinity, where direct experience is fulfilling. Some current commentators on mysticism see a close connection between the Christian mystic and the traditional shaman, the mystic, like Julian of Norwich, going through an initiatory illness in a way that is remarkably shamanic.

In Western spirituality, we have lived through a long period in which the intellectualization and moralization of religion have kept us culturally disenchanted and divided into competitive groups. The increasingly intimate encounter between different forms of religion and spiritual practice, like the meeting of the mystic and the shaman, promises a breaking up of those old patterns and a new imagination of the spiritual life. What is happening is not a borrowing of one religion from another as much as a rediscovery of spiritual perspectives and opportunities within one tradition through association with another.

In this respect, one of the most remarkable events of the past fifty years in America has been Thomas Merton's entering a strict monastic life, his stretching that life to its limits and making the world aware of his experience through his widely read writings, and then his death while on an extraordinary visit to Bangkok for a conference of monks from the East and the West. Merton's imagination is much in my mind as I write about an expanded notion of theology, since in his many writings he drew connections among nonviolent social action, race relations, Eastern appreciation of nature, mystical traditions of all places, international peace, poetry and the other arts, ritual and modes of contemplation, and ground-breaking theologies such as that of Dietrich Bonhoeffer.

I look forward to the day when governments can call on nondenominational theologians to offer advice on matters of peace, crime, housing, planning, economics, education, and all other aspects of a society's daily life. Speaking about and for the mysteries that make life humane, we might effect a radical cultural change that restores the spiritual life to the center of culture and helps re-enchant a world that is suffering the loss of magic.

Theos

For too long we have imagined the *theos* of theology to be the limited image of divinity that we jealously protect and hold as the only valid and true version. But *theos* is perhaps the most mystery-filled word of all. Translated usually as "God," it is a word that fails every time it is defined, described, or translated. It is an evocative word, which calls forth the spirit that is often described as infinite, unnameable, beyond any statement about it, and yet the source of all life. For some, *theos* is an invitation to silence, the emptying of all understanding, beyond language and story, and yet fully present as the active spring from which time and events flow.

Dietrich Bonhoeffer wrote from his Nazi prison: "God is beyond in the midst of our life. The church stands not at the boundaries where human powers give out, but in the middle of the village." I understand "church" not in any institutional sense but as that spirit which gathers us together to acknowledge the ultimate mysteries that frame a human life. This "church" stands in the middle of culture, an infinite spring from which the deepest, and sometimes the darkest, human actions and ideas emerge. *Theos* is not something set apart from life, but it is the very heart and substance of the most ordinary dimension of everyday life. It is the ultimate source of enchantment, so that to seek the spell of dreamlike immersion in the boundless sea of life is to live religiously, worshiping the God who is beyond any definition or idea of God, the God who appears, as God appeared to Bonhoeffer, in the face of utterly inscrutable insanity and inhumanity. Taken to the brink of rationality, we look into the absurd abyss and behold pure divinity, beyond any institutional description, far beyond any moral prescription, and infinitely beyond any convenient, defensive, anxious, provincial, narcissistic, or belligerently argued notion.

This theology is the ultimate basis for an enchanted life. It restores magic as a principle of mature living rather than an aberration in the course of human experimentation, and it gives utter seriousness to our theme: the re-enchantment of everyday life.

Today many people frustrated with the inadequacies they see in mainstream religion express their love of spirituality and their disdain of religion. They want to address their spiritual concerns without being distracted and impeded by the politics of religion. But this new, unattached spirituality is often itself limited by the particular needs and narrow vision of its practitioners. Tradition and community offer a necessary grounding for the spiritual quest.

But I believe the new searchers are expressing an important and authentic issue of our postmodern world: the need for tradition and community liberated from belief and dogmatic coercion. They also demonstrate in their occasional narcissism and wandering, their attachments to questionable philosophies and leadership, the need we all have for nonsectarian theologians who have studied the traditions and can help us find in our honest explorations community that is neither literal nor dogmatic.

Enchantment needs its own specialist, and mystery its own lobbyist. A theology of daily life, practiced by us all, would open our eyes to a dimension solidly sealed off by the modern secularistic imagination, and it would restore soul, because soul is fed by the eternal and the spiritual as much as it finds nourishment in the temporal and the physical. Our universities and political institutions could begin to take theology seriously, placing it in the middle of the village rather than on the fringe, releasing it from its imprisonment in sectarianism, granting long-withheld life to our society, which confesses its hunger for the spirit and its longing for the soul.

Astrology's Truth

*I*F YOU WANT a brief course in enchantment, go outdoors on the next clear night and look up at the sky. Our scientists tell us authoritatively that the twinkling stars and circumambulating planets are just balls of rock, ice, and gas, but our feelings confirm that the sky is full of charm and magic. The stars cast a spell on us, and as we look at them we fall easily into a meditative trance, a significant and valid experience for the soul that need not be dismissed by our scientific sophistication.

Our scientific prejudice convinces us that it is superstitious in the extreme to consider any alternative to a cold-blooded physical appraisal of the sky, but the sacred literature and poetry of eons takes a different point of view, as in the following verses from a Passamaquoddy Indian poem:

> For we are the stars. For we sing.
> For we sing with our light.
> For we are birds made of fire.
> For we spread our wings over the sky.
> Our light is a voice.
> We cut a road for the soul
> for its journey through death.

This extraordinary poem is a primer in enchantment, teaching us that the light of the stars has a voice. We can be enchanted by listening to that voice with our eyes and hearing it merely by being present to it. If there is any spark of imagination left in us, as we stand beneath the stars, trusting the emotions and intuitions that rise up in us, we can feel with bodily certainty that these birds of fire have an impact on human life, an influence that is undeniable. Our habitual literalism and scientific, materialistic rationalism may convince us to dismiss our feelings as romantic or childish, but if we could sustain the pristine attitude of wonder occasioned by the stars and entertain the questions that come to mind under their influence, we might discover an escape from our modernism and a way into the enchanted universe.

Once, while listening to a roundtable discussion by distinguished reporters and news analysts, I was stunned to hear one of them refer to a politician's outrageous statement as "astrology." The word was spoken in the most disdainful tones, and everyone on the panel seemed to get the joke. Perhaps because I have spent years reading poetry and religious literature from Europe, the Americas, Africa, India, and China, all assuming an astrological point of view, I felt the smug rationalism of the reporters sharply and wondered if we will ever be able to recapture the most fundamental source of enchantment available to us: the brilliant, mysterious, and suggestive night sky.

Have you ever been stopped in your tracks at the appearance of a huge, yellow, egg-shaped moon rising on the horizon on a warm summer night? Have you ever commented on the thrilling sight of a purple-and-orange sunset casting its magic over thousands of people in a valley or flatlands? Have you ever gone to the trouble of rising early to see the sunrise on the other side of a lake or over the peak of a mountain? If you have done these things, then in my definition you are an astrologer, or at least an aspiring one.

Astrology begins, and perhaps its essence resides, in the undeniable power the sky has over our moods and emotions. The heart of astrology is not to be found in horoscopes and tables of houses and longitudes, although these tools are important and effective for a certain way of reading the sky. We can become astrologically astute by gradually attending to ordinary celestial events, by cultivating an awareness of the changing moon, the position of the sun, and the arrangement of planets and stars, noticing both traditional symbols and perhaps coming up with original stories and pictures. We might keep an eye on Orion's movements, or we might develop our own idea about the moon's comings and goings. Astronomy leads to a certain appreciation of the sky through measurement, while astrology invites us to stories and images about human life stimulated by patterns and qualities of light in the sky.

It's traditional in astrology to speak of the "influence" of planets and stars, and this idea is a stumbling block to many. Theologians and philosophers have fulminated in their defense of free will, which they see challenged by the idea of astrological influence, while our modern problem with celestial influence stems from our scientific knowledge about the sky and the apparent absurdity of imagining that a lifeless body could have any effect on our lives.

Yet, if we're emotionally affected by a sunrise or a beautiful moon, why not call this an "influence"? We can be "influenced" by a person or a book or a movie without engaging in moralistic harangues about the loss of will. Why not consider the same kind of relationship with the sky? A cloudy day certainly influences our mood differently than does a sunny day, and, more mysteriously, many people sense a foreboding atmosphere around a full moon.

From beyond recordable history people have refined their plain appreciation of the stars into images that guide life on earth. The stars form a zodiac, a belt of living mythological beings, a zoo of animals and other figures, that holds us in its crescent lap. In the course of time, observers of the sky have construed relationships among all the various celestial bodies, developing a system of aspects, or angles of position, rulership, planetary character, transits, and the interpretation of all these factors. Traditional astrology, East and West, is an intricate mythology of the soul, requiring a wealth of information and skill for its practice, and far deeper and more solidly based than superstition in its power to animate the imagination.

It is not unusual in general to find the natural world stimulating the imagination into story and poetry. As a way of explaining stories, scholars have often tried to trace traditional tales to their roots in nature, but we can reverse that principle and see nature as the source of the major mythologies of the world. Astrology is a form of imagination emerging from nature and having direct relevance for everyday life. It's an applied poetics, a vision of life on earth stimulated by movements in the heavens, which can take us into areas of self-reflection as no other system of symbols and images can.

Astrology, based on one of the most fundamental of human experiences—the feeling of wonder occasioned by celestial movements—is among the few self-contained symbol systems that can help make sense out of the chaos of life. When we feel confused and lost, we can use the sky for guidance.

And the sky has indeed been widely used: as the basis for religious ritual, as the inspiration for great mythological stories, for hints at making civic and military decisions, as the spark for powerful paintings, and as a guide to personality and daily living. It's impossible to look at most medieval paintings, cathedrals, or books of philosophy without running into an astrological vision. Most religions use some kind of astral technology, from rock observatories like Stonehenge to medieval European tables and formulas for setting the date of Easter, linking religious festivals and rituals to the celestial bodies. Shakespeare is riddled with astrology, as are the songs, psalms, and prayers of people in many religions around the earth. In his sermon on the Magi, Ficino says that those who study the stars are guided by none other than the angel Gabriel—a strong theological statement in support of the astrological vision.

Benefits of an Astrological Worldview

The advantages of an astrological viewpoint begin with living in tune with nature rather than in alienation from it. Even if we stay within the limits of the rudiments of astrology, we can find guidance to the rhythms and qualities of our most intimate lives. Watching a sunrise, or simply being aware of dawn as night turns into day, can present a subtle theology of hope on an ordinary morning. The approach of night, too, in a colorful sunset or in the lengthening of shadows or darkening of a room day after day, generates a sense of life's basic tempos and rhythms, teaching us important truths about our own lives and our own nights and days.

In his lecture on the sun, Ficino points out that Socrates often stood motionless, watching the sunrise, and gave special honor to the sun all his life. For this reason, Ficino says, Socrates was judged by the oracle of Apollo to be the wisest among his people. Ficino goes on to say that in his state of ecstasy, Socrates "admired not just the visible Sun, but its other, hidden aspect." There is an occult side to all of nature, and to the stars and planets in particular, but not "occult" only in the modern sense of being esoteric. The hidden aspect of nature is its microcosmic parallels in human life: a person's solar, lunar, mercurial, venusian, orionic, black hole-like, dawning, cometic, meteoric qualities.

The image of astrology that most people get from the typical newspaper shorthand, a clever and entirely personalistic reading of the sky, is far too literal and limited compared to the powerful sensitivity to life, inner and outer, that astrology can create. Astrology not only gives us images of emotional qualities; it also provides an intricate sense of time and timing especially relevant to the rhythms of human life.

At a simple level, we could be guided by astrology to avoid trying to accomplish anything important when the moon is "void of course," when it has no current relationship to a planet. We might refrain from activities like writing, speaking, or doing serious business when Mercury is moving backward as seen from Earth. When Venus is at a ninety-degree angle to Virgo, in a "square" aspect, it might be a good time to consider the paradoxes and struggles presented by sexual desire and the need for personal integrity and independence. We could understand this kind of guidance neither as a literal belief in physical planets nor as mere metaphor, but as a way to be connected to the world around us by means of a vivid, concrete, trusting imagination.

Through an astrological sensibility, we could learn that our personal and social rhythms are not unrelated to the rhythms of the world around us and that life is not as fully subjective as modern social sciences would lead us to believe. We could sense for ourselves that we are indeed microcosms, small worlds sharing many of the characteristics of the immense macrocosm.

We could cultivate a subtle and sophisticated sense of time as experienced, and not merely measured, by living in tune with our own felt rhythms and looking to the world outside us for models of timing. We could expand our notion of clock time with an appreciation for cosmic time. Where am I in my own daily, monthly, and yearly cycles? Is this the time to make endings or to dare beginnings? If we live our lives according to a mechanical clock, then our lives necessarily have a mechanical tone. Alternatively, we could become aware of our own personal seasons and tempos by noticing the blossomings and fadings of nature, by noting the special rhythms of the moon, or by contemplating the many implications of sunrise and sunset.

I find that I write best in the first hours of the morning or late at night, at those liminal times when the day's activities are beginning and ending, and so I try to incorporate that relation to the day in my work habits. Some days, thoughts and words simply don't arrive when I call for them, and then, rather than looking for some circumstance in the physical world around me to explain the "block," I assume that *my* moon is "void of course," disconnected from all the many centers that collaborate in the writing of a book, and I wait for the "sky" to change.

An astrological attitude directs attention away from the self, with its subjective, conscious, and willful decisions, toward an outer world that has its own mysterious ways of offering guidance and reflection. It gives us a concrete and explicit way to be in tune with nature, not just knowledgeable about it. Whether or not we practice astrology technically, it can show us a way to find deep guidance that transcends mere psychology. I would rather turn to astrology to expand psychology than reduce astrology to the psychological.

Keeping astrology somewhere between occult practice and modern psychology is a difficult, subtle task, demanding that our applied poetics remain both imagistic and connected to life. It's in this spirit that I read the lines of the Christian theologian Origen: "Know that you are another world in miniature and have in you Sol and Luna and even the stars" (*Homiliae in Leviticum, 5:2*). When I first read those words, twenty years ago, I began to reflect on the moon as mirrored in the interior life. Compared to the sun, the moon has a dimmer light, a faster pace, and its light is always emptying out or filling up. In poetry and art, it has been associated with the heart more than the mind, with love and romance, madness and preternatural forebodings. The dog howls at the moon and ignores the sun. The vampire comes out to enjoy the hazy light of the moon but is repelled by the sun's brilliance.

We all wax and wane and have a moonlit consciousness that is hazy, mysterious, changing, and not completely rational. Our creativity, our work, our intimate relationships, the sense that we are living a meaningful life—all of it fills and empties on a schedule not unlike that of the moon. It might help marriages if we recognized that our partner has lunar seizures and timings that may be due not to anything happening in life but rather to that person's natural unwilled lunar patterns. Beholding the moon in the sky may help us understand that it is intimately involved with our emotions and thoughts.

Unless you were to consider seriously the role astrology has had in culture for many centuries, you might not notice the considerable shift in sensibility that occurred when we lost touch with the movements of the stars and began to rely on mechanical measurements of time and its associated metaphors. The notion of time as a grid on which we can freely and independently structure a life takes away the appointments of fate and destiny. We lose the spirit of pious respect for movements and influences larger than ourselves and instead develop reliance on psychological intentionality.

With an astrological viewpoint, we can look beyond ourselves and into the world for signs of where to go and what to do. We can listen for suggestions from the world, of which we are a part, rather than initiating everything from subjective will and consciousness. This is the ethical dimension in enchanted living: deepening our sense of morality by learning the ways of nature.

Astrology is in essence not a belief, a method, a science or pseudoscience, or even an art. At base it is a form of relationship between human life and the world, a relationship in which we learn about ourselves by observing the sky. Inverting the idea that we have a sky within, we could see the heavens as our interiority turned inside out. In the mysterious dynamics of macrocosm/microcosm, the sky has a soul that to some measure overlaps with our own soul.

Robert Fludd wrote extensively about the macrocosm and microcosm, betraying his Neoplatonism and his deep astrological spirit in these words from his "Philosophicall Key": "Wherfore I cordialy admonish thee to ascende from this World unto God, that is to penetrat quite through thyself: for to clime up unto God, is to enter into thy self, and not only inwardly to visit thy dearest Soule, but also to perce into the very centre therof, to vew and behould ther thy Creatour."

In Fludd's rich imagination, astrology is a way to penetrate through yourself and enter into yourself at the very center, where a divine vision is made accessible. For him and for many of his colleagues, astrology is no mere catalog of advice but a path to self-discovery that is not limited, as modern psychology is, to purely human and subjective dimensions. It is a technology of mysticism, and although mysticism seems out of vogue in modern life, it is exactly the piece we are missing when we feel a vacancy in our hearts and in our minds, where no human love seems to satisfy and no human explanation makes absolute sense.

An astrological perspective opens up the mind, heart, and imagination, bursting the limited subjectivity that has been a harmful characteristic of modern life, embracing nothing less than the universe itself in our very definition of humankind. Many judgments, kind and unkind, are made about the European Renaissance. In my view, the greatest rediscovery of the Renaissance was the reclaiming of the cosmos as an essential element in our conception of human life. Philosophers, poets, and magi of the time were able to reconnect nature and culture and cultivate a constant interplay between human decision and natural phenomena. This aspect of the Renaissance was tenuous and didn't hold for long. Instead, we created modern technological life and abandoned magic.

Our current hope for enchantment lies in a recovery of the Renaissance appreciation of macrocosm/microcosm dynamics, spelled out so imaginatively by Fludd, Ficino, Paracelsus, and others. This could be achieved by a fresh appraisal of astrology, moving away from any hint of superstition toward an intelligent, sensitive, poetic, and existential intimacy with nature, who shows herself in the enchanting light display of the night sky. We can look deeply into that night sky and see ourselves.

Miracles of Sport

M Y UNCLE TOM spent his entire life on a small farm, but he made a few trips to the big city, and after one visit to Detroit, where he attended a Tigers baseball game, he told the story again and again of being mystified as he watched the pitcher throw a ball and then stretch out his gloved hand without looking as the ball magically returned to it. I think my uncle "got" one of the main points of sport: the spectacle of miracles.

We talk about "miracle plays," "Hail Mary passes," and "spectacular catches," because sports are full of miracles as athletes of extraordinary talent truly defy the laws of nature. They seem especially drawn to the violation of gravity, as they leap high into the air on a basketball court or baseball field, accomplish a series of somersaults on a gymnastics floor mat, dive for a catch or a tennis point, and bounce a soccer ball off their head while their feet are in the air. We spectators stand by and spectate, a more intense activity than mere watching, as we behold preternatural events as though we were still in the Garden of Eden and the laws of physics had not yet been written in stone.

The enchantment of sports, then, lies first in its capacity to take us away from the laws of nature and introduce us to a world that is real but not limited by ordinary physical laws. Like the magician, the athlete shows us the hidden potentialities of nature, and to that extent sport is an occult art. The ancient book of magic *Picatrix* defines magic in this way: "Generally we label as magical anything hidden from the senses and things most people can't explain as to how they come into being or what causes them." According to this definition, sports are filled with magic. They enchant by revealing a realm that is close to nature—most sports are eminently physical and bodily—and yet otherworldly at the same time.

Green Grass and AstroTurf

Several years ago I gave a lecture in the city of Dallas called "Dream City Dream," about the role of green places in the city. I discussed the value of gardens and trees, but I emphasized empty green areas like lawns in front of homes or in parks. Following a number of old sources, I described the open green space in a village or city as the "field" on which the soul's fate is played out. I said that it makes little difference if the field is natural grass, AstroTurf, or green felt, as on billiard tables, which are a kind of indoor village green.

We have already seen the importance of a temenos in the enchantment of culture, and the green field of baseball, soccer, tennis, football, croquet, and other sports, and of green felt tables for pool and billiards, are examples of temenos. The field is a place green in its devotion to pristine nature and open in its role of providing a place where the soul can work out its destiny.

In "The Echoing Green," the remarkable poem by William Blake, that begins at sunrise and ends at sunset, tracing the life arc of individuals and the community, the poet implies that sports are an echo of the shifting qualities of the time of life:

> While our sports shall be seen
> On the echoing green.

On the open green field of play we see the outlines of our own lives, and so we are enchanted as one who looks at the book of days and beholds the perimeters and major contours of a life.

My own sense is that when watching a professional football game in a modern stadium, the AstroTurf intensifies the sense of game and, as vividly as grass, portrays the eternal aspect of a "field." The extravagant green of the turf makes it as clear as possible that the game being played takes place in the unnatural and yet real space of sport and game, a space where the imagination is more at play than it is in life. The enchantment of the stadium is due to the enhancement of imagination made by the brilliantly artificial green and the unnaturally colorful uniforms of the players. The soul's field is revealed in that false lawn, just as it is in the felt of the pool hall.

We each have our own "fields" on which our lives play themselves out, our own course and our own turf, natural or otherwise. It's an old idea that each person has certain hazards as well—the fence of a steeplechase, the sand traps of golf, the net in tennis, and the pockets of billiards—which give life its challenge and threat and at the same time make the "game" interesting.

In their own way, sports reveal the interiority of ordinary life, another aspect of enchantment. Loss and success, for example, with their attendant emotions, are a part of everyday experience—"We win some, we lose some." And so it is in sports: One day we win the game, the next day we lose. One year a team wins the World Series, the next year another team wins. The idea of an ultimate victor is not as significant as the rhythm of success and failure, and of course the possibility of surviving losses, even when they're felt deeply and are emotionally shattering.

All of this is not merely preparation for life but the opportunity to contemplate life's dynamics and rhythms. The pleasure of sports lies not just in winning but in playing the game, in going through the entire gamut of emotions. Sports may involve theater and spectacle, because they are a form of contemplation. The playing field strips away the details of an individual life and allows us to meditate on the structures and dynamics of everyday life. Knowing those elements so well, we spectators become absorbed and emotionally involved in the play and in the outcome.

Sports and Emotion

The magus takes life with utter seriousness and yet at the same time allows the play element an important role. Could it be that since we exclude play from our serious work, in reaction we sometimes get wildly caught up in the emotions of spectator sports? A certain emotional emptiness seems to accompany extreme involvement in sports, and the jokes often told about family neglect due to a father's fanatical devotion to his team also hint at the psychological extremes that may attend sports.

Sports announcers and players talk with a degree of excitement and hyperbole that is found in religious and spiritual enthusiasm. Different sports vary, of course, in the degree of spiritual excitement they generate. A football game is like a spiritual revival meeting, while tennis and golf are more contemplative, at least as spectator sports. Baseball mixes spiritual excitement with interior contemplation, as pitchers and managers play their interior game of strategies and symbolic communications.

Sports offer important experiences of "virtual life," where actions and events have little impact on the political and social life of the culture and yet are observed with considerable passion. This virtual life is the life of the imagination, the life of the soul, the field set apart from literal activity, where things matter a great deal, even though they are not part of daily business.

Sports are especially important in our culture because apparently the soul needs to contemplate its own reality much more frequently than our style of life allows. Some cultures are almost entirely ritualistic and poetic, while our culture sees ordinary life as separate from poetry and religion. We have the arts, religion, and sports to offer us the kind of ritual contemplation we need, but with the arts made marginal to the culture as a whole and with religion in relative decline, especially in its communal ritual elements, we are left with sports as a last resort.

History teaches that sports are closely related to the arts and religion. The Olympic Games have roots in Greek religion, and we know that at one time athletic games were an important part of festivals in Rome and in the Americas. Nicholas of Cusa wrote a book about soul and fate entitled *De Ludo Globi* (The Ball Game). This fascinating exploration of the most intimate aspects of a person's life begins with a discussion comparing the ball used in the game—we could be talking about a baseball, soccer ball, or basketball—to the sphere of the world. "No honest game," he writes, "fails to teach," and "even chess and checkers contain moral mysteries."

These comments of the fifteenth-century cardinal of the Church could lead us to look further into the occult side of sports, at specific images that work both for the game and for life. Certain expressions, applying to human nature, have moved from a game into everyday life. "Three strikes and you're out," comes from baseball, and everyone knows that life gives us a certain number of opportunities but not an infinite number. If we keep making a mistake, we'll eventually run out of chances.

"Playing without a net," "playing on a level field," "scoring," "fumbling the ball"—these and hundreds of other sayings have entered daily discourse, hinting at the meaningfulness of the game. I don't want to say simply that sports teach us how to live life, but athletic games address concerns of the soul, and those concerns find their way into daily life.

Sports and Enchantment

Sports don't automatically provide enchantment, because, like art and religion, they can be used for ideological, political, and narcissistic purposes and lose their power to entrance. If a game is "fixed," the spectators suffer because the important elements of chance and contest have been manipulated out of the game. If, as sometimes happens in professional sports, the players fail really to play because their minds are on money rather than the game, then again spectators suffer, because the game has been diminished. Spectacle and festival are part of athletics, but if our stadiums become too big and too sensational, then the power of the game to satisfy the soul may falter.

The soul's need for athletic contemplation can be well satisfied in a city park where people play a simple pickup game. In fact, in such a simple setting there may be less chance of interference with the game than in a grand stadium for professional teams. The simple, the ordinary, and the intimate always give more to the heart than the extraordinary and the grand, which enhance the spirit but not necessarily the soul.

The syllogism I would present to a city council is simple: The social problems of our time are due entirely to a wounding of soul occasioned by the style of life we've adopted; their solution requires that we step outside the boundaries of that style and do all we can to nurture the soul. The local athletic field, the park green, the forest within the city limits and the surrounding farmlands and wilderness—these address the soul more than a plethora of well-intentioned but effortful plans for policing and improving the status quo. Therefore, I urge you to preserve the ballparks, the picnic areas, the commons, the tennis courts, and the running and bicycling paths. Like all magical formulas, they produce infinite benefit for the soul with inconspicuous means.

One of many excellent soulful ideas realized in our town was the transformation of an existing but unused railway line into a bicycle and walking path that takes you along miles of beautiful farmland at the edge of town, along creeks and ravines, across an old bridge spanning the wide part of our river, and into the next town. The best solutions to social problems are often humble and unusually imaginative.

The soft beauty of a quiet bicycle path is not the only value in sports, which are often brutal in their physical demands and in the spirit of competition. As we try to find a soulful entry into the realm of sport, let's not sentimentalize it. The *American Heritage Dictionary* has a curious entry for the word "athlete." It apologizes for the etymology of the word, which emphasizes competition and prize. But these, too, represent an important element in sports— winning the game, beating the opponent, and taking home the prize.

It's sometimes said that sports *sublimate* our aggressive tendencies, and sublimation is seen as a way of appeasing the drive to succeed and conquer. I'd rather understand sublimation in an alchemical sense (sublimation is the phase in alchemy where the material rises to a new level of spirituality and imagination), where we are not simply cleaning up shadowy desires but are fulfilling those desires at a more meaningful and less literal level. Following this line of thought, we could interpret literal aggressiveness in business or on the street as a failure in imagination and competition in sports as a fulfilling exercise in imagination.

Only when the athletic agony turns literal is there danger, and there the danger is literalism, not competition. In business and in politics, competition and striving for reward are worthy parts of the game; only when the combatants forget the limits and the rules do they fall into the tragic outcomes of literal aggression. It's instructive, therefore, to read in the dictionary that athletics have an ancient accent on competition and reward, and the etymological story might help us reconstruct and mitigate aggressiveness by finding a place for it in imagination.

Mythologies of Sport

One of the most charming stories in Ovid's beautiful *Metamorphoses* concerns the Diana-like runner Atalanta, who was advised by the oracle never to marry. But she was extraordinarily beautiful, and many men sought her in marriage. She made a deal with them: She would marry anyone who beat her in a race, but the losers would die.

One young man, Hippomenes, a grandson of the sea god, Neptune, thought he could beat her, and when he saw her running fast and naked, he fell in love with her. For her part, Atalanta fell in love with his youthfulness—Atalanta, as a follower of Diana, felt a special calling to protect children and adolescents. Hippomenes, whose name means horse strength, called on the goddess of love to help him, and Venus came up with a plan. She brought him golden apples and instructed him to throw the apples as a distraction and a lure for Atalanta during the race. Indeed, the shiny apples caught the young woman's eye, and she faltered as she went off the track to pick them up. The young man won the race, and the two were married.

Unfortunately, Hippomenes neglected to thank Venus adequately, and she cursed the couple by turning them into lions—the metamorphosis in this particular tale.

The story has many interesting, wide-ranging motifs and overtones, but we can use it to gain insight into sports. One of the formative deep stories in athletics, though not the only one, involves a Diana-like devotion to oneself and one's talent. It is not narcissism but rather such a loyalty to oneself that marriage of any kind seems a contradiction. I wonder if this story is behind the thought that one should not have sex before an important competition, and if any element of homoeroticism in sports is tied into it as well.

The story reveals that part of the enchantment of sports lies in the beauty of the running or the play action. We might learn from this theme the importance of emphasizing the beauty in sports and not just the muscle or the achievement. The story also hints at the desire in sports to remain apart from the ordinary business of life, protecting the boundaries of the field and the borders of the athletes' lives. Sports call for a kind of dedication that may be compared to preserving one's virginity and purity. Certainly we feel a violation of that purity when politics or business stains a college team with bribes and illegal manipulations.

Yet, as the story makes plain, that purity can be excessive, and Venus may play a role in tempering it, connecting with other aspects of life. Her golden apples, a common symbol in representations of Venus, echo the apple of Adam and Eve that accounted for their expulsion from paradise. Sports can be humanized by reconnecting them with religion and art, by taking the rituals and festivals seriously, with piety more than pomp, and by linking sports to the other arts: running and dance, football and theater, tennis and painting, baseball and architecture.

When I was a young man I liked to watch college football games, and I appreciated the music and the pageantry of halftime marching bands. But somewhere along the way, television executives decided it would be better to spend the halftime break listening to experts tally up the statistics and analyze the play—making the game more abstract and opinionated. Cutting theater and music out of the presentation of the game was a slight change but nevertheless indicative of the continual, corroding disenchantment of sports.

Recently I heard a minister on the radio begin the Sunday service by talking about the previous day's football game, and I was reminded once again of the important connection between religion and sports. That connection today is quite hidden, of course, although in the time of the early Greeks the Olympic Games were under the aegis of the father of the gods, Zeus. Vestiges remain, as when an athlete makes the sign of the cross before a free throw or the team says a prayer at the start of a game.

I don't know what it would take to desecularize our sports, but I know that if we accomplished that feat, it would mark a return to ancient practice. We could make an effort of imagination to nurture even the slightest connections among sports, beauty, and ritual and avoid the risk of offending the Venusian necessities that lie deep in the nature of things. If we offend Venus—her beauty and divinity—in our athletic prowess, we will be turned into lions, turning savage the aggression that is an essential ingredient in all sports.

Marsilio Ficino said that Venus is one of the graces that make life humane. Our story of Atalanta teaches us, too, that Venus has a role to play, keeping our sports honest and connected to life. Atalanta's beauty, the appeal of sports, can be severe and risky, unless she is slowed by the beautiful fruit of Venus. Sports can get out of hand unless we stop to admire the green lawns of tennis and polo, the outfields of baseball, the rolling fairways of golf, and the perfectly timed plays and the ingenious strategies of football.

I have begun taking tennis lessons for the first time in my life. When I'm told how to hold my hand and arm, how to address the ball, and how to follow through, I feel as though I'm back in the monastery, learning how to meditate and shape a sacred life. Tennis is yet another powerful means of finding the occult and holy imagination in the simple adjustment of a forearm. As an altar boy, I was taught to fold my hands in an attitude of prayer, while in tennis I'm told to follow through and watch the ball go where I want it to go. Nicholas of Cusa was right: the most profound mysteries are there in the ball and in the way we address it in sport.

Earthen Spirituality

ONE DAY WHEN I was walking the beach in the rain on Iona, the holy island off the coast of Scotland, looking for a stone to give my friend Alice, whose love of Iona and stories of her travels there had much to do with my walking that beach, I came across a small irregular pebble, grayish but for a strange marking in yellow. It looked as though the eons of time had etched a rune in that pebble, and then, as the image came clearer to my eyes, it appeared to be a *Y.*

The world itself asks the question "Why?" I thought. Why am I on this beach? Why did I notice this stone of all the millions of them around me?

But then my thoughts turned. The stone seemed to be addressing me. "Why are you here?"

I recalled a passage in Jung's memoirs where he tells the story of how when he was a boy he sat on a stone that eased his anxieties, a stone that had, as he expressed it, its own subjectivity, that could think and refer to itself as "I." This sense that the world is everywhere expressive is not as evident in Jung's theoretical writings as it is in his memoirs, where he describes his own long life of enchantment.

Jung also devoted many pages of his writing to the spirit of Mercury, a Roman god and also a major figure in alchemy, known in the Renaissance as the spirit in language, poetry, money, and business. Mercury is closely related to the Greek deity Hermes, guide of souls, a role that is even more fundamental and profound. The Greeks believed you could sense his spirit in a pile of stones or even in a sneeze, both indications of the unexpected expressive powers of nature.

Thinking classically, I had no doubt that Mercury had carved the *Y* in the Iona stone before me; he is the god of nature's alphabets and unexpected revelations, the *anima mundi*, Jung says, the soul of the world. He is the anima, even though anima is feminine. Like the caduceus staff, the medical emblem on which two snakes intertwine, the spirit of Mercury confounds all our attempts to divide the world in two. He mingles what we usually keep separate, hides what appears to be revealed, and reveals everything in hidden, indirect ways. He is the feminine face of the world.

Ficino says that the traditional representations of the Mercurial spirit include a man sitting on a peacock, perhaps dressed in multicolored garments, with eagle feet. Artists and magicians of Ficino's time saw in the rainbow dots on a peacock's tail the stars and planets, and alchemists sometimes described the goal of the great Work in the same imagery. It was common to portray the parts of a human life in such hybrids, and even today if you walk in Ficino's garden, just outside Florence, you will see a large sculpture of an old man in a child's body, sitting on an owl.

An alchemical illustration from Renaissance times pictures the hermaphrodite, a person, like Mercury, of two genders, while in the background is a stone carved in the perfect form of the letter *Y*. But here the meaning is the coming together in one place of opposites and differences, and so I may understand the curious stone that "caught my eye" on Iona as a hint that there, on my pilgrimage, I was experiencing a reconciliation of opposites for myself, notably in the rediscovery of spirituality in a place extraordinarily elemental and earthly.

As I imagine it, Mercury is the spirit in nature and culture that infuses all variety of activity and gives the ordinary world wings of spirit. In this Mercurial spirit we can be many things at once: worldly and otherworldly, intellectual and emotional, still and creative. Winged Mercury also gives us a way to appreciate the spirituality of the most ordinary place and everyday activities.

In the Renaissance style of elaborating Greek and Roman polytheism, Mercury is one of several ways the spirit of the world shows itself. Life's multifaceted spirituality can be seen in its Mercurial expressiveness, Venusian beauty, Saturnine mystery, and Jovial meaningfulness, to mention only a few possibilities, and each of these is a kind of spirituality.

When we perceive the world as expressive, we can then cultivate a spiritual life around it, as do the pueblo dwellers of the American Southwest, who honor their sacred mountains and build their homes in the context of those mountains. The art historian Vincent Scully describes the corn dance at Tesuque in New Mexico in language that would be familiar to the European magus: "Nature's energy is being recharged, to be released in vast, strong waves of human joy. . . . It is the place where men have power enough, through their communal life, to act with some effect in the face of nature, but also the place where, most of all, not confronting or insulting but rather praising and abetting her being, they can play a willing, vital part in her vast scheme."

Enchantment is nothing more than the recognition of the world's spirituality and the exposure to its influence. An influence is primarily an "inflow," and to be enchanted you have to allow the spirit of the world to flow into you. This is one way we live our lives in accord with the world around us and yet another way to define enchantment. We are a microcosm, a small world, a human universe, to use the inspiring phrase of Nicholas of Cusa, and as we shape our lives, we have to take into account the natural world around us. We can't adequately define and imagine who we are without including it in our definition. Not only are we a universe, but nature, too, has its own humanity, in us.

Nature Spirituality

The idea of receiving the influx of the world's spirituality was spelled out beautifully by the "philosopher of the Arabs," al-Kindi, who died in 870 and was a teacher in the House of Wisdom established by the caliph al-Mansūr in Baghdad. Al-Kindi's book *On the Stellar Rays* spells out the principles of magic by which we can be educated through the influences of nature, and it was this book that had a powerful effect five hundred years later in the work of Marsilio Ficino, who quotes al-Kindi and uses his teachings almost word for word.

In his book, al-Kindi speaks exclusively about astrological influence, but Ficino suggests many ways this magic of nature can be extended to operate in all of life. According to al-Kindi, the stars all differ in their properties and have equally varied effects through the impression of their rays on earthly life. This principle, familiar to us from our discussion of Ficino's magic, suggests that it isn't enough in an enchanted world to expose ourselves to nature, art, or technology. It is the task of our soul work to open ourselves to a wide variety of influx, to enrich our souls and expand them by receiving the many gifts life has to offer.

Al-Kindi's teaching also suggests that the attitude of receiving is as important as the work of doing and building. In modern times, it seems natural to talk about building culture and making a future. We're proud of our achievements and appreciate a "can do" spirit. One never hears how far we have advanced in our capacity to receive the influence of nature or to become conduits of past wisdom. We don't brag about being "can be done to" people, and we find most forms of passivity distasteful. Yet, as Vincent Scully suggests, we can be recharged by taking nature's spirituality into us and allowing it to transform us into natural beings. We can be fulfilled not only by developing a creative ego and a unique personality but also by living as fully as possible the nature life that flows through us in common.

The Farm Spirit

A powerful example for me of a natural spirit that dovetails beautifully with human aspiration is a simple one—the farm. For whatever reasons of fate and family, in my childhood I spent many seasons of enchantment on my uncle's small farm. I was captivated by the variety of life I found in that microcosm, a world entirely different from the one I knew and enjoyed at my home in the city. On the farm I learned to love the aromas of hay, wheat, oats, corn, and even manure. I discovered something of the habits and fascinating quirks of pigs, chickens, horses, and cows. I came to love the vistas of pasture, woods, orchard, and fields of grain. On quiet rainy days especially I studied the magical stairs, stalls, posts, walls, and floors of the old weathered barns and out-buildings, and I examined all the many nails, screws, bolts, sharpening stones, and inexplicable equipment associated with old, outmoded farm equipment. I think I learned something important, too, from living in a house without running water and from daily visits to the aromatic and always haunting outhouse.

Today, forty years later, a day is complete if I can visit a local farm or just drive past one and catch a glimpse of an animal or a cultivated field. I need an orchard, if only two fruit trees, near my own home, and love to see a hill or a field that has the spirit of pasture. I worry about our civilization losing its farms, not because we need food grown on small farms—although that is true, too—but because we need the *spirit* of the farm in our midst. If we can find any wisdom in the teachings of al-Kindi and Ficino, then we might appreciate the loss to the soul in the disappearance of farms.

The poet Wendell Berry has raised a strong voice in favor of preserving farms. "You cannot have a post-agricultural world," he says, "that is not also post-democratic, post-religious, and post-natural— in other words it will be, as we have understood ourselves, post-human." I think it's appropriate to add that a world without farms would be "post-soul." The soul is nourished by being exposed to a variety of rich spirits, especially those that emanate directly from the earth, that feed it, educate it, and fill it with value.

Some spirits are stronger than others, says al-Kindi. The farm spirit is one of the strong ones, the needed ones. The Greeks worshiped a daimon of the farm and in their stories called him Aristaeus. Known as "the best god of all," he was famous as the guardian spirit of beekeeping, orchards, and farms. He got into trouble once when he took a liking to Eurydice, wife of Orpheus, but farmers are not perfect.

We could each talk about a spirit in the world, indeed many spirits that have enchanted us and continue to sustain us with their charm and values. For myself, I could tell long stories about music, woodworking, certain rivers and lakes, a city neighborhood, a building, an office—each of them with its own fructifying daimon, its tales, and its beauty. From the point of view of enchantment, one of the greatest threats to human life today is the loss of variety in rich, elemental experiences in nature and culture. Without a base of natural spirituality, we work against ourselves and our environs in all that we do, and we lack the necessary magic that nature offers in the simplest forms, if only by pounding our feet on the earth in a dance of praise.

Piety

Sometimes spirituality implies belief in a particular doctrine or dedication to universal morals and theologies, but the spirituality of enchantment involves other qualities associated with the religious life. In particular, attitudes of piety and devotion—to nature, home, work, family, and community—help sustain an enchanted world. These words "piety" and "devotion" are not part of the modern vocabulary; both are perhaps too romantic in an age of cool rationality and mechanics. Yet they represent an attitude necessary for living in an enchanted world, where careful tending of the soul results in an atmosphere full of connections and significances.

Piety has linguistic ties to "pity," which perhaps accounts for some of the modern distaste for the word, but unlike pity, it refers to an attitude in which we give ourselves, heart and soul, to that which we revere and honor. Piety also implies some kind of behavior that expresses our devotion and respect. We can be completely dedicated to our work or to nature, but an attitude of piety adds the element of heartfelt attention. Piety also includes an acknowledgment of something sacred in whatever it is we are tending; our piety sustains the spirits that animate our world.

Acts of piety can be quite simple, like planting a tree at the birth of a child, and yet they have infinite value to the heart. In *Lady Chatterley's Lover*, D. H. Lawrence has the gamekeeper drive a nail into a tree, an old traditional example of a lover's piety. I light a candle before I write, not because I need the light, but because my heart needs to be invited into the work, and I need to write in a way that honors the angels, muses, and spirits who are the only true crafters of words. It's one thing for an artist to admit that she is not the real author of her words or pictures, that *something else* brings the ideas, and another to acknowledge this other spirit with names and small rites of reverence.

As slight as piety might appear in an age of machines and vast storehouses of information, it is the absence of this virtue that accounts in large measure for our current degradation of nature and the loss of dignity in human labor. The smallest pious act transforms any activity from a secularistic, egotistic, effortful expression of human narcissism into a holy, effective, and humane act of creativity.

In a spirit of piety we acknowledge that we humans are not the only individuals, personalities, and subjectivities in the universe. We grant Jung's stone its capacity to be an "I." We allow a particular farm to have its own personality and its role in the family history. We let a river shower its banks with a spirit that invades the people living there, and we protect that river, knowing that without its blessings the people have no source of soul but their own lives.

In a spirit of piety we honor not only our own soldiers who have fought courageously but also those we have killed. We visit the shrine at Hiroshima, and see the blood on our hands, and perhaps find a sensitivity within us that will inhibit our violent aggression in the future. Piously, we visit prisons and perhaps take to heart the adage that there, but for the grace of God, I would sit and spend my days. Piety is often the entry to initiation, to change of heart and the discovery of conscience. Piously, we visit relatives, friends, and strangers in hospitals and perhaps have a life-changing experience in the presence of death.

Piety is an attitude difficult to cultivate in a generally impious world. With its associated virtues of reverence and devotion, piety moves us to build our shrines and protect our inheritances of nature and culture. Wallace Stevens writes: "The poet feels *abundantly* the poetry of everything." His accent on abundant feeling could be applied to piety, which is an attitude that grows out of the generosity of our spirit to experience life fully. If we are not pious generally, it's because we don't think we can bear our feelings, and so we keep our emotions and attachments in reserve. Withholding oneself is the opposite of piety.

The pious person doesn't have good reasons for his or her piety, and probably doesn't understand the emotions that support it. Only in an intellectualized world would such a fundamental virtue as piety fall into neglect, because the pious person knows that you don't have to understand that to which you are devoted. Piety is a form of love, and although love and knowledge can become inseparably intimate, one is not the same as the other. Piety pours from the heart and doesn't require prior intellectual approval.

My parents are pious people, but they don't flaunt their piety, and it isn't at all saccharine. They are not terribly worldly, but their piety virtually surrounds them like an aura—piety toward family, children, and church. Near my home, a group of monks maintain a place of meditation and retreat at the top of a wooded hill. A visit to their shrine and to the surrounding terrain, filled with carefully made gates and walkways and water gardens, places you fully in an atmosphere of piety. You know the piety of the place from the evident care given to every detail of the simple surroundings.

In contrast, it isn't difficult to find yourself in a place void of piety, where nothing seems sacred and nowhere is care evident. Not long ago I found myself in the lower level of a large office complex. I was surrounded by concrete and marble and artificial light. People were walking past me quickly, their blank eyes focused on an office several minutes in front of them. I got lost and, turning a corner, I found myself going in the wrong direction. Thousands of people were stomping toward me with briefcases and doughnuts in hand. I was forced to join the flow, like a bug floating down a sewer.

When eventually I found my way to peace and quiet, I was still surrounded by granite, but there I saw ten or fifteen swarthy men planting brightly colored flowers in a concrete circle around a fountain. I could see their piety as they handled the plants knowingly and carefully, and it was clear that they had not been educated in this place and that they didn't spend their days in these offices. Piety shows itself in the grace of a hand movement and in the expression on a face that reveals love and respectful familiarity.

Emanating Spirituality

The kind of spirituality that fosters enchantment is not the variety that feeds on a creed alone. It is the kind that discovers holiness around every corner. Some forms of spirituality aim infinitely high, and we see them reflected in towering buildings and church steeples. But there is a spirituality that is more like a lowly emanation from the most humble and earthbound things: that of a particular house, a garden, a neighborhood, a grove of trees, a pristine

beach, a holy well, a field of wheat. Here spirituality is indistinguishable from enchantment, for in an enchanted world the things
of nature and even of culture reek of holiness. Enchantment is
nothing more than spirituality deeply rooted in the earth.

Every religion has in its history some attempt to find an earth-
oriented spirituality, whether in the songs of Hildegard of Bingen,
the philosophy of Teilhard de Chardin, the Zen garden, or the
Hindu temple. It is particularly exciting to encounter such exalted
expressions of spirituality connected to plants, rocks, and earth, for
there we find the marriage of heaven and earth and the reconciliation of the infinite with the finite. Human life stands between these
two realms, for human life is defined essentially by the soul, which
is the mediating element that enjoys both the aspirations of the
most transcendent spirituality and the lowliest devotion to nature
and human endeavor.

Spirits

*The world being illusive, one must be deluded
in some way if one is to triumph in it.*

W. B. YEATS

The Mediation of Angels

ONE CRISP FALL afternoon in New England, I was pushing my little daughter on a swing when she initiated a theological discussion with me. "God can't be seen, but angels can be," she said, with all the confidence and finality of a medieval bishop. She went on, and I don't know where her thoughts came from, because I had never talked about these things with her previously: "Angels can be very small." She made a measurement of about an inch with her tiny fingers. Then her final statement on the matter: "God can hear us when we talk to him, because he has a hearing aid, just like Grandpa's."

A year before this discussion took place, my wife and daughter were standing at the edge of a small lake, when out of the blue my daughter said in a matter-of-fact tone: "Do you see those angels over there?" She pointed to the opposite side of the lake.

"No, I don't see them," my wife responded.

"They're dressed all in white."

My wife looked and saw only the dappled leaves and the reflection of fall-colored trees in the lake. If there is any adult who would be able to see angels, it is my daughter's mother. I have no doubt that my daughter saw angels and that angels are as real as anything else, and I don't need to be convinced by logic, evidence, or reason that angels do or do not exist. In an enchanted world, one doesn't allow the magic to slip away through any anxious demand for certainty. Mircea Eliade wrote in his diaries: "We must content ourselves with personal certitudes, with wagers based on dreams, with divinations, ecstasies, aesthetic emotions. That is also a mode of knowing, but without arguments."

The fact that angels are included in religious traditions of every variety all over the world and that they have been painted by a multitude of artists, who portray their characteristics with remarkable consistency, is enough to convince me that angels are real and are to be taken seriously. I need no further proof, because sacred imagery is a more reliable source for the nature of religious experience than any scientific investigation or personal testimony.

I have appeared on several television programs when the topic was angels, and I have been dumbfounded by the direction of conversation: a tone of defensive testimony to the existence of angels, coupled with stories of angel sightings. The discussions sounded more to me like arguments over UFOs than serious consideration of a theological issue.

I think my daughter had the best theological approach: God is necessarily invisible, and so angels act as intermediaries between the human and the divine and therefore must be seen at certain times. I was tempted to mention the idea of *deus absconditus* to my daughter, the hiddenness of the divine, but she was only three years old and the subject seemed just a little inappropriate. A similar image is *deus otiosus,* withdrawn divinity, the god who in many cultures creates the world and then fades into the background in retirement. As Mircea Eliade says, this removal of the divine from daily human life is an aspect of divinity's sublimity and transcendence. It's the very nature of the divine to be invisible in human affairs.

My daughter made another significant and relevant theological statement in that fall discussion when she asked, again without any prodding from me or any context that I knew of: "Does God hold us like puppets?"

"What was that word?" I asked, astonished that she would think in such terms.

"Puppets."

I thought of the many raging debates in theological circles about free will and determinism, and knew that theologians do everything they can to avoid the idea that the divine relates to human life in the form of a puppetmaster.

"No, we're not puppets," I said.

The fact that we are not puppets allows for the necessity of angels, who act as messengers of the divine will. We have ways of finding out which direction our lives might take, but we're free to respond in any way we want to. If we are seriously interested in knowing the deep roots and essential characteristics of our own nature and fate, then we might do well to keep our eyes and ears open for angels, who perform the hermetic function of guiding the soul.

According to some stories and teachings, angels sometimes appear in the form of human beings or other familiar figures. This is not to say that angels are mere ordinary mortals playing the function of angels, but that the presence of the angelic order is occasioned and made manifest by a familiar person, animal, or thing. I appreciated my daughter's description of angels as about an inch high; I have seen pictures of angels as very small creatures, and I recall that the respected historian of Greek religion Jane Harrison traced the image of Eros as an angel to early depictions of love as a wasplike winged insect. Of course, angels sometimes appear in dimensions greater than human, as in the paintings of Piero della Francesca, where angels are stout figures, strong and overpowering; but even there they are eminently human in appearance.

Angels and Enchantment

It's always dangerous to compare cultures, but I suspect a close parallel between Thomas Aquinas's description of angels as "separated substances," real beings who are substantial though not the way we are, and the Navajo approach to spirits. As one Navajo describes the Holy People, Diyin Dine'é, they themselves told humans at the time of Creation: "From this day on until the end of days you shall not see them again [in person], that is final. . . . Although you apparently can see the wind [now], you will only hear its voice in the future."

Enchanted life is mystifying and frustrating. In it we don't close ourselves off to a spiritual realm by hiding within the bubble of rationalism and materialism, but neither are we certain of what we see and don't see, or what we know and don't know. The Navajo teaches that angels are like the wind and thinks he sees the Holy

People in the sights and sounds of the natural world and in the faces of people he meets in the course of a day. This is a discomforting aspect of enchanted living: the spirits sometimes can't be separated from actual people or the things of nature. The anthropologist explains that what the Navajo sees is the holiness and spirituality in people, but that explanation is surely a disenchanted conclusion. I think that angels don't like being reduced to abstractions any more than humans do.

The only way to sustain enchantment is not to speak of angels literally, materialistically, or metaphorically, and yet to speak of them with respect and seriousness. This is the way of the painters of centuries who, in European art, have left us with hundreds of images of angels: with wings and without wings, with small wings and grand wings, with musical instruments of every kind, with words flowing from their mouths on banners, speaking, singing, flying, standing, enfolding, defending, praying, and announcing.

Angels and related spirits from the world's cultures are essential to enchantment, for they are all we have left in our desire to connect with ultimacy and divinity. Without the flutter of their wings in the background of experience, we have only the grinding and purring of machines or the white noise and hum of our own ceaseless thought.

In the original Greek, *angelos* means messenger. In Pindar, a daughter of Hermes is called "angel," and Hesiod describes Iris as an angel. Hermes is the go-between of the gods, as is Iris, and they suggest that an angel is a special kind of messenger that mediates between the human and the divine. Angels deliver messages from God, as in the case of the angel Gabriel visiting the Virgin Mary to give her the news that she was pregnant by the Holy Spirit, or the same angel delivering the Qur'an to Mohammed.

The idea of mediation is central in religion. If God is hidden behind or within his work of creation, then we need some visible form, some way of perceiving the continuing work of divinity in the human sphere, and angels perform that role perfectly. How are we to commune with what we believe to be divine, the ultimate resource that gives us some chance of value and meaning? How are we to connect with the deep source of "self" that lies far beneath our understanding and control? How are we to make genuine contact with another person, without speaking inanities or playing games of power and seduction? And how are we to feel part of nature lying all around us, pressing upon us with its beauty and terror?

One solution to these problems is to find an intermediary, an angel, who can speak the words that come from a deep enough place and have a source in an existence more sublime than human consciousness, and who moves easily in the world of invisibles. Rilke's famous description of the Angel remains apropos and profound: "The creature in whom the transformation of the visible into the invisible we are performing already appears complete." As we try to live more and more fully and become more and more ourselves, we are approaching, in Rilke's terms, the place already enjoyed by the angel.

Most of modern culture is profoundly narcissistic. In religion, science, politics, education, psychology—everywhere you look, the culture is trying to get better and achieve personal transcendence. That value is usually measured by knowledge, skill, financial income, prestige, social level, or positions of power and influence. Even religion and spiritual practice often aim at the perfection of the practitioner, and students and novices narcissistically measure their success by their level of spiritual achievement.

But the angel leads us in an entirely different direction. Gabriel tells the Virgin Mary that something momentous is happening to her, but he can't explain it and she will never understand it. The same angel pours words of wisdom into the ears of Mohammed, but the prophet can do nothing but bring them, as received, to the rest of the world. The angel takes everything into the invisible world, perhaps so that through the angel we can each become *homo absconditus,* a hidden person, living the paradox of invisibility and manifest presence, who in our materialism can cease denying the invisible and begin to live it. As life goes on, we ourselves might become more like the angel, visible mainly in the natural world that surrounds us, in the beauty that we manufacture, and in the persons who are our intimates, but not visible egotistically in our personalities.

If we were to give up the "self project" so dear to many therapies and theories of psychology, education, and spirituality, we might see angels once again; for the blazing light of self-interest blanks out the glow of angels. In our communities and friendships, if we were to look for the deeply hidden presence of the angel in others, we might get past all the personal, psychological judgments that keep love out of our lives. Whether we're concerned about our own "self" or the "self" of others, that attention blocks our appreciation of the angel who stands at the doorway of the truly deep and intimate.

Yet it's clear that to speak of angels and other spirits at all, we have to speak poetically. Our words can't be denotative and definitional, as they are with other things. Angels remain hidden, in spite of our talk about them and our consideration of their presence. Long ago, in mythic time, they decided not to reveal themselves directly in human life. Like the wind, their caressing and stinging presence is felt invisibly, but fortunately we can glimpse them in the sounds and sights of nature and in the faces of those we encounter in daily life.

In my book *Care of the Soul,* I told the story of a young chemist who walked with me along a stretch of railroad track and told me in no uncertain terms that I would be a priest all my life. These words came across to me as if they had been written on an angel's banner, and it makes no difference how the young man himself might explain his words. The angel speaks through human voices sometimes, and at other times in subtle, almost purely imagined voices that seem to appear from nowhere, so thin that one wonders if they exist at all.

The disenchanted world, of course, has an infinite number of explanations for these felt sensations, each of them dismissing talk of angels, but if we would have soul in our lives, we have to deepen our imaginations, recognize that there is such a thing as holy imagining and that the object of this imagining is as real as anything else. If we do not speak, think, and live in the language of enchantment, including naming angels and recognizing spirits, and, above all, refusing to reduce experience to flat materialism, then the soul will go out of our lives and communities, and we will wonder why nothing seems to hold together and nothing is of absolute value any longer.

Generations before us have had the sacred, poetic intelligence to speak of angels and demons and fairies and ghosts, but we have forgotten that wisdom, so taken are we by the allure of facts and figures. Our ancestors knew the world by proper name, but we recognize it only in analytical description. They were so acutely aware of the personality of nature and of things that they could easily give names and faces to things we consider inanimate, and they could even imagine embodied spirits hiding in and near rocks, rivers, mountains, and forests. The fairy circles of Ireland and the stone idols that are found throughout the world attest to a people's ability to express their subtle perceptions of reality in the somewhat grosser images of experience made visible.

An aesthetic or a ritualistic primitivism will not restore the delicate balance between a spiritual perception of nature and a piety of visible images. We can't go backward, but we can move forward beyond the modernistic imagination to a new religious and artistic sensibility, where the arts once again serve the spiritual life and religion recovers its soul. Art could renew its sense of the image as icon and religion realize that spirituality is as deep as it is transcendent, as ordinary as it is infinitely extraordinary.

What has preserved angels in the past are sacred stories and uncompromised theologies and artworks focused on the iconography of religion. Theology, like psychology, sometimes tries to find respectability in being current with science and the fads of materialistic discourse, but its object lies on a different plane, even though it is to be found in the most commonplace of things. Its true concern is not the psyche, and certainly not human behavior, but the soul.

To have angels in our lives, we would have to have our imaginations regularly enriched by stories and images that teach us how angels look, what they do, and what they say. The stories of Borges, Isabel Allende, Lynda Sexson, and others give us a world that is sometimes labeled "magic realism," implying that the realm they explore is neither pure fantasy nor unadulterated literalism. They write of angels and spirits and preternatural happenings, keeping alive the traditions that account for mystery in daily life. Films by Fellini, *Like Water for Chocolate*, *The Bishop's Wife*, and *The Secret of Roan Inish*—and yes, even *It's a Wonderful Life*—show us that life is not as plain as the sciences present it, but rather takes turns and finds resolutions to conflicts through the unexplainable efforts of spirits and their magic.

Intelligent yet naive, open yet not believing, modern yet in possession of archaic sensibilities, we might once again live in a world described by early Greek philosophers as "full of spirits." These spirits are not an insult to our intelligence but are broadening and intensifying: essential for enchantment and necessary for wisdom. They are Wallace Stevens's "necessary angel of earth," in whose sight the earth is seen again.

The realm of spirits, made visible by story, shrine, painting, and sculpture, allows us to "see again," and that may be the ultimate gift of the angel. "Again" here means not twice on the same plane but both in this temporal time and in the transparent time of eternity. The angel gives us a point of view from higher than the top of the mountain, a supreme overview, a vision subtle enough to allow us to see the soul in the midst of life with its needs, sorrows, and pleasures.

Extraordinary studies are being published these days on the healing power of images and on the traditional use of statues and paintings as medicines for body and soul. Slowly, perhaps, we are just now beginning to recall what to our ancestors was common knowledge: the land of the spirits, fully compatible with grounded, up-to-date intelligence, expands our sense of what it means to have a body and a soul, and in that expansion, sustained by the fluttering wings of angels, we may discover how to live a deeply human life and even to flourish.

Devils of Enchantment

IT WOULD BE A mistake to imagine enchantment in sentimental terms, for as any ancient tale of charm and fascination makes clear, devils as well as angels crowd the air of an enchanted place. Where fairies bless and grant wishes, monsters and trolls also litter the land. Witches work for good and ill, and sometimes one doesn't know whether an enchantment is worth having.

In our modern world too, it isn't always easy to discern the enchanted from the cursed. As I ride the train into the city, whichever city I'm visiting at the moment, I often see piles of garbage and refuse on the steep sloping banks that flank the railroad tracks, and I see car after car of passing trains spray-painted with random markings and extraordinary images and calligraphies.

I imagine what those tracks would look like if they were well kept, clean, and beautiful. What kind of world would it be to live in? Would it be a place rigid and moralistic in its cleanliness, or would it be a world peaceably sane, unmarked by the excesses of its oppressed inhabitants?

I think about the fantasies that lead people to desecrate their neighborhoods and their city, and I wonder if they're trying—without thinking about it in this way—to "sacrify" with their desecrations. Graffiti "art" shows considerable skill, talent, and vision, and yet at the same time it attacks the order and cleanliness of the city.

Graffiti is in large measure "underworld writing," whose appropriate venues are toilets, trains, bridges, and subways. The graffiti "artist," of course, will also vandalize storefronts and empty walls anywhere. Perhaps the problem is that our world has become so barren of natural beauty and an artistic touch that symptomatically the "graffiti artist" reminds us in shattering and loathsome ways of our need for color and form.

Over one hundred years ago William Morris was profoundly disturbed by the collapse of culture in his industrial England, and he angrily called for a return of the artist and craftsperson. He complained that what had been lost was good workmanship and decorative elaboration—two qualities that we find in certain graffiti today, as they enter through the back door rather than at the threshold of life.

Morris said that industrialization had bred "a sort of Manichaean hatred of the world." Manichaeism was an ancient religion that taught a dualistic doctrine of light and darkness, in which the dark world of matter imprisoned the light of the soul. A modern person might live out this philosophy, without knowing anything about it, in angry neglect and even positive attacks on the things around him or her. Certainly graffiti expresses angry rejection of the way things are, but in so doing it is only reflecting a general distrust and neglect of the material world.

Challenged by graffiti, we might examine our own collective and individual philosophies of life for signs of a Manichaean hatred of the world. Whenever we place high principle over material things, we are engaging in an ancient gnostic conflict between the lightness of belief and the density of matter. The artist elicits fragments of light from material, while the one acting with political fever or in desperation for profit despises the physical world as the mere raw material of his or her fanaticism.

William Morris's hope for a return to a love of the world lay in a restoration of craft and decoration, as well as in the careful preservation of buildings and artworks of the past. He attempted to demonstrate both in theory and in practice how hands-on craft gives culture some of the values taken away by factory means of production. In the hundred years since Morris's attempts at changing this pattern, we have drifted even further from craft and are moving toward a computerized and robotic world of manufacturing.

What we need, Morris said, are two virtues: honesty and simplicity. The essence of honesty in work, in his view, involves the principle of not gaining by any person's loss, and simplicity means doing nothing wasteful. "I have never been in any rich man's house," he wrote, "which would not have looked the better for having a bonfire made outside of it of nine-tenths of all that it held."

The application of these two principles would indeed be revolutionary in our world, where consumerism breeds both waste and the exploitation of workers, but Morris would doubtless be horrified to learn how we make chemicals of such toxicity that they can't be undone or buried, that the disposal of garbage is one of the great issues of local government, and that our homes are filled with infinitely more uncrafted objects and superfluous items than in his time.

We are led, then, to another motive for graffiti: the desperate expression of individuality in a world in which manufacturing plants and offices operate more than ever on the factory model. In this view, graffiti is not an expression of the ego, not a personal statement made from a person's own anger and frustration, but a pained expression of the soul, deeper seated than any single person's psychology and emotions, an anguished utterance of the times and of the society.

Not long ago, with my family I toured the Tower of London. I was hoping to visit the cold and sparse cell in which Thomas More spent the last fifteen months of his life. We did manage to look closely at another prison tower, where we saw many names carved beautifully into the walls of the cells. I remember in particular a well-executed "Thomas," which had been cut deep into the stone in noble and sharply etched calligraphy several hundred years ago.

This poignant expression of life hidden in imprisonment is graffiti too, and it makes me wonder if the spray paint we see all over our cities, and increasingly in smaller towns, stems from a feeling of imprisonment. "I'm here," it says, "even though no one sees me." What could be worse than the sense of losing one's very being. The theologian Paul Tillich wrote in many different ways that the ultimate root of our anxiety is the threat to being. Yet our methods of work and our ways of maintaining economic growth at the expense of the majority, who don't have the power to assert their individuality, generate in many of our citizens a deep feeling of imprisonment in certain jobs, neighborhoods, and lifestyles. Given this suppression of the creative spirit, we might expect the soul to show its displeasure and hint at its repressed need in writing on the walls of whatever form its prison takes, and to sense the keen longing for enchantment in the odd beauty of its desecrations.

Mix the wastefulness of uncrafted goods with the loss of personal weight and significance, and we have violated the two principles that Morris hoped would characterize culture one hundred years beyond his own generation and would be a cure for the dehumanizing effects of industrialization. What does "dehumanizing" mean? In our modern world, many people obviously have great opportunities to become successful in their jobs and to possess the physical necessities they need, but still they may lack a piece of their humanity. Dehumanizing means not having the soul that makes us human: not having soul in our communities, businesses, public places, and private lives. Dehumanization is the chasing away of that spark of vitality and well of reflection that preserve human depth of thought and sensibility.

William Morris was a prophet of enchantment. His houses, textiles, wallpapers, weavings, and furniture are filled with signs of soul, with stylized representations of the spirits that animate ordinary life. Birds and animals and vegetation are omnipresent in his work, all manifested in vivid colors that Morris had found through constant experiment, his hands continually soaked with pigments and solutions. He was a pied piper trying to entice us out of our dreary factories and artless homes into a world where vitality could still be found. Decoration, he said, which is a rich source of art for every person, should always point beyond itself, to the presence of "gardens and fields, and strange trees, boughs, and tendrils . . . some hint of past history." Morris expressed his creative vision and his anger at society by putting his mark on walls everywhere, but he did it by making exquisite wallpaper and selling his reply to ugliness, his version of graffiti, to people who might glimpse its necessity.

An enchanted world is always connected to nature, if by no other means than wallpaper alive with animated forms, and it may always be connected to the past as well, so that, as Morris said, the past is then part of our present, feeding it and sustaining it, and not a mere dead time long gone. There is an essential difference between learning from the past and living with the past, and only the latter serves enchantment, because it is more than a mental consideration. The ghosts of our ancestors are among those spirits who keep imagination alive, for imagination is not a rational exercise but rather a world of living beings, alive in a realm that is neither mental nor literally physical and yet is utterly real, where meaning and values, love and passion, originate and find their true home. The spirits of imagination that quicken present life also include people of cultures far distant who visit us in their arts, as in the Indian rug that animates my writing studio and the Chinese mountain scroll painting that gives life to my physician's office.

Now we begin to see a closer relationship between graffiti and decoration and begin to wonder if graffiti enters the void when animated decoration recedes. Graffiti presents us with the bold intervention of a foreign culture, with a spirit that is not kindly but that wants inclusion in our way of life, with an invitation to enchantment when we are suffering the pale, lifeless culture manufactured in the absence of the spirits that would animate it.

As an American, I am invited by cultures around the world to be increased and vivified by their arts and crafts, their designs and textures, not as a perpetuation of consumerism but as a cure for consumerism. The "ism" in consumerism indicates that we are not consuming with sufficient depth and substance. A better way to purchase and to own might be to take into our homes not only things that are familiar and precious but also things alive with a spirit that is unfamiliar. Our artists are often misfits, foreigners in their own country, and therefore advocates of an alien culture that has something important to say to us.

As a white American, I have a special invitation to be animated by the arts and crafts and ethos of Native Americans, African Americans, and all other ethnic groups who dwell as co-citizens. This is not a light, optional choice to make on a whim; it is a major route to enchantment and a sure path to soul. Without soul, culture doesn't breathe, has no vitality, and is plagued with symptoms, and so to allow the spirit of other cultures to enter into our own is essential in the shape and design of our cities and homes.

Graffiti is inseparable from our buildings, which it both curses and blesses. It speaks to and of our buildings. You don't put graffiti on a piece of stationery and mail it to your congressman. Beyond its particular appeal for individuality and animation, in general it speaks of the condition of our place. At once, it marks our buildings as unacceptable, and it offers hints at how to make them come alive.

Graffiti and Eros

Graffiti may appear simply as a heart and arrow whittled into a tree or fence, proclaiming the presence *in this world* of a romance, or it may be a dark sexual invitation scrawled on the wall of a public toilet. In either case, this ancient mode of expression adds the ingredient essential to all forms of enchantment—eros. From one point of view, enchantment is the welcoming of soul into everyday life, from another, it is the sexualization of all of culture.

Enchantment brings a magician's wand to nature and culture and wakes culture from its Newtonian sleep. When we are in the presence of a living world, then each thing has its own personality and gives us the opportunity for genuine intimacy, a kind of sexuality in everyday encounters in the world—sex as attraction and mutual pleasure. A Newtonian world of mechanics is soul-denying not only because it splits subject and objects but also because it precludes a sexual relationship among the things of the world. The subject-object problem is one not only of thinking but of loving as well, for we can be present and active in the world through love and attraction, not merely through knowledge and use of the world's materials.

Graffiti can sexualize a blank wall on a city street, dress it up at least so that it is attracting and appealing—sexual words. Graffiti is especially at home in public bathrooms because they house the body's secrets, like the Marquis de Sade's underground chambers where his libertines lived out their misogynist fantasies. In a culture that tries to preserve a sexless surface for daily life, erotic life is also chased into the underground toilets, where its poetry and art appear as graffiti.

Sometimes a connection is made between the erotic paintings on the walls of ancient Pompeii and the word "graffiti," but there is a major difference between that ancient art and our own defacements. Their art was public, brought into the home and the public place. The phallus was displayed openly, and sex of many kinds was portrayed with beauty and without shame. Our graffiti betrays our embarrassment at being sexual, at being motivated by love and desire, and at entertaining a fantasy life that is polymorphous and not as strictly moral as our ideals.

In the old monasteries, the monk copiers would sometimes fill the empty margins of books with strong sexual images and language. These margins were known as gutters, and of course graffiti is at home in the gutters of society. There seems to be a general principle, embodied in those old grammars, by which any attempt to make a too ordered life and a too rationalized existence generates in the alleyways of imagination a compensatory reaction like graffiti.

Enchantment takes place easily in the margins—among marginal people and in marginal activities. But there is no reason why we can't extend the margins of our lives, toning down our practical hyperactivity to allow for the leisure that enchantment requires. Once again, grammar turns into glamour. This leisure is akin to the simplicity that William Morris recommended—a clearing of the debris of modern life so that the world hidden beneath all our activities and things might breathe again and show itself as a living being, charming and inviting.

Readers of my books have told me over and over: "I'm too busy to care for my soul." If we are indeed too busy, then it's obvious that we need to relax, to learn how to do less and behold more, to become lazy in the soul instead of hyperactive in the spirit. I don't think enchantment will enter our culture through strenuous and dedicated efforts at ritual, storytelling, meditation, and the many other means created by the muscles of spirituality. I place my trust in the capacity of enchantment simply to reveal itself once the barriers have been lifted and our busyness interrupted.

We could listen closely to the dark angels who spoil our buildings with their spray cans, and to the illnesses that keep us from our work and our busy lives, and to the natural disasters that force our attention on the powers of nature. They may throw us deep into despair but at the same time offer the smallest signals of hope.

When we respond to these destructive elements with moralism

or with grand plans to defeat them, then we simply maintain the gulf between them and us. We become more entrenched in our ways, and they have more work to do. An alternative is to listen attentively to their disturbing messages without romanticizing them or naively turning blind to their ugliness.

William Morris had a similar thought. "I think myself that no rose-water will cure us: disaster and misfortune of all kinds, I think, will be the only things that will breed a remedy." Many today are turning to "rose-water" as a way of dealing with the increasing ugliness of modern life. I fervently hope that my suggestion of enchantment will not be mistaken for rose-water; for though it is a romantic notion, it is not a superficial one. It requires courage, intelligence, and daring, as well as the willingness to appear foolish, eccentric, and out of step in the eyes of the modern world.

The shocking, disturbing, and yet fascinating paradoxes in graffiti—art and destruction, beauty and ugliness, form and effacement, love and hate—invite us to imagine a world less divided, a world of honesty and simplicity in which every person has a chance to live a human life and in which we will have restored order, beauty, and grace because we are in love with the things of the world.

The Divination of Certainty

*T*HE MODERN WAY of making life decisions is to trust the intellect—make thorough and practical investigations and then "make up your mind" quickly and firmly. You might consult experts or someone experienced in whatever it is you're deciding, and then weigh the pros and cons. Indecisiveness is considered a serious fault. The problem is that more than the mind is involved in every decision, even the most ordinary, and the other considerations—emotions, values, thoughts, vision, influences, passion—often stand in the way of clear, logical analysis and conclusion.

This is another area where I feel out of step with my times, because it often takes me a long time to arrive at a decision, and sometimes, especially in the most serious matters, circumstances in the world force me into a choice. I have the classic Libran ability to see fully the merits of both sides of an argument, and I can remain blissfully immobile before a display of options until one by one they rot, leaving no choice for me but the one remaining.

My innate distaste for logical, quick decision making has led me to take careful note of my intuitions and to trust them, and I have found that this kind of guidance feels more interior, brings up a wealth of imagination and memory, and keeps me closer to the area of life where the choice lies. At the same time, the decision-making process is slower, and its particulars are difficult to spell out.

Contemplative Decision Making

The word "intuition" comes from the Latin *tueor,* meaning to gaze, contemplate, or protect. When we are in an intuitive state, we look carefully at what is going on and gain the kind of knowledge that doesn't arise from logic. When I stand gazing at the options before me, I'm contemplating, starting up my intuitive engines, hopeful that they will lead to an eventual decision.

In our culture, we relieve the anxiety of our decision making by building up layers of reasons, explanations, tight syllogistic sequences of logic, and rationalizations. We believe that our decisions have to be correct, or we will have been failures. Some people go to therapy to gather reasons why they should make a particular decision, or to assure themselves about past choices. They grade themselves on how effective their choices prove to be, and they carry considerable guilt when their choices turn out to be the wrong ones.

This disenchanted way of getting along in life appears sophisticated and mature, but it is full of anxiety. An alternative might be to leave behind the illusion of maturity and adopt a more naive posture, the "beginner's mind" of Zen, and make choices in an atmosphere of unknowing, from a deeper place in the imagination, which has its own rules.

At one time, and even today in some cultures, people faced with tough decisions consulted astrologers or psychics. They could receive guidance from diviners, who read the sound of thunder, the entrails of animals, or the flights of birds for meaning and insight. I had an aunt who enjoyed reading tea leaves left in her cup, until one day she proclaimed that a stranger would come to the house and, within minutes, an unfamiliar man knocked at the door. She was so shocked and, I think, in her fervent Christianity so startled by the effectiveness of her "pagan" pastime, that she never read another teacup in her life.

The technology of intuition, practiced all over the world in myriad ways, is known as divination, a quest for information in which the diviner or seeker turns to a ritual or image on which to meditate and then finds the answer to a question. The ingredients of divination usually include a rite that may appear magical, the presentation of material for reflection, and possibly a conclusion about what to do or how to think. The ritual—its ceremony and its objects—may be simple, like my aunt's teacups. The material to be read may also be simple—the tea leaves. Finally, there may or may not be an interpretation offered (my aunt concluded that a stranger would knock).

I'm more interested in applying the fundamentals of divination to everyday life, softening some of their esoteric and exotic elements, than in practicing traditional divination, although many old systems are still valid and practical. Learning from the traditions, I try to read the sudden appearance of a bird, the distant roll of thunder, or an unexpected wind. More important, I use these traditional forms as a way of educating myself in intuition, so I can rely on it more and more in daily life and thereby follow the rudiment I get from Rainer Maria Rilke—live from a deeper place.

Release from the Known and Familiar

Jung is widely known for his theory of synchronicity—taking note of events that seem connected in time but not by cause and effect— which is closely related to divination and is rooted, as I read him, in his general appreciation for "primitive" thinking. In an essay on "archaic man," he makes the comment: "whims of chance seem to him a far more important factor in the happenings of the world than regularity and conformity to law." He goes on to talk about his days as a doctor in an asylum: "An old professor of psychiatry always used to say of a particularly rare clinical case: 'this case is absolutely unique—tomorrow we shall have another just like it.'" Jung comments that this kind of joke was common in the hospital and it reminded him that in an older age, people paid close attention to the singular and unusual.

In our day, of course, we don't trust the single case, or even a duplication, but trust only infinitely repeatable events. In almost every field a student has to learn how to do statistical analysis, because we rely more on repetition than on rarity. This anxiety about unique experience is another factor that makes us shy of divination, because divination doesn't depend on regularity and conformity to law. Just the opposite, it seeks out unique signs that have to be read as unique. When divination is carried out properly, you can't rely on a dictionary of symbols and their meanings for insight. Divination asks for a risky, individual reading of data rather than an appeal to quantified parallel cases.

From the point of view of the soul, a unique event or object is of great interest, but several versions of the same thing are highly suspicious. In spite of many common themes and elements, human life presents itself in particulars and individuals. So we need a method of knowing that is appropriate to unique happenings yet provides a satisfactory degree of certainty and reliability.

Faced with a problem or a quest, in the name of enchantment we may forgo logic, forgo studies and theories, and forgo common experience. We will look for a different kind of logic altogether to give us direction and insight. What we often need is not a long path of explanations and reasons leading us directly to a conclusion, but rather a jolt forcing us out of the rut of thinking we're in. Or we may simply need a freshening of imagination, a new way of looking, a deeper perspective. Until we have had a disquieting revelation by means of divination, we may even be unaware of the shallow dimensions of our reflections.

Impediments to logic sometimes offer opportunities for fresh imagination. Feeling blocked, not knowing where to go next, reaching for experts, guidance, ideas, or just a simple lead, can all put an end to encrusted thinking and invite new paths of consideration. Of course, it's also possible to be literally stuck in an endless quest for the right way to think or the proper language to use. Divination has several means of getting us out of those closed circles of fruitless searching.

A number of years ago I was giving a series of lectures to a group of astrologers and psychologists, when a note was passed to me from a woman in the audience who was from India. When the engagement was over, I read the note carefully: "Your work is going to become well known, and you will spend more money than you have." I was startled to read the note; it had the ambience of a genuine divination. This event took place long before I published *Care of the Soul,* a book that became widely read, and my work was not known at all at the time.

Rituals of divination often include, as we shall see, a test of the diviner's credentials or ability. The test not only offers some assurance that the divination will be genuine but also serves as a small rite, initiating the petitioner into the process. I'm sure I gave more credence to a note written by a mature woman dressed in Indian attire than I would have given to one presented by a neophyte psychic from a more familiar circle.

In my case, as the months and years have passed, I have been astounded at the astrologer's ability to forecast the spread of my writings, but at the same time I've been puzzled about the other part of the message. I know that I can easily spend more money than I should—I've never been a saver or at all smart about money—but I haven't yet fallen into any disastrous financial hole either. Maybe disaster is coming, or maybe that part of the message should be read more poetically.

We need to trust the diviner, suspending our disbelief enough to be affected by the divination. I can imagine getting good information from someone I might consider a charlatan, because diviners and psychics don't play into our cultural craving for credentials and authenticity. Some psychologists might explain my trust as a form of transference—my seeing this person as a projection of some trusted figure from my past or perhaps the projection of an ideal or a hope. Generally I don't see much value in the notion of projection under any conditions, and so I prefer to consider my trust as an aspect of my wish to find alternatives to mechanistic thinking. I know nothing about the astrologer who passed me the note, and yet I am still enchanted with her art.

My story also demonstrates that divination may give us a definite message to consider, but the reading of that message may take years to unravel. In this, divination differs strongly from rationality, the whole purpose of which is to arrive at an answer, a solution, or a decision. Divination stays with you, and the solution or puzzle that it presents may persist for years, influencing your thoughts without necessarily offering a course of conduct.

Edification by Puzzlement

The gradual unraveling of a mystery, the time it may take to show itself, and the conflicting readings and interpretations it spawns are all benefits of the divinatory approach. I often compare a dream to a painting, believing that we need not demand a final interpretation of any dream, just as we would never reduce a good painting to a definitive explanation. Usually when we explain a painting precisely, its mystery vanishes along with its value. The very point of a good painting is to keep us wondering, asking questions, offering interpretations, and contemplating. The same is true to a degree with divination: its value lies in the continuous influence it has over our thoughts—deepening them, turning them in new directions, even confounding our familiar modes of intelligence and offering surprising alternatives.

In a book on African divination, James Fernandez, an anthropologist, tells of consulting a Zulu diviner who worked by conjuring spirits. He went to her hut and tested her by seeing if she could detect a coin that was hidden under a companion's leg. She failed that test, but he persisted anyway. Professor Fernandez then says that the diviner "rather quickly divined that I was far away and not in satisfactory contact with my family," particularly with his ill father. She recommended getting in better contact with him.

Disappointed in the Zulu woman, he tried another diviner, who was in a group that recommended that he sacrifice a sheep. Before going to sleep, he drank a potion of herbs, sheep's blood, and gall, and followed further advice to take note of his dreams.

He dreamed he was halfway up a ladder that was leaning against the wall of a chapel. At the top of the ladder was his father, calling him up. The next day the diviner told him that the ancestors were showing him in the dream their acceptance of him and suggested that he contribute to the repainting of the chapel and the reglazing of some broken windows. He should also call his father in America.

He didn't make the call, and when he finally got back to America he found that his father was gravely ill; he died within two weeks. Gradually Professor Fernandez came to realize that the diviner's message had been accurate and important. He summarizes it: "Spend some money on your fellow humans, and don't forget to call home." And then, in an extraordinary confession for a modern scientist, he explores some of the reasons for his skepticism about African divination.

"I focused on the recommendations contained in the divination and not on the complexities of the communication itself." This is the modern tendency I've been noting: We're so interested in arriving at final conclusions and explanations that we become immune to the transformative power of the process. Professor Fernandez elegantly refers to this personal transformation as "edification by puzzlement." It's a figurative, primary process, he says, that works by indirect means. He uses such words as aleatoric, inchoate, dreamlike, enigmatic, and metaphoric to describe the nature of divinatory reflection. Innuendo and other forms of verbal art are essential to it as well. Because we moderns are extremely uncomfortable with the tension created by mystery and innuendo, we don't often feel edified by puzzlement, and yet this very reformation in imagination could bring back to us an enchanted life.

Divinatory Powers in Art

Poets and artists of all kinds are intimately familiar with edification by puzzlement. The best of them will tell you that they don't know always what their work means. In their art they use words or images in ways that speak more directly and more profoundly than reason of our world and our experience. They trust the images that come to them as being rich in implication and complex in their truthfulness.

If the arts are not sources of divination to us, then it is because we are not looking to them for it, or we are training and expecting our artists merely to "express themselves" or challenge us at a surface level as critics of culture. Stanley Hopper, my professor of poetry and religion during my doctoral studies, founded his work on the premise that we need to shift from theo-logic to theo-poetics, to a recognition, among other things, that the poets touch such deep springs of wisdom and revelation that they serve a function in society that goes beyond aesthetics and into the realm of religion. As its name suggests, divination, too, takes place in a sacred and mysterious context and is far removed from the secularism of modern methods of reason and analysis.

Divination is a numinous way of knowing, a surrender of intentionality and will, and an openness to the confounding images that appear in ritual and dream. The very idea in divination is to give over one's will to the numinous poetics of ritual. Therefore, especially in times of deep change and decision, we might turn to divination to wrap ourselves in the dissolving and restructuring suggestions of its counterlogic.

Societies that appreciate divination and other numinous rites hold together because of the power of their sources of knowledge and the depths from which they are guided. We take a poll and make decisions by majority rule, while enchanted societies consult the very foundations of imagination for signs of direction and decision. Our choices are rational, supposedly, and theirs holy; ours are focused on a clear goal, while theirs piously await revelation.

I was once anxiously driving to a meeting that I feared would be full of dark emotions. I was trying to think of some way to calm myself, and as I drove up to a stop sign on a country road, a brilliant red cardinal lighted on it. I couldn't help but think of it as a sign. I thought to myself: The bird is lovely, stately, and brightly colored; maybe this signifies that the meeting will turn out fine. But then I thought: that shade of red is very close to the color of blood, which could mean that the meeting will be terrible. The meeting turned out to be even worse than I had anticipated, and afterward I thought I had learned a lesson in divination: I have to pay special attention to the message that counters my wish and my feelings of self-protection.

The sources of divination are many. We could risk our modernist sensitivities and consult a traditional diviner in Africa and South America, or among Native Americans—anyone who lives and practices where enchantment still has power. Or we could use more available and less challenging forms like the *I Ching,* tarot cards, runes, and astrology. Or less formally, we could learn to read the common signs that are all around us.

We could incorporate the fundamentals of divination in the way we think generally. For example, we could read the signs in front of us and shape our life and work more by intuition than by logic. We could live an astrological life, to one degree or another, using the moon as a guide to the waxing and waning activities in our own lives or, following Ficino, initiating important projects in the spring or at the beginning of the week. We could turn to poets and artists, not just for beauty and entertainment, but for direction, especially for the depth of vision in which they can educate us, for their edifications of puzzlement.

This brings me back to Stanley Hopper, for whom theo-poetics is profoundly deeper than theo-logic. Certain arts, he says, are closer to archetypal consciousness than to intellectualizing theories, and so they have an extraordinary degree of reliability. Eastern religions appeal, he says, because they place us so close to our souls, as do the mystical traditions of the West. He cites Augustine: "Thou wert with me, but I was not with Thee," and Meister Eckehart: "God is nearer to me than I am to myself." But he also quotes Wallace Stevens:

> There was a muddy center before we breathed.
> There was a myth before the myth began. . . .
> From this the poem springs.

Hopper's conclusion: "What was projected in the dualistic mythological world pictures, falls back to the deep psyche and sustains us as a Presence there." Notice that he capitalizes "Presence," acknowledging the word's numinosity in this context. He also hints that theo-poetics, the category in which I would place divination, is not a dualistic enterprise. I don't try to conquer or control life, but rather I look for ways to be one with it. I don't try to determine what my life will become, but rather I do everything possible to participate in its unfolding, following the signs that lead me where my soul's desire lies and my fate awaits me.

Divination works, we might say, by placing our thoughts closer to our souls and to nature, to the way things are and operate, and out of that accomplished intimacy life decisions can be made with confidence and reliability. Yet the divinatory approach can be challenging, because we are faced not only with the mystery in our decisions and problems but with the additional mystery of the divinatory material itself.

Slow, intuitive, ritualistic, interpretive, and unique, divination differs radically from modern means of attaining knowledge. Its purpose is to affect our vision and perhaps alter the very foundations of our way of thinking. In taking us so deep in our quest, it may lead us to questions we hadn't considered in our initial search for insight, and indeed may take us in startling directions. My aunt was afraid of the power she saw only momentarily in her "game" and gave it up. The anthropologist was led to abandon certain modern assumptions that were part of his education and method. Sometimes divination helps us ask better questions or reorients our considerations.

Divination also asks us to live more in uncertainty than we may feel comfortable doing with our modern sensitivities. Intuition, especially as it requires an assortment of interpretations, may induce false leads and mistaken conclusions. For myself, I expect that using this approach, I may be wrong more than half the time; but even as I make my mistakes, I learn the subtle rules of enchanted thought, and I get better at knowing how to live intuitively and more from imagination than reason. I also have to give up a measure of control and allow the divination to take me to unfamiliar territory. I may make a decision based on intuition rather than fact, and if my trust is still in data and logic, I may feel anxious. Gradually I may learn a new source of confidence and trust, and I may learn the lesson that it may be more important to deepen my quests and questions than always to be right.

Divination won't work if it's taken up as another tool in the modern arsenal of decision making; for its value lies in serving as a form of initiation into a different way of life altogether, one that is closer, as Hopper says, to the soul and to nature. To appreciate divination, we may have to discover a path away from the modern world, returning to enchanted life, where divination is the normal way of knowing and logical analysis an aberration.

This Magical Life

THOSE OF US who have been brought up in a secular culture, sometimes complemented with a religious belief system, don't realize how much our lives have been impoverished by the lack of magic. Life may appear to be complete, with our fact-based education; ethical, scriptural, and theological religious practices; practical careers and workdays; politics rooted in nationalism and recent history; and entertainment aimed at numbing us to the "pressures of modern life." What is missing in all this is the penetrating enchantment of every experience that rises out of a world that is alive and that has deep and mysterious roots of power.

In many cultures, the magus speaks of magic as a means of exercising power, but in a society where power means dominance over others and personal gain, magic's goal of power may be misunderstood. For centuries, the thoughtful magus has tried to separate the narcissistic exercise of magical power from the respectful, more humble practice, labeling the former "black magic" and the latter "white magic." In his celebrated *Oratio* in 1487, the young Pico della Mirandola admitted that many practiced "demonic" magic, but in another form altogether, magic is a humane art, "the highest realization of natural philosophy." Pico's friend and mentor, Marsilio Ficino, turned the idea around, describing philosophy as an initiation into mysteries, and in his work one can scarcely distinguish his many roles of philosopher, priest, theologian, translator, musician, and magus.

For Ficino, magic is primarily an erotic process, emerging out of the interactions of plants, animals, humans, and earth, as well as from the interrelationships of the elements and parts of the human body, to say nothing of the sympathies of body, soul, and spirit. "The whole power of magic is founded on Eros," he writes in his book on love. In our ordinary lives, magical effect rises from our view of life as connected and related, as a community of beings in nature and among humans.

Applying this philosophy to ordinary experience suggests that we could all find considerable power for everyday life by living closer to nature, not just physically but above all in imagination. As a first step, we might become conscious of how widespread is our devotion to the mental life, how innocently we trust our sources of information, our experts, and our traditional ways of interpreting both nature and human behavior. We think that knowledge, education, and literacy will ultimately save us from the threats of nature and from our own social ills, but the natural magic of the Renaissance, which I am using as my inspiration in this manifesto of enchantment, has an altogether different basis, as it is rooted in love and in a fundamentally erotic approach to every aspect of life.

If we were to look at our personal difficulties and our social problems as matters of love, we might realize how utterly inappropriate it is to pursue intellectual solutions to those problems. The heart is not convinced by rational explanations, nor is it much affected, and yet the magical point of view sees the heart implicated in all our activities. We can influence the emotional pulse of the heart, and we can have power in life through love, but to do so we need more skill in magic than in thought. Ficino says, "the works of magic are works of nature, but art is its handmaiden." The arts of magic help us find power for the heart, for, as Ficino says pointedly in the same section on magic, "nature is a magician." Magical arts offer a way of living so intimately with the ways of nature that its magic becomes our magic, and we forge a creative and effective life by being tuned in to nature's potency.

Sympathy

The magus finds "sympathies" in relationships between things, based on similarities ignored by the scientific eye. Sympathy is an odd word to use of the things of nature and human life, so odd that many modern commentators describe it in the usual terms of cause and effect, as though sympathy were a physical law. But it is a heart word, pointing to an intimacy among things that is best expressed not as natural law but as natural affection, a kinship of qualities that gives the impression that nature is a web of connections rather than an arena of separate existences.

What is the sympathy between nutmeg and the sun? Ficino says that if you put a dash of nutmeg in your food, you may benefit from an increase in solar spirit. Here the connection is color. Olivia Shakespear, an early love of W. B. Yeats, advised him to live near water and avoid woods, which would have too much of a solar influence on him. Robert Fludd was famous for his "weapon salve," the application of ointment to the weapon that caused a wound, demonstrating another kind of sympathy. The weapon is profoundly implicated in the wound and so is also involved in the treatment.

Writing about Ficino's magic, Frances Yates makes an important point: "The magus enters with loving sympathy into the sympathies which bind earth to heaven, and this emotional relationship is one of the chief sources of his power." Paracelsus said: "What the saint is in the 'Realm of God,' the magus is in the 'Realm of Nature.'" Just as the saint is one who does not simply know theology but rather lives life fully from devotion, so the magus is one who is so devoted to nature as to live in continuous sympathy with it.

Magic is often explained in obscure and esoteric terms, but that very exoticism keeps it out of our everyday lives. Most of us know that it is easy to love things, and that things have relationships among one another. You may love an antique box, know that it gives your home unique power, and realize it can't be placed just anywhere. As we arrange our homes, we are doing so from the sympathy we notice among things and from our own relationships to things. Interior design, whether professional or amateur, is largely the practice of natural magic, an attempt to arrange life for maximum emotional and practical power.

If we were to allow things to have subjectivity and personality, we might see how they show sympathy for us. Dogs and cats give us comfort, companionship, and pleasure, and we are even now discovering scientifically how they can nurse people to health and help them live more securely in old age. Our homes hold us and protect us, while our cars take us where we want to go. My word processor—an unfortunate name for such a personal and companionable instrument—makes my work of writing infinitely easier and likes to play with me. The road near my house appears as a true friend when I've been away on a trip, and the sick tree just outside the kitchen window is a worry as its leaves fail to arrive in the spring. It's been a good companion, keeping me company as I wash dishes at the window.

I can't imagine life without birds, with their outrageous colors and habits, their cries and swoops, their acrobatic way of animating the sky, and their songs and chants. Books play a far more intimate role in life than mere utilitarian objects. Their mere presence gives much to a home or a room, and they are capable of a very long-term relationship. I still wince when I think of a particular book lost or lent away years ago, and I feel fully moved into a new home only when the books are secure on their shelves, providing their necessary warmth and companionship.

In these simple erotic connections we can see the origins of magic. Of course, magic may become complicated as it develops over time, but everything, from the early flights of the Wright brothers to cooking an egg, can become arcane and complicated as it is refined. It helps to keep the basics in mind, and the most rudimentary principle of magic is sympathy.

The quote from Frances Yates is not just about the sympathy among things but in particular about the loving connection between earth and heaven. As we saw in the section on astrology, this "heaven" is not a literal sky but more the archetypal realm, a world of essences or Platonic source images, and so this sympathy, so close to Ficino's, is a constant consonance of actual life and mythic memory, or life and imagination.

Like the mystic, the magician is in love with the world of the senses and the world of mysteries, and sees these two worlds as inherently connected with one another. Magical power derives from this special sympathy, expressed most enticingly by Ficino when he recommends that we paint our horoscope on the ceiling of our bedroom so that when we go out into the world we bring that deep awareness of our essential nature with us.

Sensation and Mystery

The magus doesn't separate, as we often do, eros and logos, love and knowledge. The magus is a grounded philosopher, who is utterly entranced by the world before his eyes. The magus knows materials, colors, temperatures, properties, and the history of many things, and in that knowledge finds power. The magus is educated and trained not just to know about things but also to live in this world effectively empowered by the things of nature and culture.

I use this word "effective" carefully. After almost twenty years of practicing psychotherapy, I'm convinced that most, if not all, psychological complaints stem from a failure to find and exercise power. In our emotional suffering, we feel victims of another person, of fate, of circumstance. As a therapist, what I have searched for is not empowerment, in the sense of ego strength, essentially a narcissistic form of power, but rather the effectiveness that comes from being attuned to the world around us. If we think we are the only subjects, the only creative ones, in this world of mineral, animal, and plant life, then we will naturally feel a loss of power, because human life doesn't thrive on the basis of such egotism. The world supports us, offers guidance and sustenance, and can help us make ordinary life extraordinarily effective.

Instead of trying to figure ourselves out and come up with a convincing plan for a healthy life, we might instead pay closer attention to the world around us. We could get to know our immediate environment. I find that reading Henry David Thoreau helps me live closer to the natural world in my own region, and even though I don't think he ever uses the word "magic," his philosophy offers an excellent grounding for a magical life. His neighbors Ralph Waldo Emerson and Emily Dickinson give similar philosophies of nature, which keep the transcendent element intact and thus preserve the magic. Emily Dickinson writes explicitly about the value of a magical approach to life.

The magus has been exploring these issues for centuries in the midst of Western industrialization. Slighted in the history books, the philosophy of magic is available to us only in books and conferences inaccessible to the average person. I would go so far as to say that we are a magic-starved society, trying to create an effective and humane culture on the limited basis of scientific method, machinery, and materialistic philosophies. Meanwhile, explorations into the more subtle and mysterious resources of nature go unnoticed and are dismissed as superstition, eccentricity, and naïveté.

Pico della Mirandola claimed: "there is no latent force in heaven or earth which the magician cannot release by proper inducements." This statement summarizes the gist of the magus's point of view: magic is concerned with latent powers in the sky and on earth that can be tapped for human purposes through artful means. The idea of "inducing" this power, drawing it out for our use, is a common one in the writings of magicians. They speak frequently of "baits," "nets," and "decoys," used to entice the hidden potentials from the density of raw nature.

Since magic works primarily on the basis of sympathies and similarities among the qualities of things, the most effective decoys are images. "Blessed are the image-makers," Ficino writes in his book of magic. If we can make images that correspond potently to the latent powers we're looking for, then we may be able to induce them into our daily lives.

In a disenchanted world, the artist works for aesthetic, expressive, and analytical purposes, but in an enchanted world the artist is the sorcerer's apprentice, the one who makes the images that assist magic. We too, by living an artful life, can fill our lives with the materials and images that strengthen the imagination and shorten the gap between our sense of self and the "outside" world.

Practical Magic

All of this needn't sound arcane and out of step with modern times. We could learn from the natural magic of Chinese *feng shui*, for instance, where to place doors in our buildings, how to design a highway intersection, and where to put a park not for practical or aesthetic purposes alone but for the power these ordinary elements offer everyday life.

Feng shui teaches that one should always have a "dragon" of support behind a home, a place of work, or your own person. I once gave an all-day workshop sitting in a chair placed somewhat precariously on a platform over an indoor swimming pool. This was not good *feng shui*.

I feel more secure writing in a chair with a high, supportive back—the "dragon" of my writing, I presume—than in something more efficient but more exposing. A lighted candle, the sound of a bell, a smoke-ring of incense, an evocative rug—these, too, bring magic into my work, so that all I have to do is sit and let the words come, because the world has been adjusted for the work. The world around me stirs my thoughts and eases my mind as I write sentence after sentence.

Magic is not just a procedure; it's a way of life. The magus lives every minute of every day magically. Ficino says that on melancholic days we should avoid walking through groves of trees but instead should seek out hills and other places exposed to the light of the sun. He gives advice, as do other magicians, on dress, diet, habits, travels, and friends. In England, John Dee recommended the magical use of poetry and music.

The art historian Edgar Wind says that Leonardo da Vinci employed the magic principle of achieving spectacular effect with inconspicuous means. This is a particularly interesting principle of magic: small effort brings great reward. I once asked a house builder, "How can you take on such a big project and not become frustrated or make mistakes that ruin the project?"

"I work one step at a time," he said, restating an ancient principle of magic.

The magus is interested in rings, stones, bells, clocks, toys, pictures, clothing, boxes, books, vessels—the small things, accessories, incidentals, all of which he or she believes to have extraordinary power to bring significant benefits to life.

We are all magicians, but now as we leave behind a moment in history characterized by rationalism and mechanistic thought, our magic is implicit and hidden in our ideas and work. Since we're not educated explicitly in magic, we aren't as articulate about it as someone in the preindustrial world might have been. The highly imagistic writings of the old magicians appear abstruse and difficult to our logical minds, and yet they beg for elucidation and translation into the terms of modern life. We could learn from them the genteel magic of living the ordinary life effectively as well as congenial ways of appropriating the more esoteric magic of spells, talismans, angel conjuring, and alphabets.

We don't have to take these arcane methods literally and super-stitiously. We might learn with Leonardo that a highly imaginative and carefully made image may have a profound effect on the life of a place. When I lived in Chicago decades ago, the city installed in a central plaza a huge sculpture of a woman's head made by Picasso, a magus if there ever was one, and the city was transformed. A woman of mystery took her place at the center of city life, and no one could disregard her, as her spirit emanated from this icon at the heart of the city.

Ficino strongly recommends making an image of the world and keeping it close at hand. One Christmas our family brought a globe into our home. More than an atlas, more than a tool for travel, its very presence has an effect on us who live with it and on visitors, who invariably touch it and spin it. It's an instrument of magic, like the Celtic harp that stands near it, both giving the illusion of prac-ticality but exuding an air of magic as well.

Certain ordinary things have a great deal of magic in them and so could be made, bought, and used on behalf of enchantment: a yo-yo allows us to ritually play out the ascent and descent we find in our dreams and in our emotions; a spinning top echoes the whirling of the planets; and a dollhouse magically shrinks the house to a size where imagination can get hold of it. Our diaries and journals could house magical letters if we brought art to their production and their keeping. And, as William Morris knew well, there is magic in wall-paper and bedsheets if we use them to entice the many life-giving spirits into our homes.

Traditionally, magicians liked to have cosmic motifs in their clothes and instruments, like a moon and stars on a witch's hat or a crystal globe in which to observe fate and the future. I once gave a workshop to artists—poets, painters, sculptors—and in one exer-cise we looked at slides of the participants' work. Almost ninety percent of the slides contained some cosmic image—a moon, sun, planet, or stars—making a connection between the main theme of the work and the sky above. This fascinating correspondence seemed to me to echo again the message of the *Emerald Tablet,* the centuries-old summary of alchemical teaching: "As above, so below." Each of us could easily practice this little piece of traditional magic by having an image of the sky in our home or at work. Children enjoy stars that are stuck on the ceiling above their beds and glow in the dark—a playful version of Ficino's ceiling horoscope. Our family has a large sun planned for the roof of our new house, and I try to keep cosmic imagery on my stationery.

One day someone brought a beautifully hollowed-out rock to our house, and we placed it in among the small trees and bushes that lead to the porch. It isn't a practical thing, although the dog drinks out of it and sometimes my daughter will take a bath in it; nor is it a merely aesthetic ornament. Every day, I walk past that rock, look at the rainwater that has gathered in its bowl, and feel its magic. In all its uselessness and its mysteriousness, it has become an important object for the family. Like magic itself, it's a perfect blend of nature and culture, and it has a fascinating outside and inside, as though some secret lay in the revelation of its interior. It, too, seems to be an image of the cosmos.

To live in an enchanted world, we have to assume the role of magician in our everyday lives: have a few objects of power within reach, live by the simple principles of magic, use poetic language and imagery in the most practical affairs, and cultivate an abiding attitude that is at home with mystery and the interiority of the world.

Emily Dickinson wrote to her cousins Louise and Frances Norcross: "Life is a spell so exquisite that everything conspires to break it." In our unmitigated pragmatism, we often casually dismiss the many spells that ordinary life casts, considering them ancillary to the real business of living. If we rediscovered the sensibility of the magus, we might not only esteem those moments of magic but seek them out and treat them as the real stuff of life. This reorientation of values would be the basis for the re-enchantment of everyday life, and the soul would be conjured back into daily experience, with all its contradictions and puzzlements, and with its gift of humanity.

Conclusion

Spelling out the fundamentals of enchantment, I've strung many colored beads on a simple necklace. It would have been disenchanting of me to have created a grand theory, and lacking in charm to have made a checklist of ways to restore enchantment. An enchanted way of thinking is not as heavy with fact and theory, or as rigid with logic and proof, as disenchanted discourse. I've tried to demonstrate in the very writing of this book how we might preserve our intelligence, even as we begin to think and speak more imagistically and act more magically.

Each section of this book begs for further elaboration, and many important themes have been left for other occasions. For instance, gender can be enchanting, when it isn't subjected to propaganda and anxious attempts to keep us divided and polarized. We could also explore the implications of a philosophy of enchantment for education at all levels. The role of magic in mainstream religion appears to be tangled and confused, as so many writers try, misguidedly in my view, to free religion of its paganism.

As we arrive at the end of a century of materialism and a millennium of moralism, many are confessing to a thirst in their souls for a different way of life, for "something more." I'm convinced that the re-enchantment of our own individual lives, as well as of the culture we live in, is one effective way to respond to that thirst. Our fundamental orientation toward life seems to be lacking an ingredient that feeds the soul. I believe that our maladjustment to the heart lies deeper than our problems with mechanistic and mental approaches to the human situation, and that this deep shortsightedness has dried out our souls. We're feeling the desiccation of our lives as though we were wanderers lost in a desert, thirsty for water but uncertain which direction to take and misled by mirage after mirage promising satisfaction.

Enchantment conjures up the juices of vitality and a renewal of childhood, play, poetry, art, natural religious virtues, and community. Its characteristic emotion is joy, and its goal deep pleasure. It may be the tonic we're looking for as we seek out ways, chemical and therapeutic, to deal with the epidemic of depression that has become the characteristic soul sickness of modernism. Make a soulless world, and there is nothing in it to lift our spirits, nothing to give us daily meaningful experiences that render life worth living and make getting up in the morning a joy. An abstract philosophy or a moralistic injunction may motivate us toward certain behaviors with urgent and heavy-handed intensity, but modest, regular exposure to an enchanted world provides a light touch and a deep desire to live a full life.

Although I decided not to make this a manual of magic, on every page I've been instructed by magicians of the past and have remembered their wisdom. Each section of each chapter is a small lesson in magic, and I expect the overall effect of a life lived according to these lessons to be a transformation in culture, a deep reorientation away from the imperial heroics of progress and futurism, toward an appreciation of a rich past and a rebirth of old wisdom, a renewal that in the fifteenth century was called "Renaissance." A rebirth of art and humane culture and a revitalization of religion, involving a discovery of the values in the much-despised pagan religion of nature, would make life both more magical and, therefore, less burdensome.

When we live by magic, we don't try to understand everything that is happening and everything we're doing. We allow nature to remain mysterious, but we tap into it to share its hidden powers. We use inconspicuous means to achieve powerful effects, and we acknowledge the potency of materials and images to render our world enchanting. We appreciate the "performance power" in language, so that our every use of words and letters, from correspondence to business, is not forgetful of magic and of the special thrust of poetry that invigorates the commonest forms of expression. We tend to accessories and incidentals, to color, sound, shape, texture, and fabric; to clothing, decor, furnishing, architecture, and transport; to libraries, parks, toys, and sports—all with a magician's hope for the fullness of life.

In our own renaissance, we may rediscover an idea largely lost in the twentieth century, though it has been revived often by our artists and writers: the depth and centrality of the imagination. We tend to consider imagination too lightly, forgetting that the life we make, for ourselves individually and for the world as a whole, is shaped and limited only by the perimeters of our imagination. Things are as we imagine them to be, as we imagine them into existence. Imagination is creativity, and the way we make our world depends on the vitality of our imagination.

And so we need to be educated above all in imagination. In an enchanted school, music and the other arts are primary and omnipresent. Science and technical skill are incomplete without them. The presence of soul requires a vivid and honored imagination, one that is developed over time through exposure to the arts, to intimate discussion, including conversation with the men and women in our past and in present cultures unlike ours. Our "media"— newspapers, magazines, television, radio, movies—could help immensely in the ongoing education in imagination by resisting temptations to be merely clever and effective, and instead giving us complex images and stories for our rumination and edification. It's worth noting that magicians of the past were deadly serious in their play with imagination, while our writers and producers are often puerile and irresponsible with the many techniques they have for working magically with images.

To re-enchant our individual lives, we could live by intuition and divination, give up all labor that has no element of play in it, express ourselves in poetry of whatever kind is suitable, live in the presence of children and the whole gamut of ages, work at sustaining neighborhoods and regions to preserve the genius of place, make shrines and temples to whatever spirits reveal themselves, and pray with faith rather than demand, hoping for compassion rather than truth.

We could preserve the family farm and the small store; and cook only those foods that retain a sense of place, that are real and lusciously loaded with fantasy and sensation. We could turn off the television and tell stories, and cancel business appointments and trips and practice not-doing at home. We could find a career that expresses our ethical enthusiasms and wakens our soul. We could make a home that is full of spirits and makes us reluctant to leave. We could discover the beauty and necessity of the useless and the nonsensical, shedding our driving rationalism and our grumpy purposefulness.

There is no way to re-enchant our lives in a disenchanted culture except by becoming renegades from that culture and planting the seeds for a new one. The revolution spelled out in these pages may seem soft and quaint, but that is because we live in a world that honors only what is hard, driving, heroic, and reasonable. We want proof before we believe anything, but an enchanted person believes first and then over time is surprised when the intelligence in that belief is revealed. There is no call for proof, which is merely an expression of the anxiety of our times.

Enchantment is a condition of unending suspension of disbelief, the willingness to live in a bungalow of stories rather than a warehouse of facts. It places imagination before information, and wisdom before intelligence—it measures its WQ rather than its IQ.

Rather than subject nature to its purposes, it listens for the occult voices in nature and looks for the personalities that populate it. It places more importance on a sculptured or painted image of those spirits than on inventing a new machine or improving an old piece of technology. It gives genuine soul to our very idea of what a machine is and what technology is all about in a humane world, and it grants human scale to all our labor and invention.

Enchantment encourages the artist to work with the scientist, the politician with the priest. A philosophy of enchantment assumes that political strife and street crime result from an anxious loss of home and homeland, or a drying up of imagination and the spirit that offers hope. Enchantment inspires deep and unconditional compassion, while disenchantment blinds a person to all but superficial notions of community.

The re-enchantment of everyday life starts with a single, small, inconspicuous step and goes on to the next inconspicuous step.

Over time, a new way of life emerges from small acts of magic. The individual dedicated to enchantment is, in the words of Wallace Stevens (understand "man" as "person"):

> The impossible possible philosophers' man,
> The man who has had the time to think enough,
> The central man, the human globe, responsive
> As a mirror with a voice, the man of glass,
> Who in a million diamonds sums us up.

The enchanted person is a "mirror with a voice," giving expression to the voice heard in nature and deep within the heart. When the innermost realm meets the outermost in an articulation that embraces them both, then we sense the enchantment, we hear the song, and we are caught in its spell. Our very natures are spelled out in this trance that sums us up in diamonds rather than in facts, and from that diamond trance we can make a world that feeds the soul, charms the heart, and praises the Mystery that is its source and sustenance.

Notes

INTRODUCTION

xx   *"How important it is":* Shunryu Suzuki, *Zen Mind, Beginner's Mind* (New York: Weatherhill, 1970), p. 22.

THE WATERS OF LIFE

14   *water is not just H2O:* Ivan Illich, *H2O and the Waters of Forgetfulness.* (Dallas: Dallas Institute Publications, 1985).

15   *"Tristan, resting trustfully":* Joseph Campbell, *The Masks of God: Creative Mythology* (New York: Viking, 1968), p. 227.

20   *"the thalassal regressive trend":* Sandor Ferenczi, *Thalassa: A Theory of Genitality,* trans. Henry Alden Bunker (New York: W. W. Norton, 1968), p. 56.

TREES THAT TALK

24   *The landscape architect:* Dan Kiley, "The Poetry of Water," in *Stirrings of Culture* (Dallas: The Dallas Institute Publications, 1986), p. 90.

25   *a woman from faerie:* W. B. Yeats, "The Friends of the People of Faery," in *Mythologies* (New York: Collier Books, 1959), pp. 117–24.

25   *trees can be planted:* Christopher Alexander et al., *A Pattern Language* (New York: Oxford University Press, 1977), p. 171.

26   *"There is no center":* John G. Neihardt, ed., *Black Elk Speaks* (New York: Pocket Books, 1972), p. 230.

29   *"Again and again":* John Fowles and Frank Horvat, *The Tree* (Boston: Little, Brown), n.p.

BLOOD FROM STONES

32   *"Transform yourselves":* C. G. Jung, *Letters,* ed. Gerhard Adler, trans. R. F. C. Hull. Vol. 2: 1951–1961, Bollingen Series XCV:2 (Princeton: Princeton University Press, 1975), p. 326.

33 *"When I hewed":* Jung, *Letters,* p. 290.

36 anima mundi: C. G. Jung, *The Structure and Dynamics of the Psyche,* trans. R. F. C. Hull, in *Collected Works,* vol. 8, Bollingen Series XX (Princeton: Princeton University Press, 1969), §190.

36 *model should be made:* See Marsilio Ficino, *Three Books on Life,* trans. Carol V. Kaske and John R. Clark (Binghamton, NY: Medieval & Renaissance Texts and Studies, 1989), p. 347 and n. 2.

ECOLOGY'S HOME

45 *"A lake . . .":* Henry David Thoreau, *Walden,* in *A Week on the Concord and Merrimack Rivers, etc.,* ed. Robert F. Sayre (New York: The Library of America, 1985), p. 471.

45 *the very notion of facts:* Donald Cowan, *Unbinding Prometheus* (Dallas: The Dallas Institute Publications, 1988), p. 5.

THE ENCHANTED CHILD

52 *"You have an acorn":* James Hillman and Michael Ventura, *We've Had a Hundred Years of Psychotherapy—And the World's Getting Worse* (San Francisco: HarperSanFrancisco, 1992), p. 18.

THE PRESENCE OF THE HAND

72 *"Industrial labor":* Eric Gill, *Last Essays* (London: Jonathan Cape, 1942), p. 82.

THE ETERNAL HOUSE

77 *"All really inhabited":* Gaston Bachelard, *The Poetics of Space,* trans. Maria Jolas (Boston: Beacon Press, 1969), p. 5.

80 *the chthonic spirits:* James Hillman, *The Dream and the Underworld* (New York: Harper & Row, 1969), pp. 35ff.

81 *procreative function:* Richard Broxton Onians, *The Origins of European Thought* (Cambridge: Cambridge University Press, 1988), pp. 123ff.

83 *"shapes in replication":* James Hillman, "Interior and Design of the City," in *Stirrings of Culture* (Dallas: The Dallas Institute Publications, 1986), pp. 83–84.

RUINS AND MEMORY

87 *name of preservation:* E. P. Thompson, *William Morris* (Stanford, CA: Stanford University Press, 1976), p. 241.

93 *"What does this tower":* The Shepherd of Hermas, trans. Rev. F. Crom-

bie, *Ante-Nicene Fathers*, vol. 2, Alexander Roberts and James Donaldson, eds. (Peabody, MA: Hendrickson Publishers, 1994), p. 41.

94   *The Luba people:* Evan M. Zuesse, "African Religions: Mythic Themes," *The Encyclopedia of Religion*, ed. Mircea Eliade (New York: Macmillan, 1987), vol. 1, p. 71.

95   *"In some strange way":* Vincent Scully, *New World Visions of Household Gods and Sacred Places* (Boston: Little, Brown, 1988), p. 4.

A GARDEN PARADISE

97   *In Jung's view:* C. G. Jung, *Psychology and Alchemy*, trans. R. F. C. Hull, in *Collected Works*, vol. 12, Bollingen Series XX (Princeton: Princeton University Press, 1968), §§154, 155.

100   *"The completely irreligious mind":* Thomas Merton, *Conjectures of a Guilty Bystander* (New York: Doubleday, 1989), p. 306.

100   *"At two-fifteen":* Ibid., p. 131.

NOISE AND SILENCE

108   *Studies have been made:* R. Murray Schafer, *The Tuning of the World: Toward a Theory of Soundscape Design* (Philadelphia: University of Pennsylvania Press, 1980), p. 187.

111   *Ficino said:* Marsilio Ficino, *Omnia Opera* (Basil, 1576), p. 651. See D. P. Walker, *Spiritual and Demonic Magic* (London: The Warburg Institute, University of London, 1958), p. 6.

THE SPIRITUALITY OF POLITICS

122   *"In tranquillity":* Wing-Tsit Chan, ed., *A Source Book in Chinese Philosophy* (Princeton: Princeton University Press, 1963), p. 209.

MYSTIC TRANSPORT

137   *"Movement is in space":* Norman O. Brown, *Love's Body* (New York: Vintage Books, 1966), p. 50.

139   *Navigation of St. Brendan: Encyclopedia of Religion*, ed. Mircea Eliade (New York: Macmillan, 1987), vol. 2, pp. 257ff.

THE PARTICULARITY OF PLACE

146   *real, haunting place:* Edward Casey, *Getting Back Into Place* (Bloomington: Indiana University Press, 1993).

147   *"Everywhere the world":* De Vita Coelitus, p. 536.

151   *"This anxiety is aroused":* Paul Tillich, *The Courage to Be* (New Haven and London: Yale University Press, 1952), p. 47.

SEX AND THE SOUL

159 *"magical act"*: Jung, *Structure and Dynamics*, §§83–85.

160 *"besides turning out"*: Thompson, *William Morris*, p. 651.

161 *no discernible meaning*: Adolf Guggenbühl-Craig, *From the Other Side* (Woodstock, CT: Spring Publications, 1995).

MARS AND AGGRESSION

165 *"To know war"*: James Hillman, "Wars, Arms, Rams, Mars: On the Love of War," in *Facing Apocalypse*, Valerie Andrews, Robert Bosnak, and Karen Walter Goodwin, eds. (Dallas: Spring Publications, 1987), pp. 118, 125.

167 *The alchemical sword*: C. G. Jung, *Psychology and Religion: West and East*, trans. R. F. C. Hull, in *Collected Works*, vol. 11, Bollingen Series XX (Princeton: Princeton University Press, 1969), §357.

168 *A Dutch alchemical painting*: Johannes Fabricius, *Alchemy* (Wellingborough, Eng.: Aquarian Press, 1976), fig. 43.

170 *"Venus was placed"*: Edgar Wind, *Pagan Mysteries in the Renaissance* (New York: W. W. Norton, 1968), p. 89.

AN EDUCATION IN DREAMS

175 *"When a frog"*: Shunryu Suzuki, *Zen Mind*, p. 83.

THE THERAPIST'S CHAIR

186 *"the psyche is a world"*: C. G. Jung, *Alchemical Studies*, trans. R. F. C. Hull, in *Collected Works*, vol. 13, Bollingen Series XX (Princeton: Princeton University Press, 1967), §75. See also James Hillman, *Anima* (Dallas: Spring Publications, 1985), ch. 5.

ARCHETYPES AND MYSTERIES

194 *Jung himself provides*: William McGuire and R. F. C. Hull, eds., *C. G. Jung Speaking*, Bollingen Series XCVII (Princeton: Princeton University Press, 1977), pp. 292ff.

200 *"They sing of all"*: Hesiod, *Theogony* 11:55ff. in *Hesiod*, trans. Richard Lattimore (Ann Arbor: University of Michigan Press, 1973), pp. 126–27.

201 *This gaining of intimacy*: See David Miller, "Orestes: Myth and Dream as Catharsis," in *Myths, Dreams, and Religion*, Joseph Campbell, ed. (New York: E. P. Dutton, 1970), pp. 26–47.

202 *Grünewald crucifixion*: Andrée Hayum, *The Isenheim Altarpiece: God's Medicine and the Painter's Vision* (Princeton: Princeton University Press, 1989).

OBJECTS OF ART

204 *"the picture begins":* Frances A. Yates, *Giordano Bruno and the Hermetic Tradition* (Chicago: University of Chicago Press, 1964), pp. 77–78.

209 *"Temple carpenters":* S. Asby Brown, *The Genius of Japanese Carpentry* (Tokyo: Kodansha, 1989), p. 24.

209 *"One should take":* Ibid., p. 35.

210 *"If you have nothing":* C. G. Jung, *The Vision Seminars,* vol. 2 (Zurich: Spring Publications, 1976), p. 487.

211 *become talismans:* Brian P. Copenhaver, "Scholastic Philosophy and Renaissance Magic in the *De Vita* of Marsilio Ficino," *Renaissance Quarterly* XXXVII, no. 4 (Winter 1984), p. 530. E. A. Wallis Budge, *Amulets and Superstitions* (New York: Dover, 1978), p. xxiii. Budge says, "No amulet could be regarded as a piece of inert and dead matter"—a principle I would apply to all matter in a condition of enchantment. Albert the Great also taught the superiority of talismans: Kurt Seligmann, *Magic, Supernaturalism and Religion* (New York: Pantheon, 1948), p. 144.

211 *Christian objects of piety:* Budge, *Amulets,* p. xxviii.

212 *"a magic rooted":* Hans Belting, *Likeness and Presence: A History of the Image Before the Era of Art,* trans. Edmund Jephcott (Chicago: University of Chicago Press, 1994), p. 185.

MUSICA HUMANA

215 *"De institutione musica":* Boethius, *The Fundamentals of Music,* trans. Calvin M. Bower, ed. Calude V. Palisca (New Haven and London: Yale University Press, 1989).

216 *"psychotherapist as* musicus*":* Thomas Moore, "Musical Therapy," *Spring 1978* (Dallas: Spring Publications, 1978), p. 130.

FURNITURE MUSIC

225 *Plato poses a question:* Plato, *Republic,* 3.410–11, in *The Collected Dialogues of Plato,* trans. Paul Shorey, ed. Edith Hamilton and Huntington Cairns, Bollingen Series LXXI (Princeton: Princeton University Press, 1961), pp. 654–56.

227 Musique d'ameublement: Alan M. Gillmor, *Erik Satie* (New York and London: W. W. Norton, 1988), p. 232.

227 *"Nothing can be":* William Morris, "The Lesser Arts," in *The Collected Works of William Morris,* vol. 22 (London: Longmans Green, 1914), pp. 23, 26.

EVERYDAY MYTHOLOGIES

235 *"go deep into yourself"*: Rainer Maria Rilke, *Letters to a Young Poet,* trans. Stephen Mitchell (New York: Vintage Books, 1986), p. 9.

STORIES IMPERFECT AND IMPOSSIBLE

242 *"If I knew at the beginning"*: George Plimpton, ed., *The Writer's Chapbook* (New York: Viking, 1989), p. 200.

244 *"We can get carried away"*: Ted L. Estess, "The Inenarrable Contraption: Reflections on the Metaphor of Story," *Journal of the American Academy of Religion* XLII:3 (September 1974), p. 432.

BOOKS AND CALLIGRAPHIES

254 *"when you climb"*: Alan Watts, *The Way of Zen* (New York: Vintage Books, 1957), p. 175.

255 *"Thus the aimless life"*: Ibid, p. 181.

256 *"If you do not understand"*: Faubion Bowers, "Calligraphy: An Overview," in *The Encyclopedia of Religion*, vol. 3, ed. Mircea Eliade (New York: Macmillan, 1987), p. 26.

SENSE IN NONSENSE

258 *obscene words have power:* Sandor Ferenczi, "On Obscene Words," in *First Contributions to Psycho-Analysis,* trans. Ernest Jones (New York: Brunner/Mazel, 1952), p. 137.

260 *"performance power"*: See Sam Gill, *Sacred Words: A Study of Navajo Religion and Prayer* (Westport, CT: Greenwood Press, 1981).

261 *the incantation:* Richard Kieckhefer, *Magic in the Middle Ages* (Cambridge: Cambridge University Press, 1989), p. 20.

262 *"Blue./Blue Moon"*: Mimi Otey, *Blue Moon Soup Spoon* (New York: Farrar, Straus & Giroux, 1993).

263 *"Fury jams the gullet"*: Anne Stevenson, *Bitter Fame: A Life of Sylvia Plath* (Boston: Houghton Mifflin, 1989), p. 138.

265 *Arnold of Villanova:* Kieckhefer, *Magic,* p. 85.

267 *"trotting out old words"*: James Hillman, "Letter to Tom Moore," *Corona 2* (1981), pp. 115–20.

268 *"To make a place"*: David Pingree, ed., *Picatrix: The Latin Version of the Ghayat Al-Kakim* (London: The Warburg Institute, 1986), p. 64.

THE HOLY WELL

276 *According to the story:* Arch Merrill, *Land of the Senecas* (Interlaken, NY: Empire State Books, 1949), p. 76.

276 *"My whole heart"*: Wilfred S. Dowden, *The Letters of Thomas Moore,* vol. 1 (Oxford: Clarendon Press, 1964), p. 77.

EVERYDAY SHRINES AND TABERNACLES

284 *painting ephemeral images:* Stephen Huyler, *Painted Prayers* (New York: Rizzoli, 1994).

286 *ordinary personal shrines:* Shaun McNiff, *Earth Angels* (Boston: Shambhala, 1995).

287 *form of sacred play:* Lynda Sexson, *Ordinarily Sacred* (New York: Crossroad, 1982).

288 *"Moving to a new house":* Ibid., pp. 22–23.

TEMENOS AND SANCTUARY

296 *"give you a sense":* Christopher Alexander, Sara Ishikawa, and Murray Silverstein, *A Pattern Language* (New York: Oxford University Press, 1977), p. 1110.

296 *He recommends:* Ibid., p. 536.

296 *"memory theater":* Frances A. Yates, *The Art of Memory* (Chicago: University of Chicago Press, 1966), p. 131.

NUMINOSITY AND LUMINESCENCE

300 *"When something sacred":* Mircea Eliade, *Journal II 1957–1969,* trans. Fred H. Johnson, Jr. (Chicago: University of Chicago Press, 1989), p. 268.

301 *"The feeling of it":* Rudolf Otto, *The Idea of the Holy,* trans. John W. Harvey (London: Oxford University Press, 1958), p. 12.

302 *"They lose their":* C. G. Jung, *The Symbolic Life,* trans. R. F. C. Hull, in *Collected Works,* vol. 18, Bollingen Series XX (Princeton: Princeton University Press, 1976), §582.

302 *"A person is made perfect":* Jung, *Structure and Dynamics,* §388.

THEOLOGY OF THE WORLD

307 *"As I stand":* Trudy Griffin-Pierce, *Earth Is My Mother, Sky Is My Father: Space, Time, and Astronomy in Navajo Sandpainting* (Albuquerque: University of New Mexico Press, 1992), p. 33.

309 *"Mistress":* Euripides, *Hippolytus,* trans. Robert Bagg (New York and London: Oxford University Press, 1973), p. 24.

312 *Some current commentators:* Elisabeth K. J. Koenig, "Suffering Love Is the Way Home: Christian Spirituality in the Light of Theology and History," *Christian Spirituality Bulletin* 3:1 (Spring 1995), pp. 10–14.

313 *"God is beyond":* Dietrich Bonhoeffer, *Letters and Papers from Prison,* ed. Eberhard Bethge (New York: Collier Books, 1971), p. 282.

ASTROLOGY'S TRUTH

315   *"For we are the stars":* Jerome Rothenberg, ed., *Technicians of the Sacred* (Berkeley: University of California Press, 1985), p. 45.

318   *Socrates "admired":* Marsilio Ficino, *The Book of the Sun (De Sole),* trans. Geoffrey Cornelius, Darby Costello, Graeme Tobyn, Angela Voss, and Vernon Wells, in *Sphinx* 6 (1994), p. 145.

321   *"Wherfore I cordialy":* Allen G. Debus, *Robert Fludd and His Philosophicall Key* (New York: Science History Publications, 1979), p. 31.

MIRACLES OF SPORT

326   *"No honest game":* Nicholas de Cusa, *De Ludo Globi, the Game of Spheres,* trans. Pauline Moffitt Watts (New York: Abaris Books, 1986).

EARTHEN SPIRITUALITY

332   *he sat on a stone:* C. G. Jung., *Memories, Dreams, Reflections,* trans. Richard and Clara Winston, ed. Aniela Jaffé (New York: Pantheon, 1973), pp. 20, 42.

333   *man sitting on a peacock:* Marsilio Ficino, *De Vita Coelitus Comparanda,* ch. 18.

334   *"Nature's energy":* Scully, *New World Visions,* p. 13.

334   *Al-Kindi's book:* Al-Kindi, *On the Stellar Rays,* trans. Robert Zoller, ed. Robert Hand (Berkeley Springs, WV: Golden Hind Press, 1993).

336   *"You cannot have":* Wendell Berry, "Conserving Communities," *Resurgence* 170 (May/June 1995), p. 8.

THE MEDIATION OF ANGELS

343   *"We must content ourselves":* Eliade, *Journal II,* 1965, p. 267.

344   deus otiosus: See Eliade, ed., *Encyclopedia of Religion,* vol. 4, pp. 314ff.

345   *I suspect:* I have no direct knowledge of Navajo sacred imagination. I'm relying here on the splendid book by Griffin-Pierce, *Earth Is My Mother, Sky Is My Father,* pp. 31–32.

347   *"The creature in whom":* Rainer Maria Rilke, *Duino Elegies,* Trans. J. B. Leishman and Stephen Spender (New York: W. W. Norton, 1967), p. 129.

DEVILS OF ENCHANTMENT

352   *honesty and simplicity:* William Morris, "The Art of the People," *Collected Works,* vol. 22, p. 47.

353   *"I have never been":* Ibid., p. 48.

354 *"gardens and fields":* William Morris, "Textiles." See Thompson, *William Morris,* p. 107.

358 *"I think myself":* Thompson, *William Morris,* p. 245.

THE DIVINATION OF CERTAINTY

361 *"whims of chance":* C. G. Jung, *Civilization in Transition,* trans. R. F. C. Hull, in *Collected Works,* vol. 10, Bollingen Series XX (Princeton: Princeton University Press, 1970), §121.

364 *"rather quickly divined":* James W. Fernandez, "Afterword," in *African Divination Systems,* Philip M. Peek, ed. (Bloomington and Indianapolis: Indiana University Press, 1991), p. 213.

367 *"What was projected":* Stanley Romaine Hopper, "Myth, Dream, and Imagination," in *Myths,* ed. Joseph Campbell, pp. 11–137.

THIS MAGICAL LIFE

369 *"the highest realization":* Giovanni Pico della Mirandola, *Oration on the Dignity of Man,* trans. A. Robert Caponigri (South Bend: Gateway Editions, 1956), p. 53.

369 *initiation into mysteries:* Ioan P. Couliano, *Eros and Magic in the Renaissance,* trans. Margaret Cook (Chicago: University of Chicago Press, 1987), p. 37.

370 *"The whole power":* Marsilio Ficino, *Commentary on Plato's Symposium on Love,* trans. Sears Jayne (Dallas: Spring Publications, 1985), p. 127. Ficino spells out the connection between eros and love in Chapter 10, Book VI.

370 *"the works of magic":* Ibid.

371 *Olivia Shakespear:* A. Norman Jeffares, *W. B. Yeats: A New Biography* (New York: Farrar, Straus & Giroux, 1989), p. 88.

371 *"The magus enters":* Yates, *Giordano Bruno,* pp. 126–27.

371 *Paracelsus said:* Quoted in James Robinson Howe, *Marlowe, Tamburlaine, and Magic* (Athens, Ohio: Ohio University Press, 1976), p. 20.

374 *Mirandola claimed:* Edgar Wind, *Pagan Mysteries in the Renaissance* (New York: W. W. Norton, 1968), p. 110.

Index